Natural Resources and Economic Development

Natural Resources and Economic Development explores a key paradox: why is natural resource exploitation not yielding greater benefits to the poor economies of Africa, Asia and Latin America?

Part One examines this paradox both through a historical review of resource use and development and through examining current theories that explain the under-performance of today's resource-abundant economies, and proposes a frontier expansion hypothesis as an alternative explanation. Part Two develops models to analyse the key economic factors underlying land expansion and water use in developing countries. Part Three explores further the "dualism within dualism" structure of resource dependency, rural poverty and resource degradation within developing countries, and through illustrative country case studies, proposes policy and institutional reforms necessary for successful resource-based development.

EDWARD B. BARBIER is currently the John S. Bugas Professor of Economics in the Department of Economics and Finance, University of Wyoming. He has over twenty years' experience as an environmental and resource economist, working mainly on the economics of environmental and development issues.

Natural Resources and Economic Development

EDWARD B. BARBIER

CAMBRIDGE
UNIVERSITY PRESS

333.709172
B23n

CAMBRIDGE UNIVERSITY PRESS
Cambridge, New York, Melbourne, Madrid, Cape Town, Singapore, São Paulo

CAMBRIDGE UNIVERSITY PRESS
The Edinburgh Building, Cambridge CB2 2RU, UK

Published in the United States of America by Cambridge University Press,
New York

www.cambridge.org
Information on this title: www.cambridge.org/9780521823135

First published 2005

Printed in the United Kingdom at the University Press, Cambridge

A catalogue record for this book is available from the British Library

ISBN-13 978-0-521-82313-5 hardback
ISBN-10 0-521-82313-7 hardback

This country has become rich because nature was good to us.
President John F. Kennedy
Speech at the University of Wyoming
Laramie, Wyoming
September 25, 1963

Contents

Figures

Tables

Acknowledgments

I am grateful to a long list of people who have helped in various ways to make this book possible. First and foremost, I would like to thank Chris Harrison of Cambridge University Press for encouraging me in this project, and for waiting patiently over the years as it proceeded from draft proposal to final manuscript.

I am indebted to Erwin Bulte, Jo Burgess, Chris Harrison and Margie Reis for reading the entire first draft manuscript, and for providing such helpful comments on the whole draft that assisted me in subsequent revisions. I am grateful to Dan Bromley, Ron Findlay, David Pearce and Gus Speth for also reading the draft.

Much of this book is based on research that I have conducted in recent years that has been written up, presented and sometimes published in various forms. I owe numerous individuals their thanks for collaborating on this research or for providing invaluable comments on previous versions of the resulting papers and presentations. I will try my best to acknowledge this help chapter by chapter.

Chapter 1 benefited from the comments of Dan Bromley, Jo Burgess, Richard Damania, Bob Deacon, Ramón López, Joe Stiglitz, Michael Toman and fellow participants in the Environment and Sustainable Development Task Force of the Initiative for Policy Dialogue. I am also grateful for the research assistance of Tessa Leonce for helping me find and compile some of the data for the stylized facts presented in the chapter. I am also indebted to the Department of Agricultural & Applied Economics, University of Wisconsin, Madison for inviting me to present the 2003 Hibbard Lecture in April 2003, and the Department of Economics, Adelaide University, Adelaide, Australia for inviting me to present the 2002 Joseph Fisher Lecture, which was published in *Australian Economic Papers*.

Chapter 2 was helped enormously by discussions with Ron Findlay, Jay Shogren and Gavin Wright, and by the insightful comments of Jo Burgess and Chris Harrison.

Chapter 3 benefited from discussions with Bob Deacon, Ron Findlay and Gavin Wright, and from the comments by Erwin Bulte and Jo Burgess.

Chapter 4 is largely based on a paper presented at the Session on Environmental Economics at the 78th Annual Conference of the Western Economic Association International, Denver, CO, July 12, 2003, which was eventually published in *Contemporary Economic Policy*. Thanks also to Rich Carson, Nick Flores, Michael Hoel, Chuck Mason, Carol McAusland, Jay Shogren, Luis Sosa, Gavin Wright and seminar participants at the Economics Department, University of Colorado and the 6th Occasional Workshop on Environmental and Resource Economics, University of Santa Barbara California for invaluable comments and suggestions on previous versions of this paper. Thanks to Seong-Hee Kim and Margie Reis for research assistance.

Chapter 5 is a much expanded version of a paper presented for the principal paper session "Panel Data Evidence on Economic Development and the Environment in Developing Countries" at the 2004 American Agricultural Economics Association annual meeting, August 1–4, 2004, Denver. This paper and others from this session appear in *American Journal of Agricultural Economics*. I am grateful to Wade Brorsen, Ian Coxhead, Gerry Shively and Doug Southgate for comments.

Chapter 6 is comprised of two separate research efforts, and earlier drafts of the papers based on these papers benefited from the comments provided by Jo Burgess, Tom Crocker, Rob Godby, Nick Hanley, Patrick Hultberg, Ramón López, Marc Nerlove, Unai Pascual and Sara Scherr. The case study on mangrove loss in Thailand is based on research undertaken as part of the Project "Demographic and Economic Factors Determining Coastal Land Conversion into Commercial Shrimp Farms, Thailand," funded by the Population, Consumption and Environment Initiative (PCE) of the John D and Catherine T MacArthur Foundation. I would like to thank the MacArthur Foundation, and the PCE Director, A. Kumar, for their support. The original case study paper on mangrove loss in Thailand appears in *Land Economics*, and I would like to thank my co-author, Mark Cox, for collaborating on this research and all the work we undertook under the MacArthur PCE Initiative. I would also like to thank our collaborating researchers on the Project at the Institute for

Social and Economic Policy, Bangkok, in particular S. Sathirathai, R. Tokrisna, S. Aksornkoae, W. Sungunnasil, I. Sarntisart and S. Suwannodom, who have all provided valuable help and advice on all aspects of this research. Finally, I would like to acknowledge the research assistance of S. Chanyaswad. The case study on pre-NAFTA deforestation in Mexico that appears in the chapter is based on a paper that appears in *Economic Inquiry*. I am grateful to Jo Burgess for her research collaboration on the original project that was the basis of this research, a report prepared for the Latin American and the Caribbean Country Department of The World Bank and the Government of Mexico. I would also like to thank Colleen Clancy, Michael Collins, Luis Constantino and Augusta Molnar.

Chapter 7 is based partly on my Invited Address Conference of Australian Economists Glenelg, South Australia, Australia October 1–3, 2002. A version of this address appears in the *Economic Record*. I am grateful to Richard Damania, Keith Hancock, Patrik Hultberg, Chuck Mason for helpful comments, and to Lee Bailiff for research assistance. The Nigeria case study is based on work over the years that I have conducted with several researchers, Gayatri Acharya, Bill Adams, Kevin Kimmage and Julian Thompson. This research also benefited from many conversations and assistance provided by the late Ted Hollis, Richard Thompson, Gert Poulet and David Thomas. The Nigeria case study work was funded by the IUCN Wetlands Program, and I am grateful for this assistance to Richard Acreman and Jean-Yves Pirot. I was able to pull together and summarize this research into the case study that appears in the chapter thanks to the project "Economic Analysis of Upstream-Downstream Water Allocation in Developing Economies," funded by Stanford University and the Hewlett Foundation. I am grateful to Ken Arrow and Larry Goulder for this support and for their guidance. The research of the Nigeria case study has been published by IUCN and also by *Agricultural Economics*, *Ambio*, *American Journal of Agricultural Economics* and *Water Resources Research*.

Chapter 8 benefited from conversations over the years with Gordon Conway, Ian Coxhead, Partha Dasgupta, Sisira Jayasuriya, Ramón López, Anil Markandya, David Pearce, Richard Sandbrook, Gerry Shively and Doug Southgate. I am also indebted to Randy Bluffstone and Partha Dasgupta for their comments. I would also like to thank Ramón López, Joe Stiglitz, Michael Toman and fellow participants in the Environment and Sustainable Development Task Force of the Initiative for Policy Dialogue.

Chapter 9 is based partly on a paper for the NBER Summer Institute 2004 Workshop on Public Policy and the Environment, Cambridge, Massachusetts, August 2–3, 2004. I would like to thank Don Fullerton, Scott Taylor and Gavin Wright for helpful comments on previous versions of this paper.

Chapter 10 benefited from the comments by Jo Burgess and Margie Reis.

Finally, thanks to Partha Dasgupta for inspiring me to explore the role of natural resources and economic development, and to David Pearce and Richard Sandbrook for providing so many opportunities for me to do so. I am grateful to all my colleagues with whom I worked at the London Environmental Economics Centre and the International Institute for Environment and Development, especially Bruce Aylward, Josh Bishop, Gordon Conway, Anil Markandya and Tim Swanson. I am also grateful to the Environment Department, University of York, and especially Charles Perrings. I would also like to thank my colleagues at the Department of Economics and Finance, University of Wyoming, in particular Tom Crocker, Jay Shogren and John Tschirhart.

Thanks to my mother, Marietta Barbier Falzgraf, and to the Rolnicks, the Scheeles, the Burgesses and the Gebbies, for their support, encouragement and love over the years.

Above all, I will always be indebted to Jo Burgess: for believing in what we do and for working with me in trying to make it so, and for following her heart and giving her love so generously to our family, friends and me. And, finally, thanks to Becky, James and Lara for always teaching me what life is really all about.

Introduction

A s the title indicates, this book intends to explore the contribution of natural resources to economic development. The main geographical focus will be on the so-called "developing world," i.e. the low and middle-income countries of Africa, Asia and Latin America. There has been increased interest in the application of natural resource economics in these countries, now that it has been recognized that the environment is not a "luxury" for economic development but contains natural "capital" fundamental to growth and development in poorer economies.

Most economic texts and monographs do not address the role of natural resources in economic development in much detail. This is unfortunate, as the environmental problems faced by developing countries are considerably different from those occurring in industrialized economies. Many rural populations depend on the direct exploitation of natural resources, for agriculture, livestock raising, fishing, basic materials and fuel, both to meet their own subsistence requirements as well as to sell in markets for cash income. The lack of basic water supply, sanitation and other infrastructure services suggests that increased public provision of resource-based services is highly valued by many households. Rapid land use change has meant that many natural environments and habitats are disappearing quickly, with the result that critical ecological resources and functions are being disrupted or lost. Growing populations have further increased the demand for natural resource use and conversion. Finally, for many low and middle-income economies resource-based development and primary commodity exports are the main engines for growth and long-term development.

In short, this book begins with the premise that how natural resources are used for economic livelihoods and development in the low and middle-income countries of Africa, Asia and Latin America is fundamentally different from other economies of the world. Or, as the quote at the beginning of Chapter 8 from Partha Dasgupta (1993, pp. 269 and 273) puts it: "People in poor countries are for the most part agrarian and pastoral folk ... Poor countries are for the most part *biomass-based subsistence economies*, in that their rural folk eke out a living from products obtained directly from plants and animals".

Ultimately, this book is about the actual and potential contribution of natural resources to the *sustainable economic development* in such economies. Natural resources are clearly central to this process: many low and middle-income economies are highly dependent on the exploitation of their "natural capital" to secure the needs of the present generation as well as to develop and meet the needs of future generations. However, the evidence presented throughout this book indicates that increasing economic dependence on natural resources in today's low and middle-income economies is associated with poorer economic performance. This poses an intriguing paradox: why is it that, despite the importance of natural capital for sustainable economic development, increasing economic dependence on natural resource exploitation appears to be a hindrance to growth and development in today's low and middle-income economies?

Historically there appear to be many examples of successful resource-based development, which would suggest that this paradox appears to be unique to the current era. In fact, one could argue, as the historian Walter Prescott Webb (1964) first proposed in analyzing the exploitation of the world's "Great Frontier," that much of the 500 years of global economic development has been characterized by a pattern of capital investment, technological innovation and social and economic institutions dependent on "opening up" new frontiers of natural resources once existing ones have been "closed" and exhausted. Such development was so successful, particularly during the Golden Age of Resource-Based Development (1870–1913), that some of the early theories in development economies, such as the staples thesis and the vent-for-surplus theory of trade, took it for granted that natural resource abundance, trade and growth were mutually reinforcing (Innis 1930 and 1940; Myint 1958; Watkins 1963).

However, with the benefit from hindsight afforded by the present era, we now know that, simply because a developing economy or region is endowed with abundant natural resources, the country may not necessarily end up exploiting this natural wealth efficiently and generating productive investments. Or, as Wright (1990, p. 666) suggests: "there is no iron law associating natural resource abundance with national industrial strength".

Several theories have been proposed to explain why increasing economic dependence on natural resources in today's low and middle-income economies is associated with poorer economic performance. One popular explanation is the *resource curse hypothesis*, i.e. the poor potential for resource-based development in inducing the economy-wide innovation necessary to sustain growth in a small open economy, particularly under the "Dutch disease" effects of resource-price booms. Other theories have suggested an *open access exploitation hypothesis*, i.e. trade liberalization for a developing economy dependent on open access resource exploitation or poorly defined resource rights may actually reduce welfare in that economy. Finally, some economists have proposed a *factor endowment hypothesis*. The abundant natural resources relative to labor (especially skilled labor), plus other environmental conditions, in many developing regions have led to lower economic growth, either *directly* because relatively resource-abundant economies remain specialized for long periods in primary-product exports or *indirectly* because some factor endowments generate conditions of inequality in wealth and political power that generate legal and economic institutions inimical to growth and development.

As suggested in this book, it is likely that these three hypotheses could be complementary rather than competing in their explanations as to the poor economic performance of resource-rich developing economies. It is possible that the processes outlined by all three hypotheses could operate simultaneously, and even interact, to militate against "sustainable" natural capital exploitation in low and middle-income economies: resource endowments (broadly defined) may shape institutions, and institutions in turn affect the management regime of natural resources (open access, rent-seeking and other failures) and both influence the long-run performance of the economy (the resource curse).

However, this book also argues that these three hypotheses focus mainly on explaining only two "stylized facts" concerning natural resource use in low and middle-income economies, namely the tendency for these economies to be resource-dependent (in terms of a high concentration of primary product to total exports), and for increasing resource dependency to be associated with poor economic performance. None of the current hypotheses address two additional and equally important "stylized facts": development in low and middle-income economies is associated with land conversion, and a significant share of the poor population in low and middle-income economies is concentrated in fragile lands.

Thus this book offers another perspective on the resource-development paradox, which could be termed the *frontier expansion hypothesis*. The starting point for this hypothesis is the two stylized facts of resource use in developing countries that are often overlooked in the current literature on the role of natural resources in economic development: namely, the tendency for resource-dependent economies to display rapid rates of "frontier" land expansion, and for a significant proportion of their poorest populations to be concentrated in fragile areas. From this pattern of development several conclusions emerge. First, in many developing countries much frontier land expansion occurs in order to absorb the rural poor. Second, policy and market failures in the resource sector and land markets, such as rent-seeking behavior and corruption or open-access resource exploitation, contribute further to the migration of the rural poor to the frontier and excessive land conversion. Finally, as a result, frontier-based development in many poor countries is symptomatic of a pattern of economy-wide resource exploitation that leads to insufficient reinvestment in other productive assets of the economy, and thus does not lead to sustained growth. There is clearly a "vicious cycle" of underdevelopment at work here: frontier land expansion and resource exploitation does little to raise rural incomes and reduce poverty in the long run, and results in few efficiency gains and additional benefits for the overall economy.

The consequence is that such frontier-based development and resource exploitation in many present-day low and middle-income economies often falls far short of the minimum conditions for attaining sustainable development. What little rents have been generated from this development process have not led to sufficient investments in other productive assets and in more dynamic sectors of the economy. Instead, many poor economies exhibit a "dualism within dualism" economic structure characterized by continuing dependence of the overall economy on mainly primary product exports, a large proportion of the population concentrated on fragile land, and a high degree of rural poverty. Any resource rents that are earned from frontier "reserves" are often reinvested in further land expansion and resource exploitation. The frontier remains an isolated enclave, and there are very little economy-wide efficiency gains and benefits. In addition, this process tends to be inequitable. The resource rents accrue mainly to wealthy individuals, who have increased incentives for "rent-seeking" behavior that is in turn supported by policy distortions that reinforce the existing pattern of allocating and distributing natural resources. The poor are therefore left with marginal resources and frontier land areas to exploit, further reducing their ability to improve their livelihoods, and of course, to generate and appropriate significant rents.

This book could end with these rather pessimistic observations. However, that would be neither fruitful nor helpful to anyone interested in encouraging successful resource-based development in today's low and middle-income economies. Instead, this book addresses an additional, very pertinent question: Is there some way in which policies and institutions in developing countries could be modified to change their current pattern of resource-based development from a "vicious" to a "virtuous" cycle? The short answer is "yes," but not without difficulty. This requires achieving four important long-run goals:

• Reinvesting resource rents in more productive and dynamic sectors of the economy, which in turn are linked to the resource-exploiting sectors of the domestic economy.
• Developing political and legal institutions to discourage rent-seeking behavior by wealthy investors in the natural resource sectors of the economy.
• Instigating widespread reform of government policies that favor wealthier investors in markets for valuable natural resources, including arable land.
• Targeting additional policies and investments to improve the economic opportunities and livelihoods of the rural poor, rather than relying on frontier land expansion and urban migration as the principal outlet for alleviating rural poverty.

Achieving the first goal requires fostering resource-augmenting technological change, frontier-mainstay integration and economy-wide knowledge spillovers. On available evidence, this seems to be a tall order for many present-day low and middle-income economies. As discussed in the concluding chapter, however, there are three countries – Botswana, Malaysia and Thailand – that may provide instructive examples as to how this might be accomplished. As for the other three objectives, achieving them will mean overcoming pervasive policy, market and institutional distortions that, on the one hand, encourage problems of rent-seeking and corruption, especially in frontier resource-extractive activities, and on the other, perpetuate inequalities in wealth and rural poverty. Attaining these objectives will clearly be a tall order for many low and middle-income economies. Yet, in failing to do so, these developing countries will perpetuate being trapped in the "vicious cycle" of unsuccessful frontier land expansion and resource exploitation that is symptomatic of underdevelopment rather than sustainable economic development.

In addressing the above themes, this book is clearly not examining some important areas in which natural resources may interact with global economic development.

One such area is the global scarcity of biological diversity, key ecological services and unique natural assets that are leading the international community to place greater value on the conservation of certain natural resources in developing countries, such as tropical forests, wildlife and their habitat, mangroves and wetlands, coral reefs and, of course, biodiversity.

However, this particular natural resource problem and the economic approach to its resolution is fundamentally different from the themes addressed in this book. As I have argued elsewhere, economists usually depict the current disincentives to conserve the world's remaining biological diversity as a problem of *global market failure* (Barbier 2000). A country may have a biological rich natural asset that is, or may potentially be, producing benefits of global significance, but as there is no market or any other institution at the global level to enable the country to "capture" this value, it is unlikely to consider these global benefits in its decision whether to conserve, exploit or develop the asset. That is, unless a country receives compensation in some form for the management of its stock of biodiversity to provide values of global significance, then the country has little incentive to do so. Creating such an incentive mechanism essentially involves explicit recognition at the international level of a host country's right to "sell" global benefits and the creation of the institutional means for this to occur. This could happen through various mechanisms, such as the ratification of a comprehensive international biodiversity agreement that embodies payment or exchange mechanisms for providing these global benefits or through bilateral and multilateral payment and financial schemes that allow the host country to receive compensation from the international community for conserving specific global biodiversity benefits.

Originally, I intended to discuss the theory as well as recent developments of such international mechanisms and institutions in this book. However, I have not done so principally for two reasons. First, it would have added at least two chapters to an already long book. Second, since the problem of global market failure concerning transboundary biodiversity and other natural resource benefits does diverge somewhat from the main themes addressed in this book, this problem is best explored in a separate book altogether.

A second issue that is not addressed by this book is whether "fundamental inequalities" in the existing "world economic order" are further perpetuating the poor economic performance of resource-dependent developing economies. This view is discussed to some extent in Chapter 2, which is referred to as the doctrine of "unequal development." As noted in the chapter, the failure of primary product exports to provide the "engine of growth" for developing economies in the post-World War II era led some authors to conclude that there was something inherently wrong in the "core-periphery" trading relationships underlying the pattern of trade and international division of labor characterizing the world economy. According to this view, the core-periphery trading relationship benefits overwhelmingly the industrial core states of the world economy at the expense of the primary-producing and exporting developing economies, thus creating an inherent tendency for international inequality to increase. The result is that, whereas the core industrial states in the world economic system continue to develop and grow, international trade fails to spread development to the periphery. Instead, the periphery is trapped in a perpetual state of underdevelopment and remains specialized in the production and export of primary products.

This view is still very prevalent today, and features in many critiques of the failure of "globalization" to generate benefits to poor countries and the poor within those countries. Many of these critiques focus on averting financial crisis in the developing world and on reforming the international economic "world order" – the system by which the international economic and financial system are governed – in order to make globalization more humane, effective, and equitable for poorer countries. Even prominent mainstream economists, such as Joe Stiglitz (2003), have criticized globalization from the latter perspective, arguing that globalization could be a positive force for alleviating poverty and fostering development provided that the main institutions that govern globalization – The International Monetary Fund, the World Bank and the World Trade Organization – reform their operations and overall strategies for assisting poor countries.

This book does not address the above debate concerning the pros and cons of globalization and its implications for resource use and development in low and middle-income economies. Some readers may consider this a serious omission. However, I have several reasons for not addressing the globalization debate. First, a serious discussion of how reforms of the world trading system and key multilateral institutions would lead to improvements in the economic development of poor economies is clearly a separate topic for another book (such as the one by Stiglitz (2003)). Second, before one can examine how proposed reforms might affect natural resource exploitation and the prospects for sustainable economic development in poor countries, one must first explore and understand this resource-development relationship more fully. That is the objective of this book, which, as I have noted, appears to be the first to explore this relationship in such detail. Third, from a more pragmatic perspective, with the exception of possible debt alleviation for poor economies (which I wholeheartedly endorse), the prospects of major global economic and financial reforms are not good over the short and medium term. This implies that developing countries must take the existing world economic order as "given", and cannot expect much help from the international community in terms of changing existing trading rules, financial mechanisms and lending institutions to improve either access to markets, the availability and the terms of foreign aid, or the conditions for loans and grants. Although I wish this were not the case, I would also argue that the lack of widespread reforms of international economic and financial conditions should not be an excuse for developing countries to "do nothing". Instead, as emphasized in this book, the key to successful resource-based development appears to be sound policies and favorable institutions, especially those aimed at attaining the "virtuous cycle" growth path of reinvesting resource rents, developing sound policies and institutions and lessening a "dualism within dualism" economic structure. Although more favorable international conditions would surely make this task easier for developing country governments, there is clearly a substantial policy and reform agenda that these governments could undertake themselves in order to transform current patterns of natural resource exploitation and use within their countries.

The ten chapters of this book comprise three parts. Part One, which consists of the first four chapters, provides a broad overview of the role of natural resources in economic development. The objectives of these introductory chapters are to understand better the degree of dependence of low and middle-income countries on natural resource exploitation and to examine further the key paradox concerning the role of natural resources in economic development. Why is natural resource exploitation not yielding greater benefits to the poor economies of the world? This paradox is explored both through a historical review of resource use and development and through examining current theories explaining the under-performance of today's resource-abundant economies. An important conclusion to emerge from this discussion and analysis is that frontier-based economic development still plays an important role in the economies of many developing regions, and this in turn is symptomatic of the inefficient and unsustainable way in which natural resources are used in present-day economic development. This argument leads directly to the *frontier expansion hypothesis* as an explanation of the resource-development paradox.

A key feature of frontier-based development is widespread land use change. Equally, water resource use and allocation is changing rapidly in developing countries as a result of increased economic and population growth. Part Two of the book, comprising Chapters 5, 6 and 7, explores in more detail the economic factors underlying rapid land and water use change in low and middle-income countries, and illustrates the issues with case study examples. Understanding the factors underlying these two important processes of resource use within developing countries is in turn important for devising appropriate policies and reforms to mitigate the economic losses caused by these processes.

Part Three of this book consists of Chapters 8, 9 and 10 and is concerned with developing economy-wide policies and reforms to encourage sustainable resource-based development in low and middle-income economies. The contribution of Chapter 8 is to draw the link between two types of "dualisms" found in developing economies: their "resource dependency" within the world economy and the tendency for the rural poor within these economies to be "trapped" in a poverty-environmental degradation cycle. The chapter concludes by identifying how developing countries break out of this pattern of development and ensure that natural resource exploitation does confer sustained growth and poverty alleviation. Chapters 9 and 10 elaborate further on the necessary policies, institutions and reforms that are required. For instance, Chapter 9 demonstrates that it is at least *theoretically* possible to break this vicious cycle through reinvesting resource rents in more productive and dynamic sectors of the economy, which in turn are linked to the resource-exploiting sectors of the domestic economy. Chapter 10 continues this analysis by providing further discussion and illustrative cases indicating what type of complementary policy and institutional reforms are needed. This is accomplished through a broad overview of these reforms and a review of the lessons learned from three present-day examples of successful resource-based development: Botswana, Malaysia and Thailand.

1 | Natural resources and developing countries: an overview

O VER the past twenty years, a major change has occurred in economic thinking. No longer do we consider the economic process of producing goods and services and generating human welfare to be solely dependent on the accumulation of physical and human capital. An increasing number of economists now accept that there is a third form of "capital" or "economic asset" that is also crucial to the functioning of the economic system of production, consumption and overall welfare. This distinct category consists of the natural and environmental resource endowment available to an economy, which is often referred to as *natural capital*.

Figure 1.1 depicts the basic relationship between physical, human and natural capital and the economic system.

Human-made, or physical, capital (K_P), human capital (K_H) and natural capital (K_N) all contribute to human welfare through supporting the production of goods and services in the economic process. For example, K_P, consists of machinery, equipment, factory buildings, tools and other investment goods that are used in production; K_H includes the human skills necessary for advanced production processes and for research and development activities that lead to technical innovation; and K_N is used for material and energy inputs into production, acts as a "sink" for waste emissions from the economic process, and provides a variety of "ecological services" to sustain production, such as nutrient recycling, watershed protection and catchment functions, habitat support and climate regulation. However, all three forms of capital also contribute directly to human welfare independently of their contributions through the economic process. For instance, included in physical capital, K_P, is fine architecture and other physical components of cultural heritage; increases in K_H also contribute more generally to increases in the overall stock of human knowledge; and

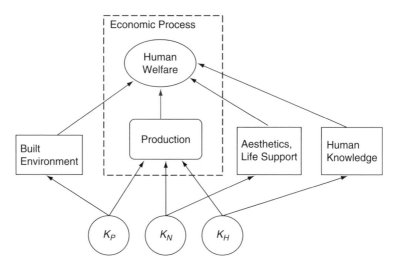

Source: Adapted from Pearce and Barbier (2000).

Figure 1.1. Human, physical and natural capital and the economic system

K_N includes aesthetically pleasing natural landscapes, and provides a variety of ecological services that are essential for supporting life.

There are some important general issues and debates concerning the role of natural resources in economic development. This introductory chapter elaborates further on these issues and debates. In particular, the chapter has three objectives.

First, the chapter highlights some of the current economic thinking concerning natural capital, growth and development. For example, it is clear from Figure 1.1 that the services provided by natural capital are unique, and in the case of the ecological services and life-support functions of the environment, are not well understood. As a result, there has also been considerable debate in economics over the role of natural capital in "sustainable" economic development. That is, does the environment have an "essential" role in sustaining human welfare, and if so, are special "compensation rules" required to ensure that future generations are not affected adversely by natural capital depletion today?

A second debate has emerged over whether environmental degradation in an economy may initially increase, but eventually declines, as per capita income increases. Empirical verification of this *environmental*

Kuznets curve (EKC) hypothesis has occasionally been cited as evidence that economies will be able to overcome certain environmental problems through continued economic growth and development. The next two sections discuss in greater detail the current debates over the role of natural capital in sustaining economic development and the implications of empirical evidence on the EKC hypothesis for economic growth and the environment.

A third objective of this introductory chapter is to provide an overview of the importance of natural capital to economic development in present-day low and middle-income countries in Africa, Asia and Latin America. The key structural features, or stylized facts, of these economies are also important for explaining the focus of the remainder of the book. In particular, four such facts will be emphasized in this chapter.

First, most low and middle-income economies are highly dependent on the exploitation of natural resources. For many of these economies, primary product exports account for the vast majority of their export earnings, and one or two primary commodities make up the bulk of exports.

Second, recent evidence suggests that increasing economic dependence on natural resources is negatively correlated with economic performance. The implications for low-income countries is that the "take off" into sustained and structurally balanced economic growth and development is still some time away, and thus the dependence of their overall economies on natural resources will persist over the medium and long term.

Third, development in low and middle-income economies is accompanied by substantial resource conversion. In particular, expansion of the agricultural land base in these economies is occurring rapidly through conversion of forests, wetlands and other natural habitat. In addition, many developing regions of the world are also placing greater stress on their freshwater resources as a result of increasing population and demand.

Fourth, a substantial proportion of the population in low and middle-income countries is concentrated in marginal areas and on ecologically fragile land, such as converted forest frontier areas, poor quality uplands, converted wetlands and so forth. Households on these lands not only face problems of land degradation and low productivity but also tend to be some of the poorest in the world.

Natural capital and sustainable development

The relationship between human, physical and natural capital and the economic system that is outlined in Figure 1.1 is also an important starting point for understanding sustainable development. All three types of capital essentially form the *total capital stock* underlying an economy, and it is the management of this total stock that is critical to determining whether or not the economy is on a sustainable development path.

The importance of the total capital stock concept to sustainability is illustrated further in Figure 1.2, which summarizes broadly the economic view of sustainable development. Most economic interpretations of sustainability take as their starting point the consensus reached by the World Commission on Environment and Development (the WCED, or Brundtland Commission). The WCED defined sustainable development as "development that meets the needs of the present without compromising the ability of future generations to meet their own needs" (WCED 1987).

Economists are generally comfortable with this broad interpretation of sustainability, as it is easily translatable into economic terms: an increase in well-being today should not have as its consequences a reduction in well-being tomorrow.[1] That is, future generations should be entitled to at least the same level of economic opportunities – and thus at least the same level of economic welfare – as currently available to present generations. Consequently, economic development today must ensure that future generations are left no worse off than present generations. Or, as some economists have succinctly put it, per capita welfare should not be declining over time (Pezzey 1989).

As noted in Figure 1.2, it is the *total* stock of capital employed by the economic system, including natural capital, that determines the full range of economic opportunities, and thus well-being, available to both present and future generations. Society must decide how best to "use" its total capital stock today to increase current economic activities and welfare, and how much it needs to "save" or even "accumulate" for tomorrow, and ultimately, for the well-being of future generations.

However, it is not simply the aggregate stock of capital in the economy that may matter but also its composition, in particular whether present generations are "using up" one form of capital to meet the needs of today.

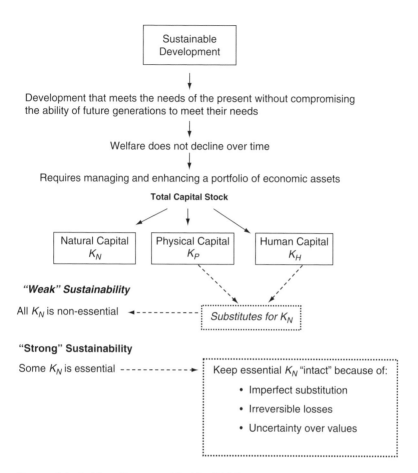

Source: Adapted from Pearce and Barbier (2000).

Figure 1.2. Sustainable economic development

For example, much of the recent interest in sustainable development has arisen out of concern that current economic development may be leading to rapid accumulation of physical and human capital, but at the expense of excessive depletion and degradation of natural capital. The major concern has been that, by depleting the world's stock of natural wealth irreversibly, the development path chosen today will have detrimental implications for the well-being of future generations. In other words, according to this view, current economic development is essentially unsustainable.

While it is generally accepted by most economists that economic development around the world is leading to the irreversible depletion of natural capital, there is widespread disagreement as to whether this necessarily implies that such development is inherently unsustainable. From an economic standpoint, the critical issue of debate is not whether natural capital is being irreversibly depleted, but whether we can compensate future generations for the current loss of natural capital, and if that is possible, how much is required to compensate future generations for this loss (Mäler 1995).

Economists concerned with this problem appear to be divided into two camps over the special role of natural capital in sustainable development. The main disagreement between these two perspectives is whether natural capital has a unique or "essential" role in sustaining human welfare, and thus whether special "compensation rules" are required to ensure that future generations are not made worse off by natural capital depletion today (see Figure 1.2). These two contrasting views are now generally referred to as *weak sustainability* versus *strong sustainability*.[2]

According to the *weak sustainability* view, there is essentially no inherent difference between natural and other forms of capital, and hence the same "optimal depletion" rules ought to apply to both. As long as the natural capital that is being depleted is replaced with even more valuable physical and human capital, then the value of the aggregate stock – comprising human, physical and the remaining natural capital – is increasing over time.[3] Maintaining and enhancing the total stock of all capital alone is sufficient to attain sustainable development.

In contrast, proponents of the *strong sustainability* view argue that physical or human capital cannot substitute all the environmental resources comprising the natural capital stock, or all of the ecological services performed by nature. Consequently, the strong sustainability viewpoint questions whether, on the one hand, human and physical capital, and on the other, natural capital, effectively comprise a single "homogeneous" total capital stock. Instead, proponents of strong sustainability maintain that some forms of natural capital are "essential" to human welfare, particularly key ecological services, unique environments and natural habitats and even irreplaceable natural resource attributes (such as biodiversity). Uncertainty over the true value to human welfare of these important assets, in particular the value that future generations may place on them if they become increasingly scarce, further limits our ability to determine whether we can adequately compensate future generations for irreversible losses in such essential natural capital today. Thus the strong sustainability view suggests that environmental resources and ecological services that are essential for human welfare and cannot be easily substituted by human and physical capital should be protected and not depleted. The only satisfactory "compensation rule" for protecting the welfare of future generations is to keep essential natural capital intact. That is, maintaining or increasing the value of the total capital stock over time in turn requires keeping the non-substitutable and essential components of natural capital constant over time.

The two sides in the debate between weak and strong sustainability are not easy to reconcile. Recent extensions to the economic theory of sustainable development have not so much resolved this debate as sharpened its focus.

Nevertheless, the weak versus strong sustainability argument is an important one, especially for developing countries that are dependent on the exploitation of natural capital for their current development efforts. As we discuss further below, this dependence of low and middle-income economies on natural resources is a key "stylized fact" for these economies, and should shape our perspective on the role of efficient and sustainable management of natural capital to foster long-run development.

Growth, environment and the EKC

Figures 1.1 and 1.2 and the discussion so far have identified the importance of natural capital as a component of the total capital stock supporting economies, and in turn, the role of maintaining this stock in order to enhance sustainable economic development. However, for many developing countries, maintaining natural capital is not a viable option in the short and medium run. As these economies grow and develop, natural resource degradation and increased pollution are likely to be increased. A critical issue for developing economies, therefore, is whether at some point in the future they are able to attain levels of economic development that will coincide with improving rather than deteriorating environmental quality.

This issue has become the focus of a new area of enquiry in economics. This recent literature is concerned with the analysis of *environmental Kuznets curves* (EKC), i.e. the hypothesis that there exists an "inverted-U"-shaped relationship between a variety of indicators of

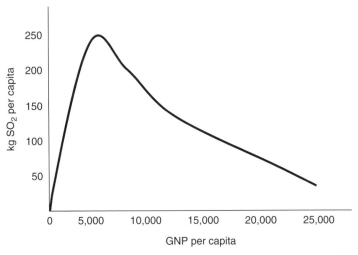

The above curve is the environmental Kuznets curve for sulfur dioxide (SO_2) estimated across rich and poor countries of the world by Panayotou (1995). The "peak" or "turning point" level of per capita income where SO_2 levels start to fall is around US$5,000.

Source: Adapted from Panayotou (1995).

Figure 1.3. An Environmental Kuznets Curve for sulfur dioxide

environmental pollution or resource depletion and the level of per capita income.[4] The implication of this hypothesis is that, as per capita income increases, environmental degradation rises initially but then eventually declines. The emerging EKC literature has important implications for sustainable development, and in particular, for whether or not developing economies may be able eventually to overcome certain environmental problems through continued economic growth and development.

Figure 1.3 shows a typical EKC estimated for sulfur dioxide (SO_2). Although estimations of such EKC relationships began in the early 1990s, interest in these studies is likely to continue for some time. There are several reasons for this.

First, the EKC is a falsifiable hypothesis that can and will continue to be tested through empirical investigation. Thus an increasing number of studies are attempting to determine whether the EKC hypothesis holds for various indicators of environmental degradation, both over time and across countries, regions, states, districts and even cities.

Second, the EKC hypothesis poses an important intellectual challenge. Explanations as to why environmental degradation should first increase then decline with income have focused on a number of underlying causes, including:

- the effects of structural economic change on the use of the environment for resource inputs and to assimilate waste;
- the effects of increasing income on the demand for environmental quality; and
- the types of environmental degradation and ecological processes.

It is not yet clear which of these factors, if any, explain why we might observe an EKC relationship. For example, many of the original explanations of the EKC hypothesis focused on changes in the composition of goods and services due to structural shifts in the economy, the efficiency of resource use, the composition of inputs, and technological innovation. However, increasingly it has been recognized that the effect of such changes on environment-income linkages are not "exogenous" processes – determined by factors outside the economy – but are influenced by policy choices (Andreoni and Levinson 2001; Dasgupta *et al.* 2002; López 1994; Panayotou 1995 and 1997; Stern *et al.* 1996; World Bank 1992). Similarly, previous conjecture that environmental quality is simply a "luxury good", and thus the demand for improved environmental quality increases more than proportionately with income, is proving difficult to substantiate (Lieb 2002; McConnell 1997). Finally, it is possible that EKC studies are providing misleading information on environment-income linkages (Stern *et al.* 1996). There is much that we do not know about key ecological processes and functions, as well as the valuable services that they provide. Even if we observe EKCs for certain indicators of pollution and resource depletion, it does not necessarily follow that the overall health and functioning of ecosystems will also improve as income increases.

Third, and perhaps most importantly, the EKC hypothesis has revived interest in the long-standing debate over the environmental implications of economic growth (Ansuategi *et al.* 1998). Some authors interpret such estimated curves to imply that economies will eventually "grow out of" many environmental problems (Beckerman 1992). Taken to its extreme, this argument suggests that we do not have to regard the environment as anything special. As people get richer they will increase their demand for the environment and improve it, initially with public health legislation, then clean air, then conservation generally.

However, other commentators have been more cautious, noting that conclusive evidence of an EKC relationship applies only to a few pollutants, thus making it difficult to use this evidence to speculate more generally about growth-environment linkages (Arrow *et al.* 1995). Still others have pointed out that, even for those pollutants displaying EKC characteristics, aggregate global emissions are projected to rise over time, demonstrating that the existence of an EKC does not necessarily imply that, at the global level, any associated environmental damage is likely to disappear with economic growth (Selden and Song 1994; Stern *et al.* 1996). Policy makers are following this renewed debate with interest. From their perspective, the critical policy issue is whether economic growth should continue to be the main priority, with protection of the environment as a secondary consideration to be addressed mainly in the future, or whether explicit policies to control environmental degradation at the local, national and global level are required urgently today.

To date, the empirical evidence suggests that, where EKC relationships do hold, they are more likely to apply only for certain types of environmental damage, e.g. pollutants with more short-term and local impacts, versus those with more global, indirect and long-term impacts such as carbon dioxide and other greenhouse gases (Arrow *et al.* 1995; Barbier 1997a; Cole *et al.* 1997; Dasgupta *et al.* 2002; Selden and Song 1994). In terms of types of "localized" environmental damage, the EKC hypothesis seems mainly to be valid for air pollution, in particular sulfur dioxide (SO_2) and to a lesser extent solid particulate matter (SPM). The evidence for other localized forms of environmental damage, such as water pollution, deforestation, urban waste and toxic metals, is more mixed (Barbier 1997a; Cole *et al.* 1997).

Moreover, environment-income relationships appear to vary across individual countries. For example, a study for Malaysia found SPM to be increasing with income (Vincent 1997), whereas a study for the United States indicated that SPM and other major air pollutants decline with increasing levels of income (Carson *et al.* 1997). De Groot *et al.* (2004, p. 509) also conclude that for China "the relationship between pollution and income is highly dependent on the type of pollution that is considered and on how environmental impact is being measured (that is, in terms of levels of pollution, pollution per capita, or pollution per unit of real gross regional product (GRP)." The authors find, for example, in the case of wastewater that it declines monotonically with income, regardless of whether wastewater is measured in absolute levels, per capita levels or per unit of GRP. This suggests that water quality in China should increase with income and overall regional development. In contrast, in the case of solid waste the authors find that if pollution is measured in terms of absolute levels then an N-shaped relationship results. However, if solid waste is measured per unit of GRP, then a downward-sloping curve occurs, and if measured in per capita terms there is no significant environment-income relationship. Of all the main pollutants in China, only waste gas appears to follow the typical inverted-U EKC relationship, but only if it is measured in absolute levels. When waste gas emissions are modeled in per capita terms, the relationship is monotonically increasing in per capita income, and when measured per unit of GRP, the relationship is decreasing.

However, even when an EKC relationship is estimated, often the turning point on the curve, where environmental degradation starts to decline with per capita income, proves to be very high relative to the current per capita GDP levels of most countries of the world (Barbier 1997a). For example, the turning point for sulfur dioxide in Figure 1.3 is just under US$5,000 per capita. In another recent analysis, none of the estimated EKC turning points for various environmental indicators are below the minimum income level of the sample of countries analyzed, and the turning points for nitrates, carbon dioxide, energy consumption and traffic volumes are well above the maximum income of the countries in the data set (Cole *et al.* 1997). In the case of those EKC estimates for tropical deforestation that are robust, the per capita income levels of most developing countries are also well to the left of the estimated turning point peaks (Barbier and Burgess 2001a; Bhattarai and Hammig 2004; Cropper and Griffiths 1994; Koop and Toole 1989).

Overall, such results suggest that most countries have not yet reached levels of per capita income for which environmental improvement is likely to occur. The implications are a worsening global problem of environmental degradation as the world economy and populations expand, even for those environmental indicators that display EKCs (Selden and Song 1994; Stern *et al.* 1996). This can be seen clearly in Figure 1.4. This figure shows the future trend in global sulfur dioxide emissions based on the estimated EKC for SO_2 depicted in Figure 1.3 and employing aggregation of individual country projections of population and economic growth over 1990 to 2025. The resulting projections show a rise in global sulfur dioxide emissions throughout this

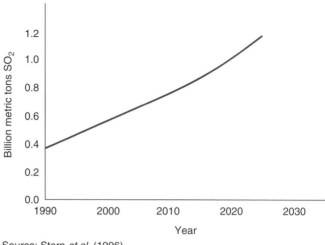

Source: Stern *et al.* (1996).

Figure 1.4. Projected trends for global SO$_2$ emissions

period. For example, total global emissions of SO$_2$ rise from 383 million metric tons in 1990 to 1,181 million metric tons in 2025, or from 73 to 142 kg per capita (Stern *et al.* 1996).[5]

Where the EKC relationship does appear to hold, especially for certain air pollutants with localized or short-term effects, there is evidence that the eventual reduction in emissions associated with higher per capita income levels may be attributable to the "abatement effect" that arises as countries become richer (Andreoni and Levinson 2001; López 1994; Panayotou 1997). Also, both the willingness and the ability of political jurisdictions to engage in and enforce improved environmental regulations, to increase public spending on environmental research and development, or even to engage in multilateral agreements to reduce emissions may also increase with per capita income levels (Carson *et al.* 1997; de Bruyn 1997; Komen *et al.* 1997).[6] The estimated EKC relationship may also be influenced by changing trade patterns, including the impact of trade liberalization on the environment, which will differ from country to country, as opposed to growth-induced abatement alone (Antweiler *et al.* 2001; Cole 2003). However, it is a great leap of faith to conclude from these results that economic growth on its own will foster environmental improvement automatically. As Panayotou (1997) has concluded, "when all effects are considered, the relationship between growth and the environment turns out to be much more complex with wide scope for active policy intervention to bring about more desirable (and in the presence of market failures) more efficient economic and environmental outcomes."

This conclusion may be particularly relevant for low-income and rapidly industrializing developing countries, whose current per capita income levels are well below the turning points of most estimated EKCs. In the absence of national and multilateral policy interventions, environmental degradation will continue in these countries as per capita income increases, at least over the medium term. In this regard, the observation of Vincent (1997) from his analysis of Malaysia is very apt: "The lack of evidence of EKCs in Malaysia does not prove that EKCs do not exist anywhere. It does indicate, however, that policy makers in developing countries should not assume that economic growth will automatically solve air and water pollution problems."

In sum, the implications of the EKC literature for sustainable development are fairly straightforward. Regardless of whether one is an adherent of the weak sustainability or strong sustainability view, estimated EKC relationships on their own do not help us determine which actual policies are required in the economy to manage its total capital stock, including its stock of natural capital. Although recent EKC studies appear to have revived the wider "growth versus the environment" debate, these studies offer very little support for the view that economic growth alone is the solution to all environmental problems. Rather, it is clear from the EKC literature that specific policies to protect the environment are necessary to reduce environmental damages that are imposing real welfare losses. As Arrow *et al.* (1995) have succinctly put it: "Economic growth is not a panacea for environmental quality; indeed it is not even the main issue."

Natural capital and developing economies: some "stylized facts"

So far, we have examined how management of environmental and natural resources, i.e. the *natural capital stock*, of a country is important for achieving sustainable economic development. This argument was summarized in Figures 1.1 and 1.2, which illustrate the current economic thinking on the relationship between natural capital and the sustainability of the economic process. We have also reviewed the recent findings of the EKC literature to make the case that the causal relationship is from improved environmental management to enhanced economic development and welfare, and not the other way around.

The key question now is: what do these current debates over the relationship between natural capital, growth and development imply for present-day low and middle-income countries in Africa, Asia and Latin America? However, before we can explore such implications further, we need to understand some of the key structural features, or stylized facts, of natural resource use in these economies.

Stylized fact one: the majority of low and middle-income countries are highly dependent on primary product exports

Most low and middle-income economies today are highly dependent on the exploitation of their natural resource endowments for commercial, export-oriented economic activities. For these economies, primary product exports – and often one or two main commodities – account for nearly all export earnings.

Returning to Figure 1.1, this suggests that natural capital (K_N) is a vital input into the production process of developing economies. More importantly, as Figure 1.2 indicates, efficient and sustainable management of the natural capital stock is essential for the long-run development prospects of many poor economies, because natural resources form the basis of the important export-earning activities of these economies. The resource rents earned from these activities in turn are the main source of investment in physical and human capital, and the export revenues finance the necessary imports of capital goods, services and technology that are critical for long-term development efforts.

Table 1.1 depicts the export concentration in primary commodities for 95 low and middle-income economies.[7] As indicated in the table, 72 of the countries – more than three-quarters – have 50% or more of their exports from primary products, and 35 countries – more than a third – have an export concentration in primary commodities of 90% or more.

Table 1.1 also indicates the share in total exports of the two main primary commodities for each country. For those low and middle-income countries with an export concentration in primary products of 50% or more, two commodities account for most of these exports and for a large share, if not the majority, of total exports. On average, for countries with a primary product export share of 50% or more, the two main commodities accounted for about 60% of total exports. For

Table 1.1 Export concentration in primary commodities for low and middle-income developing economies

	Export share 1990/99[a]	Export share 1980/81[b]	Export share 1965[b]	Main export commodities[c]			
				1		2	
90%–100%							
Yemen A. R.	100	49	100	Fisheries	31.3%	Petroleum	14.1%
Botswana	100[c]	NA	NA	Diamonds	92.7%	Beef	5.3%
Angola	99	NA	82	Petroleum	77.1%	Coffee	2.6%
Nigeria	99	99	97	Petroleum	94.2%	Cocoa	2.5%
Mali	99	83	97	Cotton	41.9%	Groundnuts	0.8%
Ethiopia	99[d]	99	99	Coffee	66.6%	Sugar	1.1%
Iran	99[c]	NA	96	Petroleum	98.1%	Fisheries	0.2%
Rwanda	99[c]	99	100	Coffee	68.8%	Tea	8.4%
Eq. Guinea	99[c]	91	NA	Cocoa	53.5%	Timber	38.0%
Sao Tome & Pr.	99[d]	100	NA	Cocoa	95.5%[d]	Copra	1.8%
Yemen PDR	99[d]	NA	94				
Burkina Faso	98[d]	85	95	Cotton	27.3%	Livestock	26.8%[d]
Zambia	98[c]	99	100	Copper	93.3%	Zinc	1.8%
Liberia	98[c]	98	97	Iron Ore	60.4%	Rubber	20.4%
Sudan	97	99	99	Cotton	30.0%	Oilseed Cake	1.6%
Niger	97	98	95	Ores/Metals	67.0%[e]	Food	29.0%[e]
Uganda	97	100	100	Coffee	95.8%	Cotton	1.6%
Mauritania	97[d]	99	99	Fisheries	41.9%	Iron Ore	37.0%

Table 1.1 (*continued*)

	Export share 1990/99[a]	Export share 1980/81[b]	Export share 1965[b]	Main export commodities[c]			
				1		2	
Algeria	96	99	96	Petroleum	34.9%	Phosphate	0.2%
Benin	96	96	95	Cotton	26.0%	Cocoa	16.0%
Malawi	95	93	99	Tobacco	53.5%	Tea	15.4%
Libya	95	99	100	Petroleum	90.5%		
Iraq	95[c]	NA	99	Petroleum	94.4%	Tobacco	0.1%
Somalia	95[d]	99	86	Bananas	18.6%	Fisheries	3.5%
Ecuador	94	93	98	Petroleum	43.6%	Fisheries	15.8%
Gambia, The	94	NA	NA	Groundnuts	17.2%	Groundnut Oil	12.0%
Guyana	94[c]	NA	NA	Bauxite	39.5%	Sugar	35.7%
Congo, Dem. Rep. (Zaïre)	93[d]	94	92	Copper	35.9%	Coffee	14.3%
Nicaragua	92	92	94	Coffee	40.9%	Cotton	21.2%
Comoros	92[d]	86	NA	Cloves	41.7%[d]	Vanilla	33.3%[d]
Cameroon	91	97	94	Petroleum	48.1%	Coffee	13.1%
Congo, Rep.	91[c]	94	37	Petroleum	83.2%	Timber	5.7%
Saudi Arabia	90	99	99	Petroleum	88.5%[e]	Food	1.0%[e]
Papua N. G.	90	100	90	Copper	31.0%	Coffee	15.2%
Lao PDR	90[d]	100	94	Timber	51.7%[d]	Electricity	19.0%

	Export share 1990/99[a]	Export share 1980/81[b]	Export share 1965[b]	Main export commodities[c]	
				1	2
80%–89%					
Burundi	89[c]	96	95	Coffee 83.5%	Tea 4.2%
Venezuela	89	NA	98	Petroleum 55.7%	Aluminum 3.7%
Myanmar	89	81	99	Timber 40.3%	Rice 28.1%
Chad	89[d]	96	97	Cotton 33.2%	Oilseed 0.2%
Oman	88	96	NA	Petroleum 90.0%	Fisheries 0.7%
Cote d'Ivoire	88[d]	90	95	Cocoa 30.5%	Coffee 18.5%
Paraguay	87	NA	92	Cotton 16.4%	Soybeans 14.9%
Gabon	87[c]	NA	NA	Petroleum 70.5%	Manganese 8.1%
Guinea-Bissau	87[d]	71	NA	Fisheries 13.9%	Groundnuts 10.4%
Togo	86	85	97	Phosphate 31.7%	Cotton 11.8%
Ghana	86	98	98	Cocoa 49.2%	Aluminum 11.3%
Chile	85	90	96	Copper 42.9%	Fisheries 11.6%
Tanzania	84	86	87	Coffee 44.1%	Cotton 11.3%
Panama	81	91	98	Fisheries 31.3%	Bananas 22.5%
Honduras	80	89	96	Bananas 35.4%	Coffee 28.0%
Peru	80	83	99	Copper 17.3%	Zinc 12.3%
Guinea	80	NA	NA	Bauxite 72.8%	Aluminum 19.4%
Cuba	80[c]	NA	NA	Sugar 74.9%	Fisheries 2.3%
70%–79%					
Mozambique	79[c]	NA	NA	Fisheries 55.7%	Sugar 7.1%
Bolivia	78	100	95	Tin 18.6%	Zinc 3.4%
Syrian Arab Republic	77	NA	90	Petroleum 40.1%	Cotton 7.9%

Table 1.1 (*continued*)

	Export share 1990/99[a]	Export share 1980/81[b]	Export share 1965[b]	Main export commodities[c]			
				1		2	
Maldives	77[d]	70	NA	Fish	57.1%[d]	Tea	22.2%
Kenya	74	88	94	Coffee	31.7%	Bananas	4.1%
Colombia	72	72	93	Coffee	46.7%	Bananas	6.7%
Zimbabwe	71	63	85	Tobacco	19.7%	Cotton	6.7%
Guatemala	71	71	86	Coffee	39.2%	Bananas	6.5%
	60%–69%						
Argentina	69	84	94	Oilseed	9.5%	Wheat	8.7%
Trinidad and Tobago	68	86	93	Petroleum	41.7%	Sugar	1.3%
Madagascar	67	92	94	Coffee	36.8%	Fisheries	8.8%
Uruguay	61	70	95	Beef	12.0%	Wool	8.5%
Senegal	60	81	97	Fisheries	39.9%	Phosphate	8.5%
	50%–59%						
Egypt	58	92	80	Petroleum	39.3%	Cotton	7.4%
Sierra Leone	58[c]	57	39	Bauxite	18.0%	Cocoa	16.3%
El Salvador	57	63	83	Coffee	63.6%	Sugar	3.0%
Central African Republic	57[c]	74	46	Coffee	26.0%	Timber	18.0%
Indonesia	54	96	96	Petroleum	31.1%	Rubber	4.7%
Morocco	50	72	95	Phosphate	16.9%	Fisheries	11.9%
	40%–49%						
Costa Rica	49	68	84	Coffee	31.4%	Bananas	20.0%
Jordan	47	57	81	Phosphate	22.1%	Wheat	0.3%
Brazil	46	59	92	Coffee	8.5%	Iron Ore	6.6%

	Export share 1990/99[a]	Export share 1980/81[b]	Export share 1965[b]	Main export commodities[c]			
				1		2	
Malaysia	33	80	94	Petroleum	12.5%[e]	Food	10.0%[e]
Sri Lanka	33	79	99	Tea	28.7%	Rubber	7.3%
	30%–39%						
South Africa	37	26	68	Ores/metals	16.0%[e]	Petroleum	8.5%
Mexico	36	73	84	Petroleum	49.6%	Coffee	3.3%
Thailand	30	68	95	Fisheries	10.7%	Rice	9.0%
Jamaica	30	40	69	Aluminum	34.5%	Bauxite	16.5%
	20%–29%						
Mauritius	29	69	100	Sugar	38.7%	Fisheries	1.5%
Tunisia	26	56	82	Petroleum	32.5%	Fisheries	3.1%
India	25	47	51	Tea	4.6%	Iron Ore	4.2%
Vietnam	24[c]	NA	NA	Fisheries	10.3%	Rubber	4.0%
Dominican Rep.	21	81	98	Sugar	20.6%	Nickel	15.4%
Philippines	20	49	95	Coconut Oil	7.0%	Copper	5.1%
	10%–19%						
China	19	43	NA	Petroleum	12.5%	Cotton	1.7%
Pakistan	18	36	64	Cotton	12.1%	Rice	8.4%
Bangladesh	16	39	NA	Fisheries	12.5%	Jute	12.5%
Haiti	15	NA	NA	Coffee	15.5%	Cocoa	1.8%
Nepal	11	48	NA	Rice	3.6%	Oilseed	1.6%
	0%–9%						
Korea, Rep.	7	9	40	Fisheries	3.1%	Sugar	0.2%

Table 1.1 (continued)

	Export share 1990/99[a]	Export share 1980/81[b]	Export share 1965[b]	Main export commodities[c] 1	Main export commodities[c] 2
Lesotho	5[c]	NA	NA	Wool 4.8%	
Lebanon	2[c]	NA	66	Tobacco 1.3%	Wool 0.2%
Total No. of Countries	95				
Avg export share of all countries	71				
Median export share of all countries	84				
Countries with export share >90%	35				
Countries with export share >50%	71				

Notes: Low and middle-income countries in Africa, Latin America, Asia and Oceania, based on World Bank definition (countries with GDP per capita in 1994 at 1987 constant purchase power parity US$ of less than US$10,500 and an average of US$2,691).

[a] Based on United Nations Conference Trade and Development (UNCTAD), *Handbook of International Trade and Development Statistics, 2001* unless otherwise stated.

[b] Based on various editions of the following World Bank documents: *World Development Report, Trends in Developing Economies, Commodity Trade and Price Trends* and *African Economic and Financial Data.*

[c] Based on World Bank, *Commodity Trade and Price Trends, 1989–91 Edition.*

[d] Based on World Bank, *Commodity Trade and Price Trends, 1989–91 Edition.*

[e] Based on World Bank Development Indicators.

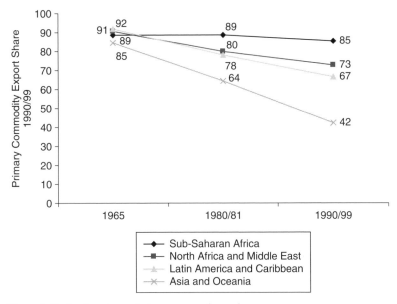

Figure 1.5. Regional trends in resource dependency

those countries with a primary product export share between 10–50%, the two main primary commodities still account for over 25% of total exports.

Throughout this book the first "stylized fact" captured by Table 1.1, that the majority of low and middle-income countries are highly dependent on primary product exports, is an important observation. For shorthand, we shall refer now to the share of primary products in total exports as the degree of *resource dependency* of a developing economy.[8] As we shall see in later chapters, we will characterize those economies with a primary product export share of 50% or more as being *resource-dependent*.

Although since the 1960s, some low and middle-income countries have reduced their resource dependency, there are important regional differences. Figure 1.5 shows the average regional changes from 1965 to 1990/99 in primary product export concentration for Sub-Saharan Africa, North Africa and the Middle East, Latin America and the Caribbean, and Asia and Oceania. In 1965 low and middle-income economies in all four regions had on average 85–92% of their exports based on primary commodities, but over the next thirty years regional trends varied considerably. In the 1990s, African countries still remained highly dependent on primary product exports (86%), and North African and Middle Eastern countries also maintained high resource dependence (73%). Latin American and Caribbean economies reduced their primary commodity export share much more, but still have a relatively high export share (67%). Only in Asia and Oceania has resource dependency fallen dramatically over the thirty-year period, to less than half of all exports (42%).

The World Bank has attempted to measure the extent to which the overall "wealth" of an economy consists of natural capital. For low and middle-income countries dependent on export revenues from primary commodities (other than petroleum), 20% of their national wealth comprises natural capital (World Bank 1997). These economies are typically located in the Caribbean, East and Southern Africa, the Middle East, South Asia and West Africa. As a comparison, natural capital accounts for only 5% of wealth for developed economies in North America, and 2% for developed economies in the Pacific and Western Europe. The most important source of natural capital in resource-dependent low and middle-income countries is agricultural land, especially for economies without substantial petroleum reserves. For example, in the poorest countries, agricultural cropland comprises around 80% of the natural capital.[9]

Stylized fact two: resource dependency in low and middle-income countries is associated with poor economic performance

Low and middle-income countries tend to be dependent on their natural resource endowments for economic growth and development because in poor economies natural capital may be the only source of capital readily available to them. Moreover, many countries are fortunate to have abundant natural resources to exploit, although as we have just seen, the most likely form of natural capital available to the poorest countries is likely to be land.

Given our discussion earlier in this chapter on the importance of natural capital to sustainable development, one might conclude that greater resource abundance should improve economic performance. That is, economies that have a greater endowment of natural resources must surely have a much better chance of attaining higher economic growth rates and prosperity than relatively resource-poor economies.

This must be particularly true with respect to low and middle-income countries, whose economies are generally more dependent on exploiting their natural capital stock in the transition to developing industrial and service sectors and the "take off" into higher and more balanced rates of long-run growth.

As we shall discuss further in Chapter 3, it has been difficult to determine from the empirical evidence whether greater *resource abundance*, in the terms of a larger natural resource endowment or stocks, is associated with higher or lower long-run growth in developing economies. However, recent evidence provides some indication that *resource dependency* may be associated with poorer economic performance.[10] For example, many low-income and lower middle-income economies that can be classified as highly resource-dependent today, in terms of primary product export share as in Table 1.1, also currently display low or stagnant growth rates (Barbier 1999).

Cross-country analysis has confirmed that countries with a high ratio of natural resource exports to GDP have tended to grow less rapidly than countries that are relatively resource poor (Rodríguez and Sachs 1999; Sachs and Warner 1997). Economies with a high primary product export share of GDP in 1971 also tended to have low growth rates during the subsequent period 1971–89 (Sachs and Warner 1995b). This finding is confirmed for the 1970–90 period, even when direct controls for the influence of geography, climate and growth in the previous decade are included (Sachs and Warner 2001). Table 1.2 replicates the results for the analysis that controls for growth in the 1960s.

There is also evidence that low and middle-income economies that are more resource-dependent tend to have lower levels of GDP per capita. Figure 1.6 indicates this relationship. The average export share of primary commodities in the total exports of low and middle-income countries over 1990/99 appears to be negatively correlated with the real GDP per capita of these countries in 1994.[11]

Finally, low and middle-income economies that are more resource dependent tend to have higher poverty levels. Figure 1.7 illustrates this relationship. Resource dependency appears to be positively correlated with a higher proportion of the population living in poverty.

In sum, this second stylized fact poses an intriguing paradox. Why is it that, despite the importance of natural capital for sustainable economic development, greater economic dependence on natural resource

Table 1.2 Economic growth and resource dependency, 1970–90

Dependent variable: Real GDP growth per capita, 1970–90 Explanatory variables	Coefficient (t-statistic)
Log GDP per capita 1970	−1.8
	(8.87)
Primary product share	−9.9
(Exports of natural resources, % GDP, 1970)	(6.50)
Trade openness	1.3
	(3.2)
Log investment	0.8
	(2.4)
Rule of law	0.4
	(3.8)
Terms of trade change	0.1
	(2.1)
Growth 1960–1969	0.02
	(0.2)
R^2	76%
Sample size	69

Source: Sachs and Warner (2001).

exploitation appears to be a hindrance to growth and development, particularly in today's low and middle-income economies? As this paradox goes to the heart of the role of natural resources in economic development, it is a critical issue worth exploring further in the remaining chapters of Part One.

Stylized fact three: development in low and middle-income economies is associated with increased land conversion and stress on available freshwater resources

As noted above, in low and middle-income economies, especially those without oil and natural gas reserves, the most important source of natural wealth is agricultural land. In these economies, expansion of this agricultural land base is occurring rapidly through conversion of forests, wetlands and other natural habitat. In addition, many developing regions of the world are also placing greater stress on their

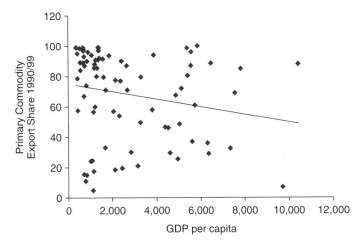

Figure 1.6. Resource dependency and GDP per capita in low and middle-income economies
Notes: Primary commodity export share is the average export share 1990/99 for low and middle-income countries in Table 1.1. GDP per capita in 1994 at 1987 constant purchase power parity US$, from World Bank Development Indicators. Correlation coefficient, $r = -0.205$. Number of observations = 82.

freshwater resources as a result of increasing population and demand. This trend for greater land and water use appears to be occurring in all low and middle-income countries, regardless of their resource dependency or economic performance.

López (1998b) identifies most of Sub-Saharan Africa, parts of Asia and the tropical forests of South America as regions with "abundant land" and open-access resource conditions that are prone to agricultural expansion. Widespread land and resource conversion is also occurring in Central America, parts of Mexico and tropical South America and some East and South East Asian countries, mainly due to the high degree of integration of rural areas with the national and international economy as well as population pressures. Agricultural land expansion in many tropical regions is also spurred by the prevailing structural conditions in the agricultural sectors of many developing countries, such as low irrigation and fertilizer use as well as poor crop yields (FAO 1997).

Table 1.3 indicates the dependence of developing countries on agricultural land expansion for crop production. Over 1970–90 increased

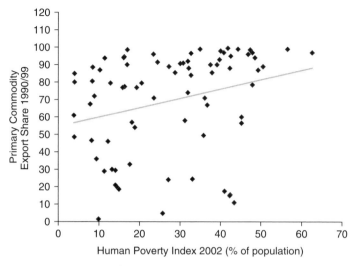

Figure 1.7. Resource dependency and poverty in low and middle-income economies
Notes: Primary commodity export share is the average export share 1990/99 for low and middle-income countries in Table 1.1. Human Poverty Index 2002 from the United Nations Development Program, *Human Development Report 2002*. Correlation coefficient, $r = 0.275$. Number of observations $= 77$.

harvested area accounted for 31% of the additional crop production in these countries, and over 1990–2010 this contribution is expected to rise to 34%. However, some of the increase in harvested area is likely to come from cropping intensity (i.e. multi-cropping and multiple harvests on the same land area). Although improvements in cropping intensity and yields are expected to reduce the developing world's dependency on agricultural land expansion over 1990–2010, about 19% of the contribution to total crop production increases in poorer economies are likely to be derived from expansion of cultivated land. Cropland expansion is expected to be particularly prevalent in Sub-Saharan Africa, East Asia (excluding China) and Latin America (including the Caribbean).

Fischer and Heilig (1997) combined the results of the FAO (1995) study summarized in Table 1.3 with recent UN population projections to estimate the demand for additional cultivated land in developing countries in 2050. Their results are indicated in Table 1.4. All developing countries are expected to increase their demand for cultivated cropland

Table 1.3 Trends in crop production and harvest area in developing regions

	Crop production				Harvested land		
	1970–90 Contribution (%) of increases in:		1990–2010 Contribution (%) of increases in:		1990–2010 Contribution (%) of increases in:		1990–2010 Percentage of crop production from new land
Region	Yields	Harvested area	Yields	Harvested area	Arable land	Cropping intensity	
Sub-Saharan Africa	53	47	53	47	64	36	30
Near East and North Africa	73	27	71	29	31	69	8
East Asia[a]	59	41	61	39	82	18	34
South Asia	82	18	82	18	22	78	4
Latin America[b]	52	48	53	47	60	40	29
All developing countries	69	31	66	34	62	38	19

Notes:
[a] Excludes China.
[b] Includes the Caribbean.
Source: FAO (1995).

Table 1.4 Demand for cultivated land in 2050 in developing regions

Region	Cultivated crop land in 1990 (1000 ha)	% of production increase from new land	Additional cultivated land required in 2050 (1000 ha)	% of new lands from forest and wetland conversion
Africa	252,583	29	241,703	61
Asia[a]	456,225	10	85,782	73
Latin America[b]	189,885	28	96,710	70
All developing countries	899,795	21	424,194	66

Notes:
[a] Excludes China.
[b] Includes the Caribbean.
Source: Fischer and Heilig (1997).

considerably, leading to extensive conversion of forests and wetlands. Throughout the developing world, cultivated land area is expected to increase by over 47% by 2050, with about 66% of the new land coming from deforestation and wetland conversion.

Recent hydrological projections of the world's freshwater resources have pointed to an emerging global threat, the dwindling supply of freshwater relative to the growing demand for water worldwide (Falkenmark *et al.* 1998; Revenga *et al.* 2000; Rosegrant *et al.* 2002; Vörösmarty *et al.* 2000). According to various scenarios, water scarcity is expected to grow dramatically in some regions as competition for water increases between agricultural, urban and commercial sectors. The cause of this global water crisis is largely the result of population growth and economic development rather than global climate change (Vörösmarty *et al.* 2000). The problem is expected to be particularly severe in low and middle-income countries, especially in selected river basins within those countries (Rosegrant *et al.* 2002).

The most common measure of aggregate freshwater availability is the total renewable water resources of a country or region, which consists of adding up average annual surface runoff and groundwater recharge from endogenous precipitation, and typically includes surface

Table 1.5 Water withdrawal by volume and by share of total renewable supplies

Region/Country	Total water withdrawal (km^3)			Total withdrawal as a percentage of renewable water supply (%)		
	1995	*2010*	*2025*	*1995*	*2010*	*2025*
Asia	2,165	2,414	2,649	17	19	20
Latin America	298	354	410	2	2	3
Sub-Saharan Africa	128	166	214	2	3	4
West Asia/North Africa	236	266	297	69	81	90
Developing countries	2,762	3,134	3,507	8	9	10
Developed countries	1,144	1,223	1,265	9	9	10
World	**3,906**	**4,356**	**4,772**	**8**	**9**	**10**

Source: Rosegrant *et al.* (2002), Table 4.1.

inflows from other countries or regions (Faurés *et al.* 2001; Gleick 2000). Hydrologists usually measure the degree of water stress or scarcity by comparing total renewable water supply to the total water withdrawals per year in a country or region. Withdrawal refers to water removed or extracted from a freshwater source and used for human purposes (i.e. industrial, agricultural or domestic water use).[12] The ratio of water withdrawals to total freshwater resources per year is often referred to as *relative water demand* or the *water criticality ratio*. Hydrologists typically consider criticality ratios for a country or a region between 0.2 and 0.4 to indicate medium to high water stress, whereas values greater than 0.4 reflect conditions of severe water limitation (Cosgrove and Rijsberman 2000; Vörösmarty *et al.* 2000).

Table 1.5 indicates recent global projections over 1995 to 2025 for total water withdrawal and the share of withdrawal to renewable water supply.[13] Already, developing countries account for 71% of global water withdrawal. Water demand in these countries is expected to grow by 27% over 1995 to 2025. Although criticality ratios are projected to remain low across all developing countries, there are important regional exceptions. By 2025 Asia is expected to show signs of medium to high stress. West Asia/North Africa is currently facing severe water limitation, and this problem is expected to reach critical levels by 2025.

As shown in Table 1.6, the problem of water stress and scarcity is likely to be worse for key developing countries and regions. The two most populous countries of the world, China and India, together account for around 35% of global water withdrawal. Both countries are already displaying medium to high water stress, which is expected to worsen by 2025. However, the problem is worse still for specific river basin regions within each country. Some of these river basins have or will have in coming years critical ratios exceeding 100%, suggesting chronic problems of extreme water scarcity. Other countries facing worsening water stress and scarcity include Pakistan, the Philippines, South Korea, Mexico, Egypt and virtually all other countries in West Asia/North Africa.

Increasing land conversion and stress on freshwater resources in developing countries may be symptomatic of a more general correlation between environmental deterioration and growth in these economies. A World Bank study noted that GDP growth and higher incomes in developing economies are associated with better sanitation and improved water supply, as well as investments in cleaner technologies (Thomas *et al.* 2000). However, the same study tested for a correlation between growth and an overall environmental quality change index (EQI) across developing countries, where the EQI was constructed by attaching equal weights to changes in indicators of water quality, air quality and deforestation. For 56 developing economies, the study found a statistically significant negative correlation ($r = -0.27$) between EQI and growth rates over 1981–98. Countries with higher growth rates displayed deteriorating overall environmental quality.[14]

In sum, there is ample evidence to suggest that, in low and middle-income economies, processes of land conversion, stress on freshwater resources and other forms of environmental degradation will continue for some time. Part Two of this book (Chapters 5–7) will explore more fully the economic factors underlying widespread and rapid land and water use change in low and middle-income countries.

Stylized fact four: a significant share of the population in low and middle-income economies is concentrated on fragile lands

Between the years 2000 and 2030, the world's population is expected to increase by more than a third, from 6.06 billion to 8.27 billion (Population Division of the United Nations 2001). Virtually all of this population growth will occur in the less developed regions, and

Table 1.6 Developing countries and regions with critical water ratios

Region/Country	Total water withdrawal (km³)			Total withdrawal as a percentage of renewable water supply (%)		
	1995	*2010*	*2025*	*1995*	*2010*	*2025*
Huaihe	77.9	93.7	108.3	83	100	115
Haihe	59.2	62.1	62.9	140	147	149
Huanghe	64	71.1	79.5	89	99	111
Changjian	212.6	238.5	259.1	23	26	29
Songliao	51.5	59.2	67.6	26	30	34
Inland	89.5	98.9	111.2	299	330	371
Southwest	8.3	9.7	12.3	1	1	2
ZhuJiang	77.1	84.9	96.9	19	21	24
Southeast	38.8	41.4	47.7	27	29	33
China total	**678.8**	**4,356**	**845.5**	**26**	**29**	**33**
Sahyadri Gats	14.9	18.7	20.8	14	17	19
Eastern Gats	10.5	13.7	11.6	67	87	74
Cauvery	11.8	12.8	13.1	82	89	91
Godavari	30.2	33.3	38.8	27	30	35
Krishna	46.2	51.4	57.5	51	57	63
Indian-Coastal-Drain	34.8	46.9	43.6	108	145	135
Chotanagpur	7.2	10.9	14.3	17	26	34
Brahmari	25.5	27.2	31	24	22	26
Luni River Basin	41.9	43.1	50.8	148	140	166
Mahi-Tapti-Narmada	31.4	34.3	36.3	36	39	42
Brahmaputra	5.5	7.2	9.2	1	1	1
Indus	159.1	178.7	198.6	72	81	90
Ganges	255.3	271.9	289.3	50	54	57
India total	**674.4**	**750**	**814.8**	**30**	**33**	**35**
Pakistan	**267.3**	**291.2**	**309.3**	**90**	**98**	**105**
Philippines	**47**	**58.2**	**70**	**24**	**29**	**35**
South Korea	**25.8**	**34.9**	**35.9**	**56**	**75**	**78**
Mexico	**78.6**	**86.2**	**94.2**	**24**	**26**	**29**
Egypt	**54.3**	**60.4**	**65.6**	**89**	**99**	**108**
Other West Asia/North Africa[a]	**143.2**	**156**	**171.5**	**116**	**125**	**139**

Notes:
[a] Excluding Turkey.
Source: Adapted from Rosegrant *et al.* (2002), Table B.3.

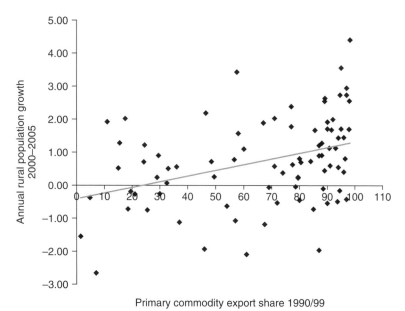

Figure 1.8. Resource dependency and rural population growth in low and middle-income economies
Notes: Primary commodity export share is the average export share 1990/99 for low and middle-income countries in Table 1.1. Annual rural population growth 2000–2005 from Population Division of the United Nations Secretariat, World Urbanization Prospects: The 2001 Revision. Correlation coefficient, $r = 0.465$. Number of observations = 94.

mainly in urban areas. Rural populations are expected to fall in more developed regions over 2000–30, from 0.29 billion to 0.21 billion. Only a modest rise in rural populations will occur in less developed regions over the same period, from 2.90 billion to 3.08 billion.

However, these aggregate trends in world population obscure two important facts concerning rural populations in developing countries. First, rural population growth is much higher for those low and middle-income economies that are more resource dependent, and second a large share of the rural populations in these economies are concentrated on poor, or fragile, lands.

Figure 1.8 illustrates that rural population growth rates are positively correlated with the degree of resource dependency in low and middle-income economies. The trend line in the figure indicates that, on average, rural populations are expanding at 1% per year in developing economies that have a primary commodity export share of 70% or higher. In contrast, for those economies with a primary product export share of 25% or less, rural populations are stagnant or even declining.

The World Bank has launched a major study of the concentration of rural populations in developing economies on fragile lands, which they define as "areas that present significant constraints for intensive agriculture and where the people's links to the land are critical for the sustainability of communities, pastures, forests, and other natural resources" (World Bank 2003, p. 59). The main findings of the study are:

- Since 1950, the estimated population on fragile lands in developing economies has doubled.
- Currently one quarter of the people in developing countries – almost 1.3 billion – survive on fragile lands. More than 1.2 billion people on fragile lands are in the developing regions of Latin America, Africa and Asia (see Table 1.7).
- The developing country populations on fragile lands include 518 million living in arid regions with no access to irrigation systems, 430 million on soils unsuitable for agriculture, 216 million on land with steep slopes and more than 130 million in fragile forest systems.
- These populations living on fragile land in developing countries account for many of the people in extreme poverty, living on less than US$1 per day.

The World Bank study also identified specific developing countries with significant shares of their populations on fragile lands, i.e. from 20–30% of their population, to 30–50%, to 50–70% to over 70% (World Bank 2003, Table 4.3). Seventy-two low and middle-income economies from Table 1.1 can be grouped into these four categories.

The results are indicated in Figure 1.9, which shows that resource-dependent low and middle-income economies contain large concentrations of their populations on fragile lands. Moreover, greater resource dependency is associated with a large percentage of population on fragile land. For example, as the concentration of populations on fragile lands in low and middle-income economies increases from 20–30% to 30–50% to 50–70% to over 70%, the average share of primary products in exports rises from 62.9% to 72.8% to 87.6% to 98.3% respectively.

In sum, a large share of the population in low and middle-income countries is concentrated on fragile lands and remains dependent on agricultural and other renewable resources for their livelihoods. Many

Table 1.7 Global population on fragile lands

	Population in fragile lands		
Region	Population in 2000 (millions)	Number (millions)	Share of total (%)
Latin America and the Caribbean	515.3	68	13.1
Middle East and North Africa	293	110	37.6
Sub-Saharan Africa	658.4	258	39.3
South Asia	1,354.5	330	24.4
East Asia and Pacific	1,856.5	469	25.3
Eastern Europe and Central Asia	474.7	58	12.1
OECD Group[a]	850.4	94	11.1
Other	27.3	2	6.9
Total	**6,030.1**	**1,389**	**23**
Total developing economies[b]	**5,179.7**	**1,295**	**25**
Total Latin America, Africa and Asian developing economies[c]	**4,677.7**	**1,235**	**26.4**

Notes: Fragile lands are areas that present significant constraints for intensive agriculture and where the people's links to the land are critical for the sustainability of communities, pastures, forests, and other natural resources.

[a] OECD Group: Australia, Austria, Belgium, Canada, Denmark, Finland, France, Germany, Greece, Iceland, Ireland, Italy, Japan, Luxembourg, Netherlands, New Zealand, Norway, Portugal, Spain, Sweden, Switzerland, United Kingdom and United States.

[b] World Total less OECD Group.

[c] World Total less OECD Group, East Europe and Central Asia and Other.

Source: Adapted from World Bank. 2003. *World Development Report 2003*. World Bank, Washington DC, Table 4.2.

of these households are extremely poor, living on less than US$1 per day. Both rural population growth and the share of population on fragile lands seem to increase with the degree of resource dependency of a developing economy. These trends have several implications for an economic approach to encouraging resource-based development in poorer economies. First, it appears that, in many of these economies, frontier land expansion and fragile land areas are serving as an outlet for absorbing substantial numbers of the rural poor. Second, we need to

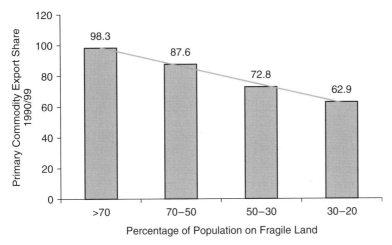

Figure 1.9. Resource dependency and share of population on fragile lands in low and middle-income economies

Notes: Primary commodity export share is the average export share 1990/99 for low and middle-income countries in Table 1.1. Share of population on fragile land is from World Bank, *World Development Report 2003*, Table 4.3. Fragile land is defined in the report as "areas that present significant constraints for intensive agriculture and where the people's links to the land are critical for the sustainability of communities, pastures, forests, and other natural resources" (p. 59). Number of observations = 72, of which 2 (>70%), 8 (70–50%), 33 (30–50%) and 29 (20–30%).

understand better the linkages between rural poverty and resource degradation in order to understand why the environment-poverty "trap" is so entrenched in many poor rural areas. Third, in order to overcome both of these problems, we need to develop specific policies and institutions to overcome this "vicious cycle" between frontier land expansion and resource exploitation, poor rural resource management and entrenched poverty. Part 3 of this book (Chapters 8, 9 and 10) addresses these concerns relating to frontier-based development, resource management and rural poverty in low and middle-income countries.

Final remarks

The view that environmental and natural resources should be treated as important economic assets, which can be called natural capital, is becoming more accepted. Armed with this concept, economists are now able to show the conditions under which depletion of this natural capital stock may or may not lead to more sustainable economic development.

However, the services provided by natural capital are unique and, in the case of the ecological and life-support functions of the environment, are not well understood. Improving our knowledge in this area is a critical task (Barbier *et al.* 1994). Better understanding of complex environmental problems and of the value of ecological services may also help eventually to resolve the "weak" versus "strong" sustainability debate in economics. Although this debate is unlikely to be resolved in the near future, it is clear that the *very minimum* criterion for attaining sustainable economic development is ensuring that an economy satisfies *weak sustainability* conditions. That is, as long as the natural capital that is being depleted is replaced with even more valuable physical and human capital, then *the value of the aggregate stock –* comprising human, physical and the remaining natural capital – should be increasing over time. This in turn requires that the development path of an economy is governed by principles somewhat akin to Hartwick's rule (Hartwick 1977), which states: First, environmental and natural resources must be managed efficiently so that the welfare losses from environmental damages are minimized and any resource rents earned after "internalizing" environmental externalities are maximized. Second, the rents arising from the depletion of natural capital must be invested into other productive economic assets.

The conclusion that efficient environmental resource management is the minimum condition necessary for sustainable economic development may surprise those who believe that the causality might run in the other direction. Proponents of the latter view argue that the environmental Kuznets curve literature provides evidence that environmental problems are likely to lessen as economies grow and develop. However, the EKC literature does not support such a conclusion. Rather, many EKC studies suggest that specific policies to protect the environment and manage resources are necessary for curbing certain forms of pollution and resource depletion, both currently and in the future. How key environmental indicators change with rises in per capita income is an important issue, but what is of more fundamental concern is how different policies can affect this relationship. This is particularly critical for developing economies that are overwhelmingly dependent on exploitation of their natural capital. The role of policies in managing natural resources for efficient and sustainable economic development in poor countries is an important recurring theme throughout this book.

Finally, this chapter has also focused more specifically on the importance of natural capital to economic development in present-day low and middle-income countries in Africa, Asia and Latin America. Four key structural features, or stylized facts, of resource use in these economies were identified. These facts are also directly relevant to themes explored in the remainder of this book.

Of particular interest for the rest of Part One is the intriguing paradox raised by the second stylized fact: why is it that, despite the importance of natural capital for sustainable economic development, increasing economic dependence on natural resource exploitation appears to be a hindrance to growth and development in the low and middle-income economies of the world? As this paradox goes to the heart of the role of natural resources in economic development, it is explored further in the next three chapters. For instance, Chapter 2 provides a brief summary of the evolution of economic thinking on the contribution of natural resource exploitation to historical processes of economic development. In Chapter 3, we discuss in more detail possible explanations of this second stylized fact, and also the conditions that may have promoted past and present counter-examples of successful resource-based development. Finally, Chapter 4 offers another perspective on why the structural economic dependence of a small open economy on exploiting its natural resource endowment – in particular its dependence on processes of "frontier expansion" through land conversion – may not lead to sustained and high rates of economic growth.

Notes

1. Although as Bishop (1993) has pointed out, the objective of "sustainability" is different from that of the standard economic objective of "efficiency". That is, there are potentially an infinite number of development paths for an economy, only some of which are sustainable. Efficiency therefore does not guarantee sustainability, as some efficient paths are not sustainable. At the same time, there is no reason why an economy could not be both efficient and sustainable.
2. For further discussion of this distinction between weak and strong sustainability see Howarth and Norgaard (1995); Pearce, Markandya and Barbier (1989); Pearce and Barbier (2000); Toman, Pezzey and Krautkramer (1995) and Turner (1993).

3. Note, however, that rapid population growth may imply that the value of the per capita aggregate capital stock is declining even if the total value stays the same. Moreover, even if the per capita value of the asset base were maintained, it may not imply non-declining welfare of the majority of people. These considerations also hold for the "strong sustainability" arguments discussed below.

4. The concept of an environmental Kuznets curve (EKC) relationship draws its inspiration from the income distribution theory developed by Kuznets (1955), who hypothesized that there is an "inverted-U" relationship between an indicator of income inequality and the level of income. However, the exact origins of the EKC hypothesis are somewhat ambiguous, and appear to be the product of numerous studies conducted simultaneously in the early 1990s. Most sources point to the analysis by Grossman and Kreuger (1995) of air quality measures in a cross-section of countries for different years, which was part of a wider investigation into whether the claims that the economic growth accompanying the North American Free Trade Agreement might foster greater environmental degradation. Similarly, the study by Shafik (1994) was originally a background paper for the World Bank's enquiry into growth and environment relationships for the *World Development 1992* (World Bank 1992). Finally, Panayotou (1995) offers perhaps the earliest and most detailed explanation of a possible "Kuznets type U-shape relationship between the rate of environmental degradation and the level of economic development" in analysis conducted for the World Employment Programme of the International Labour Office in 1992.

5. Selden and Song (1994) conduct similar projections for the four air pollutants for which they estimate an EKC relationship, SO_2, SPM, nitrogen oxides (NO_x) and carbon monoxide (CO). Their results show world emissions increasing for all four pollutants through 2025, and for SPM and NO_x, emissions rise through 2050.

6. On the other hand, corruption and bureaucratic inefficiency may also explain why EKCs "break down" for certain countries. See López and Mitra (2000).

7. As indicated in Table 1.1, the designation of "low and middle-income countries" in Africa, Latin America, Asia and Oceania, is based on the World Bank's definition. The World Bank lists a total of 142 such countries in these regions. However, many of the countries not included in Table 1.1 are small island states and nations (e.g., Antigua and Barbuda, Gaza Strip, Cook Islands, Kiribati) or countries for which export data are not readily available (Democratic Peoples' Republic of Korea). The 95 economies listed in the table have GDP per capita in 1994 at 1987 constant purchase power parity US$ of less than US$10,500 with an average of US$2,691 and a median of US$1,604.

8. Using the term "resource dependency" to describe the degree to which a developing economy is "dependent" on primary product exports may be misleading if exports are not that important to that economy. However, the latter problem does not appear to arise for the vast majority of developing economies. For all the low and middle-income countries depicted in Table 1.1 for which the data are available (88 countries), the average export share of GDP is 31.4%. For those countries with a primary product share of 50% or more, the export share of GDP is 29.6%. As the importance of exports across low and middle-income economies is fairly stable across these countries, around 30% of GDP, this suggests that the percentage share of primary products to total exports is a fairly good indicator of the degree of resource dependency of these economies. In fact, the importance of exports increases slightly with the degree of resource dependency. For economies with an export concentration in primary products of 70% or more, the export share of GDP is 30.7%; for those countries with a primary product export concentration of 90% or more, the export share rises to 34.6%.

9. Although the vast majority of the low and middle-income countries listed in Table 1.1 can be considered *resource dependent*, in terms of 50% or more of their exports are primary products, the latter countries do not contain the majority of the developing world's population. For example, the total population estimate (in 1999 or nearest year) for 94 of the countries listed in Table 1.1 is just under 4.52 billion, whereas the population in resource-dependent economies totals around 1.33 billion (30% of the total). That is because five of the most populous developing countries, China, India, Brazil, Pakistan and Bangladesh, cannot be classified as resource-dependent as defined in this book, as each has less than 50% of the exports from primary products.

10. As will be discussed further in Chapter 3, much of the claims of a "resource curse" hypothesis – that resource-abundant economies grow less fast than resource-poor ones – is based on empirical estimations by Jeffrey Sachs and colleagues. However, these authors use primary products exports as a percentage of GDP as the measure of a country's "resource abundance" (e.g., see Table 1.2). Strictly speaking, such a variable cannot be a true indicator of "resource abundance" *per se*, as it is not a measure of the total resource endowment or stocks of a country. In fact, as we shall see further in Chapter 3, there is an on-going debate in the "resource curse" literature over what indicator should be used as a measure of "resource abundance," with most authors agreeing that some measure of total resource stock availability, such as total land area per capita, cropland per capita and mineral resources per capita, would be the preferred indicators (Auty 2001b). As already discussed earlier, throughout this book, indicators

such as primary products exports as a percentage of GDP or of total exports will be referred to as measures of a country's *resource dependency*. Such indicators are really a measure of the degree to which an economy is dependent on natural resource-based exports, and as Table 1.1 and subsequent figures of this chapter show, the degree of resource dependency of an economy can be easily measured across a large number of developing economies, and in turn, has some important correlations with other key development indicators. Hence, the second stylized fact is stated in terms of the correlation between resource dependency, and not abundance, with poor economic performance in low and middle-income countries.

11. As indicated, the relationship depicted in Figure 1.6 is for the low and middle-income developing economies listed in Table 1.1 and for the 1990s. Rodríguez and Sachs (1999) appear to obtain the contradictory finding that GDP per capita is positively associated with "resource abundance." However, the latter relationship is established by regressing the log of GDP per capita in 1970 on exports of natural resources, in percent of GDP, also in 1970. Clearly, the results of Rodríguez and Sachs are for a different era, just before the oil and commodity price boom of the 1970s and early 1980s. In addition, as the authors indicate, their data set includes predominantly mineral and energy exporting countries, and countries other than the low and middle-income economies listed in Table 1.1.

12. Hydrologists distinguish two concepts of water use: water withdrawal and water consumption (Gleick 2000, p. 41). However, some water withdrawal may be returned to the original source, albeit with changes in the quality and quantity of the water. In contrast, consumptive use is water withdrawn from a source and actually consumed or lost to seepage, contamination, or a "sink" where it cannot economically be reused. Thus water consumption is the proportion of water withdrawal that is "irretrievably lost" after human use. For example, in 1995 total global freshwater withdrawals amounted to $3,800 \text{ km}^3$, of which $2,100 \text{ km}^3$ was consumed.

13. The projections in Tables 1.5 and 1.6 correspond to the "business as usual" baseline scenario in Rosegrant *et al.* (2002).

14. Controlling per capita income in 1981 also yielded a correlation coefficient of −0.27 that was significant at the 95% confidence level.

2 | Natural resource-based economic development in history

T HE preceding chapter ended with posing a key paradox concerning the role of natural resources in economic development: why is it that, despite the importance of natural capital for sustainable economic development, increasing economic dependence on natural resource exploitation appears to be a hindrance to growth and development in the majority of low and middle-income economies of the world?

Of course it is important to examine this paradox in light of the use of natural resources by today's developing economies and how current economic theories represent this use. In fact, Chapters 3 and 4 will do precisely that.

The purpose of this chapter is to provide an insightful summary of the evolution of thinking on the contribution of natural resource exploitation to historical processes of economic development over key periods of time. The era of human history covered by this review is long; it ranges from 8,500 BC until the present day. In order to make sense of this long history, in terms of the role that natural resources play in shaping economic development, the chapter focuses on several key historical epochs or phases: the agricultural transition (8,500 BC to 1 AD), the era of Malthusian stagnation (1 AD to 1000), the emergence of the world economy (1000 to 1500), the Great Frontier and the rise of Western Europe (1500 to 1913), the Atlantic economic triangular trade (1500 to 1860), and the golden age of resource-based development (1870 to 1913). Finally, the chapter looks at two alternative interpretations of historical patterns of natural resource use and their implications for contemporary economic development in present-day low and middle-income economies: the center-periphery trade, resource dependency and the theory of "unequal" development (1918 to present) and the colonial origins of comparative development (1500 to present).[1]

This chapter's review of these historical phases and various theories is relevant to the main theme of this book for several reasons.

First, the exploitation of natural resources has clearly been an important aspect of economic development for most of global history.[2] For instance, Joseph Schumpeter, who was one of the first economists to explore the meaning of "economic development," defined the latter concept as "the carrying out of new combinations of the means of production," one of which is "the conquest of a new source of supply of raw materials or half-manufactured goods, again irrespective of whether this source already exists or whether it has first to be created" (Schumpeter 1961, p. 66). As we shall see shortly, there are many examples in history where finding and exploiting "a new source of supply of raw materials" has been fundamental to the process of economic development. In essence, that is what is meant by the term *resource-based development*.

Second, by examining past cases where important advances in economic development were influenced by natural resource exploitation, perhaps we will gain some further insights into the role of natural resources in low and middle-income economies today. To facilitate such insights, the main focus of this chapter will be on explaining various theories of the role that natural resource exploitation has played in the historical development of the present-day developing world.

Finally, as Findlay and Lundahl (1999, p. 1) succinctly put it: "The story of resource-based growth has been told before, but there is no consensus as to the conclusions." That is, much of the current debate on resource-based development is linked to past disagreements in economics over this process. Although there are obvious ideological differences motivating such disagreements, what is striking is how such widely differing perspectives can arise from examining even the same historical epoch. Thus, as a prelude to understanding current thinking on resource-based development it is useful to examine some of the key economic theories that have emerged – and diverged – in explaining the role that natural resource exploitation has played in important historical periods.

Given the purpose of this chapter, it will not embark on a conventional review of economic theories of natural resource scarcity and development since Adam Smith.[3] Nor, will it begin with an arbitrary date, such as the year 1500, which is the date chosen by most historians to mark the division between "modern" and "pre-modern" times (Kennedy 1988; McNeil 1999; North and Thomas 1973). Nor is it possible to survey the entire realm of human history over the past 50,000 years, which has been identified as the era in which "we are dealing with biologically and behaviorally modern humans" and thus "human history at last took off" (Diamond 1999, p. 39).

Instead, as noted above, the focus of the chapter will be on explaining various theories of the role that natural resource exploitation has played in the historical development of the present-day developing world during certain key historical epochs. We therefore begin with one of the more remarkable, and important, *processes* of economic development ever to occur in global history: the rise of agriculture and the demise of hunter-gatherers.

The agricultural transition (from 8500 BC to 1 AD)

As argued by Toynbee (1978, pp. 40–41), "agriculture and animal-husbandry have certainly been the most important of all human interventions to date. They have not ceased to be the economic foundations of human life, even at times and places at which they have been overshadowed by trade and manufacture."[4] Yet for most of the course of the last 50,000 years of the history of "modern humans," and in fact since the emergence of our species, the predominant economic system around the world was based on hunting-gathering:

For most of the time since the ancestors of modern humans diverged from the ancestors of the living great apes, around 7 million years ago, all humans on Earth fed themselves exclusively by hunting wild animals and gathering wild plants, as the Blackfeet still did in the nineteenth century. It was only within the last 11,000 years that some peoples turned to what is termed food production: that is, domesticating wild animals and plants and eating the resulting livestock and crops. (Diamond 1999, p. 86)

The demise of hunting-gathering and the rise of agriculture across the globe is often referred to as the "agricultural transition" because it took several millennia to take hold and spread through many regions of the world (Diamond 1999; Livi-Bacci 1997; McNeil and McNeil 2003). For example, the most rapid spread of food production was from its original development in Southwest Asia (the Fertile Crescent) across western Eurasia, including Great Britain and Southern

Scandinavia, yet even this dissemination took from ca. 8,500 to 2,500 BC (Diamond 1999, pp. 180–182). In North America, the "agricultural transition" process was much slower: "Some time between 12,000 and 3,000 years ago the early Americans turned from an exclusively hunting and gathering culture to one based more and more on agriculture" (Smith 1975, p. 733). Similar agricultural transition periods occurred in other regions of the world (McNeil and McNeil 2003).[5]

Despite the length of time it took to evolve, the agricultural transition still represents one of the foremost examples of successful resource-based development – in terms of the Schumpterian interpretation of "development" discussed above – ever to occur. For one, the era of agricultural transition corresponded with one of the first major global demographic transitions. During the 30,000 years of the hunting-gathering period until 10,000 BC, population growth averaged around 0.008% per year, and the total human population reached 6 million at most. In contrast, during the historical period that spanned the agricultural transition, from 10,000 BC to 1 AD, annual population growth rates increased to 0.037% and the world's population expanded from 6 million to over 230 million (See Tables 2.1 and 2.2).[6] In addition, the era of agricultural transition ushered in a long period of agricultural-dominated economic systems globally. Since this period and over the next millennium and a half, there were numerous inventions that improved cultivation and animal husbandry techniques, such as biannual and triannual rotations, breeding better seed and animal varieties, developments of plowing techniques and the use of air and water power, but all of these inventions improved the efficiency of agricultural-based economic systems and their ability to generate surpluses rather then lead to their replacement by another principal means of production (Livi-Bacci 1997). Thus Cipolla (1962, pp. 45–46) notes: "It is safe to say that until the Industrial Revolution man continued to rely mainly on plants and animals for energy – plants for food and fuel, and animals for food and mechanical energy."

Finally, the agricultural transition and rise of agricultural-based systems also allowed the creation of "surpluses" that were instrumental to the beginnings of urbanization, manufacturing and trade (Cipolla 1962; Livi-Bacci 1997; McNeil and McNeil 2003). Some writers have argued that such conditions also led to the emergence of the classic "core-periphery" resource-based trade relationship, which persists to this day in the world economy, whereby an economically dominant,

Table 2.1 *World population, 40,000 BC to 2001 AD*

	Total numbers ('000)										
	40,000BC	10,000BC	1AD	1000	1500	1820	1870	1913	1950	1973	2001
1. Western Europe			24,700	25,413	57,268	133,040	187,504	260,975	304,941	358,825	392,101
~ France			5,000	6,500	15,000	31,250	38,440	41,463	41,829	52,157	59,658
~ Germany			3,000	3,500	12,000	24,905	39,231	65,058	68,375	78,950	82,281
~ Italy			7,000	5,000	10,500	20,176	27,888	37,248	47,105	54,797	57,845
~ Netherlands			200	300	950	2,333	3,610	6,164	10,114	13,438	15,981
~ Spain			4,500	4,000	6,800	12,203	16,201	20,263	28,063	8,976	40,087
~ United Kingdom			800	2,000	3,942	21,239	31,400	45,649	50,127	56,210	59,723
2. Eastern Europe			4,750	6,500	13,500	36,457	53,557	79,530	87,637	110,418	120,912
3. Former USSR			3,900	7,100	16,950	54,765	88,672	156,192	179,571	249,712	290,349
4. Western Offshoots[a]			1,170	1,960	2,800	11,231	46,088	111,401	176,457	250,841	339,839
~ United States			680	1,300	2,000	9,981	40,241	97,606	152,271	211,909	285,024
5. Latin America			5,600	11,400	17,500	21,705	40,399	80,935	165,938	308,399	531,213
~ Mexico			2,200	4,500	7,500	6,587	9,219	14,970	28,485	57,643	101,879
6. Asia			174,200	182,900	283,800	710,400	765,229	977,361	1,382,447	2,248,260	3,653,504
~ China			59,600	59,000	103,000	381,000	358,000	437,140	546,815	881,940	1,275,392
~ India			75,000	75,000	110,000	209,000	253,000	303,700	359,000	580,000	1,023,590
~ Japan			3,000	7,500	15,400	31,000	34,437	51,672	83,805	108,707	126,892
7. Africa			16,500	32,300	46,610	74,236	90,466	124,697	227,333	390,034	821,088
World[b]	500	6,000	230,820	267,573	438,428	1,041,834	1,271,915	1,791,091	2,524,324	3,916,489	6,149,006

Notes:

[a] Australia, Canada, New Zealand and the United States.

[b] World population levels for 40,000 BC and 10,000 BC are from Livi-Bacci (1997), pp. 30–32 and Table 1.2.

Source: Adapted from Maddison (2003), Table 8.a., unless otherwised indicated.

Table 2.2 World population growth rates, 40,000 BC to 2001 AD

	40,000–10,000BC	10,000BC–1AD	1–1000	1000–1500	1500–1820	1820–1870	1870–1913	1913–1950	1950–1973	1973–2001
					Annual average rate of growth (%)					
1. Western Europe			0.00	0.16	0.26	0.69	0.77	0.42	0.71	0.32
~ France			0.03	0.17	0.23	0.42	0.18	0.02	0.96	0.48
~ Germany			0.02	0.25	0.23	0.91	1.18	0.13	0.63	0.15
~ Italy			−0.03	0.15	0.20	0.65	0.68	0.64	0.66	0.19
~ Netherlands			0.04	0.23	0.28	0.88	1.25	1.35	1.24	0.62
~ Spain			−0.01	0.11	0.18	0.57	0.52	0.88	0.94	0.50
~ United Kingdom			0.09	0.14	0.53	0.79	0.87	0.25	0.50	0.22
2. Eastern Europe			0.03	0.15	0.31	0.77	0.92	0.26	1.01	0.32
3. Former USSR			0.06	0.17	0.37	0.97	1.33	0.38	1.44	0.54
4. Western Offshoots[a]			0.05	0.07	0.44	2.86	2.07	1.25	1.54	1.09
~ United States			0.06	0.09	0.50	2.83	2.08	1.21	1.45	1.06
5. Latin America			0.07	0.09	0.07	1.25	1.63	1.96	2.73	1.96
~ Mexico			0.07	0.10	0.67	0.67	1.13	1.75	3.11	2.05

Annual average rate of growth (%)

	40,000–10,000BC	10,000BC–1AD	1–1000	1000–1500	1500–1820	1820–1870	1870–1913	1913–1950	1950–1973	1973–2001
6. Asia[b]			0.00	0.09	0.29	0.15	0.55	0.92	2.19	1.80
~China			0.00	0.11	0.41	−0.12	0.47	0.61	2.10	1.33
~India			0.00	0.08	0.20	0.38	0.43	0.45	2.11	2.05
~Japan			0.09	0.06	0.22	0.21	0.95	1.32	1.14	0.55
7. Africa			0.07	0.07	0.15	0.40	0.75	1.64	2.37	2.69
World[c]	0.008	0.037	0.01	0.10	0.27	0.40	0.80	0.93	1.93	1.62

Notes:

[a] Australia, Canada, New Zealand and the United States.

[b] Excludes Japan.

[c] World population growth rates for 40,000–10,000 BC and for 10,000 BC–1AD are from Livi-Bacci (1997), pp. 30–32 and Table 1.2.

Source: Adapted from Maddison (2003), Table 8.a., unless otherwise indicated.

relatively industrial and urbanized "core" state would trade its manufactures for basic raw materials and primary products from less-developed "periphery" states. As suggested by Chew (2001, pp. 19–21), this "core-periphery" trade relationship can be seen with the first major civilization to emerge during the era of agricultural transition, the urbanized states of southern Mesopotamia in 3,000 BC:

> The intensive consumption of natural resources by core urbanized centers such as Mesopotamia to meet its reproductive needs not only impacts on its immediate ecological landscape but extends beyond its territorial boundaries. The set of ecological relationships that resulted from such transformations was not restricted to the immediate surroundings of these urbanized communities but was extended to their hinterland areas … All this urbanization meant that the intensive utilization of natural resources of the immediate surroundings and also the importation of some natural resources such as timber from distant reaches (Indus valley) of the economy system. High-quality timber from Zagros and Taurus mountains, the Caspian area, the eastern Mediterranean, Punjab and the Indus valley were obtained via military expeditions and trade.

Numerous theories have been proposed as to why early modern humans chose to forego hunting-gathering in favor of agriculture, but there is general consensus on some issues.[7] First, there were many features of hunting-gathering that made it relatively attractive compared to agriculture; for example, as emphasized by Sahlins (1974), hunter-gatherers may have had low levels of material wealth but they were not necessarily poverty-stricken, and there is substantial evidence that the average productivity, in terms of the amount of effort required in obtaining food, was much higher in hunter-gathering compared to early agriculture. However, Sahlins (1974) also emphasizes that hunting-gathering was subject to substantial diminishing returns; i.e. after only a modest level of hunting and gathering effort, any additional effort is unlikely to yield significant gains in food output. As a consequence, as long as there were substantial large herding animals available in the wild, such as mammoth, bison, camel and mastodon, the combination of low hunting cost and high kill value would make hunting-gathering a relatively attractive economic activity compared to agriculture (Smith 1975). On the other hand, the slow growth, long lives and long maturation of these large mammals also made them prone to extinction.

It therefore follows that the rise of agriculture was linked to the gradual extinction of the large mammals that were the principal sources of wild game for hunter-gatherers.[8] To illustrate how this might have occurred, Smith (1975) develops a model of a primitive hunter-agrarian economy, in which the population has the choice of allocating its labor to hunting a wild species of biomass, M, as well as to growing a subsistence crop. In Smith's economy, it is possible for the population to specialize in the long run in hunting only or to combine both hunting and agriculture in a mixed economy. However, the most interesting scenario is the case in which along an optimal development path the economy perpetually depletes the stock of wild game and thus evolves from a pure hunting culture, to a mixed economy, and finally to a pure agrarian economy. The conditions for the latter scenario are depicted in Figure 2.1.

Figure 2.1 depicts the optimal development path of the primitive economy in terms of the biomass stock of wild game, M, and its marginal value, ξ. The curve $E(\xi)$ indicates all combinations of M and ξ that correspond to a constant value of wild game (i.e. $d\xi/dt = 0$). This condition implies that the marginal value product of the game stock net of any biological growth is equal to the discount rate, which represents the opportunity cost to the economy of maintaining the stock. The curve $B(\xi)$ represents the bioeconomic equilibrium of a constant game stock (i.e. $dM/dt = 0$), which occurs if harvest intensity equals average biological growth of the stock. However, in the scenario depicted in Figure 2.1 where $B(\xi) > E(\xi)$, Smith demonstrates that for all levels of the game stock, its value will always be bounded by $\xi_0^b \geq \xi \geq \xi_0^e$. This in turn means that, along the optimal development path of the economy, hunters will always harvest faster than the biological growth of the game stock and the opportunity cost of maintaining wild game (the discount rate) will always exceed the net value of the marginal product of the stock. As shown by the optimal development path P, the economy will deplete the stock of wild game continually, and most eventually drive the stock to extinction, and thus specialize thereafter in agriculture.

Smith also shows that, even under an alternative scenario favoring a mixed hunter-agrarian economy in the long run, this outcome may be vulnerable to extinction if certain conditions change. For example, the prospect for extinction is greater the lower the biological reproduction rate of the wild game species, the higher the value placed on meat, the higher the preference for present over future consumption and the lower the efficiency of labor in agriculture relative to hunting.

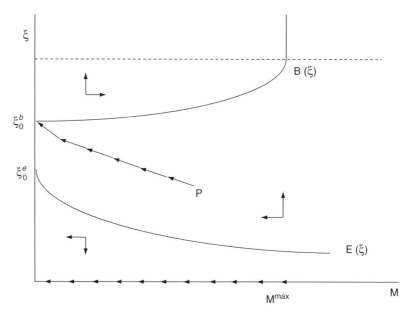

Source: Adapted from Smith (1975).

Figure 2.1. Extinction and the rise of agriculture

The latter result may seem counter-intuitive, but it gets to the heart of a key paradox concerning the era of agricultural transition: why should hunting and gathering societies that were highly efficient at these activities have an economic incentive to switch to agriculture? From Smith's model, the solution to this paradox is straightforward: An economy that is relatively more efficient at hunting will allocate more of its labor to this activity, but if the game is a slow-growing mammal species, then the result is a greater likelihood of over-harvesting and extinction. In the long run, once the species is extinct, the economy has no choice but to specialize in agriculture. Thus the more efficient the economy is at hunting slow-growing prey, the more likely that it must evolve into an agrarian economy eventually.[9]

Smith's model of the agricultural transition has important implications for resource-based development generally.

First, development that is based on exploitation of a single, strategic resource (e.g. large and slow-growing wild species) does not necessarily lead to collapse of the economy when that resource is irrevocably depleted. In fact, Smith shows the opposite incentive effect: under certain conditions, the extinction of wild game was the important driving force in inducing hunting-gathering societies to evolve into fully agrarian economies. As we shall see later in this chapter, this optimistic outcome of resource depletion has important parallels with other eras of successful resource-based development, such as the exploitation of successive frontier resources in North America and other "Great Frontier" global regions, which gave rise to the staples thesis of resource trade and development.

Second, as noted above, the more efficient a society is at its main resource-exploiting activity (e.g. hunting and gathering), the more likely it is to deplete that resource, thus leaving the society no choice in the long run but to adopt a different resource-based economic activity (e.g. agriculture). Whether they were aware of it or not, as early humans improved their skills and efficiency at hunting and gathering, they were actually increasing the likelihood of the demise of these activities and the onset of the agricultural transition. But of course, early human societies could engage in this behavior because, whether they knew it or not, they always had agriculture as their "backstop" technology once the wild game were depleted. Historical and archaeological evidence shows that this is indeed the case; hence, the era of agricultural transition. However, this begs the question what happens to the pattern of resource-based development if there is no alternative to the main resource-exploitation activity? As we shall see in the next section, under very different conditions the outcome may not be so fortunate for some resource-dependent economies.

The era of Malthusian stagnation (from 1 AD to 1000)

From 1 AD until 1000 the world's population is thought to have increased at an annual rate of only 0.01% (see Table 2.2). Over the same period, very little economic growth took place as well. For example, Maddison (2003) estimates that real Gross Domestic Product (GDP) per capita either was stagnant from 1 AD to 1000 or fell in certain key regions, such as in Western Europe (see Table 2.3). Thus, for many centuries after the agricultural transition, global economic development appeared to be at a standstill. This has led some scholars to view this long period as the era of "Malthusian stagnation" (Galor and Weil 1998; Kremer 1993).

Table 2.3 World gross domestic product per capita, 1 to 2001 AD

| | 1990 International dollars | | | | | | | | |
	1AD	1000	1500	1820	1870	1913	1950	1973	2001
1. Western European average	450	400	771	1,204	1,960	3,458	4,579	11,416	19,256
~ France			727	1,135	1,876	3,485	5,271	13,114	21,092
~ Germany			688	1,077	1,839	3,648	3,881	11,966	18,677
~ Italy			1,100	1,117	1,499	2,564	3,502	10,634	19,040
~ Netherlands			761	1,838	2,757	4,049	5,996	13,082	21,722
~ Spain			661	1,008	1,207	2,056	2,189	7,661	15,659
~ United Kingdom			714	1,706	3,190	4,921	6,939	12,025	20,127
2. Eastern Europe	400	400	496	683	937	1,695	2,111	4,988	6,027
3. Former USSR	400	400	499	688	943	1,488	2,841	6,059	4,626
4. Western offshoots average[a]	400	400	400	1,202	2,419	5,233	9,268	16,179	26,943
~ United States	400		400	1,257	2,445	5,301	9,561	16,689	27,948
5. Latin American average	400	400	416	692	681	1,481	2,506	4,504	5,811
~ Mexico			425	759	674	1,732	2,365	4,845	7,089
6. Asian average[b]	450	450	572	577	550	658	634	1,226	3,256
~ China	450	450	600	600	530	552	439	839	3,583
~ India	450	450	550	533	533	673	619	853	1,957
~ Japan	400	3	500	669	737	1,387	1,921	11,434	20,683
7. Africa	430	425	414	420	500	637	894	1,410	1,489
World	445	436	566	667	875	1,525	2,111	4,091	6,049

Notes:
[a] Australia, Canada, New Zealand and the United States.
[b] Excludes Japan.
Source: Adapted from Maddison (2003), Table 8.c, unless otherwise indicated.

Two conditions characterize a Malthusian economy (Barbier 1989; Galor and Weil 1998; Brander and Taylor 1998b). First, at least one factor of production, such as land, is both essential and fixed in supply, implying decreasing returns to scale for all other factors.[10] Second, any increase in real income would lead to increases in population growth, which in the long run dissipates fully the initial income gains. The latter effect occurs regardless of changes in productivity arising either from the discovery of new resources (such as land and natural resources) or from technological innovation. According to Galor and Weil (1998, p. 150):

The Malthusian model implies that there exists a negative feedback loop whereby, in the absence of changes in the technology or in the availability of land, the size of the population will be self-equilibrating. More significantly, even if available resources do expand, the level of income per capita will remain unchanged in the long run: better technology or more land will lead to a larger, but not richer, population.

This "self-equilibriating" feature of a Malthusian economy explains why during the first millennium AD per capita GDP remained stagnant while global population grew only modestly. From 1 AD to 1000 the world's population expanded from 231 to 268 million, although this period also included important cycles of population growth and decline (Livi-Bacci 1997, Table 1.3). In addition, important innovations did occur in the technology of the agricultural-based economic systems of the time. As noted above, the improved techniques included biannual and triannual rotations, breeding better seed and animal varieties, developments of plowing techniques and the use of air and water power (Livi-Bacci 1997). Although these inventions improved the efficiency of agricultural-based economic systems and their ability to generate surpluses, their cumulative effect appears mainly to have been to increase periodically the populations dependent on these systems. Hence, the "Malthusian model" appears to portray accurately much of the global economy over the first millenium AD.

Under favorable conditions, the Malthusian resource-based economic system will lead to constant per capita income and population. Any change in the productivity of the system, such as the result of discovering new resources or technological innovation, simply leads to a new long-run equilibrium in which a higher level of population and production is sustained but per capita income is left unchanged.

However, under unfavorable conditions, the Malthusian economy can actually collapse. Initial resource exploitation leads to rapid population growth, but in the long run population rises above the level that can be sustained by the resource base, and thus a cycle of resource depletion and population decline ensues. Brander and Taylor (1998b) develop such a model to show the conditions under which such a collapse might occur, and apply the model plausibly to explain the rise and fall of the Easter Island economy from 400–1500 AD. Brander and Taylor also indicate how similar conditions may have caused the collapse of other Malthusian resource-dependent economies on other Polynesian islands and in other regions of the world.

Recent evidence suggests that Polynesians migrating from other islands settled on Easter Island around 400 AD (Brander and Taylor 1998b). The early economy of the island was based on abundant palm tree forests and fish, and the human population exploiting these resources grew quickly. The famous Easter Island statues were carved between 1100 and 1500, and the human population reached its peak of about 10,000 people around 1400 AD. However, about this same time, the palm forest was completely depleted, and over the next century both the number of people and food consumption began to decline sharply. By the time of European contact in the early eighteenth century, the island's population had fallen to around 3,000 inhabitants, who lived at a meager subsistence level.

To describe the dynamics of the rise and fall of the resource-based Easter Island economy, Brander and Taylor develop a Ricardo-Malthus model of open-access renewable resource exploitation. In essence, their model is a variation on the standard predator-prey dynamic relationship, where human population, L, is the predator, and the island's resource stock, S, is the prey.[11] However, underlying this relationship is a simple Ricardian economy, in which the single input of human labor (equal to the total population) is allocated to either extracting the open-access renewable resource harvest, H, or producing a composite numeraire good, M. The result is two dynamic equations denoting net change in the resource stock and population, respectively

$$\dot{S} = dS/dt = G(S) - H = rS(1 - S/K) - \alpha\beta LS \qquad (2.1)$$

$$\dot{L} = dL/dt = L(b - d + F) = L(b - d + \phi\alpha\beta S). \qquad (2.2)$$

In equation (2.1), the biological growth of the resource, $G(S)$, is assumed to be logistic, with r denoting the intrinsic growth rate and K the carrying capacity of the environment. The parameter α represents the constant coefficient in the Schaefer harvesting function, and β reflects consumers' "taste" for the output of the harvest good. Thus (2.1) indicates that the resource stock will increase if its biological growth exceeds harvesting by the human population. In equation (2.2), b is the proportional birth rate, d is the proportional death rate, F is the human fertility function $F = \phi H/L$, and ϕ is a positive constant. If birth and fertility exceed deaths, then the population will increase.

Brander and Taylor demonstrate that the dynamic "predator-prey" system represented by (2.1) and (2.2) may yield a long-run steady state where both resources and human population are constant, i.e. $\dot{S} = \dot{L} = 0$, and there is a steady-state resource stock level, S^*, and population, L^*.[12] However, a number of important conditions dictate the dynamic behavior of the system and determine whether an "interior" steady state (i.e. $S^* > 0$ and $L^* > 0$) is attainable. Three of the outcomes explored by Brander and Taylor are particularly interesting for such a Malthusian economy:

- If the environmental carrying capacity, K, is sufficiently small, then there is no interior steady state; i.e. the resource stock is run down to a level that causes extinction of the human population.
- If the intrinsic growth rate, r, is sufficiently large, then the economy will adjust monotonically to an interior steady state; i.e. both the resource stock and the human population will converge eventually to their long-run steady-state values, S^* and L^* respectively.
- If the intrinsic growth rate, r, is sufficiently small, then the economy will adjust cyclically to an interior steady state; i.e. initially abundant resources will cause human populations to "overshoot" their steady state, causing resource stocks to fall, which in turn cause population to decline and resource stocks to recover, and the cycle repeats itself until eventually the long-run steady-state values, S^* and L^*, are reached.

Brander and Taylor consider the first case to be a good approximation of what may have happened to the twelve "mystery islands" that were once settled by Polynesians but were unoccupied the time of first European contact. In contrast, the second case is representative of what happened on the other major islands of Polynesia, excluding Easter Island. Throughout the rest of Polynesia, the main forest resources are

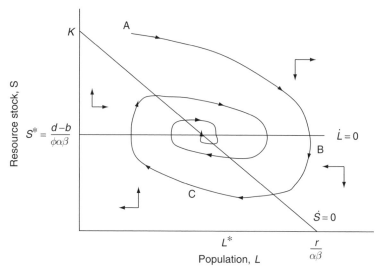

Source: Adapted from Brander and Taylor (1998b).

Figure 2.2. A long-run development path for a Malthusian economy

the coconut and Fiji fan palms, both of which are relatively fast-growing trees that reach fruit-bearing age in approximately seven to ten years. Finally, the third case resembles the Easter Island economy. The Jubea palm growing on Easter Island was not only unique to this island but also grew very slowly, reaching the fruit-bearing stage after forty to sixty years.

Figure 2.2 illustrates the dynamics underlying the "Malthusian trap" of the Easter Island economy. Point A represents the first arrival of Polynesians to Easter Island in 400 AD, when the initial population is small and the resource is at its carrying capacity, K. For several centuries, humans have very little impact on the resource stock. However, population begins to increase rapidly, and because the main resource on the island is the slow-growing Jubea palm, the resource stock starts to fall. The human population "overshoots" its steady-state level, L^*, and over-harvests resources. Eventually, the decline in resource stocks will cause population to fall. For example, point B represents some time during 1400–1500 AD, when the Easter Island population exceeded its peak of 10,000 people, and the main resource of the composite stock, the Jubea palm, was pretty much depleted. Population falls rapidly thereafter, and there is some recovery of stocks (but excluding the extinct Jubea palm). Point C represents the first arrival of Europeans to Easter Island in the early 1700s.[13]

Brander and Taylor suggest that the problem of population "overshooting" and resource collapse may also explain the demise of other Malthusian economies globally, during the era of Malthusian stagnation. The examples they cite include: the collapse of the Mayan civilization (600–1200 AD) due to deforestation and soil erosion; the demise of the Mesopotamian civilizations of Assyria, Babylonia and Sumeria (2000 BC to 1200 AD) due to soil salinization; and the Chaco Anasazi in southwestern United States (1000 to 1200 AD) due to soil degradation. Thus, the authors conclude: "our analysis of Easter Island and the other cases suggests that economic decline based on natural resource degradation is not uncommon" (Brander and Taylor 1998b, p. 134).

The emergence of the world economy (from 1000 to 1500)

Although much of the global economy could be characterized as "Malthusian" for nearly a millennium, and possibly longer for some regions, by the end of that era an important development took place that would have profound implications for world economic history. This development was the burgeoning expansion of international trade between some countries and regions, which represented the first signs of a truly "world" economy.

The expansion in international trade during 1000 to 1500 ushered in an unprecedented period of growth in global population and GDP per capita, thus ending the era of Malthusian stagnation once and for all. For example, by the end of this 500-year period, the average world level of GDP per capita had increased from US$436 per person to $566 (see Table 2.3). The annual average population growth rate also rose to 0.1%, and world population increased from 268 to 438 million (see Tables 2.1 and 2.2).

The emergence of the world economy was also critical for the subsequent rise of Western European nations as global economic powers from 1500 AD and the Industrial Revolution two and a half centuries later (Cipolla 1976; Jones 1987; Kennedy 1988; Marks 2002; McNeil 2003; North and Thomas 1973; Pomeranz 2000).[14] For example, over 1000–1500 AD, the experience gained through trade and commerce first by the Italian city states of Venice and Genoa, and later by Spain, Portugal, England, Holland and France, was pivotal in their subsequent evolution into world economic and political powers. However, it is important to recognize that the European city-states and nations had at best only a peripheral role in the emergence of the world economy. As pointed out by Findlay (1998, p. 98), "Western Europe in 1000 was the least developed of the major regions." Instead, this was the era of the "Golden Age of Islam" in North Africa and West Asia (ca. 1000–1492) and the Sung Dynasty in China (960–1279).

From around 1000 to 1492, various Islamic states flourished and expanded as the result of growing trade, making the Islamic world the dominant economic power involved in the rise of international trade.[15] This was despite the fact that over this period, there was no single Islamic empire as such. Or, as Toynbee (1978, p. 429) puts it: "Islam's domain was thus expanding conspicuously at a time when the unitary Islamic state was disintegrating."[16]

During this Golden Age of Islam, the Islamic states in North Africa and West Asia were at the center of a vast network of regional and international trade (Findlay 1998). The Islamic world had the leading manufacturing industries of the time: silk, linen, woolen and cotton textiles, ceramics, glass and leather, paper and various processed agricultural products. The main imports were primary products, such as furs from Russia, tropical spices from Southeast Asia, precious metals and gold from the Sudan, lumber, cotton and wool from Western Europe, and slaves from Africa and Eastern Europe.

The Sung Dynasty in China (960–1279) also saw the emergence of a dominant economic power fostered through greater trade, especially maritime trade. This became a necessity for the survival of the Sung Empire, especially after it lost all of its territory north of the Yangtse River Basin to the semi-nomadic Jurchen tribes in 1126 and was now willing and able to end its economic isolation and "open up" to sea and land trade with its Asian neighbors. As Toynbee (1978, p. 421) notes:

Thus by 1126, China, whose people had once believed that theirs was the only civilization in the World, had become the "Middle Kingdom" of half the World ... and all East Asian countries were now in touch, both by sea and land, not only with South-East Asia and with India, but also with the Islamic World on the far side of the Indian subcontinent.

Although China was able to engage in some trade across the Indian Ocean with the Islamic states, it is clear that this East-West pattern of trade was dwarfed by China's own trade with the rest of Southeast Asia: "China exported porcelain, silk and other manufactures to South-East Asia in exchange for spices, medicinal herbs and other natural resource products. Lucrative as was the South-East Asian spice trade with the Middle East and Europe, it must have been dwarfed by the volume of trade with China" (Findlay 1998, p. 94).

The emergence of the world economy and the expansion of international trade were therefore linked directly to the growth and development of two regional economic powers, the Islamic states (which included most of India) and the Sung Dynasty of China (Marks 2002). As a result, in 1000 and for several centuries later, China, India and Africa each had a share of world GDP that far exceeded the entire share of Western Europe (see Table 2.4).[17]

Moreover, even at its nascent stage, the world economy was already characterized by the classic pattern of "North–South" trade. As Findlay (1998, p. 87) remarks, an ironic twist to this pattern during the Golden Age of Islam in the Western Hemisphere is that the dominant "North" was not Western Europe:

Thus the pattern of trade between the Islamic world and Europe, from Spain to Russia, was of the familiar "North–South" or "colonial" pattern of exchange of manufactured for primary products and labour-intensive goods, of which the most labour-intensive is of course slaves. The difference from the nineteenth-century pattern was the Islamic world constituted "the North" and Europe "the South."

Equally, in the Eastern Hemisphere, "the North" consisted of China and "the South" was the myriad small states in Southeast Asia that supplied spices and other natural resource products.[18]

As we shall see presently, there is a continuing disagreement among economists as to whether such patterns of North–South trade lead to beneficial development in the resource-trade-dependent South. For example, those economists who believe that specialization and trade in resource-based exports may be ultimately beneficial to industrialization and economic development of the South cite as their example the Golden Age of Resource-Led Development (1870–1914). It is also clear, for reasons discussed below, that by 1500 Western Europe had benefited considerably from its "South" role in the emerging world economy. In contrast, proponents of the "unequal development" doctrine would argue that "trade with developed nations prevents industrialization in

Table 2.4 Share of world gross domestic product, 1 to 2001 AD

Share of world total (%)

	1AD	1000	1500	1820	1870	1913	1950	1973	2001
1. Western Europe	10.8	8.7	17.8	23.0	33.0	33.0	26.2	25.6	20.3
~ France			4.4	5.1	6.5	5.3	4.1	4.3	3.4
~ Germany			3.3	3.9	6.5	8.7	5.0	5.9	4.1
~ Italy			4.7	3.2	3.8	3.5	3.1	3.6	3.0
~ Netherlands			0.3	0.6	0.9	0.9	1.1	1.1	0.9
~ Spain			1.8	1.8	1.8	1.5	1.2	1.7	1.7
~ United Kingdom			1.1	5.2	9.0	8.2	6.5	4.2	3.2
2. Eastern Europe	1.9	2.2	2.7	3.6	4.5	4.9	3.5	3.4	2.0
3. Former USSR	1.5	2.4	3.4	5.4	7.5	8.5	9.6	9.4	3.6
4. Western offshoots[a]	0.5	0.7	0.5	1.9	10.0	21.3	30.7	25.3	24.6
~ United States			0.3	1.8	8.8	18.9	27.3	22.1	21.4
5. Latin America	2.2	3.9	2.9	2.2	2.5	4.4	7.8	8.7	8.3
~ Mexico			1.3	0.7	0.6	0.9	1.3	1.7	1.9
6. Asia[b]	75.1	67.6	61.9	56.4	36.1	22.3	15.4	16.4	30.9
~ China	26.1	22.7	24.9	32.9	17.1	8.8	4.5	4.6	12.3
~ India	32.9	28.9	24.4	16.0	12.1	7.5	4.2	3.1	5.4
~ Japan	1.2	2.7	3.1	3.0	2.3	2.6	3.0	7.8	7.1
7. Africa	6.9	11.7	7.8	4.5	4.1	2.9	3.8	3.4	3.3
World	100.0	100.0	100.0	100.0	100.0	100.0	100.0	100.0	100.0

Notes:
[a] Australia, Canada, New Zealand and the United States.
[b] Excludes Japan.

Source: Adapted from Maddison (2003), Table 8.b., unless otherwise indicated.

less-developed countries," and thus "there is an inherent tendency for international inequality to increase" (Krugman 1981, p. 149).

In fact, the North–South model of "unequal development" developed by Krugman (1981) fits well the stylized facts of the North–South pattern of trade in the emerging world economy described above. As suggested by Krugman (1981, p. 149), if trade reinforces and sustains the economic dominance of the leading region, it is because "a small 'head start' for one region will cumulate over time, with exports of manufactures from the leading region crowding out the industrial sector of the lagging region." This appears to be the case with the two leading regions of the early world economy: the Islamic world remained the leading region in the Western Hemisphere through its specialized trade in manufactured exports for almost five centuries, and the Sung Dynasty dominated the Eastern Hemisphere trade for nearly three hundred years, until its overthrow by Mongol invaders from the North. Thus Krugman's theoretical model explains the long-term dominance of the two economic powers very well, without suggesting that there was anything unique about the type of trade that occurred in that era compared to more recent eras of North–South trade (i.e. since colonial times to the present day).[19]

In his model, Krugman assumes that there are two trading regions, North (N) and South (S), each producing two goods, a manufacturing good, M, and an "agricultural" good, A. Although referred to as "agricultural," the latter good is more generic and could represent any natural resource product or raw material (e.g., cotton, wool, furs, precious metals and spices). The two regions have equal and constant labor forces, $L_N = L_S = L$. The agricultural good is produced by labor alone (e.g., one unit of L produces one unit of A), and there is a single world price of manufactures relative to agricultural products, P_M. However, in either region, manufacturing is the growth sector, and requires both labor and capital, K. The reason is that manufacturing exhibits increasing returns to scale, i.e. the unit capital requirements, c, and the unit labor requirements, v, are decreasing functions of each region's aggregate capital stock:

$$c_S = c(K_S), \ v_N = v(K_N), \ v_S = v(K_S), \ c' < 0, \ v' < 0. \qquad (2.3)$$

In each region the output of manufactured goods depends on the capital stock, but output of agricultural goods is determined solely by that sector's role as a residual claimant on labor. In addition, Krugman assumes that there is an upper limit on the amount of capital accumulated in each region, K_{max}, corresponding to when the region completely specializes in manufacturing and no more labor can be drawn out of agriculture:

$$M_i = \frac{K_i}{c(K_i)}, \quad A_i = L - v_i M_i, \quad v(K_{max})\frac{K_{max}}{c(K_{max})} = L, \quad i = N, S \quad (2.4)$$

Given production requirements in the agricultural sector, the wage rate is 1 in terms of the agricultural good (and thus $1/P_M$ in terms of manufactures), and the rental per unit of capital is a residual. If capital is produced by labor alone, then the rental per unit of capital, ρ, is the profit rate, and Krugman adopts the classical assumption on savings generation that all profits and only profits are saved:

$$\rho_i = \frac{(P_M - v_i)}{c_i} = \rho(P_M, K_i), \quad \rho_1 > 0, \quad \rho_2 > 0, \quad \frac{\dot{K}_i}{K_i} = \rho_i, \quad i = N, S$$

$$(2.5)$$

Finally, a fixed proportion, μ, of wages are spent on M, and $1 - \mu$ on A, and P_M is determined by world demand and supply:

$$P_M[M_N + M_S] = \mu[L_N + L_S] \rightarrow P_M = \frac{2\mu L}{\left[\dfrac{K_N}{c(K_N)} + \dfrac{K_S}{c(K_S)}\right]}, \frac{\partial P_M}{\partial K_i} < 0, i$$

$$= N, S \quad (2.6)$$

Combining (2.5) and (2.6) yields the dynamic equation for capital accumulation:

$$\frac{\dot{K}_i}{K_i} = g(K_i, K_j), \quad g_1 < 0, \quad g_2 < 0, \quad i = N, S, \quad j \neq i \quad (2.7)$$

As long as both countries produce the agricultural good, A, wage rates will be equalized by trade. Because of the increasing returns to scale in producing manufactures, M, condition (2.7) guarantees that whichever region has the larger capital stock initially will have a higher profit rate and grow faster.[20] The result is an ever-increasing divergence between regions, until K_{max} is reached by the leading region, whereas the other region will have no capital and thus produces only the agricultural good.

Figure 2.3 illustrates the dynamics of this process of uneven regional development. The long-run equilibrium is along the 45-degree line

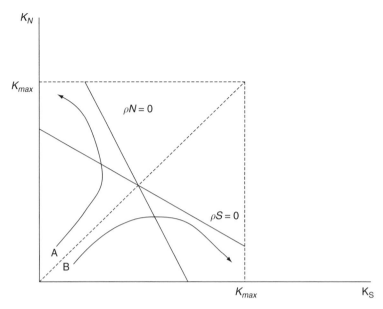

Source: Adapted from Krugman (1981).

Figure 2.3. The dynamics of unequal development and North–South trade

where the rate of profit in each region is zero and $K_N = K_S$. However, if either region starts with an initial capital stock greater than the other region (i.e. point A or B), then there follows a period in which both regions grow, but the already more developed region grows faster. As manufacturing capital grows, the relative price of industrial goods falls, until eventually a point is reached when the lagging region's industry cannot compete and begins to shrink. Once this starts, there is no check because costs rise as the scale of the industry falls. Eventually the lagging region's manufacturing sector disappears whereas the favored region specializes completely in manufactures (i.e. reaches K_{max}).[21]

There are several reasons to believe that the Islamic world and the Sung Dynasty in China had an initial "head start" that would give them an economic advantage over other regions. For example, Findlay (1998, p. 86) notes that there occurred "a 'green revolution' in the agriculture of the Islamic world over the period 700–1100" and that "this agricultural revolution enabled extensive growth of urbanization" that was the stimulus to developing leading manufacturing industries. There was a similar agricultural revolution in China that "led to a massive increase in the population of China from 50 million at the height of the Tang in 750 ... to well over 100 million in the eleventh century under the Sung" (Findlay 1998, p. 92). Similarly, "by the later decades of the eleventh century there existed an enormous iron industry in North China, producing around 125,000 tons per annum ... this production figure was far larger than the British Iron output in the early stages of the Industrial Revolution, seven centuries later" (Kennedy 1988, p. 5).

The remaining regions involved in the burgeoning world economy were clearly more peripheral, and therefore specialized in and traded chiefly raw material and natural resource products (e.g., cotton, fish, timber, wool, gold, fur and spices) or labor in the form of slaves. Unable to compete with the industry from the leading regions, the economies of the "lagging" regions never developed beyond this specialization in natural resource-based products in trade.

However, there was one important exception. By 1400–1500, compared to other "underdeveloped" regions, Western Europe had managed to establish a comparative advantage in a unique set of goods and services for the world economy. First, Western Europe specialized and traded in a distinct type of natural resource products compared to other regions: "Probably the most important characteristic of this commerce was that it consisted primarily of *bulk* products – timber, grain, wine, wool, herrings, and so on, catering to the rising population of fifteenth-century Europe, rather than the luxuries carried on the oriental caravans" (Kennedy 1988, p. 22). As populations recovered in post-Black Death Europe, demand for these products rose, which in turn stimulated the development of processing industries for some products, notably cotton and wool textiles, in Northern Italy, Flanders and England (Cipolla 1976).[22] Second, mainly because "there existed no uniform authority in Europe which could effectively halt this or that commercial development," there occurred "decentralized, largely unsupervised growth of commerce and merchants and ports and markets," to such extent that "gradually, unevenly, most of the regimes of Europe entered into a symbiotic relationship with the market economy, providing for it domestic order and a nonarbitrary legal system (even for foreigners), and receiving in taxes a share of the growing profits from trade" (Kennedy 1988, pp. 23–24). The result was that Europe became specialized in innovative commercial and banking services and institutions that lowered the considerable transaction costs involved in trade, including the development of deposit banking, direct loans to underwrite long-distance transactions and even foreign exchange (North and Thomas 1973).[23] Finally, Western Europe developed and specialized in "middleman" maritime transport services that became crucial to the expansion of global trade (Marks 2002). The city-states of Italy particularly dominated these services, as "both Venice and Genoa were involved in a major revolution in nautical technology during this era," such as the invention of the stern-post rudder and the mariner's compass (Findlay 1998, p. 103). As a result, "they continued to be the middleman between Europe and the East, until the French, Dutch and English supplanted them in the early seventeenth century" (Findlay 1998, p. 115).

By the twelfth and thirteenth century, with its specialization in select natural resource products, including some processed products, and key services such as commerce and maritime transport, Western Europe was no longer an "underdeveloped" region but more of a "semi-developed" or "middle-income" region. By 1500, Western Europe had the highest per capita GDP levels in the world, and had the largest share of global GDP after China and India.[24]

Interestingly, Krugman (1981, pp. 158–160) extends his analysis to include the possible rapid development of a "middle-income" region in a three-region model of the world economy, and also allowing for perfect mobility of capital between regions. He draws three important conclusions from this analysis: First, "the trend of international inequality may at some times be ambiguous, with a middle-income region growing faster than either high- or low-income regions." Second, "the direction of international capital movements" are unilateral and goes "from the high-income region to the middle-income region, not to the poorest areas." Finally, *which* poor region becomes industrialized at this stage is arbitrary, and can be determined by historical accident or by small differences in the conditions of production between the two backward regions."

Following this interpretation, it is clear that by 1500 and possibly before Western Europe already had in place important "differences in the conditions of production" compared to other "underdeveloped" regions of the world. However, what would particularly propel the rapid rise and economic development in the next few centuries would be these production "differences" combined with an important "historical accident": the discovery and exploitation of the vast natural resources of the "Great Frontier."

This "historical accident" of the discovery of the New World, coupled with the other fortuitous advantage of the discovery and use of coal as a cheaply available energy resource in eighteenth-century northwestern Europe, may also explain why in only a few centuries Western Europe was able to "leap ahead" of other global economic powers such as China. For example, Pomeranz (2000) argues that many of the market conditions that were characteristic to Europe were also prevalent in China, in particular access to overseas markets, trade and commerce, and in fact, as noted above China was the greater economic power over much of the 1000–1500 era. Thus these conditions alone cannot explain why the industrial revolution occurred in Europe and not China, enabling the former region and not the latter to take off into dynamic growth and world dominance. Instead, Pomeranz points to two key "exogenous" advantages that Europe had compared to China, in order to explain this "great divergence": By the eighteenth century, Western Europe not only had the geological advantage of cheap and accessible coal resources but also the geographical advantage of discovering the New World first and its cornucopia of natural resources.[25] It is the importance of the "Great Frontier" that we will particularly focus on next.

The Great Frontier and the rise of Western Europe (from 1500 to 1913)

As noted by Findlay (1998, p. 113): "Though a world economy had been operating for centuries, and even millennia, the decade of the 1490s which saw the voyages of Columbus and da Gama was undoubtedly *the* decisive moment in the formation of the world economy as we know it today." For one, it meant that finding new frontiers, or reserves, of natural resources to exploit became the basis of much of global economic development for the next four hundred years (Cipolla 1976; di Tella 1982; Findlay 1992; Findlay and Lundahl 1994; Webb 1964). Such frontier-based economic development can be characterized by a pattern of capital investment, technological innovation and social and economic institutions dependent on "opening up" new frontiers of natural resources once existing ones have been "closed" and exhausted (di Tella 1982; Findlay and Lundahl 1994).[26]

However, recognition of the role of the frontier in modern global economic development has only occurred over the past century or so. The first "frontier thesis" was put forward by Frederick Jackson Turner in his now infamous 1893 address to the American Historical Association, *The Significance of the Frontier in American History*: "the existence of an area of free land, its continuous recession, and the advance of American settlement westward, explain American development" (Turner 1986, p. 1). Critical to this frontier expansion was the availability of "free" land and resources: "Obviously, the immigrant was attracted by the cheap lands of the frontier, and even the native farmer felt their influence strongly. Year by year the farmers who lived on soil whose returns were diminished by unrotated crops were offered the virgin soils of the frontier at nominal prices. Their growing families demanded more lands, and these were dear. The competition of the unexhausted, cheap, and easily tilled prairie lands compelled the farmer either to go west and continue the exhaustion of the soil on a new frontier, or to adopt intensive culture" (Turner 1986, pp. 21–22).

Turner's frontier thesis was further extended by Walter Prescott Webb to explain not just American but global economic development. Webb (1964) suggested that exploitation of the world's "Great Frontier," present-day temperate North and South America, Australia, New Zealand and South Africa, was instrumental to the "economic boom" experienced in the "Metropolis," or modern Europe: "This boom began when Columbus returned from his first voyage, rose slowly, and continued at an ever-accelerating pace until the frontier which fed it was no more. Assuming that the frontier closed in 1890 or 1900, it may be said that the boom lasted about four hundred years" (Webb 1964, p. 13). Or, as summarized also by Findlay (1992, p. 161), "it is beyond doubt that Europe as a whole gained vast new regions, with access to enormous amounts of natural resources that fuelled her expansion for centuries ... These overseas territories provided the raw materials and the markets, the field for profitable investment, and eventually the destination for massive emigration from Europe."[27]

It is clear that Western European states benefited from the exploitation of the natural resource wealth of the "Great Frontier," and that their rise to world dominance was linked directly to this exploitation (see Tables 2.3 and 2.4). As we shall see presently, it also seems that the emerging nations of the Great Frontier, particularly the United States and Canada, also benefited from the exploitation of their abundant natural resources. However, what about the rest of the world, particularly the present-day "developing regions" of Latin America, Asia and

Africa? Did they also benefit from their resource-based trade with Western Europe? After all, for much of the period from 1500 until 1900, both the Great Frontier regions and other regions of Latin America, Asia and Africa were "colonized" by the major Western European states, and virtually all these "colonized" regions contained abundant natural resources to exploit. Is it the case that only the colonies and former colonies of the Great Frontier seem to gain from resource-based trade with Western Europe, whereas today's developing regions were made comparatively worse off by their colonial experience? If so, why?

To this day, there is considerable disagreement among economists over the answers to these important questions. Moreover, the answers seem to vary depending on which era, as well as which "developing" regions, they are examining. Finally, the various answers to these questions may also help us resolve the key paradox stated at the beginning of this chapter: if natural capital is so important for sustainable economic development, why do the majority of resource-dependent low and middle-income economies tend to under-perform in terms of growth and development? In the next chapter, we will look at current economic theories that attempt to explain (or refute) this paradox. In the remainder of this chapter we will look at two import eras within the period of the exploitation of the "Great Frontier," the Atlantic economic triangular trade (from 1500 to 1860) and the "Golden Age of Resource-Based Development" (from 1870 to 1913), and we will also examine two different explanations of how the legacy of colonial and post-colonial trading relationships may have shaped the present-day pattern of resource-dependent development in the low and middle-income countries of today.

The Atlantic economy triangular trade (from 1500 to 1860)

Along with the rise of the Western European states, the pattern of international trade in the World Economy changed considerably. First the Italian city-states, followed by the French, English and Dutch, took over the East–West trade in spices, tea and coffee. The race for this trade also precipitated an era of colonization of Asian states in South and East Asia. Second, a new three-regional pattern of trade also emerged in the Atlantic Economy to replace the old Europe-Islamic world-Africa trade in raw materials, manufactures, and slaves. As described by Findlay (1993, p. 322),

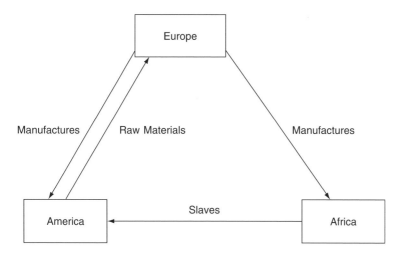

Source: Findlay (1993).

Figure 2.4. The triangular trade of the Atlantic economy, 1500–1860

the pattern of trade across the Atlantic that prevailed from shortly after the time of the discoveries down to as late as the outbreak of the American Civil War came to be known as the "triangular trade," because it involved the export of slaves from Africa to the New World, where they produced sugar, cotton, and other commodities that were exported to Western Europe to be consumed or embodied in manufactures, and these in turn were partly exported to Africa to pay for slaves.

Figure 2.4 illustrates the regional pattern of the Atlantic economy triangular trade. The European states imported raw materials from their colonies and former colonies in North and South America: sugar from the Caribbean, cotton from the American colonies and later the United States, and gold and other raw materials from Brazil and the Spanish Americas. The European states, and in particular England and to some extent France, then exported manufactures and processed raw materials (e.g., cotton textiles, construction materials, refined white sugar and rum) back to the Americas. Similarly, the European states also exported manufactures (and gold) to Africa, in exchange for slaves. However, instead of bringing the slaves to Europe they were instead shipped to the plantations in the Americas where they became the principal labor force for the production of the key raw materials exported from the New World. This triangular trade continued for centuries, until abolition of the slave trade by European states and the United States by the mid-nineteenth century ended a key component of the Atlantic economy, and the natural increase of the slave population in the Americas meant that new sources of supply were no longer necessary anyway.

In fact, the triangular trade had implications beyond the Atlantic economy. First, much of the intra-European trade was actually part of the complex triangular trade described by Figure 2.4. For example, Findlay (1993, pp. 343–344) notes:

Portugal required its colonial possessions to direct their trade through the mother country, but it was unable by itself to meet the rising Brazilian demand for manufactured goods ... British exports to Portugal, the famous exchange of Cloth for Wine in Ricardo's example, were to a considerable extent undertaken for the ultimate satisfaction of Brazilian and not Portuguese demand ... The Anglo-Portuguese trade ... had its counterpart in the Franco-Spanish relationship, which provided an outlet for French manufactures in the American possessions of Spain.

Second, the triangular trade of the Atlantic economy also had significant links with other important regional trade routes in the world economy:

For most of the eighteenth century, the textiles that were exchanged for slaves on the west coast of Africa were manufactured in India and exported by the British and French East Indian Companies. Thus the "European" manufactures of our schema can be thought of as initially exchanged for these Indian cloths, which were better suited to African tastes and climates. (Findlay 1993, p. 322).

Finally, the triangular trade was instrumental to the export-led "take-off" of growth and development in Great Britain that is commonly known as the Industrial Revolution: "There is therefore little doubt that British growth in the eighteenth century was 'export-led' and that, among exports, manufactured goods to the New World and re-export of colonial produce from the New World led the way" (Findlay 1993, p. 342).

Although Britain, France and other European states clearly benefited from the triangular trade of the Atlantic economy, the implications for other regions involved in the trade, either directly or indirectly, were more mixed. For instance, the triangular trade fits neatly into the "stylized facts" of the three-region version of the "unequal development" model of Krugman (1981) discussed above. Europe was obviously the "high-income" region and Africa the "low-income" region. Thus, the model would predict that Europe would gain from the triangular trade, whereas Africa would remain a low-income, resource-dependent region. However, one could make the case that the third trading area, the Americas, was also split into low and middle-income regions. In fact, only one region in the Americas could be considered truly a middle-income region, and that would be the United States, particularly the North. As noted by Findlay (1993, p. 344) cotton was a "comparative latecomer to the triangular trade, becoming significant only in the 1780s," and although it initially came from the West Indies and Brazil, ultimately the South of the United States was the major source of raw material for the cotton mills of Great Britain up to the outbreak of the Civil War. However, cotton from the South also was an important raw material for the nascent textile industries in the Northern states. Thus, one of the important consequences of the American Civil War was not only the permanent political reintegration of the United States but also the diversion of the previous Atlantic cotton and other raw material trade from the US to Britain to an internal trade within the United States from the South and other regions to Northern industries.[28]

In contrast, much of tropical Latin America did not fare as well as the United States (see Tables 2.3 and 2.4). Like Africa, this region remained largely underdeveloped and dependent on primary product exports long after the triangular trade ended. Likewise, India also suffered from its indirect involvement in the triangular trade. In fact, Krugman (1981, p. 156) used the example of India's textile industry collapsing as a classic case of the long-run results of his "unequal development" model, whereby the lagging region's manufacturing sector disappears as industry in the leading region (i.e. Great Britain) expands: "This is of course precisely what is supposed to have happened to the Indian textile industry in the eighteenth century. In effect, the lagging region's nascent industrial sector is destroyed by manufactured exports from the leading region ..."

The Golden Age of Resource-Based Development (from 1870 to 1913)

However, the demise of the triangular trade did not necessarily correspond to a decline in the world economy. To the contrary, over the period

1870–1913 many economies grew rapidly, and this economic boom was precipitated by the export-led industrial expansion in Western Europe and the United States. This was also the era of rapid migration of settlers and inflows of foreign capital into the "Great Frontier" regions identified by Webb (1964): temperate North and South America, Australia, New Zealand and South Africa. The economies of these regions therefore also expanded as a consequence of the world economic boom. Finally, a number of primary-producing "developing" or "periphery" regions, also experienced considerable growth as a consequence of growing world demand for raw materials and food. These included not only temperate Argentina but also a number of tropical countries that exported cash and food crops to the rest of the world.

The main stimulus for this economic boom was, on the one hand, the need of the rapidly industrializing European economies to exploit the cheap natural resources of the New World, and on the other, the need for imported capital and labor in the New World in order to expand its capacity to supply resource-based exports. Although this pattern of trade and factor movements had existed since the discovery of the vast potential resources of the New World in the late fifteenth century, it was the transport revolutions of the late nineteenth century that greatly accelerated the flow of primary product exports from the New World to Europe, and the corresponding emigration and capital export from Europe to the New World. As summarized by Taylor and Williamson (1994, pp. 348–349) with regard to the Atlantic trade:

After 1492, the central problem for Old World Europe was to exploit the cheap natural resources in the New World. Since the resources were immobile, the exploitation could take the form of only imports of resource-intensive commodities. That trade, in turn, was economically feasible only with the introduction of the investment and technologies that lowered freight rates on such low-value, high-bulk products. By the late nineteenth century, freight rates had fallen far enough to have created a partial convergence of resource-intensive commodity prices between the two sides of the Atlantic. The problem for the New World was to augment its capacity to supply more resource-intensive exports so as to exploit gains from trade. The economies of the New World were characterized by a dual scarcity: dear labor, dear capital, and cheap resources. The problem was to augment the supplies of labor and capital that combined with the abundant resources. The Old World helped the process along with emigration and capital export, and this process reached a crescendo between 1870 and 1913.

Thus because over the 1870–1913 period so many "periphery" regions benefited from exporting primary products to the "industrial" core of the booming world economy, this era is often referred to as the Golden Age of Resource-Based Development (Findlay and Lundahl 1999; Green and Urquhart 1976; Taylor and Williamson 1994; Schedvin 1990). Moreover during this Golden Age, in contrast to the predictions of the "unequal development" North–South models, such as the one by Krugman (1981) that we have discussed earlier, "the world economy behaved very much in the fashion captured by North–South models of trade and capital flows [e.g. Findlay, 1980, Burgstaller and Saavedra-Rivano, 1984] where a growing industrial North is linked to and transmits growth impulses to a primary-producing South via the terms of trade and international capital mobility" (Findlay and Lundahl 1999, pp. 5–6).

Findlay and Lundahl (1994 and 1999) suggest that five types of developing economies benefited from resource-based growth over 1870–1914: regions of recent settlement (Argentina), plantation-based tropical economies (Brazil), peasant-based tropical economies (Burma, Siam, Gold Coast), "mixed" peasant and plantation-based economies (Colombia, Costa Rica, Ceylon and Malaya), and finally, mineral-based economies (Bolivia, Chile, South Africa). As suggested by Findlay and Lundahl, the economic development in these four types of economies conform largely to the *staples thesis*, which has argued that the development of many countries and regions has been led by the expansion of export sectors, and in particular, natural resource exports, and the *vent for surplus theory*, which suggested that trade was the means by which idle resources, and in particular natural resources in poor countries, were brought into productive use (Chambers and Gordon 1966; Innis 1930 and 1940; Myint 1958; Smith 1976; Southey 1978; Watkins 1963). A common theme in both the staples thesis and the vent for surplus theory is the existence of excess resources – "land" and "natural resources" – that are not being fully exploited by a closed economy. The function of international trade is to allow these new sources of natural resources that previously had no economic value to be exploited, for increased exports and growth. Thus, as both the staples thesis and vent-for-surplus arguments have been mainly concerned with "surplus" natural resources as the basis for the origin of trade and export-led growth, it is not surprising that both theories derived their inspiration from the Golden Age of Resource-Based Development.

For example, the staples thesis was largely an attempt to explain the very substantial inflows of capital and labor into the most successful "regions of recent settlement" of the era, notably Canada and the United States (Chambers and Gordon 1966; Innis 1930 and 1940; Southey 1978; Watkins 1963). Other areas of recent settlement, notably Argentina and Australia, are also thought to follow the "staples" model of development in the late nineteenth and early twentieth centuries.[29] It is also claimed that the staples model is applicable to tropical economies that benefited from resource-based growth during the Golden Age, although Findlay and Lundahl (1999, p. 17) note that "tropical staples production" tended to differ from "staples of production in the regions of recent settlement" in that "there was no specialized manufacturing sector but just subsistence agriculture combined with handicrafts during the dead season." Equally, Myint (1958) argued that the classical vent-for-surplus theory of trade is a much more plausible explanation of the start of trade in a hitherto "isolated" country or region with a "sparse population in relation to its natural resources" such as "the underdeveloped countries of Southeast Asia, Latin America and Africa when they were opened up to international trade in the nineteenth century." Again, this may have typified the plantation, peasant, mixed and mineral-based economies of the Golden Age.

Lundahl (1998) provides a simple model to explain how the opening up of a previously "closed" economic region to "staples-led trade" can lead to economic development. This model is particularly relevant to the growth that occurred in tropical economies during the Golden Age of Resource-Based Development. The model is replicated in Figure 2.5.

Before trade, there are two sectors: subsistence agriculture and handicrafts. The given labor force is $0L_u$. Land is in unlimited supply, and is always combined with labor in fixed proportions to yield a constant marginal and average product (MP_S). The prices of food and wages are the same, and normalized to one. The handicraft sector displays diminishing returns to labor (MP_H). $0L_H$ labor will be employed in handicrafts, and the remainder of the unskilled labor force is in subsistence agriculture. Thus wages in the economy are dictated by the returns in the subsistence agricultural sector.

After trade there is a new, third sector: resource-intensive goods, R. Four factors are used in this sector: skilled and unskilled labor, capital and the natural resource. World markets determine the price of the resource, the return on capital and the wage for skilled workers. The

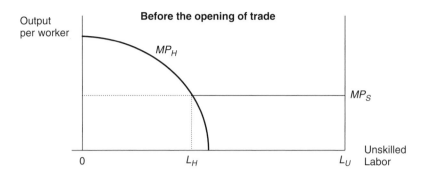

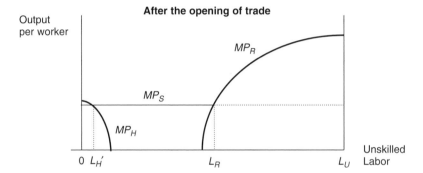

Source: Adapted from Lundahl (1998).

Figure 2.5. The opening of staples trade (vent for surplus)

unskilled wage is still controlled by the unlimited supply of land. Thus all four factors will be employed in such quantities as to make factor rewards equal to the values of the respective marginal products. This will dictate the rate of return to the natural resource, and if this return is attractive compared to the return in other countries, exploitation will take place. Imported manufactures that are close substitutes will also arrive, and if producers abroad (e.g. in developed countries) have a cost advantage, then the price of handicrafts will fall as trade is opened. The MP_H curve shifts downward, and employment shrinks in the handicrafts sector $(0L_H')$ and may even be wiped out. The new resource sector displays diminishing marginal returns (MP_R), and the marginal productivity of labor in the sector relative to subsistence agriculture determines employment, $L_R - L_U$. The remaining unskilled labor in the economy, $L_H L_R$, is employed in subsistence agriculture. Skilled workers, capital and the owner of natural resources earn comparable rates of return as world rates. Unskilled workers in subsistence agriculture and the resource sector gain, as the price of handicrafts/manufactures falls relative to wages, which remain fixed due to the unlimited supply of land. Indigenous capitalists in the handicrafts sector incur losses, and may be forced out of business.

More recent theories have focused on characterizing the "endogenous" or "moving" frontier as the basis for attracting inflows of labor and capital into a region or economy (di Tella 1982; Findlay 1995; Findlay and Lundahl 1994; Hansen 1979). Such "surplus land" models essentially postulate a Ricardian land frontier, whereby additional land can be brought into cultivation through investment of labor and/or capital, provided that the resulting rents earned are competitive with the returns from alternative assets. Thus frontier expansion becomes an "endogenous" process within a general equilibrium system of an economy, sometimes incorporating trade and international capital flows, with the supply and price of land determined along with the supplies and prices of all other goods and factors. As a consequence, changes in relative commodity and factor prices, as well as exogenous factors such as technological change and transport revolutions, induce adjustments in the supplies of the specific factors including expansion of the land frontier. As in the case of the staples and vent for surplus theories, these "endogenous frontier" models have been used mainly to explain the inflows of capital and labor into the regions of recent settlement, i.e. Webb's "Great Frontier of Canada, the United States, Argentina and Australia," and export-led colonial agricultural development in certain tropical countries, during the Golden Age of Resource-Based Development.[30]

Perhaps the most robust of the endogenous frontier models is the Findlay-Lundahl model of the effects of trade as a stimulus to frontier land exploitation and resource-based development (Findlay and Lundahl 1994). The authors suggest that various versions of their model represent the stylized facts of staples and vent for surplus theories of resource-based development, which correspond to three distinct historical cases during the Golden Age:

- The "basic model" applies to the regions of recent settlement, e.g. Canada, the United States, Argentina and Australia ("staples" thesis).
- The first "modified model" applies to tropical plantation economies, e.g. Malaya rubber economy and Costa Rica banana/coffee economy ("vent for surplus").

- The second "modified model" also applies to staple-exporting tropical peasant smallholder economies, e.g. Gold Coast (later Ghana) cocoa economy and Burma rice economy ("vent-for-surplus").

However, in contrast to the vent-for-surplus and staples theory, the key additional feature of the Findlay-Lundahl model is the concept of an endogenous frontier, i.e. the stimulus from rising prices and expanding world markets for the exported resource commodity leads to an extension of the land frontier. The authors suggest that, in the regions of recent settlement, the frontier consisted of the uninhabited prairies of North America, the pampas of Argentina or the Australian outback. In tropical plantation and peasant export economies the frontier was malarial swamps and jungles.[31]

Many of the key features are illustrated in the basic Findlay-Lundahl model. The model begins with a closed economy and assumes two sectors: agriculture, A and manufactures, M, with constant returns to scale technology. Agriculture depends on natural resource input or land, N, and labor, L_A, so that the basic production relationship is $A = A(N, L_A)$. Manufacturing depends also on labor, L_M, and capital, K_M, so that $M = M(K_M, L_M)$. The total labor force, L, is given, i.e. $L_A + L_M = L$. The capital stock K_M is in perfectly elastic supply in the long run and depends on the interest rate, ρ, determined by domestic time preference. Manufactures are the numeraire, so p is the relative price of A and w is the real wage, both in terms of M. The key "endogenous frontier" assumption is that more land (or natural resources) can be brought into production through incurring a rising marginal cost in terms of capital, K_A:

$$K_A = \phi(N), \quad \phi'(N) > 0, \quad \phi''(N) > 0, \qquad (2.8)$$

where $\phi' > 0$ represents the "marginal cost" of clearing a unit of land (in terms of the additional capital resources required).

Due to constant returns to scale, the production functions for agriculture and manufactures can be rewritten in intensive form (i.e. per worker) and denoted by small letters respectively (i.e. k now represents capital per worker). The profit-maximizing equilibrium under perfect competition in the manufacturing sector results in the equilibrium level of capital employed and the real wage, $m'(\bar{k}) = \rho$ and $\bar{w} = m(\bar{k}) - m'(\bar{k})k$, with equilibrium values denoted by a "bar". Perfect competition and free mobility of labor between sectors means that, given the equilibrium wage, there is a unique equilibrium value of land per capita, n, determined by the relative agricultural price, p:

$$p[a - a'(\bar{n})\bar{n}] = \bar{w}, \; a' > 0, a'' < 0 \tag{2.9}$$

Equation (2.9) states that the value marginal product of labor employed in agriculture must equal the equilibrium wage in the economy. However, this equation can also be inverted to solve for $\bar{n}(p)$ and $a'(\bar{n}(p))$, with $\bar{n}'(p) < 0$.[32]

Combining (2.8) and (2.9), and using the zero-profit condition in agriculture, results in the frontier land-clearing condition:

$$\frac{pa'(\bar{n}(p))}{\phi'(N)} = \rho. \tag{2.10}$$

Condition (2.10) states that, in the long run, the rate of return on clearing land must be equal to the rate of interest.[33] The numerator is the marginal value product of land per capita. As already indicated, from (2.9) this marginal product is a function of the relative agricultural price, p. The denominator is the marginal cost of land expansion, in terms of the additional capital required.

Equation (2.10) can also be solved to determine the equilibrium amount of land on the frontier, N, that is cleared in the long run. As noted above, from (2.9) a rise p will cause land per capita to fall and therefore a rise in the numerator of (2.10). Since the marginal cost of clearing land is convex in N, there must be an increase in land use in order for condition (2.10) to hold. This implies that frontier land use, N, is an increasing function of p:

$$\bar{N} = N(p), \; N'(p) > 0. \tag{2.11}$$

Since $N'(p) > 0$ and $n'(p) < 0$, it follows that both L_A and A are increasing functions of p:

$$\bar{A} = A(p), \; A'(p) > 0. \tag{2.12}$$

Equation (2.12) is essentially the positively sloped supply curve for agricultural output.

Although capital per worker in manufacturing is determined uniquely by the interest rate, ρ, an increase in agricultural labor due to a rise in p means less labor in manufacturing. This implies that L_M is a decreasing function of agricultural prices and thus the supply curve for manufactures is a positive function of its own relative price, the reciprocal of p:

$$\bar{M} = M\left(\frac{1}{p}\right), \ M'\left(\frac{1}{p}\right) > 0 \qquad (2.13)$$

The result of the economy opening to trade is that there will be a rise in the price of primary products as agricultural goods are exported at the world market price, p^*. As the small open economy is a price taker, $p^* > p$, and it is clear from (2.11)–(2.13) that the following effects will occur: additional frontier land expansion will take place, $N^* > \bar{N}$, which will also pull more labor out of manufacturing and into agriculture, $L_A^* > \bar{L}_A$ and $L_M^* < \bar{L}_M$, and agricultural production will expand and manufactures decline, $A^* > \bar{A}$ and $M^* < \bar{M}$. Since the interest rate and wages remain the same, capital per worker in manufacturing must be the same. However, this implies that the capital employed in manufacturing must decline, $K_M^* < \bar{K}_M$.

The results of the Findlay-Lundahl model are similar to those shown in Figure 2.5: the main effect of opening of trade is to cause expansion of a resource-based sector and the contraction of domestic manufactures (handicrafts). If the resource-based sector is dependent on bringing new land into production, then frontier land expansion and greater employment in the sector will occur. Frontier expansion requires increased capital investment, and so the owners of capital will also benefit from increased resource-based production. These results appear to fit well with the stylized facts of developing economic regions that "opened up" to trade and resource exploitation for export during the Golden Age of Resource-Based Development, 1870–1913. The fact that the driving force for the Golden Age was a world economic boom that boosted international primary product prices further lends credence to the predictions of these models.

However, the Findlay-Lundahl and similar models also provide some clues as to why resource-based development, along the pattern established during the Golden Age, may be successful initially but may not be sustainable. First, the shrinking of the domestic manufacturing sector implies that, opened to trade, the economy will become specialized in primary product exports. As long as world demand and prices for raw materials and other primary products are buoyed, then the resource-based economy will continue to expand. On the other hand, if the domestic manufacturing sector disappears altogether, then the resource-dependent economy remains vulnerable to falls in the international price of primary products relative to manufactures. Once specialized in resource-based exports, the economy may have difficulty in reversing this specialization and developing a modern industrialized, export-led manufacturing sector. In short, in the global economy, the seeds of "unequal development" may be set, with a rapidly developing "core" of industrialized nations trading with a slower developing "periphery" of primary product exporters.

Center-periphery trade, resource dependency and unequal development (from 1918 to the present)

Although much has changed in the world economy since the Golden Age of Resource-Based Development, as Findlay and Lundahl (1999, p. 36) have argued, very little has changed with the fundamental pattern of international trade and the division of labor:

The period from the industrial revolution to World War I can be viewed as the period when the fundamental characteristics of the present international division of labor were cemented. A new era was dawning. The industrial revolution spread. Economic tasks were divided between regions according to comparative advantage. Labour and capital moved from areas of comparatively low to areas of comparatively high returns. An industrial core was created which traded with primary producers in other parts of the world.

Unfortunately, during this modern era, very few resource-abundant developing economies have been able to join the world's "industrial core," with consequences for their long-term development prospects: "One of the main lessons of the world economic history of the past two hundred years is that the road to sustained growth goes via industrialization ... far from all of the primary exporters managed to develop a viable industrial sector. By and large, the regions of recent settlement succeeded and the rest failed" (Findlay and Lundahl 1999, p. 32). In the twentieth century, populations in Africa, Asia and Latin America have exploded (see Tables 2.1 and 2.2). However, advances in GDP per capita have been less impressive, although less resource-abundant countries such as China, India and Mexico, have managed to industrialize and develop faster in recent decades (see Tables 2.3 and 2.4). Overall, as we saw in Chapter 1, the economic performance of today's low and middle-income *resource-dependent economies* – economies mainly in Africa, Asia and Latin America with 50% or more of their exports from primary products – has been relatively poor over the long term.

Without question the most successful "regions of recent settlement" in the modern world economy has been the United States (See Tables 2.3 and 2.4). Moreover, the economic rise of the US can be directly attributable to that country's exploitation of its vast natural resource wealth. For example, the origins of rapid industrial and economic expansion in the US over 1879–1940 were strongly linked to the exploitation of abundant non-reproducible natural resources, particularly energy and mineral resources (Romer 1996; Wright 1990). In particular, during 1880–1920, the intensity of US manufacturing exports in terms of non-reproducible resources grew both absolutely and relative to the resource-intensity of imports. However, there is also evidence that there were other factors that made this historical situation in the US unique. For example, Wright (1990) maintains that, over this era:

- the United States was not only the world's largest mineral-producing nation but also one of the world's largest countries and markets;
- high international transport costs and tariff barriers for manufactured goods compared to highly efficient and low cost domestic transportation meant that the United States was a vast free trade area for internal commerce and industrial expansion that benefited from "economic distance" from the rest of the world; and
- because of the quantities of resources that were available combined with the large internal markets for goods, increasing investment in basic technologies for extracting and processing natural resources was highly profitable.

As Wright (1990, pp. 665 and 661) suggests: "the abundance of mineral resources, in other words, was itself an outgrowth of America's technological progress," and in turn, American producer and consumer goods were often specifically designed for a resource-abundant environment.

However, it is doubtful that the unique circumstances over 1879–1940 that allowed the United States to achieve "congruence" between intensive resource use and basic processing and manufacturing technologies, and thus attain rapid economic expansion, are applicable to resource-abundant developing economies today. For one, after 1940, this unique "congruence" had clearly ended for the United States, largely due to changes in the international economy, even though the US still had abundant resources. As Wright (1990, p. 665) points out:

the country has not become "resource poor" relative to others, but the unification of world commodity markets (through transportation cost reductions and elimination of trade barriers) has largely cut the link between domestic resources and domestic industries ... To a degree, natural resources have become commodities rather than part of the "factor endowment" of individual countries.

As some researchers have pointed out, the changed international conditions during the post-war era may have also affected the role of primary-product export promotion as the "engine of growth" for developing economies. During this era, the main source of economic growth in developing countries has not been primary-product based exports but labor-intensive manufactured exports (Findlay and Wellisz 1993).[34]

The failure of primary product exports to provide the "engine of growth" for developing economies in the post-World War II era led some authors to conclude that there was something inherently wrong in the "core-periphery" trading relationships underlying the pattern of trade and international division of labor characterizing the world economy. This was the doctrine of "unequal development": The core-periphery trading relationship benefits overwhelmingly the industrial core states of the world economy at the expense of the primary-producing and exporting developing economies, thus creating an inherent tendency for international inequality to increase. The result is that, whereas the core industrial states in the world economic system continue to develop and grow, international trade fails to spread development to the periphery. Instead, the periphery is trapped in a perpetual state of underdevelopment and remains specialized in the production and export of primary products.

Proponents of the unequal development doctrine included Marxist and *dependencia* writers (Amin 1974; Baran 1957; Emmanuel 1972; Frank 1967 and 1978; Furtado 1970; and Wallerstein 1974), and also less radical authors (Dixon and Thirwall 1975; Myrdal 1957; Prebisch 1950 and 1959; Seers 1962; Singer 1950). Although this literature contains a diverse range of models and theories to explain the conditions of unequal development, many of the key features of this doctrine are captured in the North–South model of trade developed by Krugman (1981), which was described and discussed earlier in this chapter.[35]

One of the more unique explanations as to why unequal development should occur between the industrial core and the primary-producing periphery in the world economy is the Prebisch-Singer thesis. Examining long-run international data, Prebisch (1950 and 1959) and Singer (1950) noted that the terms of trade of developing countries' primary product exports relative to imports of manufacturing goods were falling. The long-run tendency for international prices of primary products to fall in relation to manufactures may not in itself be a problem, e.g. if they are the result of increased technical progress they allow a country to export more and improve its world market position. However, Prebisch and Singer argued that falling terms of trade do affect a developing country's growth prospects given that the income elasticity of demand for manufactured goods is much higher than the income elasticity for primary commodities. The combination of relatively low income elasticities and falling terms of trade for developing countries' exports means that their capacity to pay for imported capital goods is lowered, thus affecting development and growth prospects.

Empirical evidence on whether the long-run relative terms of trade of primary products are falling remains fairly mixed, with recent studies suggesting a modest fall in the region 0 to 0.8 percent annually (Bleany and Greenaway 1993; Ziesemer 1995). More importantly, the basic premise of the Prebisch-Singer thesis, the tendency of long-run (non-oil) primary product prices to fall relative to manufacturing prices, is now generally accepted and is no longer "such a heretical proposition as in 1950" (Raffer and Singer 2001, p. 23). What has changed is that the thesis is no longer used, as Prebisch (1950 and 1959) argued, to justify import substitution policies in developing countries as a means to reduce dependency on primary product exports and jump start industrialization. Most protectionist import substitution efforts in the post-war era have produced disappointing, if not disastrous, results for developing countries, largely "because protectionism has led to imports of capital goods higher than the imports substituted by domestic production" (Ziesemer 1995, p. 18). Instead, as suggested by Raffer and Singer (2001, p. 25), the policy recommendations emerging from the Prebisch-Singer thesis seem to accord with more "mainstream" economic advice to developing countries:

It appears that poorer countries with static comparative advantages in (non-oil) primary commodities, or in low-tech manufactures, would be well advised to try to create different and more dynamic comparative advantages in higher-tech manufactures or services. Otherwise, they may well be caught in the trap of deteriorating terms of trade and may be at the wrong end of the distribution of gains from trade and investment. Hence our conclusion emphasizes the importance of education, and development of skills and of technological capacity. In the light of recent mainstream thinking on growth and trade, there is nothing startling about this conclusion.

The colonial origins of comparative development (from 1500 to the present)

A different perspective as to why some resource-dependent economies have developed more successfully than others is that the key to this success may have to do more with the interplay of critical exogenous factors, such as geography, climate and institutional legacy. To some extent these factors may explain why certain regions of "recent settlement" in temperate zones, such as Australia, Canada, New Zealand and the United States, emerged in the twentieth century as comparatively "developed" economies compared to the resource-dependent tropical plantation and peasant-based economies of Africa, Asia and Latin America.

Acemoglu *et al.* (2001, p. 1370) propose such an explanation with their "theory of institutional differences among countries colonized by Europeans." Their theory is based on three related hypotheses:

- Different colonization strategies created different sets of institutions. At one extreme, following Crosby (1986), "neo-Europes" were created, whereby colonial settlers tried to replicate European institutions with strong emphasis on private property and checks against government power. Primary examples of such "neo-Europes" were Australia, Canada, New Zealand and the United States. At the other extreme, "extractive states" were created, which created institutions that did not emphasize or protect private property nor provided checks and balances against government expropriation. "In fact, the main purpose of the extractive state was to transfer as much of the resources of the colony to the colonizer" (Acemoglu *et al.* 2001, p. 1370). The primary example of the extractive state was the Belgian Congo.
- The colonization strategy was influenced by geography, climate, disease and other environmental factors that influenced settlement by Europeans. In environments that were less conducive to

settlement and caused high mortality among settlers (e.g. tropical diseases such as malaria and yellow fever), the formation of extractive states was more likely. In environments more favorable to settlement, the creation of "neo-Europes" occurred. In short, what really mattered was "whether European colonists could safely settle in a particular location: where they could not settle, they created worse institutions" (Acemoglu *et al.* 2001, p. 1373).[36]

• Long after former European colonies became independent, the colonial legacy of their institutions persisted. That is, their current institutions, and thus economic performance, are largely based on whether they were former "extractive states" or "neo-Europes."

Thus, through careful empirical analysis, the authors provide substantial support for their hypothesis that "settler mortality affected settlements; settlements affected early institutions; and early institutions persisted and formed the basis of current institutions" (Acemoglu *et al.* 2001, p. 1373).

In a related analysis, Engerman and Sokoloff (1997) have argued that the *factor endowments*, broadly conceived, of New World colonies were instrumental in generating the economic conditions and institutions that determined why some of the colonies (e.g. the United States and Canada) developed faster than others (Latin American and the Caribbean countries). Engerman and Sokoloff (1997, p. 275) consider that the relevant factor endowments were not just relative abundance of land and natural resources to labor in the New World but also include "soils, climate, and the size or density of native populations," and that the impact of these factor endowments "may have predisposed those colonies towards paths of development associated with different degrees of inequality in wealth, human capital, and political power, as well as with different potentials for economic growth." Here, the authors emphasize that the key causal relationship is between factor endowments (i.e. resource and environmental conditions), social and economic inequality and the development of key institutions that generate long-term economic development and growth. As Sokoloff and Engerman (2000, p. 220) note:

What is new . . . is the specific focus on how the extremely different environments in which the Europeans established their colonies may have led to societies with different degrees of inequality, and how these differences might have persisted over time and affected the course of development through their impact on the institutions that evolved.

Sokoloff and Engerman (2000, p. 220) develop their thesis to explain that, whereas "the great majority" of New World colonies "were characterized virtually from the outset by extreme inequality in wealth, human capital, and political power," the exceptions were the United States and Canada. The result is that, in the latter countries,

both the more-equal distributions of human capital and other resources, as well as the relative abundance of the politically and economically powerful racial group, would be expected to have encouraged the evolution of legal and political institutions that were more conducive to active participation in a competitive market economy by broad segments of the population (Engerman and Sokoloff 1997, p. 268).

The authors consider this to be "significant" because "the patterns of early industrialization in the United States suggest that such widespread involvement in commercial activity was quite important in realizing the onset of economic growth. In contrast, the factor endowments of the other New World colonies led to highly unequal distributions of wealth, income, human capital, and political power early in their histories, along with institutions that protected the elites. Together, these conditions inhibited the spread of commercial activity among the general population, lessening, in our view, the prospects for growth" (Engerman and Sokoloff 1997, pp. 271–272).

The notion that "inherited" colonial institutions might influence long-term growth prospects in developing economies is not new. For some time scholars have suggested that the quality of institutions are an important determinant of economic performance, and that in particular among former European colonies, ex-British colonies have prospered relative to the former colonies of other European imperial powers (e.g., France, Spain, Portugal, Belgium and Germany), because of the good political and economic institutions inherited from Great Britain (Jones 1987; Landes 1998; La Porta *et al.* 1998 and 1999; North and Thomas 1973). However, the recent theories outlined above imply that the quality of inherited institutions may depend just as much on the geographical and environmental conditions of colonial states as on who was the original European colonizer.[37] This is again best stated by Acemoglu *et al.* (2001, p. 1373):

In contrast to this approach, we emphasize *the conditions in the colonies.* Specifically, in our theory – and in the data – it is not the identity of the colonizer of legal origin that matters, but whether European colonists could safely settle in a particular location: where they could not settle, they created worse institutions.

Two implications emerge from this perspective.

First, it provides an important insight into why regions of recent settlement, e.g. Australia, Canada, New Zealand, and the United States have emerged in the modern era from being resource-dependent "periphery" states to join the world economy's industrial core, whereas other resource-dependent former colonies, notably those in Africa, Asia and Latin America, have not done so. That is, over the past 250 years natural capital may have been important for fostering economic development but in two distinct ways. An endowment of unexploited natural resources may foster the impetus for much resource-based development worldwide, especially under favorable world trade conditions, but such an endowment alone is clearly not sufficient for sustaining economic growth and development. Equally if perhaps not more important are the environmental conditions of the country or region that encouraged European settlement and the transfer of "good" colonial institutions, which in turn have evolved into the type of institutions that are most likely to foster economic progress in the modern world economy.

The second implication follows from the first. If environmental conditions are important determinants of institutional development, then this should be the case in the modern era as well. In fact, this perception is not new, but was an important component of the original "frontier thesis" put forward by Frederick Jackson Turner: "the existence of an area of free land, its continuous recession, and the advance of American settlement westward, explain American development" (Turner 1986, p. 1).[38] In short, if the presence of "frontiers" of abundant land and natural resources influences the evolution of institutions, then economic development in a resource-based economy that is dependent on frontier expansion and resource exploitation will clearly be affected by this pattern of development. This may be particularly true of the former colonies, and now low and middle-income economies, in Africa, Asia and Latin America that were largely "extractive states" with a poor set of inherited institutions from the colonial era. As we saw in Chapter 1, many of these economies are still heavily dependent on the extraction of their natural resources and frontier land expansion. Could it be that this type of frontier-based and resource-dependent development is helping to perpetuate an "extractive state" institutional structure, thus further perpetuating the poor economic performance of these economies? This is an important issue that we will address further in the subsequent two chapters, which focus on current theories explaining the comparatively poor development of today's resource-dependent low and middle-income economies.

Conclusion

As emphasized in the introduction, the purpose of this chapter has been to review the role of natural resources in economic development during certain key historical epochs and to examine various economic theories that explain this role. In keeping with the main theme of this book, the chapter has focused in particular on various theories of how natural resource exploitation has affected the historical development of today's low and middle-income economies. Consequently, some interesting insights have emerged that will be particularly useful for the next two chapters, in which we will explore current theories as to why natural resource exploitation and frontier land expansion in developing economies appear to be a hindrance rather than a boon to their sustained growth and development.

First, it is clear that, throughout history, simply because a developing economy or region is endowed with abundant natural resources, the country may not necessarily end up exploiting this natural wealth efficiently and generating productive investments. Or, as Wright (1990, p. 666) suggests: "there is no iron law associating natural resource abundance with national industrial strength."

To the contrary, we have seen that from the beginning of international trade and the emergence of a "world" economy (1000–1500 AD) there was evidence of a very familiar North–South pattern of trade, in which the North consists of an "industrial core" that specializes in manufactured trade whereas the South is the resource-abundant "periphery" that specializes in primary products trade. However, such North–South patterns of international trade do not necessarily imply the "immiserization" of the South. There are historical examples in which specialization and trade in resource-based exports have proven to be ultimately beneficial to industrialization and economic development in the resource-abundant "periphery." This is certainly true of Western Europe in 1400–1500, which used its specialization in select natural resource products and key services such as commerce and maritime transport to become a "middle-income" and ultimately a "developed" region in the world economy. Similarly, over 1870–1940, the United States coupled exploitation of its natural resource abundance with expansion of its large and relatively protected domestic market to develop successfully a resource-intensive manufacturing sector that eventually became dominant internationally.

Thus throughout history abundant natural resources and favorable conditions in the world economy have combined often to generate successful resource-based development in many economies. However, other factors are also important. In particular, favorable institutions that encourage efficient and sustainable economic development, including the reinvestment of resource rents into more dynamic economic sectors, such as manufacturing, commercial services and transport infrastructure, appear to be critical as well. Ironically, recent evidence suggests that environmental conditions may also be extremely important in determining whether or not countries develop "good" institutions. That is, the inhospitable tropical climate and diseases prevalent in many African, Asian and Latin American countries may explain why these countries failed to attract mass European settlement, and thus to develop into "neo-Europes" with favorable institutions for economic development. The fact that many of the low and middle-income economies may still be dependent on resource exploitation and frontier land expansion for their economic development may in turn be perpetuating their "extractive state" institutions.

These issues lead us to the next two chapters, which discuss current theories of natural resource use and economic development in present-day developing economies. We are also closer to understanding the key paradox identified in the previous chapter: Why is it that, despite the importance of natural capital for sustainable economic development, increasing economic dependence on natural resource exploitation appears to be a hindrance to growth and development in the majority of today's low and middle-income economies?

Notes

1. In writing this chapter I have benefited from many recent developments in "world history," and its emphasis on "connections" across regions and national boundaries. For an insightful introduction to this rapidly growing field and useful references, see Manning (2003).

2. Indeed, some economists analyzing problems of growth and development in low and middle-income might consider natural resources to be relatively less important to these problems today. For example, in his excellent essay on the problems facing economic development in the "tropics" today, Easterly (2001) hardly mentions the role of natural resources, except in the context of linking present-day "environmental concerns" to the "over-population" problem (see Chapter 5). However, as Easterly (2001, p. 91) concludes that "the general wisdom among economists ... is that there is no evidence one way or the other that population growth affects per capita growth," then presumably this also allows him to dismiss "environmental concerns" arising from over-population as well as being possible constraints on growth. However, for an alternative view, see Hayami (2001), who considers the fundamental development problem in low-income countries today to be rapid population growth rates that have increased the relative scarcity of natural resources, especially land, relative to labor and thus reducing the endowment of arable land per agricultural worker significantly.

3. Such reviews are, of course, instructive for other purposes; e.g., such as illustrating how economic approaches to environmental and natural resource problems have evolved since the classical economics of Smith, Malthus and Ricardo. See, for example, Barbier (1989).

4. One illustration of the remarkable ingenuity of the initial agricultural and animal husbandry domestications has been their completeness, as well as their longevity, over the past 3,000 years or more. For example, Diamond (1999, p. 128) notes: "Thus, by Roman times, almost all of today's leading crops were being cultivated somewhere in the world." Similarly, "the era of big mammal domestication began with the sheep, goat and pig and ended with camels. Since 2000 BC there have been no significant additions" (Diamond 1999, p. 166). See also McNeil and McNeil (2003, ch. 2) for a catalogue of induced agricultural and social innovations that resulted during the era of agricultural transition in many regions of the world.

5. According to Diamond (1999, p. 177): "The main such spreads of food production were from Southwest Asia to Europe, Egypt and North Africa, Ethiopia, Central Asia, and the Indus Valley; from the Sahel and West Africa to East and South Africa; from China to tropical Southeast Asia, the Philippines, Indonesia, Korea, and Japan; and from Mesoamerica to North America."

6. As Livi-Bacci (1997, pp. 95–99) points out, although scholars agree generally that the era of agricultural transition corresponded with an era of demographic transition, there is widespread disagreement on the direction of causation. For example, traditional theory has suggested that the direction of causation is from agricultural and husbandry inventions to more

productive agriculture to population growth. The alternative view is that causation occurs in the opposite direction: once hunter-gatherers settled all the available land, additional demographic growth meant that they had to evolve agricultural and husbandry techniques. Of course, as suggested by Diamond (1999, p. 111), both views may be correct and there was a "two-way link between the rise in human population density and the rise in food production", i.e.: on the one hand, "food production tends to lead to increased population densities because it yields more edible calories per acre then does hunting-gathering. On the other hand, human population densities were gradually rising through the Pleistocene anyway, thanks to improvements in human technology for collecting and processing wild foods. As population densities rose, food production became increasingly favored because it provided the increased food outputs needed to feed all those people." McNeil and McNeil (2003, p. 35) also argue that climate change may have had an impact on the rise of farming and cattle herding in some regions, notably sub-Saharan Africa.

7. Of course, not all hunter-gatherers did convert to agrarian economies, with often tragic consequences. For example, Diamond (1999, p. 112) asserts "... in most areas of the world suitable for food production, hunter-gatherers met one of two fates: either they were displaced by neighboring food producers, or else they survived only by adopting food production themselves ... Only where especially geographic or ecological barriers made immigration of food producers or diffusion of locally appropriate food-producing techniques very difficult were hunter-gatherers able to persist until modern times in areas suitable for food production." Note that, although his analysis does not take into account the importance of such "geographic or ecological barriers," Smith (1975) does illustrate through his model the conditions under which a pure hunting society is maintained even in the long run.

8. Employing a different modeling approach, Horan *et al.* (2003) examine the related question – why did early North Americans exterminate their large, potentially domesticable animals such as horses and camels, whereas early Europeans preserved a similar group of animals for domestication? As the authors demonstrate, the role of hunting innovations relative to the abundance of wild game plays a crucial role in resolving this paradox.

9. In one version of his model, Smith (1975) is even able to show the affects of an increase in population on the outcome of a long-run mixed hunting-agrarian economy. In such a mixed economy, increasing the human population causes no change in the stock of wild game but reduces hunting effort and per capita income. The former effect implies that more labor will be devoted to agricultural activities. If one considers the mixed economy as an intermediate process leading up to the transition from a hunting-gathering to

an agrarian economy, then Smith's results conform to recent theories that increasing population was, at least in part, a stimulus towards greater agricultural production in hunting-gathering societies, and that the period leading up to agricultural transition was characterized by a decline in living standards and nutritional levels (Livi-Bacci 1997, pp. 95–97).

10. With virtually no growth occurring over the period 1 to 1000 AD, then presumably both physical and human capital were also fixed in supply. Following the discussion in Chapter 1, this implies that another economic condition during the Mathusian era was the lack of substitution possibilities of physical or human capital for natural capital as the latter became depleted or degraded.

11. Brander and Taylor (1998b, pp. 122–123) suggest that "it is convenient to think of the resource stock as the ecological complex consisting of the forest and soil" and to "think of (broadly defined) harvest as being food (i.e., agricultural output from the soil and fish caught from wooden vessels made from trees)."

12. As Brander and Talyor (1998b, Figure 1 and p. 126) demonstrate, the interior steady state for their economy has distinctly Malthusian properties. For example, if the economy has already attained this steady state but then the intrinsic growth rate of the resource, r, rises. The biological growth of the resource, $G(S)$, will increase, and at stock level S^* the rate of harvest will be less than resource growth and so S must increase. Per capita consumption of the resource good rises, causing population growth. As L rises, so do harvest levels. The resource stock must therefore return to its steady state level, S^*, and population growth falls to zero. However, there is now a new and higher steady-state human population but per capita income is unchanged.

13. As Brander and Taylor (1998b) recount, the economy of the Easter Island was never allowed to complete its long-run cyclical development path to its natural steady state. In the late nineteenth century, the arrival of slavers and smallpox decimated the remaining human population and changed its Malthusian economy irrevocably.

14. Marks (2002, p. 33) suggests that a true "world economy" first emerged some time during the 1300s: "During the fourteenth century, the Old World – the Eurasian continent and Africa – had been connected by eight interlinking trading zones within three great subsystems. The East Asia subsystem linked China and the Spice Islands in equatorial Southeast Asia to India; the Middle East-Mongolian subsystem linked the Eurasian continent from the eastern Mediterranean to central Asia and India; and the European subsystem, centered on the fairs at Champagne in France and the trading routes of the Italian city-states of Genoa and Venice, linked Europe to the Middle East and the Indian Ocean. Moreover, these

subsystems overlapped, with North and West Africa connected with the European and Middle East subsystems, and East Africa with the Indian Ocean subsystem."

15. Most scholars consider 1492 the end of the Golden Age of Islam because of two key events that year that would mark the rise of Western Europe: the fall of the Cordoba Caliphate, the last Islamic foothold in Western Europe and the discovery of the American continents by Christopher Columbus.

16. Even at its most unified (and largest), the Islamic World was still split into three empires. According to Toynbee (1978, p. 476), "In 1555 the Islamic World was larger than it had been in 1291, and the greater part of it was now embraced politically in three large empires: the Osmanli (Ottoman) Turkish Empire in the Levant, the Safavi Empire in Iran, and Timurid (mis-named Mughal) Empire in India." However, the rise of the Ottoman Empire in the late thirteenth century and until its peak in the mid-sixteenth century also signaled the end of the Golden Age of Islam. Particularly in later periods, the Ottoman Empire did not foster the same attitudes to innovation, trade and growth as previous Islamic states. Thus, Kennedy (1988, p. 13) notes: "Ottoman imperialism, unlike that of the Spanish, Dutch, and English later, did not bring much in the way of economic benefit."

17. As suggested by Maddison (2003, p. 242) another indicator of the comparative economic development of a country is its urbanization ratio, which measures the proportion of the population living in towns with more than 10,000 inhabitants: "In the year 1000, this ratio was virtually zero in Europe (there were only 4 towns with more than 10,000 inhabitants) and in China it was 3 per cent. By 1800 the West European urban ratio was 10.6 per cent, the Chinese 3.8 per cent. When countries are able to expand their urban ratios, it indicates a growing surplus beyond subsistence in agriculture, and suggests that the non–agricultural component of economic activity is increasing."

18. In addition to the geographical specialization in the pattern of trade, Findlay (1998, p. 87) notes another common North–South feature of the emerging world economy: "Another North–South syndrome that we are familiar with is that the 'North' is the source of scientific thought and that technological progress is diffused from the North to the South." Geography also played an important role in establishing the initial "comparative advantage" of the North: "Because of its central location, the Islamic world had the greatest geographical knowledge of its time" (Findlay 1998, p. 88). Equally, as noted previously, geographical location was a paramount reason why the Sung dynasty turned to maritime trade, once they were pushed out of northern China by the Jurchen: "When

access was cut off by the powerful semi-nomadic states of the western Hsia and the Khitans in the northeast, it was natural that they turn to that other avenue, the sea. Trade with Korea and Japan increased under the Sung, but the main channel of contact was to the south, with Java, Sumatra and other Indonesian isles, Annam and Champa in Vietnam, and ultimately with the lands of the Red Sea and the Persian Gulf" (Findlay 1998, p. 93).

19. In fact, Krugman (1981, p. 150) remarks that his model of North–South trade is totally consistent with standard neoclassical trade results: "One of the surprising things that emerges from the analysis is that the theory of uneven development fits in very well with the Hecksher-Ohlin theory of trade." Thus, it is the relative initial starting points of the two regions – i.e. the relative competitive advantage of the leading region over its trading partner – that causes the uneven development, and not trade *per* se.

20. In (2.7) $g_2 < 0$ derives directly from (2.6); i.e. an increase in the other region's capital stock will reduce the terms of trade of manufactures. However, $g_1 < 0$ assumes that the worsening terms of trade effect of an increase in K_i outweighs the reduction in the unit input requirements of an increase in K_j. Although this assumption weakens the forces for uneven development, divergence still occurs.

21. Krugman (1981) considers other long-run equilibria other than that depicted in Figure 2.3, where the leading region specialized fully in manufactures and the other region in agriculture. An interesting, and possibly more realistic alternative, long-run equilibrium is where "the 'underdeveloped' region has specialized completely in agriculture, while the 'developed' region contains both agricultural and industrial sectors" (Krugman 1981, pp. 154–155).

22. Livi-Bacci (1997) notes that global populations fluctuated considerably during 1000 to 1500, with largest variations occurring in Europe. For example, in the three centuries leading up to the Black Death, ca. 1000 to 1340, global population increased from 253 to 442 million, with the largest rise occurring in Europe (30 to 74 million). The demographic consequences of the Black Death were equally devastating. From 1340 to 1400, world population fell from 442 to 375 million, with Europe again experiencing the largest relative decline (74 to 52 million).

23. For example, North and Thomas (1973, pp. 54–55) note: "The Champagne Fairs, centrally established in France during the twelfth and thirteenth centuries, played a prominent role in the commerce between Southern and Northern Europe ... As goods in considerable and growing quantities were exchanged, the fairs became both a major market for international trade and a center of an embryonic international capital market, providing an organized and systematic locus for international credit transactions and the mechanism to make payments ... This

was in effect a freely fluctuating exchange rate which mirrored the demand and supply of different European currencies, reflecting the international balance of payments between the trading areas ... The periodic fairs began to decline in the thirteenth century, increasingly replaced by permanent markets located in centrally placed urban areas, a process which had occurred earlier in Italy."

24. In fact, Maddison (2003, p. 249) suggests that Western Europe "drew level" in development terms with China in the fourteenth century.

25. However, see Maddison (2003, pp. 249–251) for a critique of Pomeranz's characterization of the "great divergence" between China and Western Europe, which Maddison considers to have occurred much earlier (e.g. during the 1000–1500 period) and for different reasons. McNeil (1999, p. 253) also notes that "in the eleventh and twelfth centuries something approaching the sort of economic development that transformed western Europe after the eighteenth century also came to pass in China. Thus, for example, the Chinese built up a massive iron industry using coal for fuel some seven hundred years before England did the same." However, McNeil goes on to argue that "the beginnings of what might be called a proto-industrial revolution failed in the end to change older social patterns." The latter included Confucian principles that "regarded merchants as parasites," official control of economic activity and the social dominance of the gentry class.

26. In an interesting series of essays, Pomeranz and Topik (1999) document the global growth of many important markets and trading routes for many key resource commodities from 1400 to the present.

27. At the end of the previous section it was explained why Western Europe appeared to have gained a competitive advantage over other "less developed" regions of the world economy by 1500. However, one of the great historical questions explored by scholars is why did Western Europe end up exploiting the "Great Frontier" and not the non-European economic powers of that time? Scholars seem to agree that this outcome was due to the "outward-looking" approach of Western Europe to trade as a source of government revenue and economic development as opposed to the "inward-looking" approach of the Islamic and Asian empires, which were more dependent on domestic agriculture as a source of revenue and development (see, for example, Findlay 1992 and 1998; Jones 1987; Kennedy 1988; McNeil 1999; Toynbee 1978). Jones (1987, pp. 227–229) provides a succinct summary of this view: "Eurasia embraced in the sixteenth, seventeenth and eighteenth centuries four main politico-economic systems. These were the Ottoman empire in the Near East, the Mughal empire in India, the Ming and Manchu empires in China, and the European states system. The Ottoman, Mughal and Manchu systems were all alien, imposed military

despotisms: revenue pumps. They were primarily responsible for the blighted development prospects of their subjects ... Europe's very considerable geological, climatic and topographical variety endowed it with a dispersed portfolio of resources. This conduced to long-distance, multilateral trade in bulk loads of utilitarian goods. Taxing these was more rewarding than appropriating them."

28. The important other regions were of course the American frontier. For example, the "frontier thesis" proposed by Turner (1986) not only examined the consequences of Western expansion as an outlet for labor migration and capital investment but also noted that the abundant resources of the frontier were important to the economic development and growth of US industry. More recently, other scholars have demonstrated explicitly how the abundant natural resources of the United States fueled its export-led manufacturing growth, especially over the period 1879–1940 (Romer 1996; Wright 1990).

29. For instance, Findlay and Lundahl (1999, p. 16) note that all four regions of recent settlement during the Golden Age, Argentina, Australia, Canada and the United States, displayed a similar pattern of economic development: "All of them based their export activities on the existence of an unexploited land frontier, all of them received both capital and labour from abroad and all of them were in the process of industrializing as World War I broke out."

30. For example, Hansen (1979) suggests that his Ricardian land surplus model is mainly applicable to the agricultural development "under old-style imperialism" (i.e. colonialism) whereby "subsistence agriculture by illiterate and uneducated native farmers takes place exclusively on vast expanses of marginal land, whereas intramarginal land is occupied by colons – knowledgeable Europeans capable of picking up and applying technical progress." Findlay and Lunduhl (1994) show how their basic "endogenous frontier" model can be modified closer to the "vent-for-surplus" theory to explain the process of rapid export expansion in key plantation and peasant export economies, such as smallholder rubber in Malaya and bananas and coffee in Costa Rica in the late nineteenth and early twentieth century, cocoa in Ghana in the early twentieth century and rice in Burma in the second half of the nineteenth century.

31. Findlay and Lundahl (1999, p. 26) argue that their model can also apply to at least three mineral-based economies, Bolivia, Chile and South Africa, who also expanded during the Golden Age, if it is recognized that for these economies "the 'frontier' now will extend vertically downwards rather than be horizontally extensive as in the case of land and agriculture."

32. Totally differentiating (2.9) with respect to p and n yields

$$\bar{n}'(p) = \frac{dn}{dp} = \frac{[a - a'(n)n]}{pa''(n)n} < 0.$$

33. Letting r denote the value of a unit of land, the zero-profit condition in agriculture requires $\pi = L[pa - w - rn] = 0$. However, it follows from (2.8) that $r = pa'(n) = \rho\phi'(N)$. That is, the value of an additional unit of land must equal the cost of obtaining, which from (2.8) must be the value of the additional capital resources required to clear a unit of land. Using the latter expression in the zero-profit condition and rearranging results in condition (2.10).

34. From their case study analysis of five open developing economies, Findlay and Wellisz (1993) conclude that over the post-war era it was economies with relatively no resources, such as Hong Kong, Singapore and Malta, that were among the earliest and most successful exporters of labor-intensive manufactures. In contrast, resource-rich Jamaica and the Philippines have done relatively poorly, whereas Indonesia and Malaysia have done comparatively better by balancing primary exports with rapid expansion of labor-intensive manufactures.

35. One of the interesting aspects of the model by Krugman (1981) is that he is able to translate the basic assumptions underlying the unequal development literature into a neoclassical model of North–South trade. Thus Krugman (1981, p. 150) comments: "One of the surprising things that emerges from the analysis is that the theory of uneven development fits in very well with the Heckscher-Ohlin theory of trade."

36. A point ignored by Acemoglu *et al.* (2001) but emphasized by others, notably Crosby (1986), Diamond (1999) and Livi-Bacci (1997), is that disease and environmental conditions also played an important role in the success of European colonization. That is, by bringing in imported diseases from Europe, such as smallpox, tuberculosis and measles, European colonists effectively decimated many indigenous populations who had no genetic resistance to such diseases. This further enhanced the ability of Europeans to establish successful colonies, regardless of whether they were "neo-Europes" with permanent settlements by Europeans or "extractive states" with minimal settlement.

37. See also Pomeranz (2000) who, as noted above, also points out Western Europe's advantage not only in terms of the discovery and colonization of the "Great Frontier" overseas but also its good fortune of having abundant and accessible coal resources to fuel the industrial revolution at home.

38. In fact, it is clear from the remainder of Turner's 1893 address to the American Historical Association, *The Significance of the Frontier in American History*, that by "American development" Turner was implying the evolution of institutions just as much as economic development. See Turner (1986).

3 | *Does natural resource dependence hinder economic development?*

THE introductory chapter highlights the structural dependence of many low and middle-income economies on natural resource exploitation. Chapter 2 reviews many theories that, on the whole, suggest that natural resource exploitation has been the main feature of economic development and trade in the developing world historically. These theories generally suggest that the exploitation of the natural resources of a country is, at the very least, an important first step in its economic development. However, the evidence presented in Chapter 1 indicates that increasing economic dependence on natural resources in today's low and middle-income economies is associated with poorer economic performance. As emphasized throughout Part One of this book, this poses an intriguing paradox. Why is it that, despite the importance of natural capital for sustainable economic development, increasing economic dependence on natural resource exploitation appears to be a hindrance to growth and development in today's low and middle-income economies?

Conventional explanations suggest that the comparatively poor growth performance of low-income countries can be attributed to failed policies and weak institutions across the economy, including the lack of well-defined property rights, insecurity of contracts, corruption and general social instability (Keefer and Knack 1997; Mauro 1995; Murphy *et al.* 1993; Pack 1994; World Bank 1992). As we shall see, weak institutions in particular may be an important part of the story as to why resource-rich countries display disappointing rates of growth and development. However, the mechanism by which institutions interact with natural resource endowments may be critical to economic development, and thus failed policies and weak institutions alone may be insufficient to explain the poor economic performance of resource-abundant countries.

Three alternative hypotheses have been proposed to explain why natural capital exploitation may inhibit economic progress in developing economies. One explanation is the *resource curse hypothesis*, i.e. the poor potential for resource-based development in inducing the economy-wide innovation necessary to sustain growth in a small open economy, particularly under the "Dutch disease" effects of resource-price booms (Auty 1993, 1994, 1997 and 2001a; Gelb 1986b and 1988; Gylfason 2001a and 2001b; Gylfason *et al.* 1999; Matsuyama 1992; Rodríguez and Sachs 1999; Ross 1999; Sachs and Warner 1995b and 2001; Stevens 2003). Other theories have suggested an *open access exploitation hypothesis*, i.e. trade liberalization for a developing economy dependent on open access resource exploitation or poorly defined resource rights may actually reduce welfare in that economy (Brander and Taylor 1997 and 1998a; Chichilnisky 1994; Hotte *et al.* 2000; Southey 1978). Finally, some economists have proposed a *factor endowment hypothesis*. The abundant natural resources relative to labor (especially skilled labor), plus other environmental conditions, in many developing regions have led to lower economic growth, either *directly* because relatively resource-abundant economies remain specialized for long periods in primary-product exports (Wood and Berge 1997; Wood and Mayer 2001; Wood and Ridao-Cano 1999) or *indirectly* because some factor endowments generate conditions of inequality in wealth and political power that generate legal and economic institutions inimical to growth and development (Easterly and Levine 2003; Engerman 2003; Engerman and Sokoloff 1997; Sokoloff and Engerman 2000).

Thus the focus of this chapter will be to review these three hypotheses, as well as the corresponding empirical evidence, that seek to explain why the long-run development of low and middle-income economies may be hindered, rather than helped, by natural resource exploitation. If natural resource exploitation is indeed "hindering" rather than "nurturing" economic development, then a critical aspect of this problem is the failure to ensure that the rents from natural resource extraction are reinvested in other forms of capital – human, physical and knowledge-based – to "sustain" economic growth in resource-rich developing countries. This is the so-called "Hartwick rule" of resource-based development. The end of this chapter therefore outlines the basic theory behind this rule, and examines recent empirical efforts to assess whether the rule is being followed in developing economies.

The resource curse hypothesis

One recently proposed explanation of the poor performance of resource-dependent economies is the *resource curse hypothesis*. According to this view, the limits of resource-based development stem from the poor potential for such development in inducing the economy-wide innovation necessary to sustain growth in a small open economy. This phenomenon is often linked to the "Dutch disease" effect arising from some exogenous influence, such as trade liberalization or a resource price boom (Auty 1993, 1994, 1997 and 2001a; Gelb 1986b and 1988; Gylfason 2001a and 2001b; Gylfason *et al.* 1999; Matsuyama 1992; Rodríguez and Sachs 1999; Ross 1999; Sachs and Warner 1995b and 2001; Stevens 2003).[1] For example, Matsuyama (1992) has shown that trade liberalization in a land-intensive economy could actually slow economic growth by inducing the economy to shift resources away from manufacturing (which produces learning-induced growth) towards agriculture (which does not). Sachs and Warner (1995b, 1999a, 1999b and 2001) also argue that the relative structural importance of tradable manufacturing versus natural resource sectors in an economy is critical to its growth performance, i.e. when a mineral or oil-based economy experiences a resource boom, the manufacturing sector tends to shrink and the non-traded goods sector tends to expand.[2]

The argument that resource abundance may lead to slower economic growth is not new. The moral philosophers that were the precursors to classical economists often believed that the "easy riches" from land and natural resources led to "sloth" and therefore would provide a disincentive to be productive (Sachs and Warner 1999b). As we have seen from Chapter 2, the classical economists and early development economists were much more mixed in their opinion on the link between resource abundance and growth. For example, Myint (1958) argued that the classical vent-for-surplus theory proposed by Adam Smith explains how trade was the means by which idle resources, and in particular natural resources in poor countries, were brought into productive use, thus leading to economic development and growth. Equally, the "staples thesis" argued that the successful development of many countries and regions in the late nineteenth and early twentieth century was led by the expansion of export sectors, and in particular, natural resource exports (Chambers and Gordon 1966; Innis 1930 and 1940; Smith 1976;

Southey 1978; Watkins 1963). However, the "unequal development" theorists were less sanguine about the ability of poorer economies to develop and grow by exploiting their natural resource endowments through promoting primary product exports. First, they argued that, due to the presence of export enclavism, the beneficial "forward" and "backward" linkages between primary export sectors and the rest of the economy would be small (Baran 1957; Myrdal 1957; Seers 1962). Second, following the Prebisch-Singer thesis, there is an inherent tendency of long-run (non-oil) primary product prices to fall relative to manufacturing prices, thus worsening the development prospects of developing countries specializing in resource-based commodities (Prebisch 1950 and 1959; Singer 1950).

In the wake of the oil-price shocks of the 1970s and 1980s, "Dutch disease" models focused on the problems caused for a primary product-exporting economy by "resource booms" that lead to over-valued commodities (Corden 1984; Krugman 1987; Neary and van Wijnbergen 1986; Torvik 2001; van Wijnbergen 1984; Wahba 1998). Either the discovery of large reserves of a valuable natural resource or a boom in commodity prices will cause an expansion in primary product exports and lead to over-valuation of the exchange rate. This will reduce manufacturing and service exports that are more conducive to growth, and may also reduce total exports eventually.

The resource curse hypothesis is related to these "Dutch disease" effects. There are two elements to this hypothesis. First, economies with large natural resource sectors relative to manufacturing and services will grow more slowly, even if no resource boom occurs. Because manufacturing and advanced services lead to a more complex division of labor and innovation, these sectors are more dynamic and will produce more economy-wide growth. Second, a resource price boom or windfall may lead to increased growth initially, but this will be only a temporary gain.[3] As a result of the boom, the natural resource sector will expand and draw economic resources away from the more dynamic sectors, such as manufacturing. The result is that in the long run the economy will become more specialized in natural resource production and export, and thus growth may even slow down.

These effects of a resource boom are illustrated in Figure 3.1. Because it specializes more in natural resources, the resource-based economy grows at a slower rate than the average growth rate of all countries. However, at some future time t_0 the natural resource-based

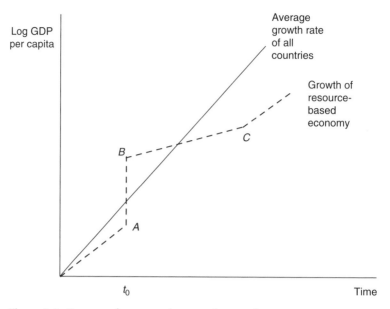

Figure 3.1. Resource booms and economic growth

economy experiences a commodity price boom or a discovery of additional valuable resource reserves. The result is an initial windfall gain and an immediate gain in GDP per capita (line *AB*). However, this gain will also mean that even more scarce economic resources are diverted to the natural resource sector, and growth will slow down (line *BC*). Eventually, the natural resource-based economy may revert to its pre-boom growth rate, but its GDP per capita will be even lower than the world average, and its lower growth rate will cause further divergence from the per capita income of other economies.

The model developed by Matsuyama (1992) provides a more elegant depiction of the "resource curse" effect.

A conventional perspective in the literature is that there are *positive* links between agricultural productivity and industrialization in economic development. Rising agricultural productivity in food production makes it possible to feed the growing population in the industrial sector and release labor to industry. Higher incomes in agriculture also stimulate domestic demand for industrial products, and increases domestic savings to finance industrialization. However, an important contribution of Matsuyama's model is to demonstrate that this conventional wisdom may hold for a closed economy but not necessarily for an open economy. Matsuyama shows that, in a closed economy, an increase in agricultural productivity will release labor to manufacturing, which is the more dynamic sector, and thus fosters economic growth. However, in an open economy with prices determined by world markets, a rich endowment of arable (or natural resources generally) may be a mixed blessing. That is, a relatively resource-abundant country will specialize in the production and exports of primary commodities. In the absence of changes in relative world prices, rising productivity in the agricultural sector would therefore attract labor away from manufacturing, thus slowing industrialization and growth.

In his model, Matsuyama (1992) assumes that there are two sectors in the economy, agriculture and manufacturing, and one mobile factor, labor, which is assumed to be constant and normalized to one.[4] Agricultural productivity is a constant, Hicks-neutral rate, A, but productivity in manufacturing, M_t, increases as a by-product of manufacturing experience. Letting n_t be the fraction of labor employed in manufacturing at time t, manufacturing output, X^M, and agricultural production, X^A, are governed by

$$
\begin{aligned}
X_t^M &= M_t F(n_t), \ F(0) = 0, F' > 0, F'' < 0, \ \dot{M}_t = \delta X_t^M, \ \delta > 0, \\
X_t^A &= AG(1 - n_t), \ G(0) = 0, G' > 0, G'' < 0.
\end{aligned}
\tag{3.1}
$$

Assume initially that the economy is closed. Letting pt be the relative domestic price of the manufacturing good, labor market equilibrium requires

$$
AG'(1 - n_t) = p_t M_t F'(n_t)
\tag{3.2}
$$

Equilibrium in the market for food, C^A, and manufactures, C^M requires

$$
\begin{aligned}
C_t^A &= \gamma L + \beta p_t C_t^M, \quad C_t^M = X_t^M = M_t F(n_t), \\
C_t^A &= X_t^A = AG(1 - n_t).
\end{aligned}
\tag{3.3}
$$

In (3.3), γ represents the subsistence level of food consumption required by the total population (labor force), L. The parameter β indicates the marginal rate of substitution of food and manufactures in consumer preferences. The relationship between the aggregate demand for food and manufactures is derived through a representative consumer utility-maximizing problem (see Matsuyama 1992 for details). In a closed economy, all output of food and manufactures is assumed to be consumed.

Combining the equilibrium conditions in (3.3) and using (3.2) to substitute for $p_t M_t$ yields

$$\phi(n_t) = \frac{\gamma L}{A}, \quad \phi(n_t) \equiv G(1 - n_t) - \beta G'(1 - n_t)\frac{F(n_t)}{F'(n_t)}, \quad \phi' < 0.$$

$$(3.4)$$

Equation (3.4) states that there is an inverse relationship between agricultural production as a function of the share of employment in manufacturing, $\phi(n)$, and agricultural productivity per capita in the closed economy, A/L. As the right-hand side of (3.4) is decreasing in A and $\phi(n)$ is declining in n, (3.4) can be solved for a unique solution for the share of employment in manufacturing in terms of agricultural productivity, A

$$n_t = n = v(A), \quad v'(A) > 0. \tag{3.5}$$

Substituting (3.5) back into the rate of change in manufacturing productivity as governed by (3.1), one obtains

$$\frac{\dot{M}_t}{M_t} = \delta F(v(A)). \tag{3.6}$$

Equation (3.5) indicates that the employment share of manufacturing, n, is constant over time but positively related to agricultural productivity. If this is the case, then (3.6) shows that output in manufacturing will increase at a constant rate, also positively related to agricultural productivity, A. Thus in a closed economy, increasing agricultural productivity will lead to both a rising share of employment in manufacturing and increased industrial innovation. The result will be greater economic growth.

Now, assume that the economy is opened to world trade. Labor is immobile across all economies, and there are no technological spillovers globally. The world economy (starred variables) also evolves according to the closed economy path of the home economy:

$$A^* G'(1 - n^*) = p_t M_t^* F'(n^*), \quad n^* = v(A^*),$$
$$v'(A^*) > 0, \frac{\dot{M}_t^*}{M_t^*} = \delta F(v(A^*)). \tag{3.7}$$

In (3.7), n^* is the equilibrium level of employment share of manufacturing in the world economy, which is constant and positively related to world agricultural productivity, A^*. In turn, n^* determines constant growth in world output in manufacturing, which is also positively related to A^*.

Under free trade, pt, is the world terms of trade for manufactures, and thus the home economy must choose its level of manufacturing employment, n_t, to equate (3.2) and (3.7) with respect to pt:

$$\frac{F'(n_t)}{G'(1-n_t)} = \frac{AM_t^*}{A^*M_t}\frac{F'(n^*)}{G'(1-n^*)} = \frac{1}{p_t} \tag{3.8}$$

By setting $t = 0$ in (3.8) and noting that the left-hand side is decreasing in n, it follows that the initial conditions for specializing in manufacturing in the home economy when it opens to trade are:

$$n_0 \overset{>}{\underset{<}{=}} n^* \quad \text{if and only if} \quad \frac{A^*}{M_0^*} \overset{>}{\underset{<}{=}} \frac{A}{M_0}. \tag{3.9}$$

Condition (3.9) states that manufacturing will account for a larger (smaller) share of the home economy's employment, compared to the rest of the world, if the home economy has a comparative advantage in manufacturing (agriculture).

Returning to (3.8) and differentiating this relationship with respect to time yields

$$\left[\frac{G''(1-n_t)}{G'(1-n_t)} + \frac{F''(n_t)}{F'(n_t)}\right]\dot{n}_t = \delta\{F(n^*) - F(n_t)\} \to \dot{n}_t \overset{>}{\underset{<}{=}} 0 \quad \text{if} \quad n_t \overset{>}{\underset{<}{=}} n^* \tag{3.10}$$

The expression in the squared bracket on the left-hand side of (3.10) is negative. This in turn implies that the employment share of manufacturing in the home economy will grow if its manufacturing sector's share of employment is larger than that of the world economy's share; otherwise, n_t will decline.

Thus, conditions (3.8) to (3.10) jointly state that when the home economy initially has a comparative advantage in manufacturing (agriculture), its manufacturing productivity will grow faster (slower) than the rest of the world and accelerates (slows down) over time. From

(3.9), an increase in agricultural productivity, A, will cause the home country to specialize even more in agriculture rather than manufacturing when the economy opens to trade. This implies that the share of employment in manufacturing will be falling (see equation 3.10). For this to occur, $\delta F(n)$ must also be lower if agricultural productivity increases in the home economy. The manufacturing share of employment in the economy will therefore be falling over time. Consequently, when the economy opens to trade, a negative link is established between rising agricultural productivity, manufacturing employment and economic growth.

In essence, Matsuyama's model suggests that a small open economy that has a comparative advantage initially in its resource (agricultural) sector will fall behind economies that have a comparative advantage in manufactures. In an open economy with less productive agriculture (relative to the rest of the world), the manufacturing sector attracts more labor, and therefore grows faster. In an open economy with more productive agriculture (relative to the rest of the world) the agricultural sector squeezes out manufacturing, and the economy declines.

Sachs and Warner (1999a) have examined evidence over the period 1960–94 for eleven major Latin American economies to test the hypothesis that any natural resource booms occurring in these countries may have had a positive impact on their growth performance.[5] First, the authors note that the main structural feature of these economies is that they have remained by and large exporters of primary commodities or manufactured products based on these commodities. Second, they suggest that a significant resource boom occurred in only four of the eleven countries (Bolivia, Ecuador, Mexico and Venezuela), and mixed evidence of a boom in another three (Chile, Colombia and Peru). However, Sachs and Warner conclude that in only one of these seven countries (Ecuador) did a resource boom have a positive and lasting effect on GDP per capita. In two countries (Chile and Colombia) there appears to be no effect of a resource boom on economic development, and in the remaining four cases (Bolivia, Mexico, Peru and Venezuela), the resource boom actually produced a negative impact on GDP per capita. On balance, resource booms appear to frustrate economic growth in Latin America, most likely through a "Dutch disease" resource-price boom effect.

Special features of certain developing countries may make them particularly vulnerable to this type of commodity-boom impact. For example, by examining eight country case studies – Cameroon, Ecuador, Gabon, Indonesia, Mexico, Nigeria, Papua New Guinea and Venezuela – Wunder (2003) maintains that the resource curse is particularly relevant for oil-producing tropical countries. In these countries, the "Dutch disease" effect of the discovery of new reserves or oil price increases caused the oil and non-traded sectors of the economy to expand at the expense of non-oil trade sectors. In tropical developing countries, such as the eight countries examined by Wunder, the key non-oil trade sectors are typically agriculture, fisheries, forestry and non-oil mining, which are likely to stagnate as a result of the rising terms of trade from the oil boom.[6] Hausmann and Rigoban (2002) show that if a country has a sufficiently large non-resource tradable sector, relative prices can be stable, even when a commodity boom in the resource sector generates significant volatility in the demand for non-tradables. However, when the non-resource tradable sector disappears, prices in the economy become much more volatile, mainly because "Dutch disease" induced shocks to the demand for non-tradables will not be accommodated by movements in the allocation of labor but instead by expenditure-switching. The inefficiency of financial markets in the country further reinforces this impact, especially as the presence of bankruptcy costs makes interest rates dependent on relative price volatility. These two effects interact causing the economy to specialize inefficiently away from non-resource tradables: the less it produces of them, the greater the volatility of relative prices, the higher the interest rate the sector faces, causing it to shrink even further until it disappears. An increase in resource income will therefore lead to specialization in the resource sector, higher interest rates and a lower level of capital and output in the non-tradable sector, ultimately causing a large and permanent decline in welfare.

As noted in connection with the second "stylized fact" discussed in Chapter 1, Sachs and colleagues have conducted other cross-country analyses in an attempt to verify the main tenet of the resource curse hypothesis, i.e. that resource-abundant economies grow less fast than resource-poor ones. Their analysis indicates that countries with a high ratio of natural resource exports to GDP have tended to grow less rapidly than countries that are relatively resource poor (Rodríguez and Sachs 1999; Sachs and Warner 1997 and 2001; see also Table 1.2).

However, these studies by Sachs and colleagues use primary products exports as a percentage of GDP as the measure of a country's resource abundance. Strictly speaking, such a variable cannot be a true indicator of "resource abundance" *per se*, as it is not a measure of the total resource endowment or stocks of a country. In fact, there is an on-going debate in the "resource curse" literature over what indicator should be used as a measure of resource abundance, with most authors agreeing that some measure of total resource stock availability, such as total land area per capita, cropland per capita and mineral resources per capita, would be the preferred indicators (Auty 2001a).

Auty (2001a) also points out that different types of natural resource endowments may have different impacts on the economic performance of a country. In particular, he distinguishes between the potential effects of *point resources* (e.g. mineral and energy resources) and *diffuse resources* (e.g. cropland). Some studies have sought to distinguish natural resource endowments in this way, and have concluded that countries endowed with abundant point resources tend to grow more slowly or be more susceptible to the "Dutch disease" impacts of a resource commodity boom (Leite and Weidman 1999; Sala-I-Martin and Subramanian 2003; Wunder 2003). Others question whether the resource curse hypothesis that resource-abundant economies perform relatively poorly is valid, even for countries endowed mainly with energy and mineral resources (Davis 1995; Manzano and Rigobon 2001). For instance, Manzano and Rigobon (2001) re-examine the period of analysis of Sachs and colleagues in the 1970s and 1980s and conclude that the poor performance of countries highly dependent on primary product exports is less likely the result of the "resource curse" but of "debt overhang":

> ... we argue that in the 70s commodity prices were high, which led developing countries to use them as collateral for debt. The 80s saw an important fall of those prices, leaving developing countries with an important amount of debt and a low flow of foreign resources to pay them. Thus, in the sample, the curse (low growth) looks close to a debt-overhang problem. (Manzano and Rigobon 2001, p. 5)

In sum, the empirical evidence linking natural resource abundance to long-run growth performance appears to be mixed. One problem is the controversy over what indicator of total resource stock ability best measures abundance, or whether certain types of resources (e.g. point resources) are more likely to be correlated with poor economic performance. In addition, other studies suggest that the reason why resource rich countries grow more slowly may have less to do with the "resource curse" than with other factors, such as debt overhang and the structural characteristics of these economies.

The evidence linking resource commodity price booms and windfalls to "Dutch disease" effects on resource-dependent economies seems more compelling. In this regard, the model and mechanism outlined by Matsuyama (1992) may be more relevant: the effects of a resource price boom is to increase the comparative advantage of the resource sector at the expense of manufacturing, thus reducing the overall growth potential of the economy. However, as we have seen from the empirical evidence, the vulnerability of a resource-dependent economy to this Dutch disease effect may have a lot to do with its structural characteristics (Hausmann and Rigobon 2002; Manzano and Rigobon 2001; Wunder 2003).

Despite the compelling evidence in favor of a "resource curse" arising from a commodity price boom, recent efforts at understanding this process have pointed to a curious conundrum: If the windfall gain from rising commodity prices or new resource discoveries is so detrimental to economic development, why do the governments of resource-dependent economies fail to take corrective measures or adopt prudent policies to correct such imbalances? Or, as Ross (1999, p. 307) puts it succinctly: "The failure of states to take measures that could change resource abundance from a liability to an asset has become the most puzzling part of the resource curse."

Thus many recent studies of the resource curse phenomenon suggest that the "Dutch disease" and other economic impacts of the resource curse cannot be explained adequately without also examining political economy factors, in particular the existence of policy and institutional failures that lead to myopic decision-making, fail to control rent-seeking behavior by resource users and weaken the political and legal institutions necessary to foster long-run growth (Ascher 1999; Auty 1994 and 1997; Baland and Francois 2000; Broad 1995; Gylfason 2001b; Karl 1997; Lane and Tornell 1996; Leite and Weidmann 1999; Mahon 1992; Ross 1999 and 2001; Sala-I-Martin and Subramanian 2003; Stevens 2003; Tornell and Lane 1998 and 1999; Torvik 2002).[7] For example, Auty (1994, p. 24) suggests several pathways for a negative "impact of a favorable natural resource base on policy choice," which result ultimately in poorer economic performance: "the richer the natural resource endowment then, first, the

longer lax macro policies are tolerated; second, the less pressure to
achieve rapid industrial maturation; third, the longer rent-seeking
groups are tolerated (and the more entrenched they become); and
fourth, the greater the likelihood of decelerating and more erratic
economic growth."

Of these various pathways, the encouragement of rent-seeking behavior has received the most attention of late (Ascher 1999; Gylfason
2001b; Tornell and Lane 1998 and 1999; Torvik 2002). In short,
natural resource abundance, windfall commodity price booms and
the discovery of valuable new reserves can all encourage private agents
to compete vigorously for the increased resource rents, and in states
with weak political and legal institutions, governments are over-
whelmed by the special interest pressures of rent seekers, thus leading
to distorted economic and resource management policies that favor the
rent seekers and generate problems of corruption, institutional breakdown and of course dissipation of resource rents. Tornell and Lane
(1998) and (1999) model formally this process, demonstrating how
natural resource booms and accompanying foreign exchange windfalls
trigger political games among powerful interest groups in a state with a
"weak legal-political infrastructure" that result in current account
deficits, disproportionate fiscal redistribution, and stagnation.
Although booms may result in an initial increase in productivity,
weak institutions provide the incentive for the rent-seeking interest
groups to compete for a greater share of production via increased
transfers, and more transfers mean less actual investment in the economy. Employing different models, Baland and Francois (2000) and
Torvik (2002) also show how, in a rent-seeking economy with weak
institutions, an unanticipated resource boom will result in more waste-
ful rent-seeking activity rather than greater entrepreneurship and
investment in productive activities.

Certain types of natural resource endowments may generate these
opportunities for rent-seeking behavior and corruption. For instance,
several studies suggest that this is the case for point resources, which
include energy and mineral resources as well as timber forests (Auty
2001a; Karl 1997; Leite and Weidmann 1999; Ross 1999; Sala-I-
Martin and Subramanian 2003). As suggested by Auty (2001a, p. 6),

The deterioration among the resource-abundant countries is more severe
where the natural resource rents emanate from "point" resources, such as

mining, rather than from "diffuse" source resources like land under peasant farms ... Point rents are associated with staples that are relatively capital-intensive and thereby concentrate ownership. They include not only mines but also plantations where the crop requires immediate processing as in the case of sugarcane. In contrast, where the staple poses more modest invest-ment barriers to entry, as with rice and maize, and some tree crops such as coffee and cocoa, the rents are likely to be more widely dispersed throughout the population.

If "bad" policies and institutions lie at the heart of translating resource abundance and windfall gains into negative economy-wide effects, then "good" policies and institutions may explain why some developing economies with resource wealth may have avoided the "resource curse." In other words, "the natural resource curse is not necessarily the fate of resource abundant countries ... sound economic policies and good management of windfall gains can lead to sustained economic growth" (Sarraf and Jiwanji 2001, p. 3). However, judging by available empirical evidence, very few resource-abundant develop-ing economies have achieved such success. For example, Gylfason (2001b, p. 566) examined the long-run growth performance of eighty-five economies and concluded:

Of this entire group there are only four resource-rich countries which managed to achieve (a) long-term investment exceeding 25% of GDP on average in 1965–1998, equal to that of various successful industrial states lacking raw materials, and (b) per capita economic growth exceeding 4% per year on average during the same period ... These countries are Botswana, Indonesia, Malaysia and Thailand. The three Asian countries achieved this success by diversifying their economies and by industrializing; Botswana without doing so.[8]

Botswana is a particularly interesting case because its economy has remained heavily dependent on mineral export earnings, principally diamonds, and has experienced substantial commodity export booms and windfalls periodically since the 1970s, yet since 1965 the country has one of the highest rates of long-term growth in the world and in the 1990s the highest ratios of government expenditures on education to GDP (Gylfason 2001b). Botswana's success in managing cycles of resource booms and busts is attributed largely to its adoption of appro-priate and stable economic policies, including managing the exchange rate to avoid excessive appreciation during boom periods, using windfalls to build up international reserves and government balances that provide a cushion when booms end, avoiding large-scale increases in government expenditure and instead targeting investments to public education and infrastructure, and finally, pursuing an economic diversification strategy that has led to modest increases in labor-intensive manufactures and services (Hill 1991; Sarraf and Jiwanji 2001). However, such long-term policies for stable management of the economy are only possible if legal and political institutions function well. Compared to most African countries, Botswana has had considerable political stability and lack of civil conflict. In addition, the government has an international reputation for honest public administration, and overall Botswana is generally rated the least corrupt country in Africa (Gylfason 2001b).

The open access exploitation hypothesis

The recent emphasis on "political economy" explanations of the resource curse phenomenon accords well with the general perception that the comparatively poor growth performance of low-income countries arises mainly from failed policies and weak institutions, including the lack of well-defined property rights, insecurity of contracts, corruption and general social instability (Pack 1994; World Bank 1992). In particular, pervasive policy and market failures in the resource sector, such as rent-seeking behavior and corruption or open access resource exploitation, will clearly provide formidable obstacles to successful resource-based development. As noted in the previous discussion of the resource curse hypothesis, there is significant evidence that resource sectors in many developing countries are prone to problems of rent-seeking and corruption, thus ensuring that natural resource assets, including land, are not being managed efficiently or sustainably (Ascher 1999; Broad 1995; Gylfason 2001b; Karl 1997; Tornell and Lane 1998 and 1999; Torvik 2002). Several studies have also noted the rent-dissipation effect of poorly defined property rights, including the breakdown of traditional common property rights regimes, in developing countries (Alston *et al.* 1999; Baland and Plateau 1996; Bohn and Deacon 2000; Bromley 1989 and 1991; López 1994; Ostrom 1990).

In fact, the pervasiveness of poorly defined property rights in the natural resource sectors of developing countries and the resulting negative economic consequences are often identified as important factors in explaining the poor performance of many resource-dependent economies. As this explanation differs somewhat from the resource curse hypothesis, we can consider the former to be a second hypothesis, the *open access exploitation hypothesis*.

For example, Brander and Taylor (1997 and 1998a) note that over-exploitation of many renewable natural resources – particularly the conversion of forests to agricultural land – often occurs in developing countries because property rights over a resource stock are hard to define, difficult to enforce or costly to administer. They demonstrate that opening up trade for a resource-abundant economy with an open access renewable resource may actually reduce welfare in that economy. As the resource-abundant country has a comparative advantage in producing the resource good, the increased demand for the resource good resulting from trade openness leads to greater exploitation, which under conditions of open access produces declining welfare in the long run.

Brander and Taylor (1997) construct a 2 × 2 (two-good, two-sector) model of a small open economy by combining open access renewable resource exploitation within a standard Ricardian model of international trade. One of the two goods is a resource good produced using labor, L, which is fixed in supply, and the resource stock. The other good is a generic "manufactures" good produced using labor, L_M. The "manufactures" good, M, is treated as the numeraire whose price is normalized to one. As one unit of labor is used to produce one unit of M, labor's value marginal product in manufacturing is also one. It follows that, given a competitive labor market, the wage rate in the economy is one. The second good is harvest, H, from a renewable resource stock, S, which is subject to the standard net biological growth relationship

$$\dot{S} = G(S) - H = rS\left(1 - \frac{S}{K}\right) - \alpha SL_H \qquad (3.11)$$

Biological growth, $G(S)$, is assumed to be logistic, with an "intrinsic" growth rate, r, and a carrying capacity level of population, K. The Schaefer harvesting production relationship is a function of a constant, α, the resource stock, S, and the amount of labor in the economy devoted to resource harvesting, L_H.

The effect of open access exploitation in the resource sector is to ensure that the price of the resource good must equal its unit cost of production. That is, as all rents from using the resource stock are dissipated, and only labor costs are incurred in harvesting, the equilibrium open access harvesting condition is always

$$p = w\frac{L_H}{H} = \frac{w}{\alpha S} = \frac{1}{\alpha S}. \tag{3.12}$$

where p is the (relative) price of the resource good. Equation (3.12) states that, under open access, the price of the resource good must equal its unit cost of production. Since the wage rate, w, in the economy is one, the unit labor requirements, and thus costs, of the resource sector are inversely related to the size of the stock.

To complete their model, Brander and Taylor assume a representative consumer endowed with one unit of labor, who has Cobb-Douglas preferences for both goods. As this implies that both goods are essential, in autarky manufactures, M, must be also be produced. The authors also show that the rate of the intrinsic growth rate to the total labor supply in the economy, r/L, determines autarky relative prices and hence Ricardian comparative advantage. Thus for some sufficiently high ratio of r/L a country would have an autarky price of the resource good less than the world price and can be considered relatively resource abundant. When the economy opens to trade, a resource abundant country with a moderate r/L ratio will specialize in the resource good at the outset of trade and along the transition path, but it will eventually become diversified in production in the long run. Although the economy gains from the opening of trade initially, utility declines eventually and in the long run. A country with a very high r/L ratio may be able to specialize in producing and exporting the resource good in the long run. However, the small economy's steady-state utility is U-shaped in the terms of trade. International trade at low or very high world relative prices for the resource good raises steady-state utility, but trade at intermediate price levels reduces steady-state utility.

Figure 3.2 illustrates the effects of opening of trade in the resource-abundant economy. Figure 3.2a compares the initial post-trade impacts and the transition to the steady state, whereas Figure 3.2b contrasts steady state utility under autarky with various trade scenarios. Denoting p^A and S_A as the autarky equilibrium resource price and stock respectively, we have from (3.12) $p^A = 1/\alpha S_A$ as the initial

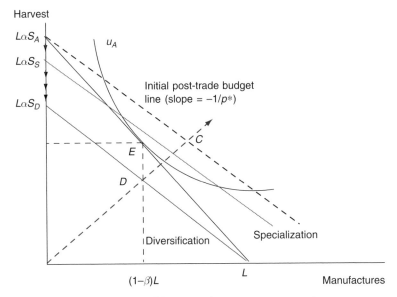

3.2a Temporary equilibrium and transition to a steady state

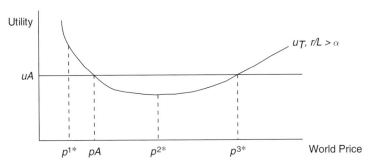

Source: Brander and Taylor (1997).

3.2b Steady-state utility and the terms of trade

Figure 3.2. Open access exploitation and trade in a resource-abundant economy

condition describing this equilibrium. In Figure 3.2a, the initial autarky production and consumption point is at E, with β and $(1 - \beta)$ representing the share of labor employed in the resource and manufacturing sectors respectively. Denoting p^* as the world price for the resource good, if $p^* > p^A$ when trade opens, then the economy immediately specializes in the resource good as $p^* \alpha S_A > 1$, implying that the value marginal product of labor exceeds the prevailing domestic wage in the resource sector. The temporary equilibrium production point moves to the vertical axis at $L\alpha S_A$, and the economy's initial post-trade budget line has a slope $-1/p^*$(represented by the dotted black line in Figure 3.2a), and it lies outside the autarky production possibility frontier. This implies that the economy exports initially the resource good, imports manufactures and experiences temporary gains from trade as the new consumption point is now C.

However, the initial trading equilibrium cannot be sustained. All labor has entered the resource sector, which will result in the temporary harvest rate rising above the steady-state autarky level. The harvest rate will exceed resource growth, and S will decline. As the resource stock falls, Schaefer production implies that harvests will also decline, and as shown in Figure 3.2a, the vertical intercept of the production possibility frontier shifts down as indicated by the arrows. Two possible steady-state outcomes may result.

First, if the resource stock stabilizes at a level that can sustain the entire labor force at a wage rate exceeding one, then the economy can specialize in production and export of the resource good in the long run. This is indicated by the line in Figure 3.2a, which is the small country's free-trade budget line that has a vertical intercept, and production level, of $L\alpha S_S$ and an intercept on the horizontal axis beyond L. As depicted in the figure, the specialized steady state would allow the country to gain from trade. However, this need not be the case. Steady-state consumption levels under complete trade specialization may not necessarily be higher than in autarky, and depending on the relationship between the terms of trade and steady-state utility, the economy may or may not have gained from trade.

Figure 3.2a also illustrates the case of steady-state diversification . In this case, the resource stock falls to a level, S_D, so that not all the labor is allocated to harvesting and its value marginal product equals one. The economy will consume at point D, and in comparison to autarky, international trade reduces the small country's steady-state utility unambiguously.

Figure 3.2b shows the consequences of trade for a resource-abundant economy, $r/L > \alpha$. The flat line labeled u^A represents the country's steady-state per capita utility under autarky, whereas u^T represents the country's steady utility under trade, which is a function of different world prices, p^* for the resource good. If the world price equals the small economy's autarky price, p^A, its trading and autarky utility are equal. At all prices below p^A the economy would export manufactures and experience steady-state gains from trade. However, if world prices fell below some level, p^{1*}, then the economy would no longer remain diversified and instead would specialize completely in manufactures. At world prices just above p^A the economy would be an exporter of the resource good but diversified in production. In this range, steady-state utility under trade would be less than it would be under autarky. However, if world prices rise to p^{2*}, the economy would specialize in the production of the resource good. This price level minimizes steady-state utility under trade. Above p^2 additional increases in the world price are beneficial to the economy, and there is some price, p^{3*}, beyond which steady-state gains from trade would occur relative to autarky.

Brander and Taylor conclude that, as the problem lies with the "open access" nature of exploitation in the resource-abundant economy, then the first–best policy would be for the small open country to switch to more efficient resource management policy through simply establishing property rights. However, as they acknowledge, there are many policy and institutional distortions that currently work against such solutions, particularly in developing countries and other resource-abundant small open economies. Consequently, Brander and Taylor (1997, p. 550) argue in favor of "second best approaches" such as the country imposing "a modified 'Hartwick's rule' (see Hartwick 1977) under which an exporting country that experienced temporary gains from selling a resource good on world markets might re-invest those proceeds in an alternative asset."

However, in an extension to the analysis by Brander and Taylor, Hannesson (2000) demonstrates that their results may depend critically on the assumption that the manufactures good sector is constant returns to scale. For example, in Brander and Taylor's model, the steady-state national income in terms of manufactures does not change, as long as the country does not specialize fully in open access resource extraction. In contrast, Hannesson argues that it is not at all unlikely for economies heavily dependent on extractive industries and with a locational disadvantage in manufacturing to have diminishing returns in the latter sector. As a consequence, the equilibrium national income of a small open economy in terms of manufactures is likely to rise from trade, even if harvested exports are exploited under open access, as the country is now able to import manufactures at a constant world price rather than having to acquire these goods through reallocating resources with diminishing returns.[9]

Hannesson also shows that, with diminishing returns to manufacturing, moving from an open access regime to optimal management may or may not lead to an improvement in welfare. Such an "immiserizing effect" of a transition from open access to optimal management will occur if the demand for the resource good is inelastic so that the value of harvested output is less with optimal management than under open access and more labor is withdrawn from the resource sector.

Although Hannesson's version of the small open economy model of Brander and Taylor (1998a) indicates that open access exploitation of natural resources may not necessarily be the only, or even the principal, cause of declining welfare, several other trade models do show that open access resource exploitation may have negative consequences for a resource-abundant economy engaged in trade.

For example, with the specific case of Latin America in mind, in which raw materials are often inputs into semi-processed or processed exports, López (1989) also develops a two-good model of a resource-rich open economy in which the open access renewable resource serves as an input into an "enclave" export-processing sector. What makes López's model particularly interesting is that it contains both features of the "resource boom" effects common to the resource curse hypothesis as well as the "overexploitation effects" from assuming that the economy is dependent on open access extraction of its natural resources. Thus, a commodity price boom leads to over-valuation of the exchange rate and misallocation of factors of production to the resource sector, but expansion of the latter leads inevitably to excessive exploitation of the open access resource and decline in stocks. The consequence is that any initial improvement in the terms of trade causes the rate of open access resource extraction and real income to increase in the short run, but in the long run inevitably the rate of open access resource extraction permanent income falls as both resource stocks decline and the exchange rate becomes over-valued. In essence, the "boom and bust" impact of the resource price windfall is reinforced by the tendency of the economy to become more dependent on over-exploiting an open access resource as an additional consequence of the exchange rate effects of the commodity price rise.

Some authors have also extended the 2 × 2 model small economy model to a two-country, or North–South, model of trade and open access resource exploitation. For example, as Chichilnisky (1994) has shown, such a North–South model of trade and resource becomes a more relevant context to analyze trade and renewable resource relationships when the two countries are otherwise identical except that they "differ only in the pattern of ownership of an environmental resource used as an input to production." This is for two reasons. First, "no trade is necessary for efficiency when the two countries are identical, yet trade occurs when they have different property-rights regimes." Second, despite the fact that neither country has an initial comparative advantage in producing the resource-intensive good, "the lack of property rights for a property rights for a common-property resource" in one country (the South) leads it to produce and export resource-intensive goods. Moreover, the South exploits its open access resource to a greater degree than is efficient and at prices below social costs, even if the all factor prices are equal across the world, all markets are competitive, and the two countries have identical factor endowments. Finally, because in the resulting world economy resource-intensive goods are under-priced, the country that has well-defined resource property rights (the North) ends up over-consuming the resource-intensive good.

Brander and Taylor (1998a) also extend their analysis of trade and an open access renewable resource beyond the small economy case to consider a two-country model. Unlike Chichilnisky (1994), however, Brander and Taylor consider both countries (North and South) to exploit a given resource stock under open access conditions. Thus each country is endowed with a renewable resource and labor, and may produce the harvested good and/or numeraire good, which again is referred to as "manufactures." The advantage of conducting such an analysis of open access resource exploitation and trade in a North–South context is that it allows the world price of the resource good to be endogenously determined within the model. This allows the authors to examine how one country's trade and resource management practices affect resource stocks and welfare elsewhere in the world.

The results for Brander and Taylor's North–South model confirm many of the authors' predictions for the small open economy (see Brander and Taylor (1997)). First, the more "resource-abundant" of the two countries has a higher rate of intrinsic growth for the resource stock relative to total labor supply, r/L. Second, with the opening of trade, the more resource abundant country will export the resource good, and may suffer long-run losses from trade. In particular, if the resource exporter is always diversified during the transition from autarky to the trading steady state, then the country loses at every point along the transition path as well as in the steady state.[10]

These welfare impacts arise from the interaction of endogenous terms of trade effects with resource depletion under open access conditions. Because of stock depletion under open access, there is over-exploitation even under autarky for both countries. However, the resource-abundant country will have a larger resource stock and a lower relative price of the resource good. This comparative advantage means that, with the opening of trade, the resource-abundant country will increase its harvest for export whereas consumers in the resource-poor (labor-abundant) country have an incentive to import the resource good. The result is depletion of the renewable stock in the resource-abundant country, and as the stock falls the labor cost of producing the harvested good rises, causing a gradual increase in its price. Because of open access conditions, resource rents remain zero and the only income is labor income, which must fall in real terms as the price of the resource good rises. In contrast, for the resource-poor (labor-abundant) country, trade induces it to export manufactures (the labor-intensive good), and thus its resource stock recovers relative to autarky. As nominal (labor) income and the price of the manufactures in the resource-poor country are the same as in autarky, while the price of the resource good is lower, real income must rise. Thus it follows that trade causes steady-state utility to fall in the resource-abundant country and to rise in the labor-abundant country, and under certain conditions, these relative losses and gains from trade will also occur at every point along the transition from autarky to the free trade steady state.

In sum, these North–South models are strikingly similar in their conclusions that "incomplete property rights in renewable resource sectors undermine the presumption that trade liberalization is necessary welfare improving" (Brander and Taylor 1998a, p. 204). It follows that, if open access conditions for resource exploitation mean that a resource-dependent developing economy may not gain from trade, then the obvious first–best solution would be to ensure that open access resources in the economy are "privatized" as quickly as possible. As discussed above, there may be political and institutional reasons why such a solution is impractical for many developing countries. However, putting these obstacles aside, allowing individuals to establish private property rights over open access resources may not necessarily lead to increased efficiency gains for the economy.

For example, several authors have examined how open access conditions can lead to an "endogenous" process of property rights establishment that may lead to excessive dissipation of resource rents and less benefits for an economy (Anderson and Hill 1990; Hotte *et al.* 2000; Southey 1978). There is ample evidence in developing economies that more secure rights over natural resources, particularly land, will lead to incentives for increased investments in resource improvements and productivity (Besley 1995; Bohn and Deacon 2000; Feder and Feeny 1991; Feder and Onchan 1987).[11] However, if many individuals are competing to establish property rights over previously unclaimed land and other natural resources, then the resulting "race for property rights" can lead these individuals to incur high costs to claiming and enforcing these rights. Any potential economic gains from more secure rights, including increased investment opportunities, may be quickly dissipated. As described by Anderson and Hill (1990, p. 177): "When property rights and the rents therefrom are 'up for grabs,' it is possible for expenditures to establish rights to fully dissipate the rents, leaving the efficiency gains from privatization in question."

The classic case of the "race for property rights" was the "land give aways" and homesteading that opened up both the Canadian and United States West in the nineteenth century (Anderson and Hill 1975 and 1990; Southey 1978). In the case of homesteading, individual farm families could establish freehold title by occupying and developing their land. In the case of land and natural resource giveaways (or grants), land and other natural resources were given away to large-scale landowners (e.g. railroad companies, ranchers, mineral exploiters) by the government as a reward for initiating development (e.g. building railways, establishing ranches, initiating mining operations). However, as argued by Southey (1978, p. 557) the latter activities could be considered "simply homesteading on a grand scale." The result is that competition among homesteaders for the best land, and large-scale landowners for the best resource grants, will lead to premature development, as well as the complete dissipation of all net capitalized rents.

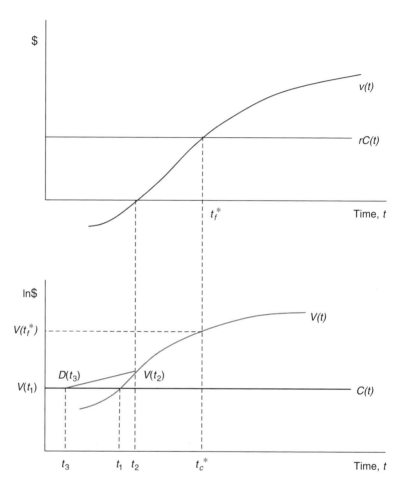

Source: Southey (1978).

Figure 3.3. The race for property rights and rent dissipation

This outcome of Southey's model can be represented in a simple diagram (see Figure 3.3). Consider the homesteading problem first. Southey separates the decision to farm the land from the decision to "break in" the land, or convert it, to a farm. For example, farming generates a stream of net annual earnings, or rents, $v(t)$, and the discounted present value of this stream of rents to some initial time can be denoted as $V(t)$. The stream of annual rents are displayed in the top diagram of Figure 3.3, whereas the present value, or capitalized, rents are indicated in logarithmic scale on the bottom diagram. Finally, breaking-in the land incurs a one-time lump sum cost, C. The latter cost is indicated on the bottom diagram of Figure 3.3, whereas the annual interest charge on this cost, rC, is shown on the top diagram.

If there is no competition among homesteaders for land, then a representative homesteading household would be free to choose the best time both to break in its parcel of land, t_c, and to farm it, t_f, so as to maximize net capitalized rents:

$$\max_{t_f,t_c} W = V(s) - Ce^{-r(t_c-s)}, \ V(s) = \int_{t_f}^{\infty} v(t)e^{-r(t-s)}dt, t_c \leq t_f. \quad (3.13)$$

Assuming breaking-in costs are constant over time, $\partial C/\partial t_c = 0$, the solution to this problem is:

$$v\left(t_f^*\right) = rC\left(t_c^*\right), t_f^* = t_c^*. \quad (3.14)$$

The homesteading household delays its breaking-in costs until the last minute, and then commences farming right away. The optimal time to farm ensures that the expected net annual rent at that date just covers the interest charge on the break-in costs incurred.

However, if there is competition among homesteaders for land, then the first household on the land is likely to establish freehold title, provided that the household not only occupies the land but also actively works it right away. The household would undertake these activities provided that the present value expected rents are positive and sufficient to cover breaking-in costs:

$$V(t) = \int_{t=t_f}^{t=\infty} v(t)e^{-r(t-t_c)}dt \geq C(t_c) \geq 0. \quad (3.15)$$

But Southey argues that if the pool of would-be-homesteaders is sufficiently large, then the first household on the land would be forced to break in the land and farm as soon as possible, i.e. as soon as capitalized rents just cover breaking-in costs $V(t_1) = C(t_1)$ at some time $t_f = t_1$. As shown in Figure 3.3, not only are net capitalized rents dissipated but also settlement and farming of the land clearly occurs prematurely.

Resource "giveaways" can also lead to premature development and dissipation of capitalized rents. That is, natural resources are given to large-scale landowners (e.g. railroad companies, ranchers, mineral exploiters) by the government as a reward for initiating development (e.g. building railways, establishing ranches, initiating mining operations). However, given the long lag-time necessary for production to begin from such developments, occupation and initial breaking in to stake the resource claim will occur long before production starts up. Thus, if production starts at some time t_2 then the present value expected rents earned will be $V(t_2)$. But if initial development takes place before t_2 at some time $t_3 < t_2$ then $V(t_2)$ discounted back to this initial breaking-in period can be denoted as $D(t_3)$, which (due to the logarithmic scale) is shown as a straight line in the bottom diagram of Figure 3.3. If there are many large-scale landowners competing for resource giveaways, there will be a race to stake and develop the best resource claims. As a consequence of this competition, the first land-owner to stake a claim will do so at the earliest possible date, which is when $D(t_3) = C(t_3)$. Once again, resource development occurs prematurely, and no net capitalized rents are made.

Factor endowment hypothesis

In Chapter 2 it was noted that some economists have proposed a *factor endowment hypothesis* as to why some resource-dependent economies have historically developed more successfully than others. For instance, Acemoglu *et al.* (2001), Engerman and Sokoloff (1997), and Sokoloff and Engerman (2000) have all suggested that the key to successful resource-based development over the long run may have to do mainly with the interplay of critical exogenous factors, such as geography, climate and institutional legacy. To some extent these factors may explain why certain regions of "recent settlement" in temperate zones, such as Australia, Canada, New Zealand and the United States, emerged in the twentieth century as comparatively "developed" economies compared to the resource-dependent tropical plantation and peasant-based economies of Africa, Asia and Latin America.

Other economists have also examined the connection between given environmental conditions, notably climate and tropical locations, and the economic performance of a country. Some, such as Hall and Jones (1999) suggest that this linkage is also indirect; i.e. they use distance from the equator as an instrument for social infrastructure, as they argue that latitude is correlated with Western influence, which leads to good institutions. Still others, such as Bloom and Sachs (1998) and Kamarck (1976) maintain that there is a direct effect of climate, or more precisely geography, on performance. As summarized by Easterly and Levine (2003, p. 7), this view maintains that

tropical location leads to underdevelopment through mechanisms such as (1) the fragility and low fertility of tropical soils, (2) high prevalence of crop pests and parasites, (3) excessive plan respiration and lower rate of net photosynthesis, (4) high evaporation and unstable supply of water, (5) lack of a dry season, cold temperatures, or long enough summer days for temperate grain crops, (6) ecological conditions favoring infectious diseases for humans, (7) lack of coal deposits, and (8) high transportation costs.[12]

In sum, there appear to be two perspectives as to how factor endowments may influence long-run economic development. The first view suggests that this influence is *direct*. Rich versus poor resource endowments, temperate versus tropical climates, whether a country is landlocked and other geographical and environmental factors influence the quality of land, labor and production technologies available to an economy and thus its long-term growth and development prospects.[13] The second view is that the impact of factor endowments on economic development is *indirect*. Environment, geography and resource endowments affect a country's economic development because factor endowments have a long-lasting influence on patterns of political and legal institutional development.

Easterly and Levine (2003) attempt to test whether factor endowments, such as temperate versus tropical location, the ecological conditions influencing the spread of disease and favorable environmental conditions for growing grains and cash crops, influence long-run economic development *directly*, or only *indirectly* through institutions. The authors also examine whether the direct or indirect impact of factor endowments on long-run economic development is superseded by the instigation of major policy changes over the past four decades. They represent factor endowments for seventy-two former colonies by four main variables: settler mortality during the early nineteenth century, the latitude of a country, crops/minerals dummy variables for whether a country produced leading world commodities in 1998–99, and a dummy variable for whether a country is landlocked or not.

The results of the analysis by Easterly and Levine provide strong support for the factor endowment hypothesis in explaining observed cross-country variation in the logarithm of per capita income levels in 1995 for seventy-two former colonies, but only through the *indirect* impact through the differences in institutional factors across countries. The factor endowment variables explain cross-country variations in institutional development, which in turn account for differences in the 1995 level of per capita income across the former colonies, even when controlling for other factors such as the origin of legal institutions, religious composition and ethic diversity of countries. However, the authors find little evidence that factor endowments have any *direct* impact on economic development. Moreover, macroeconomic policies over the past four decades appear not to have exerted any significant, additional influence on cross-country differences in income levels of former colonies. This leads Easterly and Levine (2003, p. 35) to conclude that

measures of tropics, germs, and crops explain cross-country differences in economic development through their impact on institutions ... tropics, germs, and crops do not explain economic development beyond their impact on institutions ... Furthermore, policies do not explain cross-country differences in GDP per capita once one controls for the impact of endowments on institutions and on to economic development.[14]

A variation of the factor endowment hypothesis has been proposed by Wood and colleagues, who purport to show that whether a country's exports consist mainly of manufactures or primary products depends fundamentally on whether the country is endowed abundantly with natural resources relative to the skills of its labor force (Wood and Berge 1997; Wood and Mayer 2001; Wood and Ridao-Cano 1999).

This proposition is derived from a modified version of the Hecksher-Ohlin theory of trade, which predicts that countries tend to export those goods that use intensively the factors of production with which they are relatively abundantly endowed. Although Wood and colleagues acknowledge that there are four essential factors determining inter-product differences in factor intensities – financial or physical capital, the number of workers or labor, human skill or capital and natural resources – they eliminate capital on the grounds that it is internationally mobile and they assume that manufacturing and primary products are of equal labor intensity.[15] Consequently, as Wood and Berge (1997, p. 37) suggest: "What we are assuming is simply that the biggest (and thus most important) difference in factor proportions between manufacturing and primary production arises from their relative use of the other two immobile factors, skill and land." The logic of this modified Hecksher-Ohlin outcome is based on the following argument.

Primary production is usually both more land-intensive and less skill-intensive than manufacturing. If a country with relatively abundant supplies of land to skill opens to trade, the structure of output in the country therefore will shift away from manufacturing to primary production. In addition, because the expanding primary sector uses a lower ratio of skilled to unskilled labor compared to the contracting manufacturing sector, the demand and thus the wages of skilled relative to unskilled workers will fall. The result is that greater openness to trade will tend to widen initial differences in skill supplies among countries, increasing the gap in relative factor supplies between high-skill countries with little land and low-skill countries with much land. This will further reinforce the tendency of countries of high skill-land ratios to specialize in manufactures and of countries with low skill-land ratios to specialize in primary products.

This outcome can be illustrated in Figure 3.4. The horizontal axis indicates the relative supply of skilled to unskilled workers and the vertical axis the relative skilled to unskilled wage. Country A has relatively more land than skilled workers, and so its relative supply of skilled to unskilled workers is represented by the curve S_A. Country B has relatively more skilled workers compared to land, and so its relative supply curve for skilled labor is S_B. Both supply curves are upward sloping as an increase in the wage differential between skilled and unskilled laborers would induce more workers to participate in more education and training, and give the government and firms more of an incentive to provide such opportunities. In the absence of trade, the demand curve for skilled workers dd. Country A would employ initially h_{A0} skilled to unskilled workers, and country B would employ h_{B0} skilled to unskilled workers. Given the relative scarcity of skilled laborers in country A, that country would have a higher skilled/ unskilled wage differential. Because of the difference in relative factor endowments, the opening of both economies to trade would mean that land-abundant country A would specialize in primary production and skill-abundant country B would produce manufactures. Thus country

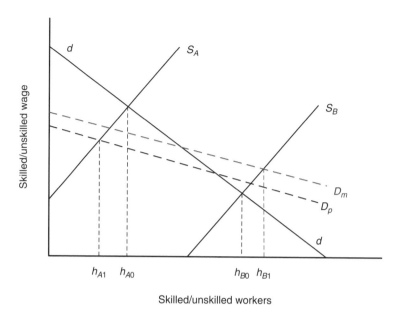

Figure 3.4. Relative skills/land endowments and trade

A faces the open economy demand curve for skilled labor associated with primary products, D_p, whereas country *B* faces the demand curve associated with manufactures, D_m. Note that $D_m > D_p$ because production of manufactures requires relatively more skilled labor. As a consequence, the land-abundant country's relatively small supply of skilled labor is reduced even further to h_{A1}, while the skill-abundant country's relatively large supply of skilled labor is increased to h_{B1}. In addition, the relative wage of skilled workers rises in country *B* but falls in country *A*. This result suggests that trade reinforces the tendency of countries with the combination of abundant skilled labor and scarce land to specialize in manufactures and countries with the combination of abundant land and scarce labor to specialize in primary products.

To test the proposition that countries with high ratios of skill to land tend to export manufactures whereas countries with low ratios of skill to land export primary products, Wood and colleagues estimate the following cross-country regression:

$$(X_m/X_p)_i = \alpha + \beta(h/n)_i + \mu_i, \beta > 0 \qquad (3.16)$$

where X_m and X_p are gross exports of manufactures and primary products respectively, h/n is the ratio of skill per worker over natural resources per worker, the subscript i identifies the country, and μ is the error term. The authors proxy "skill" by the average number of years of schooling of the population over fifteen years old and "natural resources" by total land area.

If the assumption that manufacturing and primary production are equally labor intensive is relaxed, then an alternative specification of the above model is

$$(X_m/X_p)_i = \alpha + \gamma h_i + \delta n_i + \mu_i, \ \gamma > 0, \ \delta < 0, \tag{3.17}$$

where the two factor ratios, h (skill per worker) and n (land per worker) are entered separately.

The two expressions (3.16) and (3.17) were estimated in log-linear form for all countries and different sub-groups of countries (Wood and Berge 1997; Wood and Mayer 2001). In all various samples, the coefficients of the explanatory variables have the expected sign and are statistically significant, indicating that variation across countries in their manufactured/primary export ratios can be explained simply by differences in their skill/land ratios.

It follows that, as Figure 3.4 shows, if trade reinforces the tendency of countries of high skill-land ratios to specialize in manufactures and of countries with low skill-land ratios to specialize in primary products, then greater openness to trade will tend to widen initial differences in skill supplies among countries, increasing the gap in relative factor supplies between high-skill countries with little land and low-skill countries with much land. As Wood and Ridao-Cano (1999, p. 94) maintain, the result may also be widening income differences between countries with high skills-land ratios and those with low skill-land ratios: "It thus seems rather likely that trade-induced divergence of skill supplies among countries would tend to cause long-run divergence of their *per capita* incomes."

The particular factor endowment hypothesis suggested by Wood and colleagues for explaining the poor economic performance of primary-product exporting countries shares many similarities with resource curse hypothesis discussed earlier.[16] However, Wood and colleagues stress that it is not the *absolute size* of the resource endowment of a country that is important but the *relative abundance* of natural resources to human skills in the economy that determines a country's long-run development performance. This is an important distinction, as it could explain why two countries with abundant natural resources, e.g. the United States and Venezuela, may nonetheless continue to have divergent income levels and development prospects. One country has relatively abundant levels of human skills (e.g. the United States) whereas the other country (e.g. Venezuela) has a comparatively low level of skills-resource ratio.

The factor endowment hypothesis proposed by Wood and colleagues does find common ground with one variant of the resource curse hypothesis put forward by Thorvaldur Gylfason and colleagues (Gylfason 2001a and 2001b; Gylfason *et al.* 1999). Namely, countries with an abundance of "natural capital" tend to under-invest in human capital. This may occur through the following mechanism related to rent-seeking behavior in resource-rich countries (Gylfason 2001b, p. 577):

... there is the danger that the resource rent, which flows into the hands of the main supporters of the government, which produces that rent and allocates it free of charge, may lessen both parties' interest in and understanding of the necessity of building up human capital – for example, by increasing spending by central and local governments on education, or by organizational changes to improve and strengthen the school system. Why should the recipients of the resource rent be interested in schooling and education in the name of progress? – if they have managed to line their own pockets and those of their children without acquiring an education. Thus rent seeking could partly explain why primary production tends to reduce exports ..., and also school enrolment.

If this argument is correct, it suggests that the fall in relative skill levels depicted in Figure 3.4 the low-skill and land-abundant country after the opening of trade may decline even further over time. Once the country specializes in primary production activity, opportunities for rent-seeking behavior from resource exploitation may lead to further declines of investment in human capital, thus causing relative skill levels to deteriorate even more.

Reinvesting the rents from natural capital

At the end of Chapter 1 it was suggested that the *very minimum* criterion for attaining sustainable economic development is ensuring that an economy satisfies *weak sustainability* conditions. That is, as long as the natural capital that is being depleted is replaced with even more valuable physical and human capital, then *the value of the aggregate stock* – comprising human, physical and the remaining natural capital – should be increasing over time. This in turn requires that the development path of an economy is governed by principles somewhat akin to Hartwick's rule (Hartwick 1977). First, environmental and natural resources must be managed efficiently so that the welfare losses from environmental damages are minimized and any resource rents earned after "internalizing" environmental externalities are maximized. Second, the rents arising from the depletion of natural capital must be invested into other productive economic assets.

In essence, all three hypotheses discussed above – the resource curse, the "open access exploitation" and the "factor endowment" hypotheses – provide different perspectives as to why conditions in resource-dependent developing economies may lead these economies to violate "Hartwick's rule," thus producing "unsustainable" development. In the case of the resource curse hypothesis, a commodity price boom actually *reverses* "Hartwick's rule" in that the booming natural resource sector attracts investments and factor inputs *away from* the more dynamic sectors of the small open economy, such as manufacturing. In the case of the open access exploitation hypothesis, by definition harvesting or extraction under open access condition generates no resource rents to be reinvested, and the fortunes of the economy decline in the long run as natural resource stocks become inevitably over-exploited.[17] Finally, in the case of the factor endowment hypothesis, unfavorable environmental conditions, geography, location and other "immobile" factor endowments may influence *directly* the quality of land, labor and production technologies available to an economy and thus inhibit both the efficient generation of natural resource rents as well as the returns from reinvesting any rents in other investments in the economy. Alternatively, unfavorable environmental conditions and factor endowments may have a long-lasting influence on patterns of political and legal institutional development, which in turn inhibit efficient generation of resource rents as well as their investment in other productive assets.

The remainder of this section describes in more detail the theoretical underpinnings of "Hartwick's rule". We also discuss recent efforts to measure empirically the extent to which declining natural capital in developing countries is being offset by increases in other capital in the latter economies. Both this theory and evidence helps to shed light on the basic question posed by this chapter: is the current pattern of natural resource exploitation in the majority of low and middle-income countries hindering or promoting long-term economic development?

The "sustainable development" rule identified by Hartwick (1977) is in many ways an application and extension of the models of optimal exhaustible resource extraction by Solow (1974) and Dasgupta and Heal (1974), as well as the concept of net national product as a true welfare measure as developed by Weitzman (1976). Hartwick demonstrated that, in a simplified closed economy based on non-renewable resource extraction and accumulation of reproducible capital, the condition for sustaining consumption is that investment in the capital asset must equal the depreciation of the exhaustible natural resource.[18]

"Hartwick's rule" for a closed economy exploiting an exhaustible resource has since been extended to include consideration of renewable resources (Hartwick 1978); open economies (Asheim 1986 and 1996; Hartwick 1995; Vincent *et al.* 1997); environmental externalities (Mäler 1991); interest rate uncertainty (Weitzman 1998); technical progress (Weitzman 1997) and non-optimal development paths (Dasgupta and Mäler 2000).[19]

To illustrate the main principles underlying "Hartwick's rule", it is easiest to examine the simplest case, namely for a closed economy exploiting an exhaustible resource in which aggregate consumption (broadly defined) is the only determinant of social welfare. Note that the main outcome of the rule is that depletion of the non-renewable can still satisfy the overall criterion of non-declining welfare (i.e. consumption) over time provided that "weak sustainability" is satisfied; i.e. any decline in the value of natural capital is compensated by increasing value of other forms of capital, physical and human. To simplify the analysis, we shall assume that all physical and human capital can be aggregated into one stock, K, which is distinguished from the stock of the exhaustible resource, N. Let R denote the resource extraction rate, L labor, ω the rate of depreciation of some K and δ the social discount rate. If C is aggregate consumption in the economy, and if social welfare is defined as the present value of an infinite sum of utility, $U(C)$, then the social objective of the economy is to

$$\max_{C} \int_{0}^{\infty} U(C)e^{-\delta t}, U_C > 0, U_{CC} < 0 \qquad (3.18)$$

subject to
$$\dot{K} = F(K, L, R) - C - f(R, N) - \omega K, \quad \dot{N} = -R, \quad K(0) = K_0, \quad N(0) = N_0,$$
where $F(.)$ is the aggregate production function and $f(.)$ is the cost of resource extraction. This yields the following Hamiltonian:

$$H = U(C) + \lambda[F(K, L, R) - C - f(R, N) - \omega K] - \mu R, \qquad (3.19)$$

where λ and μ are the costate variables for capital and the resource respectively. We will make use of the following first-order conditions, $\frac{dH}{dC} = 0 \rightarrow U_C = \lambda$, $\frac{dH}{R} = 0 \rightarrow \lambda[F_R - f_R] = \mu$, and we will linearize the utility function, so that $U(C) = U_C C$. Substituting the latter expressions into (3.19), and using the state equation constraints, yields

$$H = U_c C + U_C \dot{K} - U_C[F_R - f_R]R \qquad (3.20)$$

However, if consumption is the numeraire, then letting H/U_C be the dollar value of sustainable welfare or net product, SNP, then (3.20) can be rewritten as:

$$\frac{H}{U_C} = SNP = C + \dot{K} - [F_R - f_R]R = NNP - [F_R - f_R]R. \qquad (3.21)$$

In expression (3.21), NNP is net national product as conventionally defined in national accounts; i.e. NNP is the gross national product (GNP) of the economy less any depreciation (in value terms) of previously accumulated capital stocks. Thus sustainable net produce, SNP, is NNP minus an additional term, $[F_R - f_R]R$. The latter term is the "Hotelling rent" from exhaustible resource rent extraction. It represents the value of the amount of the exhaustible resource that is "used up" to produce goods and services in the economy today. Thus expression (3.21) states that a true measure of the "sustainable" net product of any economy must account not only for any depreciation in the reproducible capital stock, K, but also any natural capital depreciation.

Hartwick's rule also follows immediately from expression (3.21). According to this rule for our simple economy, the condition for sustaining consumption is that investment in the capital asset must equal the depreciation of the exhaustible natural resource. In expression (3.21) aggregate consumption is sustained if changes in C are nonnegative, i.e. $dC \geq 0$. It follows from (3.21) that the latter condition can only be met if the net growth in capital, $\dot{K}$, equals or exceeds Hotelling rents, $[F_R - f_R]R$. In other words, if all Hotelling rents are reinvested in reproducible capital, then Hartwick's rule is satisfied.

Also from expression (3.21) a more direct measure of "weak sustainability" can be derived, which is often referred to in the literature as *genuine savings* or *adjusted net savings* (Bolte *et al.* 2002; Hamilton 2003; Hamilton and Clemens 1999; Pearce and Atkinson 1993; Pearce and Barbier 2000). A conventional accounting relationship for an economy is that all gross national saving, S, is equal to gross investment, I, i.e. $S = I$. However, gross investment accounts for both depreciation in the capital stock and its increase, $I = \dot{K} + \omega K$. It follows that *net* national saving in the economy, S_N, is equivalent to the net change in the capital stock, $\dot{K}$, provided that *gross* saving is adjusted for any capital depreciation. In other words, using the notation from our above simple model however, as we have just demonstrated from (3.21), net saving as conventionally defined by the last expression is not sufficient for ensuring that the economy meets the "weak sustainability" criterion (and Hartwick's rule), unless net savings is also adjusted for any depreciation in the value of natural capital. In our simple model with a single exhaustible resource, the depreciation in natural capital is denoted by the Hotelling rents, $[F_R - f_R]R$. Thus a true measure of adjusted net savings, or genuine savings, S_G, would be

$$S_G = \dot{K} - [F_R - f_r]R = S - \omega K - [F_R - f_r]R \qquad (3.22)$$

Thus a true measure of genuine savings in the economy would be gross savings adjusted for both depreciation of reproducible capital and natural capital. Moreover, it is immediately clear that expression (3.22) would provide a direct indication of the degree to which the economy is satisfying Hartwick's rule, and thus the "weak sustainability" criterion. For example, $S_g > 0$ implies that sufficient accumulation of reproducible capital has occurred to offset the depreciation in natural capital. This in turn implies that the rents from current natural resource exploitation must have been reinvested in accumulating more reproducible capital. From (3.21) and (3.22) it follows that $S_g > 0$ implies that, in our simple model, aggregate consumption and thus social welfare must be non-declining over time. In contrast, for an economy with $S_g < 0$, welfare will be declining and thus the economy can be considered less sustainable.

The Environmental Economics Unit of the World Bank's Environment Department has been attempting to calculate genuine savings rates (now called adjusted savings rates) for as many countries as possible, from 1970 to present. In this work, genuine savings is defined as above; however, the theoretical underpinning of this work is based on a more sophisticated model that separates out physical from human capital and extends the concept of natural capital depreciation to include renewable resources and pollution (Hamilton and Clemens 1999). For example, incorporating the extensions employed by Hamilton and Clemens, some of the natural resource stock, N, is allowed to grow by an amount g; stocks of pollution, P, in the environment are increased by emissions, e, but dissipate at the rate, d, and stocks of human capital (i.e. skills), H, are an increasing function of an educational investment (i.e. current educational expenditures), $H = q(m)$, $q' > 0$. It follows that the above genuine savings rule (3.22) now becomes

$$S_G = \dot{K} - [F_R - f_r](R - g) - b(e - d) + \frac{q(m)}{q'}$$

$$= S - \omega K - [F_R - f_r](R - g) - b(e - d) + \frac{q(m)}{q'}, \qquad (3.23)$$

where b is the marginal cost of pollution abatement. For exhaustible resources that are part of natural capital, N, their rate of replenishment, g, is equal to zero. Similarly, for pure "cumulative" pollutants d is zero.

Condition (3.23) states that genuine savings consists of investments in reproducible capital, K, plus human capital, H, less the value of the depletion in natural resources and the value of accumulated pollutants. Genuine savings can also be calculated by subtracting from an economy's gross national saving, S, any depreciation in reproducible and natural capital, including damages from accumulated pollutants, while adding any appreciation in human capital.

The World Bank's measure of genuine savings follows closely expression (3.23). For example, as indicated in Bolte *et al.* (2002), the current indicator developed is the *adjusted net savings rate*, which is defined as

$$\frac{S_G}{GNI} = \left. \left(S - D_K + CSE - \sum_i R_{Ni} - CD \right) \right/ GNI, \qquad (3.24)$$

where as before S_G is adjusted net savings (genuine savings and S is gross national savings. GNI is gross national income at market prices, D_K is depreciation of reproducible capital, CSE is current (non-fixed) capital expenditure on education, R_{Ni} is the rent from depletion of natural capital stock i and CD is damages from carbon dioxide emissions. Three categories of natural resources are included in the measure of adjusted net savings: energy stocks, such as crude oil, natural gas and coal (hard and lignite); metals and minerals, such as bauxite, copper, gold, iron, lead, nickel, phosphate, silver, tin and zinc; and forest resources, measured in terms of industrial roundwood production and fuelwood. Damages from carbon dioxide emissions are the only value of "accumulated" pollution included in the adjusted net savings measure.[20]

Using definition (3.24), Table 3.1 indicates the adjusted net savings rates for various regions of the world. In past decades, developing economies as a group display rates of adjusted net savings lower than that of both transition and developed economies, although the rates in transition economies have fallen to 2% over 2000–2001. However, across different developing regions there has been considerable variation. For example, East Asia and the Pacific have generated adjusted net savings rates of 18–20% for decades. Whereas rates in past decades were low for South Asia, since the 1990s adjusted net savings have climbed to 15–18%. In both these regions, high rates of gross savings, and more recently, increased human capital investment may account for the relatively high adjusted net savings rates. In contrast, Latin America and the Caribbean have displayed consistently rates of adjusted net savings around 5–8%. The combination of low gross savings, moderate human capital appreciation and significant natural capital depreciation may be the main factors. Despite an increase to 10% in the 1990s, adjusted net savings rates in Sub-Saharan Africa are also low, around 3–5%. The region has suffered from low gross savings and human capital investment, as well as moderate natural capital depreciation. Finally, the Middle East and North Africa has displayed negative adjusted net savings rates in recent years. This suggests that the region is depleting rapidly its considerable mineral and energy

Table 3.1 Adjusted net savings as a share of gross national income

Region	1970s Average	1980s Average	1990s Average	2000	2001
All developing economies	8%	7%	9%	9%	9%
Latin America and the Caribbean	8%	5%	7%	7%	5%
East Asia and the Pacific	19%	20%	19%	18%	18%
Middle East and North Africa	6%	1%	−5%	−1%	−2%
South Asia	3%	10%	15%	17%	18%
Sub-Saharan Africa	5%	3%	10%	5%	3%
Transition economies	–	17%	13%	2%	2%
Developed economies	16%	13%	13%	14%	13%
World	12%	10%	11%	11%	11%

Source: The World Bank, *World Development Indicators 2003.*

wealth without either substantial additional investment in human or reproducible capital.

Finally, there is evidence that developing countries that are more resource-dependent tend to have lower adjusted net savings rates. Figure 3.5 indicates this relationship. The average export share of primary commodities in the total exports of low and middle-income economies over 1990–99 is negatively correlated with the adjusted net savings rates of these economies over the same period. Although the average adjusted net savings rate for all seventy-two countries was 4.7%, for those economies with a primary product export share greater than 50% the rate was only 0.3%. For economies with a primary commodity export share greater than 70%, the adjusted savings rate was –0.4%, and for countries with a primary export share greater than 90%, the rate was –1.5%. This evidence suggests that developing economies that are less resource-dependent (as defined throughout this book) tend to be more "sustainable" than countries that are more dependent on exploiting their natural resources.

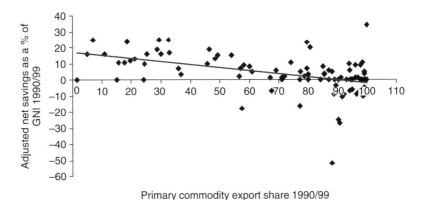

Figure 3.5. Resource dependency and adjusted net savings rates in low and middle-income economies

Notes: Primary commodity export share is the average export share over 1990/99 for low and middle-income countries in Table 1.1. Adjusted net savings rate as a percentage of Gross National Income (GNI) at market prices is the average rate over 1990/99 from the World Bank, *World Development Indicators 2003*. Correlation coefficient, $r = -0.507$. Number of observations = 72.

Conclusion

This chapter has reviewed three current explanations as to why natural resource exploitation by developing countries might hinder their economic performance. Three alternative hypotheses have been proposed to explain this phenomenon. For example, the *resource curse hypothesis* focuses on the poor potential for resource-based development in inducing the economy-wide innovation necessary to sustain growth in a small open economy, particularly under the "Dutch disease" effects of resource-price booms. The *open access exploitation hypothesis* suggests that opening up trade for a developing economy dependent on open access resource exploitation or poorly defined resource rights may actually reduce welfare in that economy. Finally, the *factor endowment hypothesis* maintains that in many developing regions the abundance of natural resources relative to labor (especially skilled labor), plus other environmental conditions, have led to lower economic growth, either *directly* because relatively resource-abundant economies remain specialized for long periods in primary-product exports or *indirectly* because some factor endowments generate conditions of inequality in wealth and political power that generate legal and economic institutions inimical to growth and development.

We also examined available evidence of the degree to which developing countries, and especially resource-dependent low and middle-income economies, are satisfying Hartwick's rule, and thus the "weak sustainability" criterion. The World Bank's adjusted net savings (genuine savings) indicator suggests that many developing countries are failing to reinvest the rents generated from natural resource exploitation in order to augment their reproducible and human capital. Even more striking, Figure 3.5 indicates that adjusted net savings rates tend to fall with the degree of resource-dependency of low and middle-income economies, and on average for those economies that with a primary commodity export share greater than 70%, the adjusted net savings rate was negative.

All three hypotheses reviewed in this chapter provide compelling explanations as to why resource exploitation by developing economies may be inherently unsustainable. According to the resource curse hypothesis, commodity price booms do not lead to the investment of resource rents in more dynamic sectors, such as manufacturing, but instead attracts investments and factor inputs into resource exploitation and away from more dynamic sectors. The open access exploitation hypothesis suggests that not only will extraction under open access condition generate no resource rents to be reinvested but also will lead to over-exploitation of the economy's natural capital in the long run. Finally, the factor endowment hypothesis maintains that unfavorable environmental conditions may directly inhibit the efficient generation of natural resource rents and the returns from reinvesting these rents in other productive assets, as well as indirectly through a long-lasting influence on patterns of political and legal institutional development.

In fact, variants of all three hypotheses suggest that natural resource abundance may interact with "weak institutions" to explain the poor development performance of resource-dependent economies. For example, Easterly and Levine (2003) provide strong support for the factor endowment hypothesis in explaining variations in economic performance for seventy-two former colonies, but only through the *indirect* impact through the differences in institutional factors across countries. In addition, many recent studies of the resource curse phenomenon suggest that the "Dutch disease" and other economic impacts of the resource curse cannot be explained adequately without also examining political economy factors, in particular the existence of policy and institutional failures that lead to myopic decision-making, fail to control rent-seeking behavior by resource users and weaken the political and legal institutions necessary to foster long-run growth (Ascher 1999; Auty 1994 and 1997; Baland and Francois 2000; Broad 1995; Gylfason 2001b; Karl 1997; Lane and Tornell 1996; Mahon 1992; Ross 1999 and 2001; Stevens 2003; Tornell and Lane 1998 and 1999; Torvik 2002). Finally, the open access exploitation hypothesis focuses directly on a major institutional failure that may be an important factor in explaining the poor performance of many resource-dependent economies: the pervasiveness of poorly defined property rights in the natural resource sectors of developing countries and the resulting negative economic consequences.

Thus, it is likely that the three hypotheses could be complementary rather than competing in their explanations as to the poor economic performance of resource-rich developing economies. It is possible that the processes outlined by all three hypotheses could operate simultaneously, and even interact, to mitigate against "sustainable" natural capital exploitation in low and middle-income economies: resource endowments (broadly defined) may shape institutions, and institutions in turn affect the management regime of natural resources (open access, rent seeking and other failures) and both influence the long-run performance of the economy (the resource curse).

However, it is also fair to say that the three hypotheses reviewed in this chapter focus mainly on explaining the first two stylized facts concerning natural resource use in low and middle-income economies, namely the tendency for these economies to be resource-dependent (in terms of a high concentration of primary product to total exports), and for increasing resource dependency to be associated with poor economic performance. None of the three hypotheses address the second two stylized facts: development in low and middle-income economies is associated with land conversion, and a significant share of the population in low and middle-income economies is concentrated in fragile lands.

To explain these additional stylized facts, requires an additional hypothesis, which we will term the *frontier expansion hypothesis*. Developing the latter hypothesis and illustrating it through a model of an open, resource-dependent developing economy is the purpose of the next chapter.

Notes

1. Auty (1993) is often credited with naming this phenomenon a "resource curse." However, Auty (1994) gives credit to Mahon (1992) for also suggesting a "variant" of the resource curse theme as an explanation of why resource-rich Latin American countries have often failed to adopt sensible industrial policies.

2. As an interesting extension, Gylfason (2001) and Gylfason *et al.* (1999) argue that "natural capital" abundance tends to crowd out investment in human capital, thus slowing economic development. For example, Gylfason (2001) shows that public expenditure on education relative to national income, expected years of schooling for girls and gross secondary school enrolment are all shown to be inversely related to the share on natural capital in wealth across countries. Gylfason (2001, p. 850) argues that "nations that are confident that their natural resources are their most important asset may inadvertently – and perhaps even deliberately! – neglect the development of their human resources, by devoting inadequate attention and expenditure to education."

3. Some economists have placed greater emphasis on the revenue volatility of primary product exports, rather than the windfall price effects of a commodity boom, as a significant factor in the resource curse (Auty 1997; Gylfason *et al.* 1999). Thus, Gylfason *et al.* (1999, p. 204) state: "... the volatility of the primary sector generates real-exchange-rate uncertainty and may thus reduce investment and learning in the secondary sector and hence also growth."

4. In his model, Matsuyama (1992) considers the agriculture sector could also represent more generally the "natural resource" sector of the economy.

5. The countries are Argentina, Bolivia, Brazil, Chile, Colombia, Ecuador, Mexico, Paraguay, Peru, Uruguay and Venezuela.

6. As will be discussed further in Chapter 5, Wunder (2003) also notes that, because these economic activities in the non-oil trade sector are also mainly responsible for much of the forest conversion occurring in oil-producing tropical countries, one unintended but potentially side effect of the "Dutch disease" impact of an oil boom is a decline in tropical deforestation.

7. Drawing from the political science literature, Ross (1999, p. 308) categories "political explanations for the resource curse" in terms of cognitive, societal and statist theories: "Cognitive, societal, and statist approaches to the resource curse each take resource windfalls (rents) as their independent variable and economic stagnation as their dependent variable. Cognitive theories suggest that windfalls produce myopic disorders among

policymakers; societal theories argue that windfalls empower social groups that favor growth-impeding fiscal or trade policies; and statist approaches suggest that windfalls can weaken state institutions that are necessary to foster long-term economic development."

8. However, Gylfason (2001, p. 566 n. 12) suggests that Indonesia should at best be considered only a qualified success, given the widespread corruption in the country and because Indonesia has recovered much less well from the 1997–98 Asian crisis compared to Malaysia and Thailand.

9. When the two goods are substitutes, and thus the indifference curves are linear, these gains from trade always dominate. However, with non-linear indifference curves, such as the case with a Cobb-Douglas utility function, the gains from trade are more ambiguous, and it is possible to obtain the same results as Brander and Taylor, even with diminishing returns in manufacturing. See Hannesson (2000).

10. Brander and Taylor (1998a) focus mainly on outcomes in which both countries remain diversified in the steady state. However, they note that if the world demand for the resource good is very high or if countries differ substantially in factor proportions, then the highly resource-abundant country might specialize in the resource good in the steady state whereas the other country is diversified. Brander and Taylor maintain that, although the specialized case "is of some interest," they consider it "as less empirically relevant" and so do not develop it further.

11. In reviewing this literature, Besley (1995) identifies three arguments for a positive link between secure land rights and investment decisions: *freedom from expropriation* (i.e. individuals do not invest if the fruits of their investment are seized by others); *increased access to formal credit markets* (i.e. if better rights make it easier to use land as collateral, then constraints on funding investments can be diminished); and *enhanced possibilities for gains from trade* (i.e. investment is encouraged if improved transfer rights make it easier for individuals to rent or sell their land).

12. As discussed in Chapter 2, scholars other than economists have also stressed the importance of tropical endowments in hindering economic development. For example, Landes (1998) suggests that tropical conditions are not conducive to a more productive work environment. Diamond (1997) suggests that germs and crops directly affect the technological development of societies in the long run. On the one hand, (colonized) tropical countries were susceptible to germs brought by European settlers and colonizers, and the latter in turn devastated by tropical diseases. On the other, productive crops and animal breeds that thrived in temperate conditions were unable to survive in the tropics. As a result, tropical countries suffer from a technological disadvantage with

regard to modern economic development. Finally, Crosby (1986) has stressed that global rise and dominance of Europe from 900–1900 was primarily the result of favorable ecological conditions that in turn produced better crops and technology as well as large populations.

13. As a number of scholars have pointed out, the view that factor endowments influence economic development has had a long history in Western thinking (Bloom and Sachs 1998; Easterly and Levine 2003; Engerman 2000). For example, Engerman (2003, p. 44) notes that "the arguments about the role of climate and natural resources in economic development have had a long history. The relation of climate to laws, social development, and economic growth was described by, among others, Plato, Aristotle, Cicero, Machiavelli, Montesqueiu, Hume and Robertson, and featured in the so-called 'dispute of the New World' about the characteristics of the areas being settled and colonized by the Europeans."

14. Easterly and Levine (2003, p. 37) note that their results seem at odds "with the large literature that relates cross-country differences in per capita *growth rates* to economic policies." The authors suggest two possible explanations for this discrepancy. First, "it could be that episodes of bad policies are associated with a temporary decrease in income, which shows up in the growth rate over a limited period, but leave no long-run impact on the income level." Second, "it could also be that bad policies are proxying for poor institutions, in those cases where they are not included in the growth regression ... bad policies are only symptoms of longer-run institutional factors, and correcting the policies without correcting the institutions will bring little long-run benefit."

15. Wood and Berge (1997, p. 37) go on to argue: "Our assumption that manufacturing and primary production are of equal labour intensity implies that wage payments account for the same share of the total cost of both goods. A change in the wage, relative to the prices of the other two factors (skill and land) would thus not alter the relative cost of production of the two goods, which is what matters for comparative advantage."

16. For example, Wood and Berge (1997, p. 54) note: "we have shown that the share of manufactures in exports depends on the availability not only of skill but also of land. Our results therefore link up with the finding in other studies that the development performance of natural-resource-abundant countries has been relatively poor ... for which one of the suggested reasons is that manufacturing has inherently greater growth potential than primary production, because of faster technical progress and more scope for learning-by-doing."

17. As noted in the discussion of the open access hypothesis, Brander and Taylor (1997, p. 550) argue that, if an economy cannot control such open access exploitation, then the second-best policy is to impose "a modified

'Hartwick's rule' ... under which an exporting country that experienced temporary gains from selling a resource good on world markets might re-invest those proceeds in an alternative asset."

18. The relevance of important contributions in the 1970s by Robert Solow (1974), Dasgupta and Heal (1974 and 1979) and Weitzman (1976) to "Hartwick's rule" is immediately apparent. For example, Hartwick (1977) bases his analytical approach on the max-min exhaustible resource model developed by Solow (1974), who showed that constant consumption as a definition of intergenerational equity. It has also become apparent that the basic proposition of "Hartwick's rule," that declines in natural capital must be offset by increases in reproducible capital, is equivalent to a rule developed by Weitzman (1976), which indicates that net national product, properly defined for an optimal growth, will yield a constant consumption path (Dasgupta and Mäler 1991 and 2000; Dixit *et al.* 1980; Mäler 1991). Finally, optimal generation of economic rents from the exhaustible resource can only occur if extraction follows Hotelling optimal extraction rule, i.e. that marginal scarcity rents rise over time at a rate equivalent to the rate of interest in the economy. The various models developed by Dasgupta and Heal (1974 and 1979) illustrate and elaborate on the significance of "Hotelling's rule" as an optimal resource extraction principle.

19. The contribution by Dasgupta and Mäler (2000) is particularly significant, as past theoretical justifications of "Hartwick's rule" have necessarily assumed that an economy is on a socially optimal path. That is, in its previous incarnations, "Hartwick's rule" demonstrates that as long as the overall stock of capital did not decline over time, consumption could be at least held constant over time, provided that: i) All prices are at their socially optimal level; ii) All resources are used efficiently (exhaustibles extracted at Hotelling efficiency rates, renewables optimally managed); iii) All stock and flow externalities are priced and internalized; iv) Any rents from resource extraction are invested in increasing other forms of capital.

20. Because (3.24) includes only three natural resources in its calculation of natural capital depreciation and only one "accumulating" pollutant, its measure of adjusted net savings is likely to over-estimate the degree of sustainability of an economy. This implies that, in using formula (3.24), an economy displays adjusted savings rates that are consistently low (e.g. 5% or lower) or negative, then there is a good chance that it is inherently "unsustainable" according to the weak sustainability (i.e. Hartwick) criterion. For example, in Table 3.1, developing economies in Latin America and the Caribbean, Sub-Saharan Africa and especially the Middle East and North Africa have displayed "unsustainable" rates of adjusted net savings in recent decades.

4 | Frontier expansion and economic development

T HE "stylized facts" reviewed in Chapter 1 suggest that the vast majority of low and middle-income economies tend to be resource dependent, in terms of a high concentration of primary products to total exports, and that these economies appear to perform poorly. In addition, development in low and middle-income countries is associated with land conversion and increased stress on freshwater resources, and a significant share of the population in developing economies is concentrated in fragile lands.

As emphasized at the end of the previous chapter, there are a number of current theories and hypotheses that attempt to explain why natural resource-abundant economies are currently failing to develop rapidly. Curiously, however, these theories have largely ignored two of the key structural features of many developing economies today, namely the tendency for these economies to display rapid rates of "frontier" land expansion, and for a significant proportion of their poorest populations to be concentrated in fragile areas.

Building on these last two stylized facts, this chapter offers another perspective on why the structural economic dependence of a small open economy on exploiting its natural resource endowment – in particular its dependence on processes of "frontier expansion" – may not lead to sustained and high rates of economic growth. Hence, this new perspective is dubbed the *frontier expansion hypothesis*.

As Chapter 2 indicates, historically "frontier expansion" has been a major part of economic development. Such frontier-based economic development is characterized by a pattern of capital investment, technological innovation and social and economic institutions dependent on "opening up" new frontiers of natural resources once existing ones have been "closed" and exhausted. Chapter 2 also cites many examples of successful resource-based development during past eras. For example, the rapid industrial and economic expansion in the US over 1879–1940 was linked to the exploitation of abundant non-reproducible natural resources, particularly energy and mineral resources (Romer 1996; David and Wright 1997; Wright 1990). During the Golden Age of Resource-Based Development (1870–1913), many tropical economies also flourished through exploiting their natural resource endowments for primary product exports (Findlay and Lundahl 1994 and 1999). Although fewer in number, there are also some examples of successful mineral-based development among today's economies (Davis 1995; Gylfason 2001; Wright and Czelusta 2002). What lessons can be learned from these past and present examples of successful resource-based development, and why are the key conditions for such success seemingly absent in the resource-dependent developing economies of today?

As the following chapter emphasizes, the first lesson to be learned is that the process of frontier-based development in low and middle-income economies today is fundamentally different from economic exploitation of the "Great Frontier" in previous eras, and in particular during the Golden Age of Resource-Based Development. Although historically frontier land expansion may have been associated with successful resource-based development, this is less likely in the case of poor countries today (Barbier 2003a and 2004a). This is for several reasons, which form the basis for the *frontier expansion hypothesis* proposed in this chapter.

First, in many developing economies a significant proportion of extremely poor households are concentrated on fragile lands, and both rural population growth and the share of population on fragile lands seem to increase with the degree of resource dependency of a developing economy (see Chapter 1 and World Bank 2003). That is, frontier land expansion appears to be serving mainly as an outlet for the rural poor in many developing countries. Second, land expansion and the migration of the rural poor to the frontier is symptomatic of the existence of policy and market failures in the resource sector and land markets, such as rent-seeking behavior and corruption or open access resource exploitation, that mitigate against successful resource-based development. The result is inefficient and inequitable rural resource use, which in turn leads to the dissipation of rents and investment opportunities.

As a consequence, in present-day developing economies frontier land expansion and resource exploitation is less likely to be associated with successful economic development. Although frontier-based economic development can lead to an initial economic boom, it is invariably short-lived. Once the frontier is "closed" and any reserves of land and natural resources available to an economy have been fully exploited or converted, some economic retrenchment is inevitable. Under certain conditions, the "bust" may start even before the frontier resource reserves are exhausted, and in some cases a repeated "boom and bust" cycle may ensue.

In the following chapter, we examine first the problems posed by the process of frontier land expansion that is so prevalent in developing countries today. That is, in today's poor economies, frontier-based development is symptomatic of a pattern of economy-wide resource exploitation that: i) generates little additional rents, and ii) what rents are generated tend to be dissipated rather than reinvested in more productive and dynamic sectors, such as manufacturing. The remainder of this chapter elaborates on this *frontier expansion hypothesis* in more detail, and secondly, develops a theoretical model of a small open economy to illustrate the main pathways suggested by this hypothesis. Finally, we end the chapter by summarizing briefly the "vicious cycle" in developing countries that is implied by the frontier expansion hypothesis.

Resource-based development and frontier expansion

We begin with the observation that an important clue to unravelling the paradox of the poor economic performance of today's resource-based developing countries can be found in the four "stylized" facts of natural resource use in these economies that were highlighted and discussed in Chapter 1. These four facts are:

- *Stylized fact one: the majority of low and middle-income countries are highly dependent on primary product exports*
- *Stylized fact two: resource dependency in low and middle-income countries is associated with poor economic performance*
- *Stylized fact three: development in low and middle-income economies is associated with increased land conversion and stress on available freshwater resources*
- *Stylized fact four: A significant share of the population in low and middle-income economies is concentrated on fragile lands.*

For example, the first three stylized facts suggest that developing countries today are embarking on a pattern of resource-dependent development that culminates in frontier resource exploitation, particularly in the form of agricultural land expansion and chronic stress on freshwater resources, but the end results do not yield much in the way of sustained economic progress. In fact, stylized fact four indicates the "symptoms" of malaise associated with frontier land expansion and resource-based development today: in many developing economies a significant proportion of extremely poor households are concentrated on fragile lands, and both rural population growth and the share of population on fragile lands seem to increase with the degree of resource dependency of a developing economy. That is, frontier land expansion appears to be serving mainly as an outlet for the rural poor in many developing countries.

But why should frontier land expansion be associated with "unsustainable" resource-based development in many low and middle-income countries today? Historically, this has not always been the case.

For instance, the brief historical overview of the role of natural resources in economic development in Chapter 2 indicates that finding new frontiers, or reserves, of natural resources to exploit became the basis of much of global economic development for the past five hundred years. Such frontier-based economic development can be characterized by a pattern of capital investment, technological innovation and social and economic institutions dependent on "opening up" new frontiers of natural resources once existing ones have been "closed" and exhausted (di Tella 1982; Findlay and Lundahl 1994). Particularly noteworthy is the period 1870 to 1913, which is often dubbed the "Golden Age" of resource-based development, because so many resource-dependent economies with unexploited "frontier" natural resources benefited from exporting primary products to the "industrial" core of the booming world economy (Findlay and Lundahl 1999; Green and Urqhart 1976; Taylor and Williamson 1994; Schedvin 1990). This was also the era of rapid migration of settlers and inflows of foreign capital into the "Great Frontier" regions identified by Webb (1964): temperate North and South America, Australia, New Zealand and South Africa. The economies of these regions therefore also expanded as a consequence of the world economic boom. Finally, a number of primary-producing "developing" or "periphery" regions, also experienced considerable growth as a consequence of growing world demand for raw materials and food. These included not only temperate Argentina but also a number of tropical countries that exported cash and food crops to the rest of the world (Findlay and Lundahl 1994 and 1999).

In addition, it has been argued that the origins of rapid industrial and economic expansion in the US over 1879–1940 were strongly linked to the exploitation of abundant non-reproducible natural resources, particularly energy and mineral resources (Romer 1996; Wright1990). Other examples of successful mineral-based development have been cited for today's economies (Davis 1995; Wright and Czelusta 2002). In the developing world, most prominent have been the mineral-led booms in the 1990s in Peru, Brazil and Chile, although Davis (1995) identifies up to twenty-two mineral-based developing economies which appear to have fared comparatively well compared to other developing countries. In his review of eighty-five "resource-rich" developing economies, Gylfason (2001) found only four to have performed successfully: Botswana, Indonesia, Malaysia and Thailand. Whereas the three Asian countries achieved this success by diversifying their economies and by industrializing, Botswana still remains fundamentally mineral-dependent.[1]

Recent reviews of successful resource-based development, both past and present, have pointed to a number of key features critical to that success (David and Wright 1997; Wright and Czelusta 2002).

First, the given natural resource endowment of a country must be continuously expanded through a process of *country-specific knowledge in the resource extraction sector*. As argued by Wright and Czelusta (2002, pp. 29 and 31):

From the standpoint of development policy, a crucial aspect of the process is the role of country-specific knowledge. Although the deep scientific bases for progress are undoubtedly global, it is in the nature of geology that location-specific knowledge continues to be important ... the experience of the 1970s stands in marked contrast to the 1990s, when mineral production steadily expanded primarily as a result of purposeful exploration and ongoing advances in the technologies of search, extraction, refining, and utilization; in other words by a process of learning.

Second, there must be *strong linkages between the resource and other, more dynamic economic sectors (i.e. manufacturing)*.

Not only was the USA the world's leading mineral economy in the very historical period during which the country became the world leader in manufacturing (roughly from 1890 to 1910); but linkages and complementarities to the resource sector were vital in the broader story of American economic success ... Nearly all major US manufactured goods were closely linked to the resource economy in one way or another: petroleum products, primary copper, meat packing and poultry, steel works and rolling mills, coal mining, vegetable oils, grain mill products, sawmill products, and so on. (Wright and Czelusta 2002, pp. 3–5)

Similarly, Findlay and Lundahl (1999, pp. 31–32) note the import-ance of such linkages in promoting successful "staples-based" develop-ment during the Golden Age: "not all resource-rich countries succeeded in spreading the growth impulses from their primary sectors ... in a number of instances the staples sector turned out to be an enclave with little contact with the rest of the economy ... The staples theory of growth stresses the development of linkages between the export sector and an incipient manufacturing sector."

Third, there must be *substantial knowledge spillovers* arising from the extraction and industrial use of resources in the economy. For example, David and Wright (1997) suggest that the rise of the American minerals economy can be attributed to the infrastructure of public scientific knowledge, mining education and the ethos of exploration. This in turn created knowledge spillovers across firms and "the components of successful modern-regimes of knowledge-based economic growth. In essential respects, the minerals economy was an integral part of the emerging knowledge-based economy of the twentieth century ... increasing returns were manifest at the national level, with important consequences for American industrialization and world economic leadership" (David and Wright 1997, pp. 240–241).[2]

However, there are three important caveats attached to the above conditions for successful resource-based development.

First, all of the past and present examples of development with the above three features are clearly based largely on minerals-based devel-opment (David and Wright 1997; Davis 1995; Wright and Czelusta 2002). A small open economy dependent on frontier agricultural land expansion may find it more difficult to foster such conditions for successful resource-based development. In fact, there is some evidence that agricultural-based development based on land expansion may be negatively correlated with economic growth and development (Barbier 2003a and 2004a; Stijns 2001). As we shall see in Chapter 10, however, present-day Malaysia and Thailand may provide important counter-examples of successful resource-based development involving frontier land expansion and resource extraction.

Second, the existence of policy and market failures in the resource sector, such as rent-seeking behavior and corruption or open access resource exploitation, will mitigate against successful resource-based development. Unfortunately, it is well documented that resource sectors in many developing countries are prone to problems of rent-seeking and corruption, thus ensuring that natural resource assets, including land, are not being managed efficiently or sustainably (Ascher 1999; Tornell and Lane 1998; Torvik 2002).[3] Several studies have also noted the rent-dissipation effect of poorly defined property rights, including the breakdown of traditional common property rights regimes, in developing countries (Alston *et al.* 1999; Baland and Plateau 1996; Bromley 1989 and 1991; Deacon 1999; Ostrom 1990).

Third, in many developing economies, inequalities in wealth between rural households also have an important impact on land degradation and deforestation processes, which may explain why so many poorer households find themselves confined to marginal lands (Barbier 1999). There is also increasing evidence in developing countries that more powerful groups use their social and economic power to secure greater access to valuable environmental resources, including land, minerals, energy, gems, water and even fuelwood, (Alston *et al.* 1999; Barbier 1999; Barbier and Homer-Dixon 1999; Binswanger and Deininger 1997; Fairhead 2001; Homer-Dixon 1999; Lonegran 1999; Swain 2001). Such problems are exacerbated by government policies that favor wealthier households in markets for these key natural resources, and especially land. For example, "rural elites" in developing countries are often "able to steer policies and programs meant to increase rural productivity into capital-intensive investment programs for large farms, thus perpetuating inequality and inefficiency" (Binswanger and Deininger 1997, p. 1996).

Both the three conditions for successful resource-based development, as well as the three important caveats, are crucial factors in understanding why current patterns of frontier resource extraction and land expansion are not generating sustained growth in many poor economies. Below, we refer to this explanation as the *frontier expansion hypothesis*. Before elaborating on this hypothesis in more detail, let us first examine some empirical evidence linking land expansion and economic performance in developing countries.

Frontier expansion and economic performance: a simple test

A fairly straightforward way of empirically verifying whether frontier-based development is associated with poor economic performance is to estimate a relationship between gross domestic product (GDP) per capita and some measure of long-run agricultural expansion. For example, if the latter indicator was some index, $\forall_{it}$, then the above hypotheses suggest that there may be a cubic relationship between per capita income, Y_{it}, and this indicator of long-run agricultural land change:

$$Y_{it} = b_0 + b_1\alpha_{it} + b_2\alpha_{it}^2 + b_3\alpha_{it}^3 \qquad (4.1)$$

Note that $b_0 > 0$, $b_1 < 0$, $b_2 > 0$, $b_3 < 0$ and $|b_1| > b_2$ would imply that i) countries with increased long-run agricultural land area would have lower levels of per capita income than countries with decreased agricultural land area and ii) per capita income would tend to fluctuate with long run agricultural land expansion.

The above relationship was estimated by Barbier (2003a) through employing a panel analysis of tropical developing countries over 1961–94. Per capita income, Y_{it}, is again represented by GDP per capita in constant purchasing power parity (1987 \$). The indicator $\forall_{it}$ is an agricultural land long-run change index, created by dividing the current (i.e. in year t) agricultural land area of a country by its land area in 1961.

The results of the analysis for all tropical countries and for low and lower middle-income countries (i.e. real per capita GDP less than US\$3,500 over 1961–94) are shown in Table 4.1. For both regressions, the estimated coefficients are highly significant and also have the expected signs and relative magnitudes.[4] Thus the estimations provide some empirical evidence that agricultural land expansion in developing countries conforms to a "boom and bust" pattern of economic development. This is seen more clearly when the regressions are used to project respective relationships between long-run agricultural land expansion and GDP per capita, which are displayed in Figure 4.1.

As indicated in the figure, an increase in agricultural land expansion in the long run is clearly associated with a lower level of per capita income than decreasing agricultural land area. For all tropical

Table 4.1 Panel analysis of per capita income and long-run agricultural expansion, 1961–94

Dependent variable: GDP per capita (PPP, constant 1987 US$)[a]
Parameter estimates:[b]

Explanatory variables	All countries (N = 1135)	Lower income countries[c] (N = 867)
Constant	14393.37	9560.07
	(23.69)**	(7.03)**
Long-run agricultural land area	−24293.31	−16645.71
change index (α_{it})[d]	(−19.04)**	(−5.30)**
α_{it}^2	15217.53	11013.18
	(11.18)**	(4.58)**
α_{it}^3	−2896.32	−2330.33
	(−6.59)**	(−3.87)**
F-test for pooled model	168.01**	126.05**
Breusch-Pagan (LM) test	6576.23**	3614.50**
Hausman test	6.85	44.02**
Adjusted R^2	0.368	0.937
Preferred model	One-way random effects	Two-way fixed effects

Notes:
[a] Mean for all countries over 1961–94 is US$2,593, and for lower income countries $1,539. PPP is purchase power parity.
[b] t-ratios are indicated in parentheses.
[c] Countries with GDP per capita (PPP, constant 1987 US$) less than US$3,500 over 1961–94.
[d] Mean for all countries over 1961–94 is 1.150, and for lower income countries 1.149.
** Significant at 1% level.
* Significant at 5% level.
Source: Barbier (2003a).

countries, the turning point is a long-run agricultural change index of 1.2. For lower income countries the turning point is 1.3. Although continued agricultural land expansion beyond these points does lead to a slight increase in GDP per capita, this impact is short-lived. For all

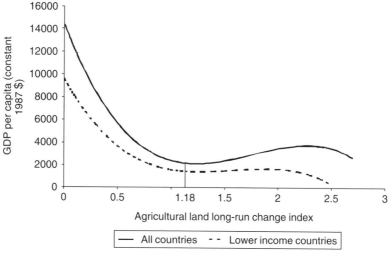

Source: Barbier (2003a).

Figure 4.1. Agricultural land expansion and GDP per capita in tropical countries, 1961–94

tropical countries, per capita income starts to fall once the land area index reaches 2.3; for lower income countries this occurs sooner at an index of 1.9. Note as well that for lower income countries, there is very little increase in GDP per capita associated with expansion of land over the 1.3 to 1.9 range.

It is revealing to compare the projections in Figure 4.1 with the actual land use situation in 1994 for developing countries. For all countries in 1994, the average land expansion index was 1.18, and for lower income countries it was 1.17. Of the 35 countries in 1994 with per capita incomes less than $3,500, only six have not experienced some agricultural land expansion compared to the 1961 base year.[5] Only eleven lower income countries are in the 1.3 to 1.9 range of agricultural land expansion, where continued expansion is associated with slightly higher levels of GDP per capita.[6] One country (Fiji) has already passed the turning point of 1.9 where further agricultural land expansion corresponds with lower levels of GDP per capita. Thus it is fair to say that, for the vast majority of lower income countries, further agricultural land expansion is likely to be associated with lower levels of GDP per capita.

The frontier expansion hypothesis

Having provided evidence that frontier-based development is not leading to sustainable economic development in poor economies, we now must try to explain why. Here, we can only sketch out the main features of this *frontier expansion hypothesis*. This hypothesis is based on four key observations of the process of frontier-based development in low and middle-income economies today (Barbier 2003a and 2004a).

First, frontier land expansion and resource exploitation may be associated with poor economic performance in resource-dependent developing countries but not necessarily a cause of it. That is, frontier-based development is *symptomatic* of a pattern of economy-wide resource exploitation that: i) generates little additional economic rents, and ii) what rents are generated are dissipated and not being reinvested in more productive and dynamic sectors, such as manufacturing, or to augment reproducible and human capital in the economy. As Chapters 1 and 3 emphasize, this pattern of resource exploitation is highly unsustainable, as it is unlikely to contribute to the long-run "take-off" into sustained growth and development for low and middle-income economies. In this chapter, we are asserting that the process of widespread frontier land conversion so prevalent in many developing countries is an important indicator that these countries have embarked on such a path of "unsustainable" resource exploitation leading to poor long-run economic development prospects.

Second, one important reason that frontier land expansion is unlikely to generate much rents is that, as such expansion results largely from conversion of forest, wetlands and other natural habitat, it is likely to yield mainly "marginal" or "fragile" land exhibiting low productivity as well as significant constraints for intensive agriculture (World Bank 2003). This in turn implies that very little effort is invested, either by poor farmers working this land or government agricultural research and extension activities, in developing *country-specific knowledge* in improving the productivity and sustainable exploitation of frontier land and resources.

Third, in contrast to past and present examples of successful minerals-based development, there are unlikely to be *strong linkages between more dynamic economic sectors (i.e. manufacturing)* and the economic activities responsible for frontier land expansion (Wright and Czelusta 2002). This in turn limits the opportunities for *substantial knowledge spillovers* arising from the exploitation and conversion of frontier resources, including land. Thus frontier-based economic activities are unlikely to be integrated with the rest of the economy. There are two reasons for this. First, as noted above, frontier land expansion appears to be serving mainly as an outlet for the rural poor in many developing countries, which suggests that much of the output is either for subsistence or local markets. Second, by definition, frontier areas are likely to be located far away from urban and industrial centers.

Fourth, as discussed in the previous section, policy and market failures, such as rent-seeking behavior and corruption or open access resource exploitation, are prevalent in the resource sectors of many developing economies. Frontier land expansion and resource exploitation is especially associated with open access. In addition, many large-scale resource-extractive activities, such as timber harvesting, mining, ranching and commercial plantations, are often responsible for initially opening up previously inaccessible frontier areas (Barbier 1997b). Investors in these activities are attracted to frontier areas because of the lack of government controls and property rights in these remote areas mean that resource rents are easily captured, and thus frontier resource-extractive activities are particularly prone to rent-seeking behavior (Ascher 1999).

All of these factors combine to ensure that frontier-based economic development is unlikely to lead to high rates of sustained economic growth. In essence, all frontier resources, including land in forests and wetlands, are "reserves" that can be exploited potentially for economic rents. However, as we have seen, conversion of frontier land "reserves" produces mainly fragile agricultural land that is largely an outlet for absorbing poor households. Such frontier land expansion does not generate substantial rents, and any resulting agricultural output will increase mainly consumption of non-tradable goods (food for subsistence or local markets). Frontier resource-extractive activities may yield more significant rents, but the rent-seeking behavior associated with these activities will mean that these rents will be reinvested into further exploitation of frontier resources. This process will continue until the economically accessible frontier resource "reserves" are exhausted and all rents are dissipated.

The lack of integration of frontier-based economic activities with the rest of the economy also decreases the likelihood that any rents generated by these activities will be reinvested in more productive and dynamic sectors, such as manufacturing. In essence, the frontier sector operates as a separate "enclave" in the developing economy. As already noted, frontier-based land expansion will result mainly in small-scale agricultural production that increases domestic, non-traded consumption. In contrast, more large-scale, frontier resource-extractive activities, such as mining, timber extraction, ranching and plantations, may generate increased resource-based exports. Such exports are more likely to result in either imported consumption or imported capital goods that are employed predominantly in the frontier resource-extractive industries.

Chapter 8 elaborates further on the above processes, focusing particularly on examples that illustrate the links between poverty, resource degradation and inequality in resource exploitation in many developing countries. Here, we will examine mainly the economy-wide implications of this process, namely why so little of the resource rents that are generated by frontier-based economic activities tend not to lead to greater economy-wide benefits and sustainable development.

There are two main reasons for this outcome. First, as noted above, the main source of rents from frontier "reserves" are large-scale resource-extractive activities that can capture these rents. But these activities and the rents they generate tend to benefit almost exclusively the wealthier households in the economy, who have a higher propensity to consume imported goods. Second, as also explained above, if these wealthier households do reinvest any of the resource rents, they are likely to take advantage of the "rent-seeking" opportunities arising from further exploitation of frontier extractive reserves. But the type of specific investments required from such resource-extractive activities are likely to result mainly in imported capital goods for this purpose, such as mining machinery, milling equipment, road-building and construction tools, etc.

It follows that, although frontier-based economic development can lead to an initial economic boom, it is invariably short-lived and the economic benefits are quickly dissipated. If the additional frontier "reserves" are used mainly to expand domestic consumption and exports (in exchange for imported consumption), then there will be little additional capital accumulation outside the frontier resource-extractive sector. This implies that any economic boom will continue only as long as the frontier resource reserves last. Once resource rents are dissipated and the frontier is effectively closed, there will be no long-term take off into sustained growth for the economy as a whole.

If during the frontier expansion phase some rents are invested in capital accumulation in other sectors of the economy as well, then the initial boom period will coincide with increased growth. However, this growth path cannot be sustained. The additional capital accumulation is unlikely to overcome the poor linkages between other economic sectors (i.e. manufacturing) and frontier-based economic activities, and therefore will not yield substantial economy-wide knowledge spillovers. As a result, any additional growth generated by this capital accumulation will last only as long as frontier expansion continues. Once the frontier is "closed" and any reserves of land and natural resources available to an economy have been fully exploited or converted, some economic retrenchment is inevitable, and an economic bust will occur.

In sum, the structural economic dependence of a small open low or lower middle-income economy on frontier land and resource expansion precipitates a "boom and bust" pattern of development that is simply not conducive to sustained and high rates of long-run economic growth. Resource dependency, frontier land expansion and populations concentrated on fragile lands are all indications that a developing economy is not exploiting its natural capital efficiently and sustainably.

A model of frontier expansion in a small open economy[7]

The previous section has explored evidence, particularly with the example of agricultural land expansion, that frontier-based development in developing countries may generate a "boom and bust" pattern in a small open economy. It was suggested that the key to this phenomenon is that the small open economy faces a trade off between allocating the production from additional frontier resources either to increase domestic consumption and exports (in exchange for imported consumption), or alternatively for capital accumulation. The rest of this section focuses on illustrating the impacts of frontier-based development further through the following model of a small open economy.

The following model includes several (but not all) of the key features of frontier land expansion and resource exploitation described above. These features include:

- Frontier activities are not integrated with other sectors of the economy.
- Frontier activities serve mainly to absorb labor; i.e. the only inputs are converted resources and labor, and the latter is increasing over time.

- Frontier resources are freely available; the only limitations on their conversion are institutional, economic and geographical constraints (e.g. distance to markets) that limit the maximum amount of conversion.
- If no profits are made, then frontier households consume all their factor income, and no rents are available to reinvest in the frontier activities (see Appendix to Chapter 4).
- However, capital accumulation will occur in the economy if aggregate output, including from the frontier sector, exceeds domestic consumption and exports.

Although these features are not as rich in detail as the process of frontier land expansion and resource exploitation described in the previous section, as we shall see from the following model, they are sufficient to generate the "boom and bust" pattern of development that cannot sustain long-run economic growth.[8]

The economy is assumed to comprise two sectors, an "established" or "mainstay" sector and a "frontier" sector. The latter comprises a variety of small-scale economic activities, such as agriculture, forestry, ranching, mining or any other basic extractive industries that are dependent on the exploitation or conversion of "newly acquired" resources available on an open, but ultimately limited, frontier. Although clearly heterogeneous, these available "frontier resources" will be viewed in the following model as an aggregate, homogeneous stock, which we can also refer to broadly as "land". Equally, the extractive activities and economic uses of these resources will be aggregated into a single sectoral output.

Thus at time $t = 0$, the frontier sector of the economy is assumed to be endowed with a given stock of accessible natural resources, F_0, which acts as a "reserve" that can be potentially tapped through the current rate of conversion, N. The output produced through converting or exploiting frontier "reserves" in turn contributes to domestic consumption, but if there is any surplus output, it could contribute to the flow of exports or alternatively augment the existing capital stock.[9] Hence, in the following model, the process of "frontier expansion" is essentially marked by the continual use and depletion of the fixed stock of frontier land resources, F_0.

To sharpen the analysis, we will not include explicitly a cost of frontier resource conversion but postulate that the existence of institutional, geographical and economic constraints limits the maximum amount of frontier exploitation at any time t to $\overline{N}$. There are two reasons for assuming that such constraints limit the extent of frontier resource conversion or depletion. First, any frontier resources are located far from population centers, and thus the rate at which these resources may be profitably converted or exploited may be constrained by distance to market and accessibility. For example, recent studies of tropical deforestation indicate that remoteness from urban areas and the lack of roads in frontier areas limit forestland conversion to agriculture (Cropper *et al.* 1999; Chomitz and Gray 1996; Nelson and Hellerstein 1997). Second, recent studies have also explored the impact on tropical land conversion of institutional factors, such as land use conflict, security of ownership or property rights, political stability, and the "rule of law" (e.g. Alston *et al.* 1999; Barbier 2002; Deacon 1994, 1999; Godoy *et al.* 1998). For example, empirical work by Deacon (1994 and 1999) suggests that formal and informal institutions that reduce ownership risk or establish the "rule of law" would constrain the extent of tropical forestland conversion.

Over a finite planning horizon, T, it follows that

$$F_0 \geq \int_0^T N \, dt, \ 0 \leq N \leq \overline{N}, \ F_0 = F(0) \tag{4.2}$$

where $\overline{N}$ is the maximum rate of frontier exploitation or conversion at any time t.

We will also assume that the other input used in frontier economic activities is labor, L^A. Thus aggregate output, A, from economic activities in the frontier sector can be denoted by the production relationship $A = A(N, L^A)$, which is assumed to be homogeneous of degree one and can be written in the following intensive form

$$a = a(n), \ a'(n) > 0, \ a'(0) = \alpha \tag{4.3}$$

where $a = A/L^A$ and $n = N/L^A$ and $a''(n) = 0$.

The second sector of the economy is the "mainstay" or "metropolis" sector. It contains all economic activities, industrial and agricultural, that are not directly dependent on the exploitation of frontier resources. Instead, production in this sector is a function of labor, L^M, and the stock of accumulated capital in the economy, K, which includes settled (i.e. non-frontier) agricultural land. Thus aggregate production in the mainstay sector can be denoted as $M = M(K, L^M)$, which if linearly homogenous can be written as

$$m = m(k), \ m' > 0, m'' < 0 \qquad (4.4)$$

where $m = M/L^M$ and $k = K/L^M$.

Aggregate labor supply, L, in the economy is therefore allocated to both sectors and is also assumed to be growing at the exogenous rate, θ, i.e.

$$L = L^A + L^M, \ L = L_0 e^{\theta t} = e^{\theta t}. \qquad (4.5)$$

We make the standard assumption that the initial stock of labor, L_0, is normalized to one. Also, it will be assumed that if the total labor supply is growing exogenously at the rate θ, so will the labor allocated to the frontier and mainstay sectors, L^A and L^M, respectively.

Utilizing the relationship $N = nL_0^A e^{\theta t}$, condition (1) can be rewritten as

$$F_0 \geq \int_0^T nL_0^A e^{\theta t} dt, \ 0 \leq n \leq \bar{n}, \ F_0 = F(0) \qquad (4.6)$$

where $\bar{n}$ is the maximum per capita amount of frontier resource conversion that can occur at any time t. Since from (4.5) frontier labor supply grows exogenously, the maximum per capita conversion rate, $\bar{n}$, must decline over time.[10]

Per capita output from either the frontier or mainstay sectors may be used for domestic consumption, c, or exported, x. To focus the analysis, we will treat domestic consumption and exports from the mainstay and frontier sectors respectively as homogeneous commodities. Let $q = c + x$ be defined as aggregate consumption, both domestic and foreign, of the economy's total output. Assuming that at any time t aggregate output $m(k) + a(n)$ that is not either consumed domestically or exported augments the economy's capital stock, then it follows that per capita capital accumulation in the economy is governed by

$$\dot{k} = m(k) + a(n) - (\omega + \theta)k - q, \quad k_0 = k(0), \qquad (4.7)$$

where ω is the rate of capital depreciation (see Appendix to Chapter 4).

In exchange for its exports, the economy imports a consumption good, z. As the country is a small open economy, the terms of trade are fixed and defined as $p = p^x/p^z$. Thus the balance of trade condition for the economy is

$$px = z \qquad (4.8)$$

Finally, all consumers in the economy share identical preferences over the finite time horizon [0, *T*] given by

$$W = \int_0^T [\beta \log(c) + \log(z)]e^{-\rho t}dt + \psi_T k(T)e^{-\rho T}, \; \rho = \delta - \theta, \; \beta > 0,$$

(4.9)

where δ is the discount rate and ψ_T is the scrap value of the terminal capital stock, $k(T)$.

Maximization of W over finite time T leads to the following Hamiltonian

$$H = [\beta \log(q - x) + \log(px)]e^{-\rho t} + \lambda[m(k) + \alpha n - (\omega + \theta)k - q]$$
$$- \mu n L_0^A e^{\theta t}$$

(4.10)

which is maximized with respect to aggregate per capita consumption, q, exports, x, and frontier resource exploitation, n. The resulting first-order conditions are

$$e^{-\rho t}\frac{\beta}{c} = \lambda$$

(4.11)

$$\frac{\beta}{c} = \frac{p}{z} \quad \text{or} \quad \frac{c}{\beta} = \frac{z}{p} = x$$

(4.12)

$$\lambda d'(n) - \mu L_0^A e^{\theta t} \begin{array}{l} < \\ = 0 \Rightarrow \\ > \end{array} \begin{array}{l} n = 0 \\ 0 < n < \bar{n} \\ n = \bar{n} \end{array}$$

(4.13)

$$\dot{\lambda} = \lambda[(\omega + \theta) - m'(k)], \quad \lambda(T) = \psi_T e^{-\rho T}$$

(4.14)

$$\dot{\mu} = 0, \; \mu \geq 0, \; F_0 - \int_0^T L_0^A n e^{\theta t}dt \geq 0, \mu \left[F_0 - \int_0^T L_0^A n e^{\theta t}dt \right] = 0$$

(4.15)

plus the equation of motion (4.7). Equation (4.11) is the usual condition requiring that the discounted marginal utility of consumption equals the shadow price of capital. Equation (4.12) is the open economy equilibrium condition, which indicates that the relative marginal value of domestic to imported consumption must equal the terms of trade, p. Condition (4.13) governs the optimal frontier resource conversion, n. If the value marginal product of frontier resource exploitation, $\lambda a'(n)$, exceeds the marginal (shadow) costs of any conversion, $\mu L_0^A e^{\theta t}$, then per capita resource conversion will be at the maximum rate, $\bar{n}$. If the costs of conversion are greater than the marginal benefits, then no frontier resource exploitation will occur. When benefits equal cost, then conversion is at the rate n where $0 < n < \bar{n}$. Equation (4.14) determines the change over time in the value of the capital stock of the economy. This value will grow if the marginal productivity of capital per worker in the mainstay sector, $m'(k)$, is less than any capital depreciation and population growth, $\omega + \theta$. In addition, the terminal value of the capital stock, $\lambda(T)$, combined with (4.11), (4.12) and (4.13) will determine the final levels of per capita domestic consumption plus exports, $c(T) + x(T)$, in the economy.

Finally, condition (4.15) states that the marginal value, μ, of the fixed stock of frontier resources, F_0, is essentially unchanging over the planning horizon. Instead, whether the scarcity value of frontier resources is positive or zero depends on whether the available stock of frontier resources, F_0, is completely exhausted through conversion, n, by terminal time, T. Combined with the other first-order conditions, (4.15) proves to be important in characterizing the optimal "frontier expansion" path of the economy.

For example, suppose that by the end of the planning horizon at time T the stock of frontier resources is not completely exhausted through "frontier expansion", i.e. $F_0 > \int_0^T L_0^A n e^{\theta t} dt$ over $[0, T]$ such that $F(T) > 0$. From (4.15) it follows that $\mu = 0$. The unlimited availability of frontier resources to the economy over the entire planning period means that these reserves have no scarcity value. However, from (4.11), the marginal value of accumulated capital in the economy is always positive ($\lambda > 0$). As a consequence, in (4.13) the value marginal product of frontier resource exploitation, $\lambda \alpha$, will exceed the costs of conversion, and thus the economy will convert frontier resources at the maximum per capita rate, $\bar{n}$, throughout $[0, T]$.

Alternatively, suppose that $F_0 = \int_0^T L_0^A n e^{\theta t} dt$ so that frontier resources are exhausted at least by the end of the time horizon, T, if not at some time $t^F < T$. These resources now have positive scarcity value, $\mu > 0$, throughout the planning period. This in turn implies that optimal paths of frontier expansion may have either an interior solution for frontier resource conversion, $0 < n < \bar{n}$, or corner solutions, $n = \bar{n}$ and $n = 0$. Since these paths have interesting and differing economic implications, we will focus mainly on them. Thus the rest of the paper will consider only the case where frontier expansion and resource conversion comes to an end some time during the planning horizon of the open economy.

We begin with the conditions for an interior solution to the choice of frontier resource conversion, $0 < n < \bar{n}$:

According to (4.13), an interior solution for n requires that the benefits of frontier exploitation equal the cost. This condition can be rewritten as

$$\lambda = \frac{\mu L_0^A e^{\theta t}}{a'(n)} \quad \text{and} \quad \dot{\lambda} = \theta \lambda \qquad (4.16)$$

given that μ is constant. Substituting (4.16) into (4.14) yields

$$\theta \lambda = \lambda[(\rho + \omega + \theta) - m'(k)] \quad \text{or} \quad m'(k_1) = \rho + \omega. \qquad (4.17)$$

The latter expression implies that the per capita capital stock remains constant at some value, k_1, and therefore $dk/dt = 0$ in (4.7). This result indicates that, if it is optimal for the economy to convert frontier resources but at a rate less than the maximum level, $\bar{n}$, then frontier expansion will be only sufficient to maintain the per capita stock of capital.

Using (4.16) in (4.11) and differentiating yields

$$-\frac{\beta \dot{c}}{c^2} = e^{\rho t}\left[\dot{\lambda} + \rho \lambda\right] \quad \text{or} \quad \dot{c} = -c[\theta + \rho] < 0 \qquad (4.18)$$

and from (4.12)

$$\dot{x} = \frac{\dot{z}}{p} = \frac{\dot{c}}{\beta} < 0 \quad \text{and} \quad \dot{q} = \dot{c} + \dot{x} = \left[1 + \frac{1}{\beta}\right]\dot{c} < 0 \qquad (4.19)$$

If the economy follows the interior solution for its frontier expansion path, then per capita domestic consumption, exports and imports will decline over time. From (4.7), a further implication of aggregate consumption, q, falling over time is that the rate of frontier resource conversion, n, must also be declining.

Clearly, a frontier expansion path that leads to declining per capita domestic consumption and exports is not very desirable. Although it is possible for the economy to choose alternative frontier expansion paths that have positive rather than negative impacts on overall economic development, at least over some initial time period $[0, t]$, it is fairly straightforward to demonstrate that such optimal paths are inconsistent with the interior solution for resource conversion outlined above.

From conditions (4.11), (4.12) and (4.14), positive growth in per capita domestic consumption and exports in the economy requires

$$\dot{q} = \dot{c} + \dot{x} = c\left(1 + \frac{1}{\beta}\right)[m'(k) - (\rho + \omega + \theta)] > 0,$$

$$\text{if } m'(k) - (\rho + \omega + \theta) > 0. \tag{4.20}$$

Economic growth will occur if the marginal productivity of capital per worker in the mainstay sector, $m'(k)$, exceeds the effective discount rate plus any capital depreciation and population growth, $\rho + \omega + \theta$. However, equation (4.14) indicates that the latter condition also implies that the value of the capital stock, λ, must be declining over time. If this is the case, (4.16) and (4.17) are no longer valid as they are based on condition (4.13) set to zero, which in turn requires λ to be positive and growing at the rate θ. Thus the interior solution for frontier resource conversion, $0 < n < \bar{n}$, is not consistent with an optimal path of the economy that leads to growth in per capita domestic consumption and exports.

With any interior solutions for resource conversion ruled out, then $n = 0$ and $n = \bar{n}$ are the only two remaining choices, if the economy wants to be on an optimal frontier expansion path that is also compatible with growth. As (4.11) and (4.20) imply that the value of the capital stock is positive but declining over time, then the optimal policy is for the economy to choose $n = \bar{n}$ first, such that $\lambda > \frac{\mu L_0^A e^\theta}{a'(n)} > 0$, to ensure that growth can at least occur for some until initial time interval $[0, t]$. However, by choosing the maximum frontier resource extraction rate over this initial period, the economy will also ensure that F_0 is exhausted at some future time, $t^F < T$, well before the end of the planning horizon. Once frontier expansion comes to an end, the economy will of course have to stop resource conversion, $n = 0$, for the remaining time in the planning period $[t^F, T]$. Thus one possibility for the economy is to pursue maximum frontier expansion until all new reserves are exhausted, and then make do with $n = 0$ until the end of the time horizon.[11]

Note that the rate of capital accumulation will also differ, as the economy switches from maximum frontier resource conversion to none at all.

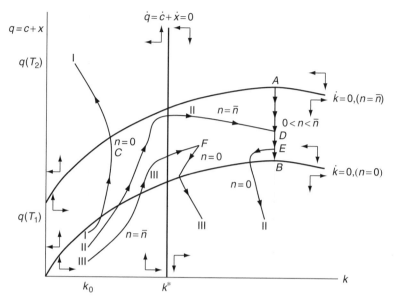

Figure 4.2. Frontier expansion paths for a small open economy

$$\dot{k} = m(k) + a(\bar{n}) - (\omega + \theta)k - q, \ n = \bar{n} \qquad (4.21)$$

$$\dot{k} = m(k) - (\omega + \theta)k - q, \ n = 0. \qquad (4.22)$$

The final dynamic equation of the economy can be found by using (4.20) and the fact that $c = \frac{\beta}{p}z = \beta x$

$$\dot{q} = \dot{c} + \dot{x} = c\left(1 + \frac{1}{\beta}\right)[m'(k) - (\rho + \omega + \theta)]. \qquad (4.23)$$

Equations (4.21)–(4.23) can be solved to yield two $\dot{k} = 0$ isoclines and a single $\dot{q} = 0$ isocline. These isoclines can be depicted diagrammatically in (k, q) space (see Figure 4.2). From (4.23), $\dot{q} = 0$ if $m'(k) = \rho + \omega + \theta$, which means that this locus is a vertical line defined at some $k = k^*$ that satisfies this condition. From (4.21) and (4.22), the $\dot{k} = 0$ isocline corresponding to $n = \bar{n}$ will be $a(\bar{n})$ distance higher than the $\dot{k} = 0$ isocline for $n = 0$. Finally, it is fairly straightforward to demonstrate that the directionals corresponding to these isoclines are $d\dot{k}/dq < 0$ and $d\dot{q}/dk < 0$.[12]

Optimal frontier expansion paths

The model above shows that the open economy can pursue three general types of paths: an interior solution path, a path of maximum frontier expansion until the frontier is closed, and a "stop-go" path alternating between maximum frontier expansion and temporary halts to resource conversion and exploitation.

Figure 4.2 depicts four trajectories that represent the first two types of possible frontier expansion paths available to the economy. Although there are two saddlepoint equilibria resulting from the intersection of the two $\dot{k} = 0$ curves with the $\dot{q} = 0$ vertical locus defined at $k = k^*$, neither of these equilibria is attainable by any of the frontier expansion paths in finite time.

For example, the frontier expansion path defined by the interior solution, $0 < n < \bar{n}$, is the trajectory labeled AB. However, as is clear from (4.17)–(4.19), the economy can only be on this trajectory if it has already attained the per capita capital stock, k_1, which then remains constant over time. This path must always be the right of k^*, since from (4.17) $m'(k_1) = \rho + \omega$ whereas from (4.23) the $\dot{q} = 0$ isocline is always defined at $m'(k^*) = \rho + \omega + \theta$. In addition, exports and consumption per capita, $q = c + x$, are always declining along this optimal path. Moreover, this trajectory is only feasible between the two parallel $\dot{k} = 0$ isoclines.[13]

As noted above, a more likely scenario is for the economy to choose an optimal frontier expansion path that is also compatible with growth, at least for some until initial time interval $[0, t]$. In this case, the optimal policy is for the economy to choose the maximum rate of frontier resource conversion, $n = \bar{n}$ at the outset. If the economy is able to maintain maximum frontier expansion until the resources are exhausted, then it will persist with this policy until the frontier is closed. Assuming that the economy starts at a given initial level of capital stock, $k_0 < k^*$, there are nevertheless several possible paths that the economy might follow, depending on the length of the planning period $[0,T]$, the available stock of frontier resources, F_0, and the terminal value of the capital stock, $\lambda(T)$. Three representative paths are depicted in Figure 4.2, and labeled I-III.

Trajectory I illustrates the case where $\lambda(T)$ is low such that terminal per capita consumption and exports are relatively high, $q(T_2)$. Along this trajectory, the economy will pursue maximum frontier resource conversion, $n = \bar{n}$, until F_0 is exhausted. Once frontier expansion ends, at point C, the economy will no longer utilize frontier resources, $n = 0$, until reaching terminal point, $q(T_2)$. Although during the initial frontier expansion phase, exports and consumption grow rapidly, per capita capital accumulation occurs only modestly. Once this phase ends and the frontier is closed, c and x continue to expand but k starts declining, and at the end of the planning period may be less than k_0. Note that if the total amount of frontier resources available to the economy is larger, then the frontier expansion phase will last longer and thus the switch to $n = 0$ would come later than depicted. The result will be that k will decline less, and at terminal time could equal or exceed k_0.

Both trajectories II and III illustrate the case where $\lambda(T)$ is relatively high so that terminal c and x are low. The result in both cases is a "boom and bust" path for the economy.

Trajectory II is representative of an economy with a larger frontier and/or time horizon. The initial phase of maximum frontier expansion, $n = \bar{n}$, coincides with the economic "boom" period in consumption, exports and capital accumulation. However, even during this phase of frontier resource exploitation, c and x begin to decline. Frontier expansion eventually leads mainly to increases in the stock of capital person. However, once the economy accumulates k_1 amount of capital, there is no incentive to increase it further, as this would result in a decline in net production, $m(k) - (\omega + \theta)k$, from the mainstay sector. Thus once k_1 is reached, the economy will follow along the segment DE of the interior solution path. The rate of frontier resource exploitation will be adjusted to $0 < n < \bar{n}$, and per capita consumption and exports will fall. At point E, frontier resources are exhausted, and since $n = 0$, the economy will depend solely on the mainstay sector until terminal point $q(T_1)$ is reached. During this last phase of trajectory II, c and x will continue to decline. Capital per person will also fall initially and then recover, but will not exceed k_1 at terminal time.

Trajectory III may be the more typical outcome if an economy has a smaller frontier stock and/or a shorter time horizon. The initial phase of maximum frontier expansion, $n = \bar{n}$, also coincides with the economic "boom" period in c, x and k. However, once frontier exploitation ends at point F, then a "bust" phase ensues. Although per capita exports and consumption continue to decline until the end of the planning period, additional capital accumulation will eventually occur. The final level of capital person will be between k^* and k_1.

How representative are these trajectories of actual development paths embarked upon by low and middle-income economies? As is the case of any theoretical model, the one developed here is a highly stylized representation of true economies. Nevertheless, the main point of the model is to illustrate some of the key features of the frontier expansion hypothesis, in particular how the structural dependence of a poor economy on frontier land and resource expansion can lead to a "boom and bust" pattern of development rather than sustained economic growth. Of course, we have also stressed that such a pattern of frontier-based development is *symptomatic* of a general pattern of unsustainable resource exploitation in many low and middle-income economies. As emphasized throughout this book so far, the fact that so few developing economies in recent decades appear to have embarked on a successful process of resource-based development – and those few success stories have tended to exploit mainly mineral resources or similar "point" resources such as timber – suggest that the key features of frontier-based development captured in the above model may have some relevance to the "unsuccessful" development efforts of many low and middle-income economies.

Final remarks

Throughout Part One of this book we have been concerned with a key paradox facing present-day low and middle-income economies: why is it that, despite the importance of natural capital for sustainable economic development, increasing economic dependence on natural resource exploitation appears to be a hindrance to growth and development in poor countries?

Previous chapters in Part One have examined the "stylized facts" of natural resource use in developing economies, provided a brief historical overview of the role of natural resources in economic development and reviewed current theories and hypotheses that attempt to explain why natural resource wealth may not be producing development benefits for poor countries. This chapter has been concerned with a new perspective on the resource-development paradox, which could be termed the *frontier expansion hypothesis*.

The starting point for this hypothesis is two stylized facts of resource use in developing countries that are often overlooked in the current literature on the role of natural resources in economic development: namely, the tendency for resource-dependent economies to display rapid rates of "frontier" land expansion, and for a significant proportion of their poorest populations to be concentrated in fragile areas. From this pattern of development several conclusions emerge. First, in many developing countries much frontier land expansion occurs in order to absorb the rural poor. Second, policy and market failures in the resource sector and land markets, such as rent-seeking behavior and corruption or open access resource exploitation, contribute further to the migration of the rural poor to the frontier and excessive land conversion. Finally, as a result, frontier-based development in many poor countries is symptomatic of a pattern of economy-wide resource exploitation that leads to insufficient reinvestment in other productive assets of the economy, and thus does not lead to sustained growth. There is clearly a "vicious cycle" at work here: frontier land expansion and resource exploitation does little to raise rural incomes and reduce poverty in the long run, and results in little efficiency gains and additional benefits for the overall economy.

The model of frontier-based expansion and economic growth developed in this chapter illustrates this pattern. The model assumes that there is a stock of frontier resources that is freely available to an economy for conversion. But if frontier land expansion and resource exploitation are used mainly to absorb a growing labor force and is not integrated with the rest of the economy, then the result is a "boom and bust" pattern of economic development rather than sustained growth. Although as shown in the model it is possible to generate optimal paths for the economy, a notable feature of all these paths is that an initial boom period can coincide with maximum conversion and exploitation of frontier reserves, but the economy will ultimately retrench considerably once the reserves are depleted.

In addition, as discussed briefly in this chapter, this process of frontier-based development tends to be inequitable in many developing economies. What resource rents are available from the frontier and existing natural capital for exploitation accrue mainly to a wealthy elite, who have increased incentives for "rent-seeking" behavior. The wealthy will also support the continuation of any policy distortions that reinforce the existing pattern of allocating and distributing natural resources. The poor are therefore left with marginal resources and frontier land areas to exploit, further reducing their ability to improve their livelihoods significantly, and of course, to generate and appropriate any substantial rents. This tendency for any frontier resource rents to benefit mainly wealthy elites and exacerbate problems of inequality and rural poverty – although not included explicitly in the model of this chapter – will be explored more fully in a later chapter (see Chapter 8).

Empirical evidence and case studies suggest that this "vicious cycle" of present-day frontier-based development is clearly very entrenched in many poor countries. Part Two of this book, comprising Chapters 5–7, will elaborate in more detail on various aspects of this "vicious cycle" by focusing on specific resource problems in developing countries. For example, these chapters examine the factors underlying two pervasive problems in developing countries: the economic forces driving land conversion and causing greater stress on freshwater resources. Finally, Part Three of the book, comprising Chapters 8–10, looks at the necessary steps and policy reforms needed to reverse the "vicious cycle" in developing countries that is implied by the frontier expansion hypothesis.

Appendix to Chapter 4

Let $p^A/p^M = p^A$ be the relative price of the frontier good, if the price of the mainstay good is the numeraire. Denoting profits in the frontier sector as $\pi^A = L^A\lfloor p^A a(n) - w - w^N n\rfloor$, equilibrium frontier production requires

$$\frac{d\pi^A}{dn} = L^A\left[p^A a'(n) - w^N\right] = 0 \quad \text{or} \quad p^A a'(n) = w^N$$

$$\frac{d\pi^A}{dL^A} = p^A a(n) - w - w^N n - \left[p^A a'(n)n + w^N n\right] = 0 \quad \text{or}$$

$$p^A\left[a(n) - a'(n)n\right] = w,$$

where w^N is the real rental price (in terms of p^M) of converted or extracted frontier resources, i.e. the "land" input into frontier economic activities, and w is the real market wage. The above two expressions indicate that the value marginal products of land and labor in the frontier sector must equal their respective input prices.

Perfect competition and free mobility of labor between the frontier and mainstay sectors also results in the following equilibrium condition for the latter sector

$$m(k) - m'(k)k = w.$$

The zero profit condition for the mainstay sector yields

$$\pi^M = L^M[m(k) - w - (r + \omega)k] = 0$$

$$\frac{d\pi^M}{dk} = L^M[m'(k) - (r + \omega)] = 0 \quad \text{or} \quad m'(k) = r + \omega,$$

where r is the real price of capital and ω is the rate of depreciation.

Let us assume that households in the mainstay sector not only sell their labor to produce the mainstay good but also own the capital used in this sector. Denoting c^M as the per capita consumption of these households and θ as population growth, it follows that per capita accumulation by mainstay households is governed by the following budget constraint

$$\dot{k} = rk + w - \theta k - c^M = m(k) - (\omega + \theta)k - c^M,$$

after using the expressions above to substitute for w and r.

Households in the frontier sector sell their labor to produce the frontier good and own the resource or converted "land" input. However, all their income is consumed. Denoting c^A as the per capita consumption of these households, their budget constraint is

$$c^A = w + w^N n = p^A a(n),$$

after using the expressions above to substitute for w and w^N.

Aggregate per capita domestic consumption, c, in terms of the numeraire mainstay price, is therefore

$$c = c^M + \frac{c^A}{p^A}.$$

Combining the last three expressions, and making use of the fact that actual domestic consumption is actually aggregate consumption less exports, $c = q - x$, yields

$$\dot{k} = m(k) - (\omega + \theta)k + a(n) - (c + x) = m(k) + a(n) - (\omega + \theta)k - q$$

Notes

1. However, Gylfasson (2001, p. 566 n. 12) suggests that Indonesia should at best be considered only a qualified success, given the widespread corruption

in the country and because Indonesia has recovered much less well from the 1997–98 Asian crisis compared to Malaysia and Thailand.

2. Wright and Czelusta (2002, p. 17) cite the specific example of the development of the US petrochemical industry to illustrate the economic importance of knowledge spillovers: "Progress in petrochemicals is an example of new technology built on resource-based heritage. It may also be considered a return to scale at the industry level, because the search for by-products was an outgrowth of the vast American enterprise of petroleum refining."

3. There is also an obvious link between rent-seeking activities in frontier areas and the lack of government enforcement of efficient regulation of these activities For example, Ascher (1999, p. 268) points out: "The weak capacity of the government to enforce natural resource regulations and guard against illegal exploitation is an obvious factor in many of the cases reviewed. In every case of land and forest use, illegal extraction and failure to abide by conservation regulations reduce the costs to the resource exploiter and induce overexploitation, while failing to make the exploiter internalize the costs of resource depletion and pollution."

4. Although only the preferred models are indicated in Table 4.1, the panel analysis was performed comparing OLS against one-way and two-way random and fixed effects models. Alternative versions of these models also employed White's robust correction of the covariance matrix to overcome unspecified heteroskedasticity. However, heteroskedasticity proved not to be a significant problem in both regressions. In the regression for all tropical developing countries, the F-test for the pooled model and Breusch-Pagan LM test were highly significant, suggesting rejection of the OLS model due to the presence of individual effects. The Hausman test was significant only at the 10 % level, suggesting that random effects specification is preferred to the fixed effects model. The one-way model tended to outperform the two-way effects model. In the regression for lower income countries, the F-test for the pooled model, the LM test and the Hausman test were all highly significant, suggesting that the fixed effects model is preferred. The two-way model tended to outperform the one-way effects model.

5. The six countries are Grenada (with a long-run agricultural land change index of 0.684), Jamaica (0.893), Bolivia (0.961), Bangladesh (0.981), Mauritania (0.998) and the Maldives (1.000).

6. The eleven countries are Sri Lanka (with a long-run agricultural land change index of 1.348), Burundi (1.397), Rwanda (1.403), Papua New Guinea (1.432), Nicaragua (1.454), Uganda (1.478), the Philippines (1.511), Vanuatu (1.610), Paraguay (1.663), Belize (1.671) and Guatemala (1.705).

7. The following model of frontier-based development in a small open economy is from Barbier (2005).

8. For instance, to make the following model more tractable, we do not include the division of the frontier sector into two types of activities: small-scale agricultural production and extractive activities that increases non-traded consumption, and large-scale extractive activities owned by wealthier households that are often the focus of rent-seeking activities. As will be clear immediately, the frontier sector is modeled here with the first set of activities in mind. Chapter 8 examines in more detail the model by Torvik (2002) that could be construed as incorporating the second type of frontier "rent-seeking" activities that also implies the existence of corruption.

9. As shown in the appendix to the chapter, the assumption of zero profits in the frontier sector and that the frontier households consume all their factor income results in the condition $c^A = w + w^N n = p^A a(n)$. However, it is possible that excess profits, or rents, are generated in this sector so that $c^A < pa(n)$. In which case, it is clear from the aggregate relationship (4.7) that any such surplus output from the frontier sector will be allocated either to increase exports, x, or capital accumulation, $\dot{k}$. Either possibility cannot be ruled out for this economy.

10. Technically, $\bar{n}$, should be subscripted to indicate that it changes over time with the growth in L_A; to simplify notation, this convention is dropped.

11. Note that it is never optimal to halt resource extraction, $n = 0$, as long as there is some frontier stock remaining, $F(t) > 0$. From (4.11) and (4.13), $n = 0$ implies that $0 < \lambda < \frac{\mu e^{(\theta - \alpha)t}}{a'(n)}$; i.e. μ is unambiguously positive. However, from (4.15), $n = 0$ also requires $\mu F_0 = 0$ and $\mu \geq 0$. Together, these conditions imply that the zero extraction policy is only optimal once the frontier resource stock is completely exhausted, i.e. when $F_0 = 0$.

12. From (4.21) and (4.22), $\frac{d\dot{k}}{dq} = -1 < 0$. From (4.23), $\frac{d\dot{q}}{dk} = c\left(1 + \frac{1}{\beta}\right)m''(k) < 0$.

13. From (4.21), at point A, on the $\dot{k} = 0$ isocline corresponding to $n = \bar{n}$, $q = m(k_1) + a(\bar{n}) - (\omega + \theta)k_1$. Since q can only increase if $n > \bar{n}$, which is impossible by definition, then any points above are infeasible for the trajectory defined by the interior solution to the problem. Equally, (4.22) rules out the possibility of points below point B as being attainable for the interior solution, since at this point $q = m(k_1) - (\omega + \theta)k_1$ and $n < 0$ is not a feasible outcome.

5 | Explaining land use change in developing countries

HE main aim of the first four chapters comprising Part One of
this book was to address a key paradox facing present-day low
and middle-income economies: why is it that, despite the
importance of natural capital for sustainable economic development,
increasing economic dependence on natural resource exploitation
appears to be a hindrance to growth and development in poor
countries?

Chapter 1 explained the importance of natural capital to sustainable
economic development, and presented four key "stylized facts" of natural
resource use in developing economies. Chapter 2 provided a historical
overview of the role of natural resources in economic development.
Chapter 3 reviewed current theories and hypotheses that attempt to
explain why natural resource wealth may not be producing development benefits for poor countries. Finally, Chapter 4 was concerned
with a new perspective on the resource-development paradox, which is
termed the *frontier expansion hypothesis*.

As emphasized in these chapters forming Part One, deforestation,
land conversion and agricultural land expansion in low and middle-
income countries are major features of the economic development
occurring in these economies. Much of the "frontier expansion" in these
economies consists of rapid land use change, mostly the conversion of
forests, woodlands and other natural habitats to agriculture and other
land-based development activities.

The purpose of the following chapter is to explore in more detail the
process of land conversion and agricultural land expansion itself as
well as recent economic explanations as to the possible causes underlying this process. The main focus will be on land use change in the
tropics, as this is where the majority of the world's poorest countries
are located.[1] The chapter first provides a brief summary of global

tropical forest and land use trends. This is followed by an overview of cross-country empirical analyses of deforestation and agricultural land expansion, highlighting the main factors and causes identified by such case studies. Four key economic approaches to cross-country analysis are then discussed – environmental Kuznets curve analyses, competing land use models, forest land conversion models and institutional analyses – and from this review a synthesis analysis is proposed and applied to a new cross-country data set.

Global tropical deforestation and land use trends

Table 5.1 displays global tropical deforestation trends over 1980–90. Over 15 million hectares (ha) of tropical forest were cleared annually, and the rate of deforestation averaged 0.8% per year. There were substantial regional differences in deforestation, however. Over 1980–90, the area of tropical forests cleared on average each year in Latin America was 7.4 million ha, almost as much as the area deforested in Asia and Africa put together. Within Latin America, the main source of total deforestation occurred in South America, around 6.2 million ha annually. However, the highest rate of deforestation (1.5% per year) occurred in Central America and Mexico. In Africa, most deforestation took place in Central and Tropical Southern Africa, although the highest rate of deforestation (1%) was in West Africa. In Asia, the highest amounts and rates of forest clearing occurred by far in Southeast Asia.

Over 1990–2000, global tropical deforestation slowed to less than 12 million ha per year, or an annual rate of 0.6% (see Table 5.2). However, this reflects less deforestation mainly in Latin America and Asia; forest clearing increased over 1990–2000 in Africa to over 4.8 million ha annually, or 0.8% per year. Whereas deforestation has declined in Tropical South America, Central Africa and Southeast Asia, it has risen significantly in Tropical Southern, West and East Sahelian Africa.[2]

The available evidence suggests that in most developing economies the decline in forest and woodlands is mainly the result of land conversion, in particular agricultural expansion for crop production (FAO 1997 and 2003). Land expansion occurring in tropical regions appears to be related to structural features of the agricultural sectors of developing economies, such as low irrigation and fertilizer use as well as

Table 5.1 Global tropical deforestation trends, 1980–90

Region	Number of countries	Land area (mn ha)	Forest cover 1980 (mn ha)	Forest cover 1990 (mn ha)	Annual deforestation 1980–90 (mn ha)	Annual deforestation 1980–90 (% per yr)
Africa	40	2,236.1	568.6	527.6	4.10	0.7
West Sahelian Africa	9	528.0	43.7	40.8	0.30	0.7
East Sahelian Africa	6	489.7	71.4	65.5	0.60	0.9
West Africa	8	203.8	61.5	55.6	0.59	1.0
Central Africa	6	398.3	215.5	204.1	1.14	0.5
Tropical Southern Africa	10	558.1	159.3	145.9	1.35	0.9
Insular Africa	1	58.2	17.1	15.8	0.14	0.8
Asia & Pacific	17	892.1	349.6	310.6	3.90	1.2
South Asia	6	412.2	69.4	63.9	0.55	0.8
Continental Southeast Asia	5	190.2	88.4	75.2	1.31	1.6
Insular Southeast Asia	5	244.4	154.7	135.4	1.93	1.3
Oceania	1	45.3	37.1	36	0.11	0.3
Latin America & Caribbean	33	1,650.1	992.2	918.1	7.41	0.8
Central America & Mexico	7	239.6	79.2	68.1	1.12	1.5
Caribbean	19	69.0	48.3	47.1	0.12	0.3
Tropical South America	7	1,341.6	864.6	802.9	6.17	0.7
TOTAL	90	4,778.3	1,910.4	1,756.3	15.40	0.8

Source: FAO (1993).

Table 5.2 Global tropical deforestation trends, 1990–2000

Region	Number of countries	Land area (mn ha)	Forest cover 1991 (mn ha)	Forest cover 2000 (mn ha)	Annual deforestation 1990–2000 (mn ha)	Annual deforestation 1990–2000 (% per yr)
Africa	**48**	**2,250.6**	**687.2**	**634.3**	**4.81**	**0.8**
West Sahelian Africa	10	528.8	47.0	43.7	0.33	0.7
East Sahelian Africa	7	501.7	109.3	96.6	1.27	1.2
West Africa	9	205.1	51.8	41.6	1.02	2.0
Central Africa	6	398.3	235.8	227.6	0.34	0.3
Tropical Southern Africa	10	557.9	230.3	212.9	1.74	0.8
Insular Africa	6	58.9	13.0	11.9	0.12	0.9
Asia & Pacific	**35**	**903.0**	**349.2**	**323.7**	**2.55**	**0.7**
South Asia	6	412.9	77.6	76.7	0.10	0.1
Continental Southeast Asia	5	190.1	87.8	80.9	0.69	0.8
Insular Southeast Asia	6	245.9	147.4	131.0	1.64	1.1
Oceania	18	54.1	36.4	35.1	0.12	0.3
Latin America & Caribbean	**41**	**1,652.3**	**957.0**	**912.9**	**4.41**	**0.5**
Central America & Mexico	7	239.7	81.0	71.7	0.9	1.2
Caribbean	24	25	7.3	7.1	0.0	0.3
Tropical South America	10	1,387.5	868.7	834.1	3.46	0.4
TOTAL	**124**	**4,805.9**	**1,993.5**	**1,870.9**	**11.78**	**0.6**

Source: FAO (2001).

poor crop yields. Low agricultural productivity and input use reflect poor agricultural intensification and development, which in turn mean more pressure is put on conversion of forests and other marginal lands for use in crop production.

The overall dependence of many developing economies on conversion of forests, wetlands and other natural habitats was an important "stylized fact" highlighted in Chapter 1. As indicated in Table 1.3 of that chapter, over the period 1990–2010 about 19% of the contribution to total crop production increases in developing regions is likely to be derived from the expansion of cultivated land. In East Asia (excluding China) the contribution to crop production from land conversion is likely to be 34%, in Sub-Saharan Africa 30% and in Latin America (excluding the Caribbean) 29% (see Table 1.3).

Stratified random sampling of 10% of the world's tropical forests reveals that direct conversion by large-scale agriculture may be the main source of deforestation, accounting for around 32% of total forest cover change, followed by conversion to small-scale agriculture, which accounts for 26% (FAO 2001). Intensification of agriculture in shifting cultivation areas comprises only 10% of tropical deforestation, and expansion of shifting cultivation into undisturbed forests only 5%. However, there are important regional differences. In Africa, the major process of deforestation (around 60%) is due to the conversion of forest for the establishment of small-scale permanent agriculture, whereas direct conversion of forest cover to large-scale agriculture, including raising livestock, predominates in Latin America and Asia (48% and 30%, respectively). Although agricultural conversion is the principal cause of tropical deforestation, in many forested regions uncontrolled timber harvesting is responsible for initially opening up previously inaccessible forested frontiers to permanent agricultural conversion and for causing widespread timber-related forest degradation and loss (Ascher, 1999; Barbier *et al.*, 1994; Matthews *et al.*, 2000; Ross 2001).

Factors determining agricultural land expansion

The discussion of the previous section suggests that the major cause of forest loss in developing countries is conversion to agriculture. Thus a cross-country analysis of agricultural land expansion should also provide insights into the factors influencing tropical deforestation.

Equally, previous studies of tropical deforestation may be able to suggest some of the possible effects of growth, income per capita and other macroeconomic factors on agricultural land expansion in the tropical developing regions of Latin America, Africa and Asia. Four distinct analytical frameworks have been proposed in the economics literature for motivating cross-country estimations of the causes of agricultural land conversion and tropical deforestation: *the environmental "Kuznets" curve hypothesis, competing land use models, forest land conversion models*, and *institutional models* (Barbier and Burgess 2001a). As the following brief review indicates, these analytical frameworks enable us to focus on certain key economic factors that may determine tropical agricultural land expansion and to choose the appropriate variables to include in our cross-country regression.[3]

The environmental Kuznets curve (EKC) hypothesis states that an environmental "bad" first increases, but eventually falls, as the per capita income of a country rises. There are a number of recent theoretical models explaining why such an inverted-U relationship between income and environmental "bads" might hold (e.g. Andreoni and Levinson 2001; McConnell 1997; Stokey 1998). Although the EKC model has generally been applied to pollution problems, there have been a number of recent studies that have also examined whether this hypothesis also holds for global deforestation (e.g. Antle and Heidebrink 1995; Cropper and Griffiths 1994; Koop and Toole 1999; Panayotou 1995; Shafik 1994). The basic EKC model for deforestation is usually

$$F_{it} - F_{it-1} = F(Y_{it}, Y_{it}^2; \mathbf{z}_{it}) = \alpha_1 Y_{it} - \alpha_2 Y_{it}^2 + \mathbf{z}_{it}\beta + \varepsilon_{it} \qquad (5.1)$$

where $F_{it} - F_{it-1}$ is the change in the forest stock over the previous period (which is negative if deforestation is occurring), Y_{it} is per capita income and $\mathbf{z}_{it}$ is a $1 \times n$ vector that includes other explanatory variables, such as population density or growth and other macroeconomic variables.[4]

The application of the EKC model (5.1) to explain deforestation trends across countries has produced mixed results. When the model is tested for both temperate and tropical countries, it is inconclusive (Antle and Heidebrink 1995; Panayotou 1995; Shafik 1994). When applied to just tropical countries, the inverted-U relationship tends not to hold for all countries but may apply to specific regions. For example, Cropper and Griffiths (1994) find some evidence that the EKC model is relevant to Latin America and Africa. However, for each of these regions the turning point – the per capita income level at which the deforestation rate is zero and is about to decline – is generally two to four times higher than the average per capita income for that region. This implies that the vast majority of the countries in these regions will have to attain much higher levels of economic development before deforestation rates slow down. Similar results are found in other EKC estimates for tropical deforestation that are robust (Barbier and Burgess 2001a; Bhattarai and Hammig 2004; Cropper and Griffiths 1994; Koop and Tole 1989). Nevertheless, as a comparison of Tables 5.1 and 5.2 indicates, tropical deforestation in most developing regions, especially in Latin America and Asia, has slowed down recently, and one possible explanation may be the EKC hypothesis.

Other empirical analyses have taken as their starting point the hypothesis that forest loss in tropical countries is the result of competing land use, in particular between maintaining the natural forest and agriculture (e.g. Barbier and Burgess 1997; Benhin and Barbier 2001; Ehui and Hertel 1989). As indicated in Chapter 1 and discussed above, the evidence across tropical regions is that substantial conversion of forest and woodlands to agriculture is occurring. From an economic standpoint, given the time and effort required to re-establish tropical forest (where this is ecologically feasible) such conversion implies that potential timber and environmental benefits from forestland are irreversibly lost. Therefore, competing land use models usually include some measure of the "price" or opportunity cost of agricultural conversion and deforestation in terms of the foregone benefits of timber production and environmental benefits from forestland

$$F_{it} - F_{it-1} = A^D(v_{it}; \mathbf{z_{it}}), \partial A^D / \partial v_{it} < 0 \qquad (5.2)$$

where v_{it} is the opportunity cost or "price" of agricultural conversion, A^D is the demand for converting forest land to agriculture, and as before $\mathbf{z_{it}}$ is a vector containing exogenous economic factors (e.g. income per capita, population density, agricultural yields).

Many country-level studies of tropical deforestation have focused on modeling the forestland conversion decision of agricultural households. There have been several such applications to rural areas of developing countries (e.g. Anderson *et al.* 2003; Barbier 2002; Barbier and Burgess 1996; Barbier and Cox 2004a; Chomitz and Gray 1996; Cropper *et al.* 1999; López 1997; Nelson and Hellerstein

1997; Nelson *et al.* 2001; Panayotou and Sungsuwan 1994; Rodríguez-Meza *et al.* 2004). Such approaches model the derived demand for converted land by rural smallholders, and assume that the households either use available labor to convert their own land or purchase it from a market. This in turn allows the determinants of the equilibrium level of converted land to be specified. In such models, the aggregate equilibrium level of cleared land across all households is usually hypothesized to be a function of output and input prices and other factors affecting aggregate conversion

$$A_{it}^D = A^D(p_{it}, w_{L_{it}}, \mathbf{w}_{it}; \mathbf{x}_{it}, \mathbf{z}_{it}), \frac{\partial A^D}{\partial p_{it}} > 0, \frac{\partial A^D}{\partial w_{L_{it}}} < 0, \frac{\partial A^D}{\partial x_{it}} > 0. \quad (5.3)$$

where p is the price of agricultural output, w_L is rural wage (labor is a key component in land clearing), $\mathbf{w}$ is a vector of other inputs, $\mathbf{x}$ are factors influencing the "accessibility" of forest areas (e.g. roads, infrastructure, distance to major towns and cities), and as before $\mathbf{z}_{it}$ represents other economic explanatory variables.

Although both the competing land use and forestland conversion models appear to work well for specific tropical forest countries, it is difficult to obtain time series data across countries for key price data in the respective models, i.e. v_{it} in equation (5.2) or p_{it} and especially w_{it} in equation (5.3). Cross-country data on important "x" variables, such as rural road expansion and road building investments, are also difficult to find. As a result, cross-country analyses of equations (5.2) and (5.3) have tended to leave out prices and "x" factors, or employed proxies. For example in their empirical estimations for deforestation across all tropical countries, Barbier and Burgess (1997) employed roundwood production per capita as a "proxy" for v_{it} in equation (5.2), as preferred measures of the "opportunity cost" of conversion (e.g., land values, timber rents) are not available across countries. Similarly, Southgate (1994) used annual population growth, agricultural export growth, crop yield growth and a land constraint dummy to explain annual agricultural land growth across Latin America over 1982–87. He found that population and agricultural export growth were positively related to land expansion, whereas yield growth and the land constraint were negatively related. Other studies have also demonstrated that structural agricultural, economic and geographic factors, which vary from country to country, are significant in explaining the different land conversion trends across countries (e.g., Barbier and Burgess 1997 and 2001a; 1999). These "structural" variables include agricultural yield, cropland share of land area, agricultural export share, and arable land per capita, which capture country-by-country differences in agricultural sectors and land use patterns, as well as other exogenous macro-economic variables, such as population growth, rural population density, GDP growth, real interest rates and debt. These factors may be particularly significant explanatory variables in a cross-country analysis, if the difficulty in obtaining cross-country time series data on key variables, such as rural wages, roads, other input prices, makes it impossible to include variables representing agricultural returns or "accessibility" of forest lands in the model.

Finally, recent empirical analyses at both the country and cross-country level have explored the impact on tropical deforestation of institutional factors, such as land use conflict, security of ownership or property rights, political stability, and the "rule of law" (e.g. Alston, Libecap and Mueller 1999 and 2000; Barbier 2002; Deacon 1994 and 1999; Godoy et al. 1998). The main hypothesis tested is that such institutional factors are important factors explaining deforestation

$$F_{it} - F_{it-1} = F(\mathbf{q}_{it}; \mathbf{z}_{it}) \tag{5.4}$$

where $\mathbf{q}_{it}$ is a vector of institutional factors and $\mathbf{z}_{it}$ represents other economic explanatory variables.

Although such models have demonstrated the importance of institutional factors in determining deforestation, it is unclear how much weight should be given to such factors in preference to explanatory variables identified by other approaches to cross-country analyses of forest loss. Nevertheless, the failure to include institutional factors in a cross-country analysis of land use change may mean that potentially important explanatory variables have been omitted.

In sum, the four main frameworks motivating cross-country analysis of tropical deforestation and land use change emphasize the following key variables: i) from equation (5.1), the inclusion of per capita income and income squared terms to test for a possible EKC relationship; ii) in the absence of adequate cross-country data for the price and "x" variables in equations (5.2) and (5.3), the inclusion of certain "structural" variables (s_{it}), such as agricultural yield, cropland share of land area, agricultural export share, and growth in agricultural value added, to capture country-by-country differences in agricultural sectors and land use patterns; and finally, iii) from equation (5.4) the inclusion of key institutional factors thought to influence land expansion and deforestation.

A synthesis model[5]

Thus a possible "synthesis" model for a cross-country analysis of the possible effects of growth, income per capita and other macroeconomic factors on agricultural land expansion in developing regions might look like:

$$\frac{A_{it} - A_{it-1}}{A_{it}} \times 100 = b_0 + b_1 Y_{it} + b_2 Y_{it}^2 + b_3 s_{it} + b_4 z_{it} + b_5 q_{it}$$
$$+ \mu_{it}, \text{ for country } i \text{ at time } t \qquad (5.5)$$

where $(A_{it} - A_{it-1})/A_{it}$ is the percentage annual change in permanent and arable cropland area and represents the dependent variable for agricultural land expansion in the analysis, Y_{it} is per capita income, s_{it} is a vector of "structural" variables representing country-by-country differences in agricultural sectors and land use patterns, z_{it} represents other exogenous explanatory variables, such as rural population growth and macroeconomic variables, and μ_{it} is the error term. Finally, as institutional factors (q_i) tend to be invariant with time, two versions of the model can be tested, one without and one including q_i.

A previous study estimated a version of equation (5.5) through applying panel analysis to agricultural land expansion in tropical countries of Latin America, Asia and Africa over 1961–94 (Barbier and Burgess 2001a). The analysis shows that the pattern of agricultural development, as represented by such structural variables as cropland share of total land area, agricultural export share of total exports, and to some extent, cereal yields, appears consistently to influence tropical agricultural land expansion. Population growth could be an additional factor, especially in Asia. Corruption and political stability may also be important institutional influences, but their significance may vary from region to region. The existence of an EKC effect for agricultural expansion appears to be highly sensitive to the model specification, and the impact of changes in GDP per capita on agricultural expansion is likely to differ considerably across tropical regions.

Building on the results of the previous study, the panel analysis of tropical agricultural land expansion of equation (5.5) has been updated for the period 1960–99, as well as modified to reflect the availability of new data and better indicators.[6] The dependent variable in the new analysis is again the percentage annual change in arable and permanent cropland area in each country. The EKC variables (Y_{it}, Y_{it}^2) are represented by gross domestic product (GDP) per capita in constant values (1995 US$) and by GDP per capita squared, respectively. The structural variables (s_{it}) are cereal yield, cropland share of total land area, agricultural export share of total merchandise exports and growth in agricultural value added. The additional explanatory variables (z_{it}) are rural population growth and the terms of trade (TOT) for each country. The latter variable is represented by an index of export to import prices ($1995 = 100$). Finally, as previous chapters suggest that the influence of changes in terms of trade on a country's export performance may be influenced by the degree of resource-trade dependence of the economy, the TOT variable has also been interacted with the share of agricultural and raw material exports as a percentage of total exports of each country.[7]

The source of data used for the above variables was the World Bank's *World Development Indicators*, which has the most extensive data set for key land, agricultural and economic variables for developing countries over the period of analysis.

Three institutional factors (q_i) were incorporated into the new analysis of model (5.5): indicators of control of corruption, political stability/lack of violence and rule of law. The source used for these data is a recent project on governance conducted by the World Bank, which put together a measure of each of the above three institutional factors and other governance indicators for 178 developing and advanced economies (Kaufmann *et al.* 1999a). As the control of corruption, political stability/lack of violence and rule of law indicators cover the broadest range of developing countries to date of any comparable indicator, it is ideal for our analysis. However, as this indicator is a single point estimate in time (based on survey data corresponding for 1997–98 according to the authors), including this time-invariant institutional index essentially amounts to incorporating a "weighted" country-specific dummy variable in the panel regression (Baltagi 1995).[8]

Unfortunately, none of the three institutional variables used in the synthesis analysis serve as a good proxy for a key institutional factor determining agricultural land conversion in tropical forest areas, namely the prevalence of open access conditions in frontier regions. An adequate cross-country data set on property rights and land ownership conditions does not currently exist for developing economies. However, as we shall see in Chapter 6, through a different modeling approach applied at the country case study level, it is possible to analyze the impacts of open access conditions on agricultural land conversion.

Finally, our synthesis analysis can also be used to test the hypothesis that institutional factors might influence economy-wide export performance, especially in countries dependent on natural resource exploitation such as the conversion of forests (Ascher 1999; Ross 2001; Wunder 2003; see also Chapters 3 and 4). That is, the degree to which there is corruption, political stability and the rule of law in a country may influence how TOT changes affect agricultural land expansion. To test this hypothesis in the empirical analysis, each of the institutional variables (control of corruption, political stability/lack of violence and rule of law) was also interacted with the TOT variable.

Table 5.3 reports the regression results. The model was first applied to the sample of all tropical developing countries, without any of the institutional variables included. Subsequent versions of the model were then tested with the inclusion of the three institutional factors comprising q_i, i.e. control of corruption, political stability/lack of violence and rule of law. Table 5.3 reports the regressions that contain each of these institutional indicators in turn, as well as an interaction term between the institutional variable and the terms of trade (TOT).[9]

Both one-way and two-way fixed and random effects models were applied. As indicated in Table 5.3, the chi-squared and F-tests for the pooled models as well as the LM statistic test for the null hypothesis of no individual effects. As these tests are significant, they suggest rejection of the ordinary least squares model. The Hausman test indicates that the random effects model is preferred over fixed effects. For all four regressions in Table 5.1, the one-way specification was chosen over the two-way random effects specification based on the likelihood ratio test. In addition, the significance of individual coefficients and the overall explanatory power of the estimation were superior for the one-way model.

The results in Table 5.3 indicate that the model is strongly robust with regard to key structural variables, s_{it}, that capture country-by-country differences in agricultural sectors and land use patterns, most notably agricultural export share, cropland share of land area, and growth in agricultural value added. Only one structural variable, cereal yield, is

Table 5.3 Panel analysis of tropical agricultural land expansion, 1960–99

Dependent variable: arable and permanent cropland expansion (% annual change)

Explanatory variables	Cross-country estimations[a]			
	No institutional variables	Control of corruption	Political stability	Rule of law
	$(N=1,526)$	$(N=1,362)$	$(N=1,362)$	$(N=1,455)$
	$(Y=0.967\%)$[b]	$(Y=0.996\%)$	$(Y=0.996\%)$	$(Y=1.039\%)$
GDP per capita (constant 1995 US$)	-1.281×10^{-4}	5.119×10^{-5}	-1.094×10^{-4}	5.555×10^{-5}
	(-0.403)	(0.162)	(-0.329)	(0.171)
GDP per capita squared	1.802×10^{-8}	-1.758×10^{-8}	3.431×10^{-9}	-1.329×10^{-8}
	(0.253)	(-0.258)	(0.049)	(-0.187)
Terms of trade (1995=100)	1.861×10^{-3}	1.210×10^{-2}	2.557×10^{-3}	5.221×10^{-3}
	(0.754)	$(2.960)*$	(0.888)	(1.417)
Agricultural export share (% of merchandise exports)	3.407×10^{-2}	4.370×10^{-2}	3.678×10^{-2}	2.985×10^{-2}
	$(2.017)*$	$(2.672)**$	$(2.183)**$	$(1.745)^{\dagger}$
Terms of trade* Agricultural export share	-2.071×10^{-4}	-2.539×10^{-4}	-2.099×10^{-4}	-1.628×10^{-4}
	(-1.588)	$(-2.006)*$	(-1.592)	(-1.211)
Growth in agricultural value added (% annual change)	1.621×10^{-2}	1.585×10^{-2}	1.562×10^{-2}	1.818×10^{-2}
	$(1.928)*$	$(1.806)^{\dagger}$	$(1.776)^{\dagger}$	$(2.094)*$
Cereal yield (kg per hectare)	7.112×10^{-5}	-8.864×10^{-5}	-1.409×10^{-4}	-1.488×10^{-4}
	(0.467)	(-0.585)	(-0.923)	(-0.939)

Table 5.3 (continued)

Dependent variable: arable and permanent cropland expansion (% annual change)

	Cross-country estimations[a]			
	No institutional variables	*Control of corruption*	*Political stability*	*Rule of law*
Rural population growth (% annual change)	2.128×10^{-1} (2.142)*	9.073×10^{-2} (0.858)	7.702×10^{-2} (0.712)	1.648×10^{-1} (1.561)
Agricultural land share (% of total land area)	-1.632×10^{-2} (−2.124)*	-1.333×10^{-2} (−1.732)†	-1.722×10^{-2} (−2.231)*	-1.282×10^{-2} (−1.647)†
Control of corruption (no control = −2.5; no corruption = 2.5)		−1.404 (−2.260)*		
Control of corruption*Terms of trade		1.510×10^{-2} (2.788)**		
Political stability (no stability = −2.5; no instability = 2.5)			3.268×10^{-1} (0.759)	
Political stability*Terms of trade			3.584×10^{-4} (0.108)	
Rule of law (no law = −2.5; full law = 2.5)				-4.056×10^{-1} (−0.775)

Dependent variable: arable and permanent cropland expansion (% annual change)

	Cross-country estimations[a]			
	No institutional variables	Control of corruption	Political stability	Rule of law
Rule of law*Terms of trade				6.212×10^{-3} (1.437)
Kuznets curve (Turning point estimate)	No ($3,555)	No ($1,456)	No ($15,946)	No ($2,089)
χ^2-test for pooled model	154.064**	114.79**	118.318**	130.181**
F-test for pooled model	2.297**	1.994**	2.059**	2.085**
Breusch–Pagan (LM) test	38.58**	15.70**	22.97**	23.10**
Hausman test	13.10	14.57	16.05	11.74
Preferred model	One-way random effects	One-way random effects	One-way random effects	One-way random effects

Notes:

[a] t-ratios are indicated in parentheses.

N = number of observations. Y = mean of dependent variable for the regression sample.

[b] Significant at 1% level,

** significant at 5% level,

[†] significant at 10% level.

Source: Barbier (2004b).

not significant in any versions of the model. Moreover, the signs of the coefficients of the significant structural variables are as expected; tropical agricultural expansion increases with agricultural export share and growth in agricultural value added, but declines with the share of permanent and arable land to total land area.

However, the regressions in Table 5.3 do not support the EKC hypothesis as an explanation of agricultural land expansion in tropical developing countries. Neither GDP per capita nor GDP per capita squared are significant explanatory variables in any versions of the model. Rural population growth is a significant explanatory variable only in the model version without institutional variables. As expected, increasing rural populations are associated with greater agricultural land expansion.

Of the regressions that include institutional variables, only the estimation with the control of corruption appears to influence agricultural land expansion. In this version of the model, not only does the control of corruption have a direct influence on land expansion but also indirectly through influencing the TOT. Also, the TOT now has both a direct influence and also an indirect one through an interaction with agricultural export share. In terms of direct effects, a TOT rise appears to spur agricultural land expansion, whereas increased (less) control of corruption slows (speeds) agricultural expansion. However, both greater corruption (i.e. a fall in the control of corruption indicator) and increased agricultural export share tend to dissipate, rather than augment, the TOT influence on agricultural expansion. Similarly, a higher TOT level tends to reduce the impacts of agricultural export share and corruption on land conversion.[10]

Both of these interaction effects have an intuitive explanation. For instance, suppose government regulations and other instruments exist to control agricultural land expansion, but if government officials are corruptible, private economic agents will bribe officials to circumvent land control policies. It follows that improved TOT and a more corruptible government will lead to higher bribes being paid for any given level of land conversion. However, if corrupt officials experience diminishing marginal utility from bribes, then the government may respond by slowing down the rate of conversion as more bribes are paid. Wunder (2003) provides another explanation of this interaction effect for some tropical countries. For example, if the TOT appreciation is due to an oil boom, then one consequence is higher rents in the oil and non-trade goods sectors. Corruptible officials will therefore be able to enrich themselves by diverting more resources away from non-oil primary product sectors, including agriculture, that are mainly responsible for deforestation. The result is again a slowing down of agricultural land expansion and forest conversion.

Equally, a rise in the TOT coupled with a higher agricultural export share will lead to greater foreign exchange earnings for any given level of land conversion. This may lead to two distinct processes to slow land conversion. First, as hypothesized by Wunder (2003), the resulting currency appreciation and simultaneous expansion of the non-trade goods sector will cause contraction in the agricultural and raw material export sector, and any resulting decline in deforestation will be larger given the importance of the latter sector to the economy.[11] In addition, increased foreign exchange may also be subject to diminishing returns, especially if there is a general increase in imported consumption, and as a result agricultural expansion may slow. The economy will be able to increase its imports, especially imported consumption goods, for a given level of agricultural land expansion. If consumers in the economy experience diminishing marginal utility of consumption of imported goods, then the result may be a decline in land conversion.

Table 5.4 indicates the total elasticity effects (or percentage changes) of the significant variables influencing tropical land conversion, including any interactions, which are evaluated at the sample regression means for the relevant variables. The most interesting results are for the regression incorporating the control for corruption indicator, which includes the interaction effects of the TOT with agricultural export share and the control of corruption. For example, a 1% rise in the TOT would have a direct impact of increasing land conversion by 1.38%. Although this elasticity effect will be moderated by any inter-action effect with agricultural export share (-0.31%), it is more than reinforced by interaction with greater control of corruption (0.70%). The result is that the total elasticity effect of a 1% rise in the TOT is an increase in land conversion by 1.77%. Equally, the moderating effect of the level of the TOT on agricultural export share suggests that a 1% increase in resource dependency may lead to only a 0.16% increase in agricultural land expansion. Finally, the interaction between the TOT and greater control of corruption may overwhelm the latter's direct influence on limiting land conversion, so that a 1% reduction in corruption may actually increase land conversion by 0.13%.

Table 5.4 Total elasticity effects

Effects[a]	No institutional variables	Control of corruption	Political stability	Rule of law
1. Terms of trade				
Terms of trade only		1.375		
Agricultural export share effect		−0.305		
Institutional variable effect		0.700		
Total effects		**1.770**		
2. Agricultural export share				
Agricultural export share only	0.364	0.463	0.390	0.297
Terms of trade effect		−0.305		
Total effects	**0.364**	**0.159**	**0.390**	**0.297**
3. Institutional variables				
Institutional variable only		−0.575		
Terms of trade effect		0.700		
Total effects		**0.125**		
4. Growth in agricultural value added	0.047	0.045	0.044	0.051
5. Rural population growth	0.329			
6. Agricultural land share	−0.303	−0.237	−0.315	−0.219

Notes:
[a] Only effects significant at 10% level or better are indicated. All effects are indicated as elasticities evaluated at the means of the respective regression samples.
Source: Barbier (2004b).

Conclusion

Much of the "frontier expansion" in low and middle-income economies consists of rapid land use change, mostly the conversion of forests, woodlands and other natural habitat to agriculture and other land-based development activities. As this chapter indicates, this is particularly the case for tropical countries. In all tropical regions of the world, deforestation is occurring at around 12 million ha per year, mainly the result of agricultural land expansion.

Previous cross-country analyses of tropical deforestation and land use change indicate that three main economic factors underlie this process: First, there may be a possible EKC relationship between deforestation and the level of economic development of tropical forest countries, such that deforestation rates will eventually decline as per capita income levels of economies increase. Second, country-by-country differences in agricultural sectors and land use patterns may be affected by certain "structural" variables, such as agricultural yield, cropland share of land area, agricultural export share, and growth in agricultural value added. Third, key institutional factors, such as corruption, political stability, the rule of law and open access frontier conditions, are also thought to influence land expansion and deforestation.

The "synthesis" cross-country analysis of agricultural land expansion of this chapter sought to investigate further the above key economic factors influencing tropical deforestation through land conversion in developing countries. Some of the significant relationships revealed by the panel analysis do suggest interesting insights, particularly in light of the overview of the role of natural resources and economic development discussed in Part One of this book.

For instance, in Chapters 1 and 4, it was suggested that economic development, especially agricultural development, in low and middle-income economies appears to be structurally dependent on frontier agricultural land expansion. This appears to be for two reasons. First, further growth in agricultural output, and in particular crop production, in many developing countries continues to require new land to be converted and brought into production. Second, frontier land expansion appears to serve as an outlet for the rural poor.

The key "structural" agricultural variables that are significant in the cross-country analysis of tropical agricultural land expansion appear to support this link between agricultural development and land conversion in poor economies. Agricultural export share, growth in agricultural value added and rural population growth are positively associated with agricultural land expansion. In contrast, the share of permanent and arable cropland in total land area is negatively associated with land conversion. Together, these two effects tell us that, if a developing economy has a sizable "reserve" or "frontier" of potential cropland available, increased conversion of this frontier land will occur as agricultural development proceeds in the economy.

The direct influence of agricultural export share and cropland expansion also suggests that greater dependency on agricultural and raw material exports in developing countries is associated with land conversion. Developing countries that are more structurally dependent on non-oil primary products for their exports are more susceptible to processes of agricultural and frontier land expansion.

However, these resource dependency effects on land conversion may depend on what happens to a country's TOT. There is some statistical evidence from the regression analysis that countries with higher TOT may reduce the resource dependency effects on land expansion. Evidence of this phenomenon is found in a study of eight tropical oil producing countries, which found that these oil countries faced fewer pressures for conversion or degradation of their forests than non-oil countries, and that forest loss was particularly less pronounced during periods of oil booms (Wunder 2003).[12] As the author points out (Wunder 2003, p. 30), the most important causal factor was "a real appreciation of the booming country's currency," and the decline in land conversion is likely to be greater given the importance of the traded non-oil primary product sector of the economy.

Corruption appears to be the only institutional factor in the cross-country regression analysis that is associated with land expansion. The direct effect is as expected; increased corruption leads to greater deforestation. However, what happens to a country's TOT may ameliorate this impact. If there is an increase in corruption, but a country has a high TOT level, then land conversion may slow down somewhat, possibly because corruptible officials experience diminishing utility from bribes as more are paid.[13]

Finally, the presence of these significant interaction effects between the TOT and corruption and primary product export dependency suggest caution in assuming that an important policy mechanism by which the rest of the world can reduce resource conversion in developing economies is through sanctions, taxation and other trade interventions that reduce the TOT of these economies. For example, our analysis suggests that such a decline in the TOT would reduce agricultural land expansion directly, but not necessarily indirectly. As Table 5.4 shows, these direct and interactive effects tend to work in opposite directions. In addition, for low and middle-income economies especially, any reduction in TOT is likely to have additional economic consequences not captured in our model, such as the loss of foreign exchange earnings that could be employed to import advanced technology and capital, or to be invested in human capital, to put the developing economy on a path that reduces its dependence on resource-based exports. Thus trade interventions may have a short-term effect of reducing resource conversion today in developing economies but the long-run consequences may be that these economies will have little opportunities to diversify away from a resource-dependent pattern of growth and trade.

Finally, the main purpose of this chapter has been to draw on economic theories and empirical evidence of the main factors behind land use change in developing countries in order to develop and test a "synthesis" model to explain agricultural land conversion across tropical developing economies. Two of the key theories emphasized in this chapter are current forest land conversion models, and the role of institutional factors in explaining deforestation. However, one key institutional factor, the prevalence of open access conditions in frontier regions, could not be included adequately in the "synthesis" panel analysis, as to date an adequate cross-country data set on property rights and land ownership conditions does not exist for developing economies. The purpose of the next chapter is to develop and present an alternative forest conversion model to explain the behavior of an economic agent who converts open access lands, and to show how this model might explain patterns of land conversion in two country case studies: agricultural land expansion in Mexico and shrimp farm expansion and mangrove loss in Thailand.

Notes

1. Throughout this chapter, the designation of countries in Latin America, Asia and Africa as "tropical" follows the classification according to the FAO's 1990 and 2000 Forest Resource Assessments (see FAO 1993 and 2001).

2. Due to changes to FAO's definition of forest cover and the incorporation of new inventory data, estimates of tropical forest cover conducted for 1990 differ in the two assessments by FAO (see FAO 1993 and 2001). In addition, as a comparison of Tables 5.1 and 5.2 indicate, more countries were added to the 2000 assessment, which of course affects the regional forest cover assessments and the estimates of deforestation. Finally the 1990 assessment used regional models driven by demographic data to generate national change rates, whereas the 2000 assessment conducted by FAO relied directly on survey reports.

3. A major problem facing cross-country analyses of deforestation is the unreliability of any international data set on forest cover. As indicated in the previous note, the FAO based its 1990 Global Forest Resource Assessment, as well as its 1995 interim assessment, on population growth projections in order to overcome an inadequate forest database for some countries and regions. Although the 2000 assessment corrected this problem by relying directly on country survey reports, FAO country forest cover data over 1990–2000 are inappropriate for cross-country analyses of deforestation that use demographic factors as explanatory variables. This in turn means that cross-country analyses that employ the FAO forest cover data since 1990 and use demographic factors as explanatory variables need to be treated with caution. An alternative source of forest area data is the FAO Production Yearbook. This includes data on forest, crop and pasture land, but does not specify land area under "closed broadleaved forest." The data are drawn from national government responses to surveys rather than using primary data sources and are generally considered to be less reliable than the Global Forest Resource Assessment data. The inappropriateness of using the FAO 1990 and 1995 assessment-based country forest cover estimates for 1990–2000 in cross-country deforestation analyses has been pointed out by Barbier and Burgess (1997) and (2001a), Cropper and Griffiths (1994) and Deacon (1999). Given the problems with recent FAO forest stock data highlighted above, some have argued that cross-country studies should concentrate on explaining agricultural land expansion, $A_{it} - A_{it-1}$, rather than deforestation across tropical countries (Barbier and Burgess 2001a).

4. Strictly speaking, deforestation is defined as (minus) the percentage change in forested area, or $(F_{it-1} - F_{it})/F_{it-1}$. However, deforestation is clearly related to the change in forest stock variable, $F_t - F_{t-1}$, in equation (5.1). In fact, various cross-country analyses have tended to use either specification as the dependent variable to represent forest loss. To simplify notation, $F_t - F_{t-1}$ is used in equation (5.1) and subsequent equations as a shorthand expression for deforestation.

5. The following synthesis model appears in Barbier (2004b).

6. Most notably, the *World Bank Development Indicators* for 1960–1999 have better coverage across countries for data on rural population growth and growth in agricultural value added, which are used in place of population growth and GDP growth from the previous analysis of Barbier and Burgess (2001a). In addition, the latter analysis did not have access to the new World Bank data set on governance indicators by Kaufmann *et al.* (1999a).

7. Further support of this interaction effect is provided by Wunder (2003), who finds evidence that an increase in an economy's TOT, principally through expansion of oil exports and price booms, might affect how other sectors, especially expansion of non-oil primary product exports, influence tropical deforestation. We discuss Wunder's hypothesis in further detail below.

8. As suggested by Baltagi (1995), including a time-invariant explanatory variable, such as the corruption index we have used, can sometimes lead to collinear regressors in a fixed effects regression. Our fixed effects regressions did not display this problem, but in general the fixed effects regressions were not very robust. Thus, as indicated by the Hausman test statistics in Table 5.3, the fixed effects regressions performed poorly compared to a random effects model. Also, as a time-invariant institutional index is in itself a "weighted" country-specific dummy variable, including the corruption index in an OLS regression will essentially imitate a fixed effects model. However, as reported in Table 5.3, our χ^2-tests and F-tests for the pooled model are highly significant, and therefore we cannot reject the hypothesis of the presence of individual effects. Given the above factors, it is not surprising that the random effects specifications always out-performed either the OLS or fixed effects models.

9. Including two or all three of the institutional indicators in the regressions often lead to collinear regressors, or to regressions that were not very robust. In addition, for our sample of tropical developing countries, these indicators prove to be highly correlated. For example, the simple pair-wise correlations between control of corruption and political stability/lack of violence and rule of law were 0.54 and 0.66 respectively.

10. For example, given the sample regression mean for the TOT variable of 113.6 and the estimated coefficients in Table 5.3, the total effects of a marginal change in agricultural export share on agricultural land expansion are $0.0437 - (0.0002539*113.6) = 0.0149$. If the TOT mean of the sample were larger, the impacts on land conversion of a marginal change in the agricultural export share would be reduced.

11. According to Wunder, this phenomenon is particularly relevant for oil producing tropical countries through a "Dutch disease" effect that

causes the oil and non-traded sectors of the economy to expand at the expense of non-oil trade sectors. In most tropical developing countries, the latter are typically agriculture, fisheries, forestry and non-oil mining, which are also the sectors most associated with forest conversion. As a consequence, a country with a large non-oil primary product export sector is likely to experience a greater slow down in forest land conversion as a result of the rising terms of trade from an oil price boom.

12. The eight countries studied by Wunder (2003) were Cameroon, Ecuador, Gabon, Indonesia, Mexico, Nigeria, Papua New Guinea and Venezuela.

13. Following the hypothesis of Wunder (2003), there may be another explanation of this interaction effect for some tropical countries. For example, if the TOT appreciation is due to an oil boom, then one consequence is higher rents in the oil and non-trade good sectors. Corruptible officials will therefore be able to enrich themselves by diverting more resources away from non-oil primary product sectors, including agriculture, that are mainly responsible for deforestation. The result is again a slowing down of agricultural land expansion and forest conversion.

6 | *The economics of land conversion*

THE previous chapter examined empirical evidence of the main factors behind land use change in developing countries. The chapter noted that many economic analyses of tropical deforestation and land conversion have emphasized the important role of institutional factors. In the "synthesis" cross-country panel analysis of agricultural land expansion in tropical countries, various institutional factors were considered, but only control of corruption appeared to be significant. However, it was also noted that one key institutional factor, the prevalence of open access conditions in frontier regions, could not be included adequately in the "synthesis" analysis, as to date an adequate cross-country data set on property rights and land ownership conditions does not exist for developing economies.

As emphasized throughout Part One of this book, the problem of open access and poorly defined property rights may have a significant influence on patterns of economic development and resource management in low and middle-income economies. One group of theories explored in Chapter 3 appears to suggest an *open access exploitation* hypothesis as an explanation of the poor economic performance of resource-dependent developing countries. According to this hypothesis, opening up trade for a developing economy dependent on open access resource exploitation or poorly defined resource rights may actually reduce welfare in that economy (Brander and Taylor 1997 and 1998a; Chichilnisky 1994; Hotte *et al.* 2000; Southey 1978). Several authors have also examined how open access conditions can lead to an "endogenous" process of property rights establishment that may lead to excessive dissipation of resource rents and less benefits for an economy (Anderson and Hill 1990; Hotte *et al.* 2000; Southey 1978). There is ample evidence in developing economies that more secure rights over natural resources, particularly land, will lead to incentives for increased investments in resource improvements and productivity (Besley 1995; Bohn and Deacon 2000; Feder and Feeny 1991; Feder and Onchan 1987). There is also counter-evidence that tenure insecurity in tropical forest frontier regions will also create the incentives for agricultural land conversion (Barbier and Burgess 2001b). Finally, Chapter 4 also cited several studies on the rent-dissipation effect of poorly defined property rights, including the breakdown of traditional common property rights regimes, in developing countries (Alston *et al.* 1999; Baland and Plateau 1996; Bromley 1989 and 1991; Deacon 1999; Ostrom 1990). That chapter noted that one principal cause of agricultural land expansion in developing economies occurs is the prevalence of poorly defined property rights in frontier regions of these economies.

Given that open access conditions and ill-defined property rights are thought to be important factors driving agricultural land expansion and forest conversion in developing countries, there needs to be developed an adequate economic model of forest land conversion under open access that can be empirically tested. The purpose of the following chapter is to illustrate one such land conversion model at the country case study level, following the approach of Barbier (2002) and Barbier and Cox (2004a). The model is based on the behavior of an economic actor who converts open access lands. Two versions of the model are developed, to contrast the role of formal and informal institutions (e.g. legal ownership rules versus traditional common property rights regimes) as constraints on the land conversion decision. The perspective on institutions adopted here follows the approach of North (1990), who defines institutions as "humanly devised constraints." The model demonstrates formally that the equilibrium level of land cleared will differ under conditions of no institutional constraints – i.e. the *pure open access* situation – compared to conditions where effective institutions exist to control land conversion. Because institutions raise the cost of land clearing, more land should be converted under pure open access. Moreover, the model is then applied to two case studies. The first case study is an empirical investigation of whether institutional constraints prevent the adjustment of the stock of converted land to the long-run equilibrium amount of land that could be cleared under open access, based on a dynamic panel analysis for agricultural planted area in Mexico at state level and over the 1960–85 period before the North American Free Trade Agreement (NAFTA) reforms were implemented.

The second case study is an empirical analysis of mangrove conversion for shrimp farming in coastal areas under pure open access conditions, based on a panel analysis of Thailand's coastal provinces over 1979–96.

Institutional constraints and forest conversion

In many tropical regions a key factor influencing deforestation is thought to be the lack of effective property rights and other institutional structures controlling access to and use of forests.[1] Where such institutions exist, they "limit" access to and conversion of forestland, thus acting as a deterrent to deforestation. In the absence of formal ownership rules, traditional common property regimes in some forested regions have also proven to be effective in controlling the open access deforestation problem (Baland and Plateau 1996; Bromley 1989 and 1991; Gibson 2001; Larson and Bromley 1990; Ostrom 1990; Richards 1997). In short, formal and informal institutions can influence the process of forest loss by imposing increased costs of conversion on farmers who clear forestland.

In this chapter we are concerned with analyzing the role of formal and informal institutions as constraints on the conversion of forestland to agriculture in developing countries. The perspective on institutions adopted here follows the approach of North (1990), who defines institutions as "humanly devised constraints that shape human interaction" and which "affect the performance of the economy by their effect on the costs of exchange and production." With this approach in mind, one can model the relationship between institutional constraints and the amount of forestland converted for use by smallholders in the following manner. First, if institutions raise the costs of land conversion, then it is possible to utilize an agricultural household model to formalize the resulting impacts on the amount of converted land used by all farming households. Moreover, the equilibrium level of land cleared will differ under conditions of no institutional constraints – i.e. the *pure open access* situation – compared to conditions where effective institutions exist to control land conversion. Because institutions raise the cost of land clearing, more land should be converted under pure open access.[2] This in turn implies that the existence of institutional constraints prevents the adjustment of the stock of converted land to the long-run equilibrium desired by agricultural households, which is the amount of land that could be cleared under open access.

The next two sections develop the two versions of the formal model of agricultural land conversion, under open access conditions and under institutional constraints governing conversion. We develop the model with the assumption that the economic agent undertaking land conversion is an agricultural household seeking to add to its existing cropland area at the expense of freely available forested land. This model is directly applicable to the case study of Mexico, where maize land expansion by peasant farmers was the main cause of forest loss in the pre-NAFTA era. However, as the Thailand case study illustrates, the same model can be applied to other processes of land conversion under open access situations, such as mangrove deforestation by commercial shrimp farms seeking to expand aquaculture areas.

A pure open access model of land conversion

The following model of land conversion is based on an approach similar to that of Cropper *et al.* (1999), López (1997 and 1998a) and Panayotou and Sungsuwan (1994). The model and the two case studies of Mexico and Thailand appear in Barbier (2002) and Barbier and Cox (2004a).

Assume that the economic behavior of all *J* rural smallholder households in the agricultural sector of a developing country can be summarized by the behavior of a representative *j*[th] household. Although the representative household is utility-maximizing, it is a price taker in both input and output markets. Farm and off-farm labor of the household are assumed to be perfect substitutes, such that the opportunity cost of the household's time (i.e. its wage rate) is determined exogenously. The household's behavior is therefore recursive, in the sense that the production decisions are made first and then the consumption decisions (Singh *et al.* 1986).

In any time period, *t*, let the profit function of the representative agricultural household's production decisions be defined as:

$$\max \pi(\,p, w, w_N) = \max_{N_j, x_j} pf(x_j, N_j) - wx_j - w_N N_j \qquad (6.1)$$

where the variable inputs include cleared land by the *j*[th] household, N_j, and a vector, x_j, of other $i, \ldots, k$ inputs (e.g., labor, fertilizer, seeds) used in production of a single agricultural output. The corresponding vector of input prices is w, and p is the price of the farm output. Finally, w_N is the rental "price" of land. If the household clears its own land from freely accessible forest, then this is an implicit price, or opportunity cost (Panayotou and Sungswuan 1994). However, if the household purchases or rents additional cleared land from a market, then w_N would be the market rental price of land (Cropper *et al.* 1999).

Utilizing Hotelling's lemma, the derived demand for cleared land by the jth household, N_j, is therefore:

$$N_j = N_j(p, w, w_N) = -\partial\pi/\partial w_N, \quad \partial N_j/\partial w_N < 0, \ \partial N_j/\partial p > 0 \quad (6.2)$$

As (6.2) is homogeneous of degree zero, it can also be rewritten as a function of relative prices, using one of the input prices, w_i, as a numeraire:

$$N_j = N_j(p/w_i, w/w_i, w_N/w_i), \ \partial N_j/\partial(w_N/w_i) < 0, \ \partial N_j/\partial(p/w_i) > 0 \quad (6.3)$$

Equations (6.2) and (6.3) depict the derived demand for cleared land by the representative j^{th} household. Assuming a common underlying technology for all rural households engaged in land clearing allows us to aggregate either relationship into the total demand for converted land by all J households. To simplify the following analysis, we will work primarily with the derived demand relationship (6.2).

In aggregating the demand for cleared land across all J agricultural households, it is important to consider other factors that may influence the aggregate level of conversion, such as income per capita, population and economy-wide policies and public investments.[3] Thus, allowing Z to represent one or more of these exogenous factors and N the aggregate demand for cleared land, the latter can be specified as:

$$N = N(p, w, w_N; Z) \quad (6.4)$$

As rural households generally provide their own supply of cleared land, N, one can view this type of supply as a kind of "production" of cleared land governed by the following conditions. The source of the cleared land (i.e. forested areas) is an open access resource, so that land is cleared up to the point where any producer surpluses (rents) generated by clearing additional land are zero.[4] The principal input into clearing land is labor, L, which is paid some exogenously determined wage rate, w_L, and the production function is assumed to be homogeneous. This production of cleared land may also be affected by a range of exogenous factors, α, that may influence the accessibility of forestland available for conversion, including roads, infrastructure, and closeness to major towns and cities.

Thus one can specify a cost function, based on the minimum cost for the rural household of producing a given level of cleared land, N, for some fixed levels of w_L and α, as:

$$C_j = C_j(w_L, N; \alpha) \tag{6.5}$$

Under open access conditions, each household will convert forest area up to the point where the total revenues gained from converting N_j units of land, $w_N N_j$, equal the total costs represented by (6.5). If a farming household clears its own land, then w_N is now the household's implicit "rental" price, or opportunity cost, of utilizing additional converted land. However, as the household is essentially supplying land to itself, then in equilibrium the implicit price ensures that the household's costs of supplying its own land will be equated with its derived demand for converted land. Then for the jth representative household the following cost conditions for supplying its own cleared land must hold:

$$w_N = c_j(w_L, N_j; \alpha), \quad \partial c_j/\partial w_L > 0,$$
$$\partial c_j/\partial N_j > 0, \quad \partial c_j/\partial \alpha < 0, \quad j = 1, \ldots, J. \tag{6.6}$$

The right-hand side of (6.6) is the average cost curve for clearing land, which may be increasing with the amount of land cleared as, among other reasons, one must venture further into the forest to clear more land (Angelsen 1999). Equation (6.6) therefore represents the equilibrium "own" supply condition for the household exploiting a pure open access resource (Freeman 2003, ch. 9). That is, in equilibrium, the household's implicit price for cleared land will be equated with its per unit costs of forest conversion, thus ensuring that any rents from clearing are dissipated. Together with the household's derived demand for converted land (6.2), equation (6.6) determines the equilibrium level of land clearing by the household as well as its implicit price. Although the latter variable is not observed, it is possible to use (6.2) and (6.6) to solve for the reduced form equation for the equilibrium level of cleared land. Substituting (6.6) for w_N in equation (6.2), and then rearranging to solve for N_j yields:

$$N_j = N_j(p, w, w_N(w_L, \alpha)),$$
$$dN_j/dw_L = \partial N_j/\partial w_L + \partial N_j/\partial w_N \partial w_N/\partial w_L, \tag{6.7}$$
$$dN_j/d\alpha = \partial N_j/\partial w_N \partial w_N/\partial \alpha > 0.$$

Aggregating (6.7) across all J households in a province or region that convert their own land, and including exogenous factors Z, leads to a reduced form relationship for the aggregate equilibrium level of cleared land:[5]

$$N^* = N(p, w_I, w_L; \alpha, Z), \quad dN/dp > 0, \quad dN/d\alpha > 0, \tag{6.8}$$

where the wage rate, w_L, is now distinguished from the vector of prices for inputs other than labor, w_I. The amount of land converted should increase with the price of output and the accessibility of forest land. However, the impact of a change in the wage rate or other input prices is ambiguous.[6]

Institutional constraints and land conversion

As discussed in the introduction, institutions can be viewed as shaping economic behavior through influencing the costs of exchange and production (North 1990). In the case of deforestation, effective formal and informal institutions may limit the ability of smallholders and others to obtain and convert forestland, thus increasing the costs of clearing compared to pure open access conditions. For example, it is straightforward to demonstrate that, if private or common property institutions enable individuals to optimally manage forest resources to supply converted land, then not only are producer surpluses being generated, but also the costs of supplying converted land will always be higher than under conditions of open access supply.

However, the conditions for establishing effective private or common property regimes to manage resources optimally in developing countries are stringent, as they involve establishing, maintaining and protecting these property rights (Baland and Platteau 1996; Ostrom 2001). It is unlikely that these conditions are met in many remote, frontier forest areas prone to agricultural conversion (Barbier and Burgess 2001b). Nevertheless, in some regions and countries, the presence of formal and informal institutions may not have led to optimal management of the supply of converted land from the forests, but they may have controlled open access exploitation by restricting land clearing and increasing the costs of conversion. If institutional constraints on forest conversion in developing countries do operate in this way, then it is straightforward to extend the model of pure open access conversion of the previous section to incorporate such impacts. This in turn can yield a testable hypothesis of the effectiveness of institutional constraints on deforestation.

Let β represent some impact of institutions on the costs of clearing land. If the presence of such effects increases the average costs of clearing, then it should follow that:

$$c_j(w_L, N_j; \alpha, \beta) > c_j(w_L, N_j; \alpha). \tag{6.9}$$

Due to the institutional constraints, β, the per unit costs of land clearing are now higher compared to pure open access conditions. Defining N^I as the aggregate amount of land cleared under the presence of such constraints, then from (6.6)–(6.8):

$$N^* > N^I = N^I(p, w, w_L; \alpha, \beta, Z). \tag{6.10}$$

The equilibrium amount of cleared land will be lower when institutional constraints are present compared to the pure open access situation.[7]

The above relationships can be used to develop a simple empirical test of whether institutional constraints may be affecting the level of agricultural-related deforestation. If D_t is the rate of deforestation caused by agricultural conversion over any time period $(t-1, t)$, then by definition $D_t = N_t - N_{t-1}$. That is, deforestation is equal to the change in the amount of agricultural land cleared and cultivated by farmers. However, equation (6.10) indicates that, if over the time period $(t-1, t)$ institutional constraints are present, then the rate of deforestation under these constraints will be less than under pure open access conditions, i.e. $D_t^I = N_t^I - N_{t-1} < D_t^* = N_t^* - N_{t-1}$. Adjustment in the level of agricultural conversion will be slower if institutional constraints raise the costs of clearing land. Assuming that the difference in the respective deforestation rates can be accounted for by some adjustment parameter, δ, it therefore follows that:

$$D_t^I = N_t^I - N_{t-1} = \delta(N_t^* - N_{t-1}) = \delta D_t^* \qquad 0 \le \delta \le 1 \tag{6.11}$$

Equation (6.11) is a basic partial adjustment model. It allows for a straightforward test of whether institutional impacts on the costs of land clearing, β, are restricting agricultural land expansion *without* having to specify the relationship between β and the amount of land cleared, N_t^I. For example, if $\delta = 1$ then this implies that institutional impacts, β, are having a negligible impact on land conversion, i.e. the actual level of land conversion is equivalent to the level under pure open access conditions, D_t^*. In contrast, $\delta = 0$ indicates that institutional constraints on land conversion are absolutely binding, and land use change is not responding to any of the factors influencing the supply and demand for cleared land, i.e. $N_t^l = N_{t-1}$. Values of δ within these two extremes will indicate the degree to which institutional impacts, β, on the costs of land clearing are "constraining" the rate of forest conversion.

Substituting equation (6.8) into (6.11) yields the partial adjustment model for cleared land. For purposes of estimation, a linear version of this model is assumed:

$$N_t^l = \delta[\gamma_0 + \gamma_1 p_t + \gamma_2 w_t + \gamma_3 w_{Lt} + \gamma_4 \alpha_t + \gamma_5 Z_t] + \lambda N_{t-1} + \delta \mu_t,$$
(6.12)

where $\lambda = 1 - \delta$ and μ_t is the error term.
Alternatively, employing the relative price specification (6.3):

$$N_t^l = \delta\left[\gamma_0 + \gamma_1 \frac{p_t}{w_{it}} + \gamma_2 \frac{w_t}{w_{it}} + \gamma_3 \frac{w_{Lt}}{w_{it}} + \gamma_4 \alpha_t + \gamma_5 Z_t\right] + \lambda N_{t-1} + \delta \mu_t,$$
(6.13)

A regression of either (6.12) or (6.13) will yield estimated coefficients $\delta\gamma_k$, which depict the adjusted impacts of the explanatory variables on land conversion under the presence of institutional constraints. The adjustment parameter δ can be calculated from the estimated value of λ. The latter value can in turn be used to derive the γ_k coefficients, which indicate the impacts of the explanatory variables under open access conditions. The regression estimates will therefore yield a direct test of the hypothesis that the presence of formal or informal institutional controls on land clearing will restrict land expansion and thus the rate of deforestation. That is, if $\lambda = (1 - \delta) > 0$, then effective institutional constraints on land clearing will reduce the rate of deforestation due to agricultural land expansion.

The next section discusses the application of the above model to the case of agricultural land expansion in Mexico during the pre-NAFTA (North American Free Trade Agreement) reform era, 1960–85.

Case study 1: agricultural land expansion in pre-NAFTA Mexico[8]

Until the early 1990s, one of the most enduring pieces of land tenure legislation in Mexico had been Article 27 of the 1917 Mexican Constitution (Brown 1997; Cornelius and Myhre 1998). Article 27 had established communal land ownership – the *ejido* – as the principal agrarian institution in rural Mexico. The *ejido* provided a framework for collectively managed, community-based land ownership. Although individual use rights of land could be assigned through a collective decision made by the community, the use rights could not be rented, sold or mortgaged. By 1991 there were 29,951 *ejidos* in Mexico accounting for 55% of the land area (Jones and Ward 1998). In addition, most of Mexico's total forest area of 49.6 million hectares (ha) was controlled by *ejidos*. Estimates suggest that as much as 70% of forested land in Mexico was owned by *ejidos*, 25% by individuals and 5% by Amerindian communities (SARH 1988; Sarukhán and Larson 2001; World Bank 1989).

Over the period 1989–94, Mexico implemented a series of major rural reforms aimed at transforming its agricultural sector to promote private investment and growth (Appendini 1998). The main impetus for such reforms was Mexico's participation in the North American Free Trade Agreement (NAFTA), although the removal of agricultural subsidies started after the 1982 debt crisis. One of the most significant NAFTA reforms were the 1992 revisions to Mexico's land tenure legislation, as enshrined in Article 27 of the 1917 Mexican Constitution.

As the *ejido* system of land management is widely believed to have been a major factor in controlling deforestation in pre-NAFTA Mexico, there are major concerns that the removal of this system of control may spur greater deforestation (Gibson 2001; Sarukhán and Larson 2001; Richards 1997). Substantial forest conversion did occur over the pre-NAFTA era, ranging from 400,000 to 1.5 million ha per year, and mainly in tropical areas (World Bank 1994). A major cause of this deforestation was the expansion of agricultural and livestock production, largely by poor rural farmers seeking new land (Barbier and Burgess 1996; Deininger and Minten 1999). Road building and timber extraction may also have contributed through "opening up" new areas of forest for encroachment by these activities.

A panel analysis conducted by Barbier and Burgess (1996) found that, prior to the NAFTA reforms, the majority of agricultural production in Mexico was essentially low input and extensive in land use, which appears to characterize much of *ejido*-based smallholder cultivation across Mexico (Brown 1997; Cornelius and Myhre 1998; World Bank 1989). A more recent study of deforestation over the 1980–90 period rejected the hypothesis that *ejido* ownership of agricultural land led to greater deforestation, leading the authors to conclude that there is little evidence that widespread communal land ownership over 1980–90 promoted increased forest conversion (Deininger and Minten 1999). To the contrary, the authors suggest that *ejido*-based communities, "valuing the safety net provided by such arrangements, have developed forms of organization capable of overcoming the 'tragedy of the commons'" (Deininger and Minten 1999, p. 334). Numerous case studies of forestry and agricultural management across Mexico and in other Latin American countries have also demonstrated the role of the *ejido* system and similar local institutional structures as a factor in controlling deforestation (Gibson 2001; Sarukhán and Larson 2001; Richards 1997).

In sum, although forest conversion to agriculture did occur during the pre-NAFTA reform era, the prevalence of *ejido* collective management of agricultural and forested lands may have deterred deforestation somewhat. During this period, such institutional constraints may have led to a lower rate of deforestation than if the remaining forested areas were under pure open access. Thus an analysis of the agricultural land expansion that occurred in Mexico during the pre-NAFTA reform period makes a relevant case study for examining the effectiveness of institutional constraints on deforestation. Such an analysis was implemented by Barbier (2002) with equation (6.13) chosen as the specification for the reduced form land conversion relationship.

The partial adjustment relationship (6.13) was estimated through a dynamic panel analysis of longitudinal data for planted agricultural area. This was applied across the thirty-one states of Mexico, plus the Federal District, and included the 1960, 1970, 1980 and 1985 time periods.[9] The latter periods coincide with the era of pre-rural reforms in Mexico, when agricultural policies were fairly stable and *ejido* ownership of agricultural and forested lands was most prevalent (Appendini 1998; Brown 1997; Jones and Ward 1998).

In the dynamic panel analysis of (6.13) the dependent variable, N^I, was agricultural area planted, which was also lagged one time period to obtain N_{t-1}. The relative price variable, p/w_i, was represented by the ratio for guaranteed maize prices to fertilizer prices, and the relative wage variable, w_L/w_i by the ratio of rural wage rates to fertilizer prices. Unfortunately, lack of data on other input prices used in agricultural production precluded the inclusion of a variable for other relative input prices, w/w_i.[10] Exogenous economic and policy factors, Z, that might also affect land clearing included population and income per capita. Exogenous factors influencing the accessibility of forested lands, α, were represented by road density.

Table 6.1 indicates the results for the random effects model, which was the preferred regression. The maize price-fertilizer ratio, population and lagged planted area are highly significant and lead to an increase in agricultural land area. The ratio of rural wage rates to fertilizer prices is also significant at the 5% level. As expected, an increase in this ratio leads to a fall in planted area. However, neither income per capita nor road density is a significant factor in explaining agricultural expansion. The negative sign of the latter variable suggests that it may be reflecting the rapid growth of urbanization in many states rather than indicating greater accessibility to frontier forest areas.

As noted, the coefficient on lagged agricultural area, $MAAP(-1)$, is both highly significant and relatively large (i.e. $\lambda = 0.868$). This implies that the null hypothesis that effective institutional constraints may have restricted the rate of land expansion cannot be rejected for the 1960–85 period in Mexico. The presence of *ejido* communal ownership of agricultural and forest lands may have exerted some degree of control on land conversion in pre-NAFTA Mexico, thus slowing down the pace of deforestation compared to pure open access conditions.[11]

The possible impacts of this effect are indicated by a comparison of the "adjusted" and "unadjusted parameter" and elasticity estimates depicted in Table 6.1. As the table shows, the adjusted responses of planted area to the key explanatory factors are significantly lower than the unadjusted estimates. This is particularly striking for the three significant variables in the regression: the maize-fertilizer price ratio, the wage-fertilizer price ratio and population. For example, the maize-fertilizer price ratio clearly had the largest impact on agricultural land use in pre-NAFTA Mexico. However, whereas the adjusted elasticity indicates that a 10% increase in the price ratio over this period caused a 11.5% increase in agricultural area planted, the $>$ unadjusted $=$ response would have been a 87% increase in agricultural land use. Compared to

Table 6.1 Mexico – random effects estimation of agricultural land expansion, 1960–85

	Dependent variable: Agricultural area planted ('000 ha)			
Explanatory variables[a]	Adjusted parameter estimates $(\delta\gamma_k)^a$	Adjusted elasticity estimates	Unadjusted parameter estimates (γ_k)	Unadjusted elasticity estimates
Maize-fertilizer price ratio (Mexican pesos (MEX$)/metric ton)	628.71 (2.995)**	1.1477	4,765.12	8.6986
Rural wage-fertilizer price ratio (MEX$/ day per MEX$/kg)	− 10,512 (− 1.986)*	− 0.4642	− 79,673	− 3.5184
Population ('000 persons)	0.025 (2.501)**	0.0943	0.19	0.7146
Income per capita (MEX$/ population)	− 0.0049 (− 1.540)	−0.0938	−0.04	−0.7106
Road density (Km/ha)	− 23.724 (− 1.593)	−0.0617	−179.81	−0.4676
Lagged agricultural area planted (lagged one period, initial period 1960)	0.8681 (17.612)**	–	–	–
Constant	−210.56 (−2.012)*	–	–	–

Estimated $\delta = 1 - \lambda = 0.1319$
Notes:
[a] t-ratios are indicated in parentheses.
** Significant at 1% level.
* Significant at 5% level.
Source: Barbier (2002).

pure open access conditions, *ejido* land management may therefore have mitigated considerably the incentives for farmers to convert forestland to agriculture in response to any increases in the maize-fertilizer price ratio during the pre-NAFTA period. Similar comparisons can be made for the influence of the wage-fertilizer price ratio and population on planted area. The adjusted response to a 10% rise in the wage-fertilizer price ratio over 1960–85 was a fall in agricultural area of 4.6%. In contrast, the unadjusted response would have been a decrease in agricultural land use of 35.2%. A 10% increase in population leads an adjusted 0.9% rise in planted area, whereas the unadjusted increase is 7.1%.

These regression results are also consistent with the theoretical model of smallholder land conversion. By far the largest, significant influence on agricultural land expansion in pre-NAFTA Mexico was the maize-fertilizer price ratio, followed by the wage-fertilizer price ratio and then population. As noted, smallholder farming in Mexico over 1960–85 was characterized by low agricultural productivity, predominantly maize-based and dependent largely on unskilled farm labor and land as its main inputs (Brown 1997; Cornelius and Myrhe 1998; World Bank 1989). Although subsidies helped to increase the use of fertilizers among farmers, these inputs tended to be underutilized, especially by poorer smallholders. Thus a rising maize-fertilizer price ratio would effectively represent greater returns to smallholder production, leading to more land being converted and brought into cultivation. Equally, an increasing population would mean more farming households and laborers, causing a further increase in the demand for agricultural land. Finally, a rise in the price of labor relative to fertilizer reduces both cultivated area and land conversion, suggesting that land is being substituted for labor in cultivation.

Although changes in the maize-fertilizer price ratio, the wage-fertilizer price ratio and population are important factors influencing forest conversion in pre-NAFTA Mexico, Table 6.1 indicates that such impacts may have been mitigated by the effective controls on land use and ownership by *ejido* collective management compared to pure open access conditions. The key issue is, of course, whether or not the 1989–94 rural reforms in Mexico – and principally the 1992 reforms of *ejido* land ownership – have affected any such institutional constraints on land conversion in the post-NAFTA era.

As summarized by Barbier (2002), there remains a degree of institutional control of forest conversion by smallholders in rural Mexico.

Forested lands continue to be held and managed collectively by *ejidos*, and there is very little evidence that the parcelling of communal agricultural land into individual plots has resulted so far in greater levels of forest conversion. Nevertheless, the widespread changes in institutional arrangements ushered in by the 1992 land tenure reforms are likely to have some influence on the rate of forest land conversion, although it may be some while yet before the effects on conversion can be detected. In addition, other NAFTA reforms and structural changes in the Mexican economy and agricultural sector will certainly also have affected agricultural land conversion (Barbier and Burgess 1996). The latter incentive effects could be considerable, and they may make it difficult to determine the impacts of the recent institutional changes on land conversion. Possibly the greatest concern for the future is what might happen to forested lands if more and more *ejidos* are dissolved or become increasingly ineffective in managing land collectively. Although legally the forest land will revert to state ownership, public authorities may have a great deal of difficulty in enforcing control of forest conversion. Throughout Latin America, the inability of central and regional governments to control illegal land clearing, squatting and land ownership disputes in remote frontier areas is not an encouraging precedent. If this occurs on a large enough scale, then the open access model of land conversion by smallholders may become a more appropriate description of the process of deforestation in rural Mexico.

Case study 2: shrimp farm expansion and mangrove loss in Thailand[12]

The issue of coastal land conversion for commercial shrimp farming is a highly debated and controversial topic in Thailand. Frozen shrimps are a major export product of Thailand, earning more than US$1.6 billion each year, and the government has been keen to expand these exports (Barbier and Sathirathai 2004; Tokrisna 1998). Yet, expansion of shrimp exports has caused much devastation to Thailand's coastline and has impacted other valuable commercial sectors, such as fisheries.

Thailand's coastline is vast, stretching for 2,815 kilometers (km), of which 1,878 km is on the Gulf of Thailand and 937 km on the Andaman Sea (Indian Ocean) (Kaosa-ard and Pednekar 1998). In recent decades, the expansion of intensive shrimp farming in the coastal areas of Southern Thailand has led to rapid conversion of mangroves (Barbier and Sathirathai 2004). The rate of mangrove deforestation slowed in the 1990s, but in the mid-1990s the annual loss was estimated to be around 3,000 ha/year (Sathirathai 1998).

Although mangrove conversion for aquaculture began in Thailand as early as 1974, the boom in intensive shrimp farming through mangrove clearing took off in 1985 when the increasing demand for shrimps in Japan pushed up the border-equivalent price to US$100 per kilogram (kg) (Barbier and Sathirathai 2004). For example, from 1981–85 in Thailand, annual shrimp production through aquaculture was around 15 thousand metric tons (KMT), but by 1991 it had risen to over 162 KMT and by 1994 to over 264 KMT (Kaosa-ard and Pednekar 1998).

Shrimp farm area has expanded from 31,906 ha to 66,027 ha between 1983 and 1996. A more startling figure is the increase in the number of farms during that period, from 3,779 to 21,917. In general, this reflects a rapid shift from more extensive to more small-scale, intensive and highly productive aquaculture systems of on average 2–3 ponds with each pond comprising up to 1 hectare (ha) in size (Goss *et al.* 2001; Kongkeo 1997; Tokrisna 1998). However, much of the semi-intensive and intensive shrimp farming in Thailand is short term and unsustainable, i.e. water quality and disease problems mean that yields decline rapidly and farms are routinely abandoned after 5–6 years of production (Dierberg and Kiattisimkul 1996; Flaherty and Karnjanakesorn 1995; Thongrak *et al.* 1997; Tokrisna 1998; Vandergeest *et al.* 1999).

Although shrimp farm expansion has slowed in recent years, unsustainable production methods and lack of know-how have meant that more expansion still takes place every year simply to replace unproductive and abandoned farms. Estimates of the amount of mangrove conversion due to shrimp farming vary, but recent studies suggest that up to 50–65% of Thailand's mangroves have been lost to shrimp farm conversion since 1975 (Dierberg and Kiattisimkul 1996; Tokrisna 1998). In provinces close to Bangkok, such as Chanthaburi, mangrove areas have been devastated by shrimp farm developments (Raine 1994). More recently, Thailand's shrimp output has been maintained by the expansion of shrimp farming activities to the far Southern and Eastern parts of the Gulf of Thailand, and across to the Andaman Sea (Indian Ocean) Coast (Flaherty and Karnjanakesorn 1995; Sathirathai 1998; Vandergeest *et al.* 1999).

Moreover, conversion of mangroves by shrimp farm is irreversible. Without careful ecosystem restoration and manual replanting efforts, mangroves do not regenerate even in abandoned shrimp farm areas. In Thailand, most of the estimated 11,000 or more hectares (ha) of replanted areas over 1991–95 have occurred on previously unvegetated tidal mudflats (Lewis *et al.* 2000). Such "afforestation" efforts have been strongly criticized as being ecologically unsound (Erftemeijer and Lewis 2000; Stevenson *et al.* 1999). However, more recent efforts at mangrove replanting in Southern Thailand have focused on ecological restoration of mangrove areas destroyed by both legal and illegal shrimp ponds, although the total area restored is very small relative to the natural mangrove forest area that has been converted (Lewis *et al.* 2000). Currently in Thailand there is no legal requirement that shrimp farm owners invest in replanting and restoring mangroves, once farming operations have ceased and the ponds are abandoned. Shrimp farming does not necessarily have to pose any environmental threat, provided that wastewater from the farm has been treated before being released. In addition, it is possible to design shrimp aquaculture systems in coastal areas that do not involve removal of vegetation and areas naturally fed by tidal conditions. However, the establishment of these farm systems is too expensive for the type of small-scale pond operations found in much of Thailand, which are dependent on highly intensive and untreated systems through rapid conversion of mangrove and coastal resources (Thongrak *et al.* 1997; Tokrisna 1998). Much of the financial investment in coastal shrimp farms is from wealthy individual investors and business enterprises from outside of the local community (Flaherty and Karnjanakesorn 1995; Goss *et al.* 2000 and 2001). Although some hiring of local labor occurs, in the past shrimp farm owners have tended to hire Burmese workers as their wage rates are much lower.

Ill-defined property rights have accelerated the rapid conversion of mangroves to shrimp farms in Thailand. Historically, this has been a common problem for all forested areas in Thailand (Feder *et al.* 1988; Feeny 1988, Feeny 2002; Thomson *et al.* 1992). Although the state through the Royal Forestry Department ostensibly owns and controls mangrove areas, in practice they are *de facto* open access areas onto which anyone can encroach. This has had three impacts on mangrove deforestation attributable to shrimp farms. First, the open access conditions have allowed illegal occupation of mangrove areas for establishing shrimp farms, in response to the rising prices and profits from shrimp aquaculture (Barbier and Sathirathai 2004).[13] Second, in Thailand insecure property rights in cleared forest areas have been associated with under-investment in land quality and farm productivity (Feder *et al.* 1987 and 1988; Feeny 1988 and Thomson *et al.* 1992). The lack of tenure security for shrimp farms in Southern Thailand appears also to be a major factor in the lack of investment in improving productivity and adopting better aquaculture methods, leading to more mangrove areas being cleared than necessary (Barbier and Sathirathai 2004). Third, several studies have pointed out how open access forest lands in Thailand are more vulnerable to rapid deforestation and conversion to agricultural and other commercial uses as the development of roads and the highway network make these lands more "accessible"(Cropper *et al.* 1999; Feeny 2002). Similar problems exist for the open access coastal mangrove areas in Southern Thailand. In particular, the geographical "spread" of shrimp farm expansion and accompanying mangrove deforestation has also proceeded from the more to less accessible areas: initially in the coastal provinces near Bangkok, spreading down the southern Gulf of Thailand Coast towards Malaysia, and more recently beginning on the Andaman Sea (Indian Ocean) Coast (Flaherty and Karnjanakesorn 1995; Raine 1994; Sathirathai 1998; Vandergeest *et al.* 1999).

Despite the lack of secure property rights and the frequently illegal occupation of mangrove areas, owners have an incentive to register their shrimp farms and converted land with the Department of Fisheries. In doing so, the farms become eligible for the preferential subsidies for key production inputs, such as shrimp larvae, chemicals and machinery, and for preferential commercial loans for land clearing and pond establishment (Tokrisna 1998; Barbier and Sathirathai 2004). Such subsidies inflate artificially the commercial profitability of shrimp farming, thus leading to more mangrove conversion, even though estimates of the economic returns to shrimp aquaculture in Thailand suggest that such conversion is not always justified (Sathirathai and Barbier 2001). Combined with insecure property rights, the subsidies also put further emphasis on shrimp aquaculture as a commercial activity for short-term exploitative financial gains rather than a long-term sustainable activity.

If shrimp farm expansion is a major cause of mangrove deforestation, then the resulting mangrove loss in any period, r_t, is directly related to the amount of land area converted by shrimp farms, i.e.

$$M_{t-1} - M_t = r_t = N_t - N_{t-1} \qquad (6.14)$$

where M represents mangrove area, and N is the amount of land cleared and used for shrimp farming. Equation (6.14) states that the land available for shrimp farming in the current period, N_t, equals the amount of productive land left over from a previous period, N_{t-1}, plus any newly cleared land, r_t. Equally, the decline in mangroves between the current and previous periods $M_{t-1} - M_t$, equals the amount of land newly converted for shrimp farming, r_t.

Equation (6.14) implies a direct link between mangrove deforestation and land conversion for shrimp farm area expansion, with the latter activity determined by the commercial profitability of aquaculture operations. For a relatively long time period $[t, t-1]$, it is possible to establish this link formally.[14] In equation (6.14), let M_{t-1} represent the amount of mangrove area available in a previous period before much shrimp farming has occurred. Thus compared to the current period, t, in the previous period, $t-1$, mangrove area will be relatively abundant, and very little of it will have been cleared for shrimp farming, i.e. $\frac{N_{t-1}}{M_{t-1}} \approx 0$. Thus dividing equation (6.14) by M_{t-1} we obtain:

$$\frac{M_{t-1} - M_t}{M_{t-1}} = \frac{N_t - N_{t-1}}{M_{t-1}} = \frac{N_t}{M_{t-1}}. \tag{6.15}$$

The left-hand side of (6.15) is a measure of the long-run proportionate change in mangrove area. It therefore represents a long-run indicator of *mangrove loss*. The right-hand side of (6.15) is the ratio of current shrimp farm area to mangrove area in a previous base period. It therefore represents a long-run indicator of *relative shrimp farm area expansion*.

Returning to the pure open access model of land clearing, recall equation (6.8), which defines an equilibrium reduced-form relationship between current shrimp farm area, N_t^*, and the output and input prices for shrimp farming, the accessibility of mangrove areas, and other economic and demographic factors:

$$N^* = N(p, w_I, w_L; \alpha, Z), \quad dN/dp > 0, \; dN/d\alpha > 0, \tag{6.8}$$

Thus it follows from condition (6.15) that our long-run indicator of relative shrimp farm area expansion, N_t/M_{t-1}, will also be determined by equation (6.8). As equation (6.15) suggests that our long-run indicators of mangrove loss and shrimp farm expansion are equivalent, then our measure of long-run mangrove loss, $M_{t-1} - M_t/M_{t-1}$, is also determined by (6.8). Thus both indicators of mangrove loss and shrimp farm expansion can be estimated, using appropriate data for the shrimp output price, p, the wage rate, w_L, other input prices, w_I, the "accessibility" of mangrove areas, α, and other economic and demographic factors that may affect the mangrove clearing decision, Z.

Alternatively, if the household-derived demand relationship (6.3) was used with (6.6) to solve for the reduced-form level of land conversion, N_j^*, then the aggregate land conversion relationship (6.8) would be specified in relative prices, i.e.

$$N^* = N(p/w_i, w/w_i, w_N/w_i; \alpha, Z). \qquad (6.16)$$

The relative-price relationship for land conversion (6.16) was estimated through dynamic panel analysis across twenty-one coastal provinces of Thailand and over 1979–96.[15] As is clear from (6.15), to use either our mangrove loss or shrimp farm expansion indicators as a dependent variable requires first choosing an appropriate base year for mangrove area, M_{t-1}. We chose 1979 as the base year for two reasons. First, both economic and mangrove data in Thailand prior to that date were not complete for all coastal provinces, and second, even though shrimp farming began prior to 1979, the major period of shrimp farm establishment and expansion in Thailand occurred over 1979–96. Thus, the dependent variable for mangrove loss, $(M_{t-1} - M_t / M_{t-1})$, is the proportion of mangrove area cleared relative to the 1979 area of mangroves, $[(M_{1979} - M_t)/M_{1979}]$, and the dependent variable for relative shrimp farm expansion, (N_t/M_{t-1}), is the proportion of shrimp farm area in the current year relative to 1979 mangrove area, $[S_t/M_{1979}]$.

Output price, p, in equation (6.16) was represented by the provincial price of shrimp in Thai baht/ton.[16] The two input prices chosen for w_L and w_I, respectively, were the minimum provincial wage and the price of ammonium phosphate. The latter is a proxy for the price of feed used in shrimp aquaculture, with which it is highly correlated (Thongrak *et al.* 1997). To estimate (6.16), these output and input prices were expressed in terms of relative prices with respect to the minimum wage. The distance of each province from Bangkok was included as the measure of the "accessibility" of provincial mangrove resources, α. Finally, several exogenous factors, Z, were chosen to represent both economic effects and demographic changes at the provincial level that might influence mangrove conversion: gross provincial product per capita (GPP), population growth, and the number of shrimp farms per total provincial land area.[17]

Table 6.2 shows the results of random effects estimations for the mangrove loss regression and for two versions of the shrimp farm expansion regressions, one with shrimp farm density and one without.[18]

The results reported for mangrove loss in Table 6.2 show that all variables have the predicted signs. In addition, the only explanatory variable that has no significant impact on long-run mangrove loss in Thailand is shrimp farm density. The relative price of shrimp has a significant and positive effect on mangrove deforestation across the coastal provinces of Thailand, whereas mangrove loss declines for those coastal provinces that are further from Bangkok. A rise in the relative feed price has a significant and negative impact on long-run mangrove loss. Provincial economic development (represented by GPP) causes mangrove deforestation, as does population growth, although the latter variable is significant only at the 10% level.

The two regressions for relative shrimp farm area expansion in Thailand vary little with respect to the sign and significance of the coefficients of three main variables: relative shrimp price, relative feed price and the accessibility of mangrove areas. All three variables are significant and have the predicted signs (see Table 6.2). Shrimp farm area expansion increases with the relative price of shrimp, but declines with the relative feed price and for those coastal provinces further from Bangkok. Population growth is significant in explaining relative shrimp farm expansion in both regressions, but only at the 10% level in the estimation that excludes shrimp farm density. Provincial economic development has a significant and negative impact on shrimp farm expansion in the regression that includes shrimp farm density, but is insignificant in the estimation without it. Finally, shrimp farm density appears to be a significant factor in shrimp farm expansion, but this variable might be endogenous in the regression.[19]

The panel analysis regressions of mangrove loss and relative shrimp farm area expansion reported in Table 6.2 are therefore consistent with the theoretical model of "open access" land conversion developed above. Further insights into the causes of mangrove loss and shrimp farm expansion can be gained from the estimated elasticities, which are indicated in Table 6.3.

The variables with the largest impacts on mangrove loss are distance from Bangkok and the price of ammonium phosphate, followed by the minimum wage, shrimp price, gross provincial product per capita (GPP) and population growth. In both regressions of relative shrimp

Table 6.2 Thailand – random effects estimation of mangrove loss and shrimp farm area expansion, 1979–96

	% Mangrove area cleared relative to 1979 $(M_{1979}-M_t)/M_{1979}$	% Shrimp farm area relative to 1979 mangrove area S_t/M_{1979}	% Shrimp farm area relative to 1979 mangrove area S_t/M_{1979}
Shrimp price-wage ratio (Thai Baht (B)/kg per B/day)	4.081×10^{-2} (5.524)**	1.795×10^{-1} (4.941)**	2.089×10^{-1} (3.769)**
Fertilizer price-wage ratio (B/kg per B/day)	-2.620×10^{-3} (−6.982)**	-8.102×10^{-3} (−7.244)**	-9.031×10^{-3} (−5.313)**
Distance of province from Bangkok (km)	-5.013×10^{-4} (−3.314)**	-1.331×10^{-3} (−2.033)*	-1.681×10^{-3} (−2.316)*
Population growth (%/year)	5.808×10^{-7} (1.769)†	5.915×10^{-6} (2.431)*	6.548×10^{-6} (1.741)†
Gross provincial product per capita (B/person)	8.466×10^{-7} (2.428)*	-2.875×10^{-6} (−2.587)**	-1.546×10^{-6} (−0.919)
Shrimp farm density (Farms/km^2)	1.071×10^{-3} (0.945)	2.380×10^{-2} (5.086)**	–
CONSTANT	0.773 (7.882)**	1.536 (3.715)**	1.780 (3.733)**

Notes:
t-ratios are indicated in parentheses.
** Significant at 1% level.
* Significant at 5% level.
† Significant at 10% level.
Source: Barbier and Cox (2004a).

Table 6.3 Thailand – estimated elasticities for mangrove loss and shrimp farm area expansion, 1979–96

Explanatory variables	% Mangrove area cleared relative to 1979 $(M_{1979}-M_t)/M_{1979}$	% Shrimp farm area relative to 1979 mangrove area S_t/M_{1979}	% Shrimp farm area relative to 1979 mangrove area S_t/M_{1979}
Shrimp price-wage ratio (Thai Baht (B)/kg per B/day)	0.158**	0.402**	0.468**
Shrimp price (B/kg)	0.156**	0.397**	0.462**
Wage rate (B/day)	0.302**	0.421**	0.450**
Fertilizer price-wage ratio (B/kg per B/day)	−0.460**	−0.824**	−0.918**
Fertilizer price (B/kg)	−0.445**	−0.796**	−0.887**
Distance of province from Bangkok (km)	−0.626**	−0.963*	−1.216*
Population growth (%/year)	0.014†	0.080*	0.089†
Gross provincial product per capita (B/person)	0.097*	−0.190**	−0.103
Shrimp farm density (Farms/km²)	0.014	0.185**	−

Notes:
** Significant at 1% level.
* Significant at 5% level.
† Significant at 10% level.

Source: Barbier and Cox (2004a).

farm area expansion, the variables with the largest effects are again distance from Bangkok and ammonium phosphate price, followed by the minimum wage and shrimp price.[20] In the estimation that includes shrimp farm density, the remaining impacts are attributed to GPP, shrimp farm density and population growth. In the estimation that excludes shrimp farm density, only population growth has a modest, but barely significant, impact on shrimp farm expansion. As expected, the effects of changes in the explanatory variables on relative shrimp farm expansion are always greater than on mangrove loss.[21]

Overall, these results reaffirm the hypothesis that the profitability of shrimp farming, coupled with "open access" land conversion decisions, is a very important underlying cause of mangrove deforestation in Thailand. Intensive shrimp farming utilizes considerable amounts of feed, the costs of which represent anywhere from 30–60% of the total costs of shrimp aquaculture in various systems across Thailand (Kongkeo 1997; Thongkrak *et al.* 1997; Tokrisna 1998). Thus it is not surprising that a change in the price of ammonium phosphate – our proxy for feed price – causes a relatively large impact on shrimp farm expansion and mangrove clearing. As indicated in Table 6.3, if ammonium phosphate and thus feed prices across Thailand were to rise by 10%, then the relative decline in shrimp farm area would be 8–9% and mangrove clearing would decrease by around 4.5%. Our results indicate that shrimp farm area expansion and mangrove loss are also responsive to changes in the price of shrimp. As discussed above, expansion of shrimp farming in Thailand has occurred rapidly since 1985, which was when a rapid rise in world demand and prices for shrimp occurred. The elasticity estimates suggest that if the price of shrimp were to rise by 10%, then relative shrimp farm area would increase by 4–5% and mangrove deforestation would expand by 1.6%.

The analysis also confirms that the "accessibility" of mangrove areas is an important determinant of mangrove clearing for shrimp farming in Thailand. This is an expected result, given that Bangkok is the major domestic market as well as the key port and terminus for both Thailand's export market and many regional domestic markets. In addition, many investors in shrimp farming operations are from outside of the coastal provinces, and in particular from Bangkok. The elasticity estimates suggest that coastal areas that are 10% further from Bangkok have 10–12% less relative shrimp farm area and have

6.3% lower mangrove clearing rates. Distance from Bangkok appears to be an important factor determining the accessibility of coastal resources, the profitability of shrimp farming and therefore mangrove conversion. The historical pattern of mangrove loss in Thailand is consistent with this result. Mangrove deforestation began initially in the coastal provinces near Bangkok, spread down the southern Gulf of Thailand Coast towards Malaysia and is now beginning on the Andaman Sea (Indian Ocean) Coast (Flaherty and Karnjanakesorn 1995; Raine 1994; Sathirathai 1998).

Table 6.3 indicates that the provincial minimum wage variable has a positive elasticity in the panel regressions. A 10% rise in the rural minimum wage causes relative shrimp farm area to increase by over 4% and mangrove clearing by 3%.[22] As discussed above, our theoretical model would suggest that the amount of mangrove land converted should decrease with the cost of labor, which is the principal input involved in clearing operations, but this effect may be counteracted by an opposite impact of a rise in the wage rate on mangrove conversion, if land and labor are substitutes in shrimp farming. Our elasticity results suggest that this latter substitution effect might be the stronger influence. As the costs of labor use in production rise, shrimp farmers may be induced to move from more intensive aquaculture operations that employ relatively more labor than land to more semi-intensive and extensive systems that require relatively more land. For example, in Thailand extensive shrimp farms (5–7 ha) have average labor costs of only US$36.1/ha, semi-intensive farms (3–4 ha) have labor costs of US$96.6/ha and intensive farms (2–3 ha) have labor costs of US$377.5/ha (Tokrisna 1998). Thus, a rise in wages may lead some shrimp farmers to expand shrimp farm area and switch to less intensive operations in order to save on overall labor costs (Goss *et al.* 2001).[23]

Shrimp farm expansion and mangrove loss may also be influenced somewhat by demographic pressures, such as provincial population change, although the significance of this impact is weak in two of the three regressions (see Tables 6.2 and 6.3). A 10% rise in population growth will cause shrimp farm area to expand by 0.8–0.9%, and mangrove clearing also increases by 0.1%.

A 10% rise in gross provincial product per capita increases mangrove loss by about 1% but the impact of GPP on relative shrimp farm area is less clear, given the possible problem of the endogeneity of shrimp farm density in the regressions of shrimp farm expansion (see

Tables 6.2 and 6.3). As noted above, mangrove loss is increasingly occurring in coastal areas due to provincial economic development activities other than shrimp farming, such as urbanization, agriculture, tourism and industrialization (Dierberg and Kiattisimkul 1996; Tokrisna 1998).[24] Such coastal economic developments are likely to lead to increases in gross provincial product per capita while at the same time putting greater pressure on remaining mangrove areas.

To summarize, this case study provides strong evidence that our "open access" land conversion model applies to shrimp farm expansion and mangrove loss in Thailand over 1979–96. However, several recent developments could greatly influence the future impacts of shrimp farming on mangrove conversion in Southern Thailand.

First, the availability of new mangrove areas suitable for conversion to shrimp farming is becoming increasingly scarce. Of the 62,800 ha of mangrove areas considered suitable for shrimp farms in 1977, between 38% and 65% were already converted by shrimp farms between 1975 and 1993 (Dierberg and Kiattisimkul 1996). Thus expansion of shrimp farms is increasingly occurring on coastal land formerly used for rubber and palm plantations and, until the recent ban, in rice paddy areas.

Second, it is still too early to gauge the effect of the ban on shrimp farming in the rice and fruit growing areas in the Central Region of Thailand. One result is likely to be greater conversion of remaining areas of coastal mangrove forests, especially the remaining pristine mangrove on the Andaman (Indian Ocean) Coast. On the other hand, to prevent this from happening, recent policy initiatives have been proposed to promote the conservation of mangroves and the participation of local communities in their management (Sathirathai 1998). For example, the Royal Forestry Department is considering banning mangrove forest concessions and regulating the use of mangrove areas, particularly those affected by shrimp farming. Furthermore, new legislation on community management of forests has been introduced, which offers the hope that the right of local communities to protect mangrove forests may receive legal recognition. The motivation for this potential change in policy arises from the recognition that the economic benefits of mangroves to local communities may be substantial, and could possibly even outweigh the returns to intensive shrimp farming that lead to mangrove conversion.

However, if Thailand is to become a model for reconciling shrimp farm production with coastal mangrove management, then this study points to two clear policy recommendations beyond what is currently being considered by the government. First, there is an urgent need to address the main *institutional failure* concerning management of mangrove resources. The present law and formal institutional structures of resource management in Thailand do not allow coastal communities to establish and enforce their local rules effectively. Nor do the current formal institutions and laws provide the incentives necessary for local and other resource user groups to resolve conflicts among themselves. The result is that any effort to resolve such conflicts incurs high risk and management costs, which in turn make it even harder for the successful establishment of collaborative resource management systems by local communities. There is also a need to address the main *policy failure* at the heart of the economic incentives for excessive conversion of mangrove areas to shrimp aquaculture. As long as government policies continue to subsidize shrimp farm establishment and production, then this activity will remain financially profitable to the commercial investor. The result is that the commercial pressure to convert mangroves and other coastal land to shrimp farming will remain, even though the actual economic returns to such investments may not always justify such conversion (Sathirathai and Barbier 2001).

For example, a new institutional framework for coastal mangrove management in Thailand might contain the following features (Barbier and Sathirathai 2004, ch. 12). First, remaining mangrove areas should be designated into conservation (i.e. preservation) and economic zones. Shrimp farming and other extractive commercial uses (e.g., wood concessions) should be restricted to the economic zones only. However, local communities who depend on the collection of forest and fishery products from mangrove forests should be allowed access to both zones, as long as such harvesting activities are conducted on a sustainable basis. Second, the establishment of community mangrove forests should also occur in both the economic and conservation zones. But the decision to allow such local management efforts should be based on the capability of communities to effectively enforce their local rules and manage the forest sustainably. Moreover, such community rights should not involve full ownership of the forest but be in the form of user rights. Third, the community mangrove forests should be co-managed by the government and local communities. Such effective co-management will require the active participation of existing coastal community organizations, and will allow the representatives of such organizations to have the right to express opinions and make decisions regarding the management plan and regulations related to the utilization of mangrove resources. Finally, the government must provide technical, educational and financial support for the local community organizations participating in managing the mangrove forests. For example, if only user rights (but not full ownership rights) are granted to local communities, then the latter's access to formal credit markets for initiatives such as investment in mangrove conservation and replanting may be restricted. The government may need to provide special lines of credit to support such community-based activities.[25]

If successful, such local management policies might act as effectively combined formal and informal "institutional constraints" on mangrove loss due to shrimp farm expansion in Thailand. As the model of land conversion developed in this chapter suggests, the result should be to slow down the rate of conversion. It may also lead to more efficient land use, including selection of the most appropriate mangrove areas for conversion to shrimp farms.

Final remarks

This chapter was concerned with analyzing the role of formal and informal institutions as constraints on the conversion of forestland to agriculture within a developing country. Given that open access conditions and ill-defined property rights are thought to be important factors driving agricultural land expansion and forest conversion in developing countries, we have developed an economic model of forest land conversion under open access that is empirically tested.

The model demonstrates formally that the equilibrium level of land cleared will differ under conditions of no institutional "constraints" – i.e. the *pure open access* situation – compared to conditions where effective institutions exist to control land conversion. Because institutions raise the cost of land clearing, more land should be converted under pure open access. This means that, where one believes institutional "constraints" on land conversion to exist, a simple test for this constraining effect can be derived using a partial adjustment mechanism for the equilibrium level of cleared land.

The first case study of Mexico was an empirical investigation of whether institutional constraints prevent the adjustment of the stock of converted land to the long run equilibrium amount of land that could be cleared under open access, based on a dynamic panel analysis for agricultural planted area in Mexico at state level and over the 1960–85 period before the North American Free Trade Agreement (NAFTA) reforms were implemented. In this case study, the presence of *ejido* communal land management was thought to act as the main "institutional constraint" on deforestation due to maize land expansion.

The second case study is an empirical analysis of mangrove conversion for shrimp farming in coastal areas under pure open access conditions, based on a panel analysis of Thailand's coastal provinces over 1979–96. The results suggest that the profitability of shrimp farming coupled with open access availability of mangrove areas in accessible coastal areas were powerful factors driving mangrove deforestation in Southern Thailand. Perhaps what is needed in Thailand is for the introduction of "institutional constraints" to slow down mangrove loss in coastal areas, through combining effective local community and government management of the resource.

Notes

1. In addition to Chapter 5, see Barbier and Burgess (2001a), Brown and Pearce (1994), FAO (1997), Kaimowitz and Angelsen (1998) and van Kooten *et al.* 1999 for recent reviews of the role of the lack of effective property rights in tropical deforestation.
2. However, formal and informal institutions governing agricultural land ownership and expansion are not uniform across developing countries or even within the same country (Baland and Platteau 1996; Burger *et al.* 2001; López 1998b). As will become clear, the following analysis is capable of only assessing two equilibrium situations: one with the presence of institutions that are effective in controlling or limiting forest conversion and one where open access prevails. Although it may be the case that a state with effective institutions may cause less deforestation than a state without, it is also possible that the transition path from a pure open access situation to a state in which effective institutions are established may result in increased deforestation during this transition period. For some possible examples, see López (1998b).
3. For reviews of relevant empirical studies, see Barbier and Burgess (2001a), Brown and Pearce (1994), Kaimowitz and Angelsen (1998), van Kooten *et al.* (1999) and Chapter 5. The assumptions as to how exogenous "macroeconomic" factors influence the aggregate demand for cleared land vary

across the different studies. For example, to derive the aggregate demand for cleared land, Cropper *et al.* (1999) multiply the household demand by the total number of agricultural households. The latter is assumed to be endogenously determined, with one of its explanatory variables being non-agricultural income. In contrast, Barbier and Burgess (1997) and Panayotou and Sungsuwan (1994) simply assume that the aggregate demand equation for cleared land includes both a population variable and income per capita as additional exogenous factors in the demand relationship.

4. The assumption that open access conditions prevail in "accessible" forest areas implies that, if there are any rents or producer surpluses generated from clearing land, then others attracted by these profits will enter the forest to clear land as well. In equilibrium, any rents will then be dissipated, and thus each individual will clear land up to the point where total revenues equal total costs. This assumption is common in bioeconomic models of unregulated open access resources, in particular fisheries (see Freeman 1993, ch. 9 and Heal 1982 for reviews).

5. Note that if the household derived demand relationship (6.3) was used with (6.6) to solve for the reduced form level of land conversion, Nj^*, then the aggregate land conversion relationship (6.8) would be specified in relative prices, i.e.

$$N^* = N(p/w_i, w/w_i, w_N/w_i; \alpha, Z)$$

6. In the case of the impacts of a change in the wage rate on land clearing, the ambiguity of the impacts arises because of two possible counteracting effects. First, a higher wage rate should make it more costly for the household to convert more land area, thus reducing the equilibrium amount of land converted. However, labor is also used in agricultural production, and if land and labor are substitutes, then a higher wage rate may also increase the use of converted land in production. Whether the equilibrium level of cleared land will increase or decrease in response to a rise in the wage rate will depend on the relative magnitude of these two effects. See Barbier and Cox (2004a) for further details.

7. The reduced form level of land conversion when institutional constraints are present, N^I, can also be specified in terms of relative prices, i.e.

$$N^I = N^I(p/w_i, w/w_i, w_N/w_i; \alpha, \beta, Z)$$

8. The following case study is based on Barbier (2002).

9. See Barbier (2002) for further details of the specific panel analysis approach.

10. In fact, land, labor and fertilizers were the predominant inputs in smallholder, mainly land-extensive and rainfed agriculture across Mexico during the pre-NAFTA period (World Bank 1989).

11. There is limited anecdotal evidence that, in some areas, the *ejido* system may have controlled deforestation better than property-owning alternatives. In Chiapas, a controlled comparison of an *ejido* with a neighboring community of property-owning individuals revealed that the former was characterized by less inequalities in wealth and land holdings, greater community solidarity and fewer social problems (Brown 1997). Since the 1950s, the *ejido* community also experienced less land use change and expansion and more stable land ownership patterns.

12. The following case study is based on Barbier and Cox (2004a).

13. This process has been a frequent occurrence historically on all of Thailand's forest lands, as noted by Feeny (2002, p. 193): "In contrast to the creation of private property rights in crop land, the commercialization of forestry was associated with the creation of state property rights in forest lands. De jure state property was often, however, de facto open access. Illegal logging and the expansion of the area under cultivation in response to market opportunities and population growth led to rapid deforestation."

14. As noted above, the conversion of mangrove area by shrimp farms has been largely irreversible in Thailand. That is, even if unproductive shrimp farms are abandoned, mangrove systems cannot regenerate naturally on this land. Moreover, to date, very little replanting of mangroves has occurred on abandoned shrimp farm land, nor are shrimp farm owners required legally to undertake such replanting (Erftemeijer and Lewis 2000; Lewis *et al.* 2000; Stevenson *et al.* 1999).

15. Although data were collected for all twenty-two coastal provinces of Thailand for this period, only twenty-one coastal provinces were used in the analysis. As no mangrove area data were recorded by the Royal Forestry Department for the coastal province of Narathiwat, we excluded this province from the analysis. See Barbier and Cox (2004a) for details.

16. In the regressions, all price variables as well as Gross Provincial Product per capita (GPP) are expressed in local currency (Thai baht) and in real terms (1990 values), using the GDP deflator for Thailand.

17. The exchange rate and real interest rate were also included as additional exogenous variables in the analysis. However, these variables are not represented at the provincial level. Neither variable was significant, and their inclusion distorted the original regression results. Both variables were therefore dropped from the final regressions. Population growth was used instead of population density as the latter was highly correlated with GPP and shrimp farm density. See Barbier and Cox (2004a) for further details.

18. The general approach advocated for panel analysis was followed in estimating equation, and in all cases the one-way random effects models

performed best. Log-log and semi-log forms of the regression were also tested but the linear form performed best. Inclusion of the variable for average distance of each province from Bangkok in the models meant that any fixed effects regression would be collinear. We tested the models with and without this variable and for the possible endogeneity of the shrimp farm density variable in the regressions. The null hypothesis that shrimp farm density is an exogenous variable could be rejected for the mangrove loss regression but not for the shrimp farm estimation. However, the standard instrumental variable (IV) technique could not be employed to correct for the endogeneity of shrimp farm density in the latter estimation. The IV technique in panel analysis requires using a two-stage fixed effects procedure, but unfortunately, a fixed effects regression is incompatible with our preferred regression that includes the "distance" variable. As an alternative, we therefore report two versions of our panel analysis of shrimp farm expansion in Table 6.2, one with the shrimp farm density variable and one without. See Barbier and Cox (2004a) for further details.

19. See previous note and further discussion in Barbier and Cox (2004a).

20. As Table 6.3 indicates, in the regression without shrimp farm density, the impact of the shrimp price on relative shrimp farm area expansion is slightly larger than the impact of the minimum wage rate.

21. As noted previously, mangrove deforestation in Thailand has also resulted from tourism, agricultural, industrial and urban developments in coastal areas, and thus is not completely explained by mangrove clearing for shrimp farming. If economic activities other than shrimp farming are responsible for mangrove loss in the coastal areas of Thailand then this might explain why in Table 6.3 the elasticities for the explanatory variables are larger for the two versions with shrimp farm expansion as the dependent variable rather than the version with mangrove loss as the dependent variable.

22. By employing relative prices in each regression, and using minimum wage as the numeraire, the impact of a rise in the wage rate will depend on the relative impacts of the shrimp price-wage ratio versus the fertilizer price-wage variables on the dependent variable. In all regressions the negative impact of the latter variable has the greater absolute effect, which is the reason why the elasticity associated with the minimum wage is positive.

23. Despite the anecdotal and empirical evidence that higher wages may induce some substitution of land for labor in shrimp farm operations, thus leading to an increase in overall mangrove clearing, this interpretation of our results must be treated with some caution. Because of the lack of disaggregate data on shrimp farm operations across all provinces in Southern Thailand over 1976–90 by type of technology – extensive,

semi-intensive and intensive – we are unable to separate out the separate effects of wages on mangrove clearing by each type of farm. By employing the aggregate shrimp farm data in our analysis, we are essentially treating all three technologies as a single technology, which could lead to a misleading prediction about the likely effects of a wage change on land use. We are grateful to an anonymous reviewer for pointing this possibility out to us.

24. Tokrisna (1998) provides some evidence of these changing trends in the rate of mangrove utilization by various coastal economic activities. Before 1980 an average of 7% of all mangrove areas in Thailand were converted to shrimp ponds. In 1986, the rate of mangrove conversion to shrimp ponds was estimated to be 30%, but declined to 17% by 1994. In contrast, the rate of mangrove conversion due to other coastal economic activities, such as urbanization, agriculture, tourism and industry, has increased rapidly from 15% before 1980, 17% in 1986 and 36% by 1994. In terms of cumulative impacts on mangrove loss, over the entire 1979–96 period, shrimp farming is still thought to have had the greatest effect, even though the rate of mangrove conversion due to shrimp aquaculture have tended to vary over this period. As reported above, estimates suggest that up to 50–65% of Thailand's mangroves have been lost to shrimp farm conversion since 1975 (Dierberg and Kiattisimkul 1996; Tokrisna 1998).

25. Other complementary policies may also be necessary to reduce the environmental damages associated with shrimp farming and other mangrove-converting activities, such as establishing concession fees and auctions for these activities, reducing subsidies for shrimp farming, introducing incentives for mangrove replanting, water pollution charges, and even environmental assurance bonds for large-scale developments. For further discussion see Barbier and Cox (2004a) and Barbier and Sathirathai (2004, ch. 12).

7 | Does water availability constrain economic development?

THE previous two chapters of Part Two focused on the economic factors and conditions determining land conversion in developing countries. The following chapter is concerned with the problem of freshwater availability and use, which was highlighted in Chapter 1 as an important "stylized fact" of the role of natural resources in economic development for many low and middle-income economies.

The future availability of freshwater supplies in developing countries is often suggested as a possible major constraint on the development efforts of these economies. That is, even if sufficient land and other natural resources are available for exploitation, the scarcity of water will limit economic development in many low and middle-income economies. The purpose of this chapter is to examine in more detail the role of water supplies and allocation in economic development. The approach taken to water in this chapter parallels that of the previous two chapters on the economics of land use change and conversion.

The chapter begins with a review of current and future sources of water supply and trends in use in developing countries. As suggested by Barro (1990) and Barro and Sala-I-Martin (1992), the actual supply of water utilized by a country, through domestic, agricultural and industrial use, has the characteristics of a government-provided public good subject to congestion. This in turn implies that the influence of water utilization on economic development can be depicted through a growth model that includes this congestible public good as a productive input for private producers. The model is then used as a basis for a cross-country analysis of the economic factors determining changes in water supply. However, many water resource problems within developing countries and trans-boundary watersheds relate to specific cases of upstream-downstream water misallocation. The remainder of the chapter is devoted to discussing the economic consequences of diverting water from downstream uses without taking into account the economic effects of such diversions. A case study of upstream diversion of water for irrigation developments in Northern Nigeria at the expense of downstream floodplain agricultural and other economic benefits is the principal focus of this discussion.

A problem of global water scarcity?

With the new millennium, the international scientific and policymaking community has focused on a number of pressing global environmental concerns facing humanity. Despite disagreement over many environmental "doomsday" scenarios, there has been remarkable agreement over one perceived global threat, the dwindling supply of freshwater resources relative to the growing demand for water worldwide. As one set of commentators have noted, "The only issue that the UN General Assembly was able to agree on at its Special Session 5 years after Rio was on the looming water crisis" (Falkenmark *et al.* 1998).

The key elements of the "looming water crisis" are summarized in a report released by the World Resources Institute: "In the twentieth century, water withdrawals have risen at more than double the rate of population increase and surface and groundwater sources in many parts of Asia, North Africa, and North America are being depleted ... Currently, almost 40 percent of the world's population experience serious water shortages. Water scarcity is expected to grow dramatically in some regions as competition for water grows between agricultural, urban and commercial sectors" (Revenga *et al.* 2000). Moreover, the cause of the global water crisis can be blamed largely on "the growth and the economic development of human population" rather than on global climate change: "We conclude that impending global-scale changes in population and economic development over the next 25 years will dictate the future relation between water supply and demand to a much greater degree than will changes in mean climate" (Vörösmarty *et al.* 2000).

However, other water resource experts, while not minimizing the potential threat of water scarcity, are less sanguine about the accuracy of future projections of global and regional water shortages. In reviewing forty years of global water scenario projections, Gleick (2000, pp. 58–59) concludes that the tendency has been for most projections to overestimate greatly future water demands by assuming that use would continue to grow at, or even above, historical growth rates. For example, actual global withdrawals for the mid-1990s turned out to be only about half of the predictions made by projections thirty years previously. The reasons for such difficulties include the failure to take into account improvements in the efficiency with which water is used in all sectors and innovations in water management institutions. Because future technical, efficiency and institutional improvements are so difficult to predict, current projections of future water use also vary widely. For example, two diverging studies projecting the increase in world water demand over 1995 to 2025 suggest that the increase could be as little as 13% or as much as 37% (Cosgrove and Rijsberman 2000).

Economics has very little to contribute to the current hydrological debate over how severe the future "water crisis" might be. As pointed out by Howe (1976) some time ago, economics has been less concerned about the physical "availability" of freshwater supplies than about the full implications of water resource development for economic growth.

However, as noted in Chapter 1, problems of freshwater availability may pose a severe threat for some developing economies and regions. Two specific trends were highlighted. First, developing countries already account for 71% of global water withdrawal, and water demand in low and middle-income economies is expected to grow further by 27% over 1995 to 2025 (see Table 1.5). Second, the problem of water stress and scarcity is likely to worsen for key developing regions and countries, notably China, India, Pakistan, the Philippines, South Korea, Mexico, Egypt and virtually all other countries in West Asia/North Africa (see Table 1.6). Finally, the problem will be worse still for specific river basin regions within each of these countries.

From an economic standpoint, therefore, it seems appropriate to investigate whether increasing water scarcity may impose constraints on the economic growth of countries. That is, if economics can make a contribution to the current hydrological debate over the future water crisis, it must be to examine the claim that increasing water scarcity may reduce the per capita income of countries. That is the purpose of the following model of water and economic growth.

A model of water use and economic growth[1]

Modeling the relationship between water use and economic growth in an economy requires first determining what type of economic good is water. Although in some economies there is increasing reliance on the involvement of the private sector in providing some water services, with little loss of generality, one can view the aggregate supply of water utilized by a country as a government-provided non-excludable good subject to congestion.[2] Following the approach of Barro (1990) and Barro and Sala-I-Martin (1992), modeling the influence of water utilization on economic growth allows the development of a growth model that includes publicly provided goods that are subject to congestion as a productive input for private producers in an economy.[3]

If water has the characteristic of a non-excludable good subject to congestion, then there are essentially two ways in which water scarcity may affect economic growth. First, as water becomes increasingly scarce in the economy, the government must exploit less accessible sources of freshwater through appropriating and purchasing a greater share of aggregate economic output, in terms of dams, pumping stations, supply infrastructure, etc. Second, it is also possible that water utilization in an economy may be restricted by the absolute availability of water. Thus the influence of water use on growth may be different for a water-constrained economy. As a consequence, the following model distinguishes between the scenario in which water is not a binding constraint in the economy and the scenario in which it is binding.

Let w be the annual per capita renewable freshwater resources of a country (in cubic meters per person per year), and let r be total per capita freshwater utilization by that country (in cubic meters per person per year). In essence, w represents the hydrologists' concept of the total annual water supplies available to an economy on a per capita basis, whereas r is the actual supply provided and used, i.e. the water withdrawal.

As suggested by Barro (1990) and Barro and Sala-I-Martin (1992), the actual supply of water withdrawn and utilized by a country, for domestic, agricultural and industrial purposes, has the characteristics of a government-provided non-excludable good subject to congestion. That is, modeling the influence of per capita water withdrawal, r, on the growth of the economy can be depicted through a growth model that includes this congestible government-provided good as a productive input for private producers.

The contribution of water utilization or withdrawal, r, to the per capita output of the ith producer, y_i, can therefore be represented as

$$y_i = Ak_i f\left(\frac{r}{y}\right), \quad f' > 0, \ f'' < 0. \tag{7.1}$$

Following Rebelo (1991), part of private production depends on constant returns to the per capita capital stock available to the producer, k_i, which is broadly defined to include both physical and human capital components, and $A > 0$ is a parameter reflecting the level of technology. In addition, production increases with respect to the amount of water utilization, which is supplied through public services. However, because of congestion, the flow of water available to the ith producer is necessarily limited by the use of water by all producers in the economy.[4] Denoting aggregate per capita output across all N producers in the economy as $y = Ny_i$, it follows that water utilization, r, has to increase relative to y in order to expand the water available to the ith producer. In contrast, an increase in per capita output relative to total water utilization in the economy lowers the water available to each producer, and therefore reduces y_i in (7.1).

Note, however, that the specification of (7.1) captures only the non-excludable aspect of immediate water utilization among producers. What is missing from (7.1) is any consideration of how aggregate water utilization in the economy may generate feedback effects over time in terms of reduced ecological services and thus aggregate output. As discussed previously, in some regions the cumulative ecological damages and losses of hydrological functions that arise from aggregate water utilization may affect the availability of freshwater, although this feedback effect may take years or even decades to manifest itself in terms of impacting economic output (Sullivan 2002).

Not only may the aggregate water supplies in an economy have the characteristic of a non-excludable good subject to congestion but also the provision of these supplies may be affected by the physical availability of these supplies, or *water scarcity*. There are two ways in which this may occur.

First, it can be generally assumed that the government provides water for use in the economy by appropriating a share of aggregate private output. For example, in modeling the supply of general public goods, Barro (1990) has argued that one can think of government simply purchasing a flow of output from the private sector (e.g. battleships and highways), the services of which the government in turn makes available to the economy as a whole. In order to provide the water utilized by the economy, r, one can also envision the government purchasing or appropriating a share, z, of aggregate economic output that is specifically devoted to water supply (e.g., dams, irrigation networks, water pipes, pumping stations, etc.). This suggests that $r = zy$. However, as per capita freshwater utilization in the economy, r, rises relative to the available annual per capita renewable freshwater resources, w, one would also expect that more aggregate output must be allocated for water supply. As water becomes increasingly scarce, i.e. water utilization rises relative to available freshwater resources, the government must exploit less accessible sources of freshwater. To do this, requires appropriating and purchasing a greater share of aggregate economic output, in terms of dams, pumping stations, supply infrastructure, etc. Denoting $\rho = r/w$ as the *rate of water utilization relative to total freshwater availability*, it therefore follows that

$$r = z(\rho)y, \quad z' > 0, \ z'' > 0, \ z(0) = 0, \ z'(0) = 0, \ z(1) = \alpha, \ z'(1)$$
$$= \beta < \infty, \tag{7.2}$$

where $\beta > 0$, $0 < \alpha < 1$, and $z(\rho) < 1$ is the proportion of aggregate economic output appropriated by the government for providing water, which is assumed to be an increasing function of the rate of water utilization by the economy relative to its freshwater resources, ρ. In addition, as aggregate output, y, rises in the economy, so does water utilization, r. Finally, as water becomes increasingly scarce, i.e $\rho \rightarrow 1$, the proportion of output appropriated by the government to supply water is bounded above by α, and the rate of appropriation by β.[5]

Water scarcity also influences water utilization in an economy by limiting the total amount of water available for withdrawal. That is, even if all freshwater resources are used (i.e. $\rho = 1$), water withdrawals are finite. Thus total per capita freshwater availability imposes the following constraint on the economy

$$r = z(\rho)y \leq w, \tag{7.3}$$

with $r = z(\rho)y < w$ if $0 \leq \rho < 1$ and $r = z(\rho)y = w$ if $\rho = 1$.

Making the standard assumption that the supply of labor and population are the same, and that population grows at the constant rate n, per capita output in the economy is allocated as

$$y = c + r + \dot{k} + (\omega + n)k, \ k(0) = k_0, \tag{7.4}$$

where c is per capita consumption, $\dot{k}$ is the change in the per capita capital stock over time and ω is the rate of capital depreciation.

Finally, all consumers in the economy are assumed to share identical preferences over an infinite time horizon, given by

$$W = \int_0^\infty e^{-\delta t}\left[\frac{c^{1-\theta}-1}{1-\theta}\right]dt, \quad \delta = v - n \geq 0, \tag{7.5}$$

where v is the rate of time preference. Maximization of W with respect to choice of c and ρ, subject to (7.1) to (7.4), yields the following Lagrangian expression, L, comprising the current-value Hamiltonian for the problem specified by (7.5) subject to (7.4), plus the constraint on the control variable ρ given by (7.3)

$$L = \frac{c^{1-\theta}-1}{1-\theta} + \lambda[(1-z(\rho))Akf(z(\rho)) - c - (\omega+n)k] \\ + \mu[w - z(\rho)Akf(z(\rho))]. \tag{7.6}$$

The resulting first-order conditions are

$$c^{-\theta} = \lambda \tag{7.7}$$

$$\lambda[(1-z(\rho))Akf'z'] - \lambda Akf(z(\rho))z' = \mu[Akf(z(\rho))z' + z(\rho)Akf'z'],$$

$$\mu(t) \geq 0, \; w - z(\rho)Akf(z(\rho)) \geq 0, \; \mu[w - z(\rho)Akf(z(\rho))] = 0. \tag{7.8}$$

$$\dot{\lambda} = \delta\lambda - \lambda[(1-z(\rho))Af(z(\rho)) - (\omega+n)] + \mu z(\rho)Af(z(\rho)) \tag{7.9}$$

$$\lim_{t\to\infty}\left\{e^{-\delta t}\lambda(t)k(t) = 0\right\}. \tag{7.10}$$

plus the equation of motion (7.4). Equation (7.7) is the standard condition that the marginal utility of consumption equals the shadow price of capital, λ. Equation (7.8) determines the optimal allocation of the rate of water utilization of the economy, including the complementary slackness condition imposed by the water scarcity constraint. The Lagrangean multiplier μ can be interpreted as the scarcity value of freshwater supplies to the economy. Equation (7.9) indicates the change over time in the marginal imputed value of the capital stock of the economy. Finally, equation (7.10) is the transversality condition for this infinite time horizon problem.

Differentiating (7.7) with respect to time and substituting into (7.9) yields

$$g = \frac{\dot{c}}{c} = \frac{1}{\theta}\left[(1 - z(\rho))Af(z(\rho)) - (\omega + n + \delta) - \mu\frac{z(\rho)Af(z(\rho))}{c^{-\theta}}\right].$$

$$(7.11)$$

The above equation indicates that growth in per capita consumption, g, is negatively affected by the government's appropriation of output to supply water, $z(\rho)$, positively influenced by the contribution of water use to the net marginal productivity of capital, $Af(z(\rho)) - (\omega + n + \delta)$, and adversely impacted by conditions of water scarcity, $\mu z(\rho)Af(z(\rho))/c^{-\theta}$.

Further interpretation of the influence of water use on growth in the economy requires examining the conditions under which the water scarcity constraint (7.3) is binding or not. We begin with the interior solution in which the economy is not constrained by per capita fresh-water availability.

Scenario 1. Water scarcity is not binding in the economy

If the water scarcity constraint (7.3) is not binding, then the complementary slackness condition requires that $w > r$ and $\mu(t) = 0$ for all t. For this interior solution, equation (7.11) reduces to

$$g = \frac{1}{\theta}[(1 - z(\rho))Af(z(\rho)) - (\omega + n + \delta)]. \qquad (7.12)$$

Although water scarcity no longer affects the growth in per capita consumption, g is still influenced by water utilization in the economy. Growth is negatively affected by the government's appropriation of output to supply water, $z(\rho)$, and positively influenced by the contribution of water use to the net marginal productivity of capital, $Af(z(\rho)) - (\omega + n + \delta)$. Moreover, it can be easily demonstrated that in this economy per capita consumption, capital and output all grow at the same rate g, and there are no transitional dynamics to this steady-state growth path. In the initial period, the socially efficient level of water use, ρ^*, that satisfies (7.8) for $\mu(0) = 0$ is chosen, along with the initial values for per capita

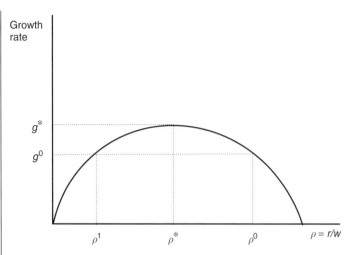

Figure 7.1. Growth and the rate of water utilization for the interior solution

consumption and output. After the initial period, $k(t)$, $c(t)$ and $y(t)$ then grow at the constant rate determined by (7.12).

It is also straightforward to demonstrate that the socially efficient rate of water utilization, ρ^*, maximizes growth in the economy. Differentiating (7.12) with respect to ρ we get

$$\frac{\partial g}{\partial \rho} \underset{<}{\overset{>}{=}} 0 \quad \text{if} \quad f(z(\rho)) \underset{>}{\overset{<}{=}} (1 - z(\rho))f'(z(\rho)). \qquad (7.13)$$

Thus the socially efficient rate of water utilization that satisfies (8) also ensures that the per capita growth rate is at its maximum, g^*.[6] Moreover, as $z(\rho)$ is strictly convex, it follows that the slope of (12) with respect to the rate of water utilization is positive for $\rho < \rho^*$, and conversely, is negative for $\rho > \rho^*$. Consequently, as depicted in Figure 7.1, the relationship between growth and the rate of water utilization is concave.

However, current policies for supplying water in most countries, even those not facing binding water constraints, are not socially efficient (Dosi and Easter 2000). For example, it is possible that water management in some countries may lead to a rate of water utilization that is too high, i.e. $\rho^0 > \rho^*$. There are two implications of this outcome. First, as is clear from Figure 7.1, over-use of water will lead to a lower rate of economic growth, i.e. $g^0 < g^*$. Second, individual producers who benefit from the provision of water are not contributing a sufficient share of the social costs of providing this non-excludable good.

A lower rate of economic growth, i.e. $g^0 < g^*$, may also result if the rate of water utilization is too low, i.e. $\rho^1 < \rho^*$. An economy in this situation may be able to increase its growth by utilizing more of its freshwater resources.

Scenario 2. The water-constrained economy

We now turn to the scenario where the water scarcity constraint (7.3) is binding in the economy, and thus the complementary slackness condition requires that $w = r$ and $\mu(t) > 0$ for all t. Equation (7.2) also implies that $z(1) = \frac{r}{y} = \frac{w}{y} = \alpha, z'(1) = \beta < \infty$. That is, the proportion of aggregate economic output appropriated by the government for providing water is now determined by the ratio of the potential water supplies to aggregate output, which is bounded by the maximum rate of appropriation, α^7.

For the water-constrained economy, growth in per capita consumption is now governed by a modified version of equation (7.11), with the rate of output appropriated by the government to supply water set at the maximum rate, α

$$g_S = \frac{\dot{c}}{c} = \frac{1}{\theta}\left[(1-\alpha)Af(\alpha) - (\omega + n + \delta) - \mu\frac{\alpha Af(\alpha)}{\lambda}\right]. \quad (7.14)$$

Growth in the water-constrained economy, g_S, is positively influenced by the net marginal productivity of capital, $Af(\alpha) - (\omega + n + \delta)$, including the contribution of water use to this productivity, but adversely affected by the government's appropriation of output to supply water, α, and by the conditions imposed by water scarcity, $\mu\alpha Af(\alpha)\lambda$. Note as well that, in a water-constrained economy, it is always optimal for the government to choose the maximum rate of appropriation of output to supply freshwater.[8]

For the water-constrained economy, condition (7.8) becomes

$$\mu = \lambda\left[\frac{f'(\alpha)}{f(\alpha) + \alpha f'(\alpha)} - 1\right] > 0.[9]$$ Using the latter expression, (7.14) can be simplified further to

$$g_S = \frac{1}{\theta}\left[Af(\alpha) - (\omega + n + \delta) - \alpha Af(\alpha)\left(\frac{f'(\alpha)}{f(\alpha) + \alpha f'(\alpha)}\right)\right]. \quad (7.15)$$

Again, it is straightforward to show that in the water-constrained economy, per capita consumption, capital and output all grow at the same rate g_S as governed by (7.15). In the initial period, the government chooses the maximum rate of appropriating economic output in order to supply freshwater, $\alpha y = r = w$, along with the initial values for per capita consumption and output. After the initial period, $k(t)$, $c(t)$ and $y(t)$ grow at the constant rate determined by (7.15).

Although in a water-constrained economy it is always optimal for the government to appropriate output at the maximum rate, α, to supply freshwater, this does not necessarily mean that economic growth will occur. From (7.15),

$$g_S \overset{>}{\underset{<}{=}} 0 \quad \text{if} \quad Af(\alpha) - (\omega + n + \delta) \overset{>}{\underset{<}{=}} \alpha Af(\alpha)\frac{f'(\alpha)}{f(\alpha) + \alpha f'(\alpha)}.$$

$$(7.16)$$

That is, growth in the water-constrained economy will occur only if the net marginal productivity of capital exceeds the negative effects on the economy of water scarcity.

In sum, in the water-constrained economy, water is always valuable in the sense that the marginal benefits of water in terms of its contribution to marginal productivity will always exceed the social cost of supply. This means that it is always optimal to allocate the maximum amount of output possible to extract the available freshwater supplies. However, whether this leads to growth or economic decline depends on whether the gains in net marginal productivity outweigh the resource costs to the economy of providing this water. An economy that has either too little or too much water relative to economic output is likely to be more adversely affected by this decision than an economy that has moderate supplies relative to overall output. The latter water-constrained economy can still provide sufficient water supplies to all its producers in order to increase net marginal productivity in the economy without allocating too much output to do so, and thus achieve economic growth.

Cross-country empirical analysis of water and growth

If the above theoretical model is to be useful for empirical analysis, there are measurement issues to address. The most common measure of aggregate freshwater availability employed by hydrologists is the FAO's definition of a country's total renewable water resources, which consists of adding up average annual surface runoff and groundwater recharge from endogenous precipitation, and typically includes surface inflows from other countries (Faurés *et al.* 2001; Gleick 1998 and 2000).[10] In the following analysis, we will use this flow indicator as our measure of the total renewable freshwater resources of a country.

Hydrologists also distinguish two concepts of water use: water withdrawal and water consumption (Gleick 2000, p. 41). Withdrawal refers to water removed or extracted from a freshwater source and used for human purposes (i.e. industrial, agricultural or domestic water use). However, some of this water may be returned to the original source, albeit with changes in the quality and quantity of the water. In contrast, consumptive use is water withdrawn from a source and actually consumed or lost to seepage, contamination, or a "sink" where it cannot economically be reused. Thus water consumption is the proportion of water withdrawal that is "irretrievably lost" after human use. For example, in 1995 total global freshwater withdrawals amounted to 3,800 km^3, of which 2,100 km^3 were consumed.

These standard hydrological definitions of water withdrawal, consumption and availability imply very limited temporal and geographical scales. Ecological damages and losses of hydrological functions may take several years to affect the availability of freshwater in a region, and in poor economies there is the additional problem that the effective supplies available to producers and households may be less than actual supplies due to lack of access to safe water and the time spent collecting water (Sullivan 2002). Assessing the freshwater supplies of a country can sometimes be arbitrary, as major rivers, lakes and other water bodies often transcend political boundaries (Gleick 2000). Thus, as argued by Sullivan (2002, p. 1205–1206), a more comprehensive water use index relative to supply should take into account "physical water availability, water quality and ecological water demand," and include as well "social and economic measures of poverty," thereby linking "macro-level hydrological data reflecting regional or catchment-level water availability and micro-level data on household water stress." However, to date, such a comprehensive water use index has yet to be developed for a cross-section of regions or countries.

In the following cross-country empirical analysis, we will use average annual water withdrawals (km^3/year) as our measure of freshwater utilization. There are two reasons for this. First, the available data across a broad range of countries is much more reliable and accurate for water withdrawals than consumption. Second, hydrologists' measures of water stress and scarcity are usually couched either in terms of water availability per person (cubic meters per person per year) or in terms of relative water demand (the ratio of water withdrawals to total freshwater resources per year).[11] When the latter measure is employed, hydrologists typically consider values for a country between 0.2 and 0.4 to indicate medium to high water stress, whereas values greater than 0.4 reflect conditions of severe water limitation (Cosgrove and Rijsberman 2000; Vörösmarty *et al.* 2000). In the following analysis, we also consider relative water demand (i.e. the *rate of water utilization relative to freshwater availability*), or what we have denoted as $\rho = r/w$, to be the critical indicator.

The results of the theoretical model suggest the possibility of a concave, or inverted-U, relationship between economic growth and water utilization (see equation (7.13) and Figure 7.1). That is, as the rate of water utilization, ρ, in an economy increases, growth, g, first increases, then stabilizes and eventually falls. This is the normal case that we would expect for an economy in which water availability is not an absolute binding constraint.

Using cross-country empirical analysis, we can therefore derive a simple test for examining the relationship between water use and growth across countries; i.e. is there any empirical evidence of an inverted-U relationship between economic growth and the rate of water utilization for a broad cross-section of countries? The rest of this section summarizes the approach developed by Barbier (2004c) to test this hypothesis through a cross-country analysis.[12]

As noted above, the key variable in this analysis is of course the rate of water utilization, ρ across countries. A recent assessment of the world's freshwater supplies provides estimates of the annual renewable water resources and the total amount of freshwater withdrawal for a single year of estimate for 163 countries (Gleick 1998 and 2000). The ratio of freshwater withdrawals, r, relative to supplies, w, can therefore serve as our cross-country measure of $\rho = r/w$.

If the hypothesized U-shaped relationship between growth and the rate of water utilization is robust, then this relationship should also hold if the normal set of "fixed" variables, x, that account for growth across countries is also included. We therefore also estimate the following basic growth regression:

$$g_{t,t+5} = b_0 + b_1\rho_t + b_2\rho_t^2 + b_x x + \mu, \qquad (7.17)$$

both for $x > 0$ and $x = 0$. Following Sala-I-Martin (1999) and Temple (1999), we choose the fixed variables, x, to be the initial level of income per capita in year t, the primary-school enrollment rate in year t and the secondary-school enrollment rate in year t.[13]

Finally, the empirical literature on growth has also identified consistently a number of other variables that appear to be significantly correlated with growth across countries. Of particular importance appear to be variables that reflect the institutional framework, the level of development and the degree of trade openness of countries (Agénor (2000), Keefer and Knack (1997), Sachs and Warner (1995a) and (1997); Sala-I-Martin (1999) and Temple (1999)). This suggests that, extending our growth model further to include these additional explanatory variables, y, should not affect the hypothesized U-shaped relationship between growth and the rate of water utilization, if that relationship is robust. Our full growth model for empirical estimation is:

$$g_{t,t+5} = b_0 + b_1\rho_t + b_2\rho_t^2 + b_x x + b_y y + \mu, \qquad (7.18)$$

where y includes, for each country in the sample, an index of political stability/lack of political violence, an index of the control of corruption, the annual population growth rate in year t, total trade as a percentage of real GDP in year t and a dummy variable indicating whether the country is classified as a developing economy.

The data for the five-year average cross-country growth rates, g, and the various variables comprising x and y were all derived from the World Bank *World Development Indicators* data set (World Bank 2001). The exceptions were the control of corruption and political stability indices, which were derived from the World Bank's study of governance across countries (Kaufmann *et al.* 1999a and 1999b), and the dummy variable for developing countries, which uses the UN Food and Agricultural Organization classification of countries.[14]

Table 7.1 summarizes the growth regression results for equations (7.17) and (7.18). All models required correction either for multiplicative heteroskedasticity using maximum likelihood estimation or for generalized heteroskedasticity using White's consistent estimator.[15] For all three models, the coefficients b_1 and b_2 not only have the expected signs but also display consistently similar magnitudes. In the basic and full growth models, for those additionally included variables that are statistically significant in explaining growth, their estimated coefficients also conform to the predicted signs. Overall, the three regression models suggest that the hypothesis of an inverted-U relationship between growth and the rate of water utilization across the diverse group of countries in our sample cannot be rejected, as this relationship appears to be remarkably robust.

For each of the models in Table 7.1 an estimate of ρ^* is computed, which corresponds to an estimate of the rate of water utilization that leads to maximum economic growth as indicated in Figure 7.1. The estimated ρ^* is fairly large across the three models, ranging from 2.9 to 3.8. However, these estimated values must be treated with caution. Only a handful of countries in our full sample of 163 countries show rates of water utilization at or exceeding these levels.[16] The vast majority of countries display rates of water utilization that are much less than one. For example, the mean of ρ in the full sample is 0.548, whereas the median is only 0.047. In essence, the data are allowing us to estimate only the part of the curve depicted in Figure 7.1 well to the left of ρ^*. Thus although these clustered observations appear to fit the hypothesized inverted U-shaped relationship, any computed value of ρ^* is essentially a projection of this estimated relationship that is likely to be far less accurate given that so few actual observations are available to verify this projection.

Table 7.1 also reports the elasticity estimates for ρ. These are fairly consistent, ranging from 0.3−0.35 across the three models. This suggests that, on average, the countries in each sample could increase freshwater utilization and achieve a modest increase in growth. For example, the full growth model predicts that an increase in the rate of water utilization by 10% could increase the average growth rate in the sample of countries from 1.30% to 1.33%.

In sum, the regression results reported in Table 7.1 provide strong support for the hypothesized inverted-U relationship between

Table 7.1 Cross-country regression of water use and growth

Dependent variable: five-year average annual growth of per capita income $(g_{t,t+5})$

Variables	Base case model[a]	Basic growth model[a]	Full growth model[b]
Constant	0.818	−1.275	9.569
	(2.432)*	(−0.685)	(2.534)*
ρ	1.614	1.647	1.947
	(5.117)**	(5.828)**	(2.515)*
ρ^2	−0.279	−0.273	−0.257
	(−6.815)**	(−7.024)**	(−2.577)**
Log per capita income in year t		−0.042	−1.538
		(−0.146)	(−3.379)**
Primary-school enrollment in year t		0.029	0.016
		(2.138)*	(1.096)
Secondary-school enrollment in year t		−0.005	0.009
		(−0.383)	(0.547)
Population growth in year t			−0.496
			(−1.748)[†]
Trade openness in year t			−0.002
			(−0.322)
Political stability indicator			1.183
			(2.421)*
Control of corruption indicator			2.454
			(3.640)**
Dummy for developing countries			2.683
			(2.258)*
Inverted-U relationship	Yes	Yes	Yes
(Estimate of ρ^*)	(2.895)	(3.025)	(3.790)
Elasticity of ρ	0.292	0.270	0.348
(Sample mean of ρ)	(0.227)	(0.229)	(0.248)
(Sample mean of $g_{t,t+5}$)	(1.155)	(1.294)	(1.298)
Number of observations (N)	$N = 143$	$N = 132$	$N = 120$

Notes:
[a] Maximum likelihood estimation after correcting the variance-covariance matrix for multiplicative heteroskedasticity.
[b] Ordinary least squares employing standard errors based on White's heteroskedasticity-consistent variance-covariance matrix.
t-statistics are in parentheses.
** Significant at 1% level.   * Significant at 5% level.   † Significant at 10% level.
Source: Barbier (2004c).

economic growth and the rate of water utilization across countries. Our estimations of this relationship also suggest that current rates of freshwater utilization in the vast majority of countries are not constraining economic growth. To the contrary, most countries may be able to increase growth by utilizing more of their freshwater resources, although there are obvious limits on how much additional growth can be generated in this way.

The latter caveat is extremely important. Even if a country could raise its growth rate by increasing its rate of water utilization, maintaining ρ greater than one is likely to be unsustainable for most countries over the long run. In fact, as our theoretical model indicates, for an economy in which water scarcity is binding, i.e $w = r$ and therefore $\rho = 1$, the resulting scarcity constraint will have very different implications for the economy's growth path (compare equations (7.12) and (7.15)). Economic growth is now determined by the ratio of the potential water supplies to aggregate output, which is equal to the maximum rate of government appropriation, i.e. $w/y = \alpha$. As condition (7.16) indicates, although in a water-constrained economy it is always optimal for the government to appropriate output at the maximum rate, α, to supply freshwater, this does not necessarily mean that economic growth will actually occur. For the economy to grow requires, first, that the net marginal productivity of capital exceeds the negative effects on the economy of water scarcity, and second, that there are sufficient freshwater resources, w, available to appropriate.

Empirically verifying condition (7.16) and the growth path of the water-constrained economy is very difficult for our data set. First, only 10 out of the 163 countries in our sample display rates of water utilization of $\rho \geq 1$. This is too small a sub-sample for conducting a separate regression.[17] Second, as noted above, our data set contains only a single-year estimate of the rate of water utilization for each country. Some countries that have rates of water utilization of $\rho \geq 1$ in a single year may not necessarily experience chronic water scarcity over a longer period of time, as implied by our model of the water-constrained economy.

Nevertheless, provided that we can use an appropriate indicator of long-run water scarcity across countries, it may be possible to test an alternative hypothesis, namely that growth rates are likely to be adversely affected in economies facing chronic water scarcity.

Hydrologists have suggested that one potential indicator of long-run water scarcity is the so-called "Falkenmark water stress index" (Falkenmark 1989; Falkenmark and Rockström 1998). The water stress index is constructed by taking a past level of renewable freshwater supply available to a country (e.g. from the 1960s to early 1990s) and dividing it by that country's population at a future date, usually in 2000 and 2025. While a country with more that 1,700 cubic meters per year per person is expected to experience only intermittent and localized water shortages, the threshold of 1,000 cubic meters is considered to be a level below which a country is likely to experience widespread and chronic shortfalls. At less than 500 cubic meters per capita annually, water availability can be considered to be so serious a problem that social and economic development may be threatened.

It is possible to devise a water stress index for our sample of 163 countries, using the single-year estimate of freshwater supply for each country divided by its population in year 2000.[18] Sixteen countries face conditions of extreme water scarcity (less than 500 cubic meters/person/year), whereas four countries experience moderate water scarcity (between 500 and 1,000 cubic meters/person/year).[19] By including dummy variables to represent the moderate and extreme water scarcity countries, respectively, in the regressions of equations (7.17) and (7.18), we can test the hypothesis that conditions of scarcity may affect adversely economic growth rates across countries.

Table 7.2 summarizes the results for the regressions with the water scarcity dummies. Once again, all models required correction either for multiplicative heteroskedasticity using maximum likelihood estimation or for generalized heteroskedasticity using White's consistent estimator.[20] The inclusion of the water scarcity dummies in the regressions produces remarkably consistent estimations compared to the previous regressions that excluded the dummies (see Tables 7.1 and 7.2). The hypothesis of an inverted-U relationship between growth and the rate of water utilization cannot be rejected, and the estimates of the turning point for ρ and its elasticity are similar. For the full growth model that includes the moderate water scarcity dummy, a 10% increase in the rate of water utilization again raises the average growth rate in the sample of countries from 1.30% to 1.33%. For the full growth model that includes both the moderate and water scarcity dummies, a 10% increase in ρ will raise growth only slightly more, to 1.34%.

Table 7.2 Cross-country regression of water use and growth: controlling for moderate and extreme water scarcity

Dependent variable: five-year average annual growth of per capita income ($g_{t,t+5}$)

Variables	Moderate water scarcity			Moderate and extreme water scarcity		
	Base case model[a]	Basic growth model[a]	Full growth model[b]	Base case model[a]	Basic growth model[a]	Full growth model[b]
Constant	0.848	−1.264	9.652	0.826	−3.508	9.567
	(2.461)*	(−0.683)	(2.553)*	(2.395)*	(−2.118)*	(2.534)*
ρ	1.602	1.652	1.939	1.917	3.404	2.100
	(5.048)**	(5.895)**	(2.509)**	(3.250)**	(9.750)**	(2.015)**
ρ^2	−0.278	−0.275	−0.255	−0.310	−0.466	−0.273
	(−6.766)**	(−7.135)**	(−2.565)**	(−4.964)**	(−11.192)**	(−2.183)**
Log per capita income in year t		−0.034	−1.550		0.375	−1.542
		(−0.120)	(−3.400)**		(1.450)	(−3.342)**
Primary-school enrollment in year t		0.031	0.017		0.040	0.017
		(2.305)*	(1.125)		(3.069)**	(1.125)
Secondary-school enrollment in year t		−0.009	0.009		−0.040	0.008
		(−0.656)	(0.535)		(−3.517)**	(0.493)
Population growth in year t			−0.483			−0.471
			(−1.691)†			(−1.653)†
Trade openness in year t			−0.002			−0.002
			(−0.321)			(−0.255)
Political stability indicator			1.159			1.142
			(2.368)*			(2.248)*

Dependent variable: *five-year average annual growth of per capita income* ($g_{i,t+s}$)

Variables	Moderate water scarcity			Moderate and extreme water scarcity		
	Base case model[a]	Basic growth model[a]	Full growth model[b]	Base case model[a]	Basic growth model[a]	Full growth model[b]
Control of corruption indicator			2.471 (3.662)**			2.492 (3.593)*
Dummy for developing countries			2.639 (2.214)			2.641 (2.215)*
Dummy for moderate water scarcity	−1.062 (−1.029)	−0.737 (−0.795)	−1.653 (−2.958)	−1.065 (−1.028)**	−1.416 (−1.754)†	−1.674 (−2.980)
Dummy for extreme water scarcity				−0.583 (−0.516)	−3.339 (−4.451)**	−0.295 (−0.233)
Inverted-U relationship (Estimate of ρ**)	Yes (2.885)	Yes (3.009)	Yes (3.798)	Yes (3.091)	Yes (3.650)	Yes (3.851)
Elasticity of ρ	0.290	0.271	0.346	0.349	0.566	0.375
(Sample mean of ρ)	(0.227)	(0.229)	(0.248)	(0.227)	(0.229)	(0.248)
(Sample mean of $g_{i,t+s}$)	(1.155)	(1.294)	(1.298)	(1.155)	(1.294)	(1.298)
Number of observations (N)	N = 143	N = 132	N = 120	N = 143	N = 132	N = 120

Notes:

[a] Maximum likelihood estimation after correcting the variance-covariance matrix for multiplicative heteroskedasticity.

[b] Ordinary least squares employing standard errors based on White's heteroskedasticity-consistent variance-covariance matrix.

t-statistics are in parentheses.

** Significant at 1% level.   * Significant at 5% level.   † Significant at 10% level.

Source: Barbier (2004c).

Table 7.2 indicates that the water scarcity dummies have the expected negative signs, although they are significant only in the full growth models and in the basic growth model in which both the moderate and extreme water scarcity dummies are included. Given the robustness of many of the additional explanatory variables in the basic and full growth models, these regressions are likely to yield more reliable estimates of growth rates across countries. Thus, based on the results of Table 7.2, it is difficult to reject the hypothesis that the presence of moderate or extreme water scarcity adversely affects economic growth.

Implications for global water scarcity

The previous empirical analysis provides strong support for the hypothesized inverted-U relationship between economic growth and the rate of water utilization across countries. Our estimations of this relationship also suggest that current rates of freshwater utilization in the vast majority of countries are not yet constraining economic growth. However, countries that are water-stressed, i.e. have limited freshwater supplies relative to current and future populations, may find it especially difficult to generate additional growth through more water use. Our empirical analysis suggests that we cannot reject the hypothesis that the presence of moderate or extreme water scarcity adversely affects economic growth.

There are some important caveats to these generally optimistic findings that increased water utilization may constrain growth only in a handful of countries.

First, a critical factor in assessing the actual amount of freshwater available in a country is that many rivers, lakes, groundwater aquifers and other water bodies often cross political boundaries. Such water sources are also often difficult to exploit for legal, technical or economic reasons (Gleick 2000).[21]

Second, while water-scarcity constraints on overall economic growth may be less likely, freshwater availability could be more problematic for key sectors in some countries, such as agriculture. For example, many hydrologists, meteorologists and water resource experts have expressed concern recently that, with world population increasing by 50% over the next 30 years, water scarcity may become a key factor behind global food insecurity, reduced production growth and rising international cereal prices (Falkenmark *et al.* 1998; Rosegrant and Cai 2001; Seckler *et al.* 1999; United Nations 1997).

Third, this chapter has focused fairly narrowly on the availability of freshwater supplies to provide economic uses of water. The wider ecological services provided by water have been ignored, and there is inevitably a trade-off between maintenance and protection of these services and the increasing allocation of water for use in the economy. As pointed out by Sullivan (2002), any resulting decline in the hydrological functions of ecosystems may in turn reduce future water availability.[22]

Fourth, although in the model of water and economic growth it was analytically convenient to view water as a congestible, non-excludable good supplied solely by a government to the private producers of an economy, it is important to note that current thinking in the economics of water management challenges the notion that a government should be the sole provider of water services in an economy. The main argument in favor of institutional reform is that, given the rapid growth of water demands over recent decades, the public sector alone is incapable of ensuring socially efficient levels of supply and water utilization in many countries (Briscoe 1996; Dosi and Easter 2000). Instead, providing an adequate supply of water to an economy and ensuring its efficient utilization constitutes a bundle of services that is best divided up between the public and private sector, with some of the services more efficiently provided by the private sector (Parker and Tsur 1997). Already, increased private sector participation and use of water markets and cost-recovery pricing has occurred in the United States, the European Union and even some developing countries (Dosi and Easter 2000; Johnstone and Webb 2001). It appears that, if the rate of water utilization is to be socially efficient so as to maximize economic growth, then public as well as private sector involvement will be required as privatization, pricing reform and water markets all have the potential for establishing the incentives for more efficient use of water in the economy than simply relying on public sector water management alone.

Finally, freshwater supplies and use rates vary considerably across the regions within a country. A country as a whole may appear to have sufficient freshwater supplies relative to demand, but specific regions and sectors may not. Variability in climate, rainfall, demographics and economic activity may also contribute to problems of localized water scarcity. In particular, arid and semi-arid regions of the world are the most vulnerable to future water stress (Vörösmarty *et al.* 2000). An important extension to the cross-country study of this paper would be to examine regional differences in growth within a country or countries, particularly where a large number of regions are experiencing moderate or severe water scarcity. As we noted in the introduction, regional conflicts over water allocation may be particularly problematic in semi-arid regions of developing countries, especially where increased water demands for population growth and economic development are favoring allocation of one water use or uses over others. As long as this allocation is efficient, then water scarcity need not be a constraint on development and welfare. However, too often in developing countries decisions over such water allocations are not efficient, with potentially serious economic consequences. We illustrate this problem next with the case of upstream water diversion of the Hadejia'Jama'are River in Northern Nigeria.

Case study: Hadejia-Jama'are river basin, Northern Nigeria[23]

In Northeast Nigeria, an extensive floodplain has been created where the Hadejia and Jama'are Rivers converge to form the Komadugu Yobe River, which drains into Lake Chad (see Figure 7.2). Although referred to as wetlands, much of the Hadejia-Jama'are floodplain is dry for some or all of the year. Nevertheless, the floodplain provides essential income and nutrition benefits in the form of agriculture, grazing resources, non-timber forest products, fuelwood and fishing for local populations (Thomas and Adams 1999). The wetlands also serve wider regional economic purposes, such as providing dry season grazing for semi-nomadic pastoralists, agricultural surpluses for Kano and Borno states, groundwater recharge of the Chad Formation aquifer and many shallow aquifers throughout the region, and insurance resources in times of drought (Hollis *et al.* 1993; Thompson and Hollis 1995). In addition, the wetlands are a unique migratory habitat for many wildfowl and wader species from Palaearctic regions, and contain a number of forestry reserves (Hollis *et al.* 1993; Thompson and Polet 2000).

However, in recent decades the Hadejia-Jama'are floodplain has come under increasing pressure from drought and upstream water developments. The maximum extent of flooding has declined from between 250,000 to 300,000 Hectares (ha) in 1960s and 1970s to around 70,000 to 100,000 ha more recently (Thompson and Hollis

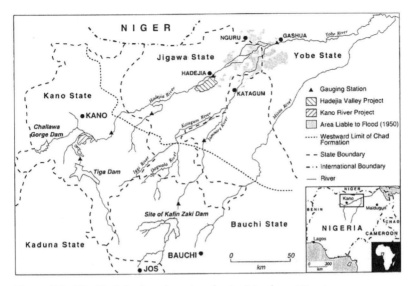

Figure 7.2. The Hadejia-Jama'are river basin, Northern Nigeria

1995; Thompson and Polet 2000). Drought is a persistent, stochastic environmental problem facing all sub-Saharan arid and semi-arid zones, and the main cause of unexpected reductions in flooding in drought years. The main long-term threat to the flooplain is water diversion through large-scale water projects on the Hadejia and Jama'are rivers. Upstream developments are affecting incoming water, either through dams altering the timing and size of flood flows or through diverting surface or groundwater for irrigation. These developments have been taking place without consideration of their impacts on the Hadejia-Jama' are floodplain or any subsequent loss of economic benefits that are currently provided by use of the floodplain.

The largest upstream irrigation scheme at present is the Kano River Irrigation Project (KRIP). Water supplies for the project are provided by Tiga Dam, the biggest dam in the basin, which was completed in 1974. Water is also released from this dam to supply Kano City. The second major irrigation scheme within the river basin, the Hadejia Valley Project (HVP), is under construction. The HVP is supplied by Challawa Gorge Dam on the Challawa River, upstream of Kano, which was finished in 1992. Challawa Gorge also provides water for Kano City water supply. A number of small dams and associated irrigation schemes have also been constructed or are planned for minor tributaries of the Hadejia River. In comparison, the Jama'are River is relatively uncontrolled with only one small dam across one of its tributaries. However, plans for a major dam on the Jama'are at Kafin Zaki have been in existence for many years, which would provide water for an irrigated area totaling 84,000 ha. Work on Kafin Zaki Dam has been started and then stopped a number of times, most recently in 1994, and its future is at present still unclear.

Against the benefits of these upstream water developments must be weighed the opportunity cost of the downstream floodplain losses. Economic valuation studies have focused on three types of floodplain benefits that are likely to be most affected by impacts on the floodplain:

- Flood-recession agriculture, fuelwood and fishing in the floodplain (Barbier *et al.* 1993).
- Groundwater recharge that supports dry season irrigated agricultural production (Acharya and Barbier 2000).
- Groundwater recharge of domestic water supply for household use (Acharya and Barbier 2002).

A combined economic and hydrological analysis was recently conducted to simulate the impacts of these upstream projects on the flood extent that determines the downstream floodplain area (Barbier and Thompson 1998). The economic gains of the upstream water projects were then compared to the resulting economic losses to downstream agricultural, fuelwood and fishing benefits.

Table 7.3 indicates the scenarios that comprise the simulation. Since Scenarios 1 and 1a reflect the conditions without any of the large-scale water resource schemes in place within the river basin they are employed as baseline conditions against which Scenarios 2–6 are compared. Scenario 2 investigates the impacts of extending the Kano River Irrigation Project (KRIP) to its planned full extent of 22,000 ha without any downstream releases. In contrast, Scenario 3 simulates the impacts of limiting irrigation on this project to the existing 14,000 ha to allow a regulated flood from Tiga Dam in August to sustain inundation within the downstream Hadejia-Jama'are floodplain. Challawa Gorge is added in Scenario 4 and the simulated operating regime involves the year-round release of water for the downstream Hadejia Valley Project (HVP), but not for sustaining the Hadejia-Jama'are floodplain. Scenario 5 simulates the full development of the four water resource schemes without any releases for the downstream floodplain. In direct comparison, Scenario 6 shows full upstream development, but less

Table 7.3 Scenarios for upstream projects in the Hadejia-Jama'are river basin, Nigeria

Scenario (time period)	Dams	Regulated releases ($10^6 m^3$)	Irrigation schemes
1 (1974–85)	Tiga	Naturalized Wudil flow (1974–1985)	No KRIP
1a (1974–90)	Tiga	Naturalized Wudil flow (1974–1990)	No KRIP
2 (1964–85)	Tiga	None	KRIP at 27,000 ha
3 (1964–85)	Tiga	400 in August for sustaining floodplain	KRIP at 14,000 ha
4 (1964–85)	Tiga Challawa Gorge Small dams on Hadejia tributaries	None 348/yr for HVP	KRIP at 27,000 ha
5 (1964–85)	Tiga Challawa Gorge Small dams on Hadejia tributaries Kafin Zaki HVP	None 348/yr for HVP None None	KRIP at 27,000ha 84,000 ha 12,500 ha
6 (1964–85)	Tiga Challawa Gorge Small dams on Hadejia tributaries Kafin Zaki HVP	350 in August 248/yr and 100 in July 100 per month in Oct-Mar and 550 in August Barrage open in August	KRIP at 14,000 ha None 8,000 ha

Notes:
1. KRIP = Kano River Irrigation Project.
2. HVP = Hadejia Valley Project.
Source: Barbier and Thompson (1998).

upstream irrigation occurs in order to allow regulated water releases from the dams to sustain inundation of the downstream floodplain.

Table 7.4 summarizes the estimated gains in irrigation benefits upstream with the downstream losses from agricultural, fuelwood and fish production in the floodplain for Scenarios 2–6 compared to the baseline Scenarios 1 and 1a. Given the high productivity of the floodplain, the losses in economic benefits due to changes in flood extent for all scenarios are large, ranging from US$2.6–4.2 million to US$23.4–24.0 million.[24] As expected, there is a direct tradeoff between increasing irrigation upstream and impacts on the wetlands downstream. Scenario 3, which yields the lowest upstream irrigation gains, also has the least impact in terms of floodplain losses, whereas Scenario 5 has both the highest irrigation gains and floodplain losses. The results confirm that in all the scenarios simulated the additional value of production from large-scale irrigation schemes does not replace the lost production attributed to the wetlands downstream. Gains in irrigation values account for at most 17% of the losses in floodplain benefits.

This combined hydrological-economic analysis would suggest that no new upstream developments should take place in addition to Tiga Dam. Moreover, a comparison of Scenario 3 to Scenario 2 in the analysis shows that it is economically worthwhile to reduce floodplain losses through releasing a substantial volume of water during the wet season, even though this would not allow Tiga Dam to supply the originally planned 27,000 ha on KRIP.

Although Scenario 3 is the preferred scenario, it is clearly unrealistic. As indicated above, Challawa Gorge was completed in 1992, and in recent years several small dams have been built on the Hadejia's tributaries while others are planned. Thus Scenario 4 most closely represents the current situation, and Scenario 5 is on the way to being implemented – although when the construction of Kafin Zaki Dam might occur is presently uncertain. As indicated in Table 7.4, full implementation of all the upstream dams and large-scale irrigation schemes would produce the greatest overall net losses, around US$20.2–20.9 million (in terms of net present value).

These results suggest that the expansion of the existing irrigation schemes within the river basin is effectively uneconomic. The construction of Kafin Zaki Dam and extensive large-scale formal irrigation schemes within the Jama'are Valley do not represent the most

Table 7.4 *Impact of scenarios in terms of losses in floodplain benefits versus gains in irrigated production, net present value (US$ 1989/90 prices)*

	Irrigation value [1][a]	Scenario 1			Scenario 1a		
		Floodplain loss [2][b]	Net loss [2] − [1]	[1] as % of [2]	Floodplain loss [3][b]	Net loss [3] − [1]	[1] as % of [3]
Scenario 2	682,983	−4,045,024	−3,362,041	16.88	−5,671,973	−4,988,990	12.04
Scenario 3	354,139	−2,558,051	−2,203,912	13.84	−4,184,999	−3,830,860	8.46
Scenario 4	682,963	−7,117,291	−6,434,328	9.60	−8,744,240	−8,061,277	7.81
Scenario 5	3,124,015	−23,377,302	−20,253,287	13.36	−24,004,251	−20,880,236	13.01
Scenario 6	556,505	−15,432,952	−14,876,447	3.61	−17,059,901	−16,503,396	3.26

Notes:
[a] Based on the mean of the net present values of per ha production benefits for the Kano River Irrigation Project, and applied to the gains in total irrigation area for each scenario.
[b] Based on the mean of the net present values of total agricultural, fuelwood and fishing benefits for the Hadejia-Jama' are floodplain, averaged over the actual peak flood extent for the wetlands of 112,817 ha in 1989/90 and applied to the declines in mean peak flood extent associated with each scenario.

Source: Barbier and Thompson (1998).

appropriate developments for this part of the basin. If Kafin Zaki Dam were to be constructed and formal irrigation within the basin limited to its current extent, the introduction of a regulated flooding regime (Scenario 6) would reduce the scale of this negative balance substantially, to around US$15.4–16.5 million. The overall combined value of production from irrigation and the floodplain would however still fall well below the levels experienced if the additional upstream schemes were not constructed.[25]

Such a regulated flooding regime could also produce additional economic benefits that are not captured in our analysis. Greater certainty over the timing and magnitude of the floods may enable farmers to adjust to the resulting reduction in the risks normally associated with floodplain farming. Enhanced dry season flows provided by the releases from Challawa Gorge and Kafin Zaki dams in Scenario 6 would also benefit farmers along the Hadejia and Jama'are Rivers while the floodplain's fisheries may also experience beneficial impacts from the greater extent of inundation remaining throughout the dry season. The introduction of a regulated flooding regime for the existing schemes within the basin may be the only realistic hope of minimizing floodplain losses. Proposed large-scale schemes, such as Kafin Zaki, should ideally be avoided if further floodplain losses are to be prevented. If this is not possible the designs for water resource schemes should enable the release of regulated floods in order to, at least partly, mitigate the loss of floodplain benefits that would inevitably result.

Currently, as a result of such economic and hydrological analyses of the downstream impacts of upstream water developments in the Hadejia-Jama'are floodplain both the States in Northern Nigeria and the Federal Government have become interested in developing regulated flooding regimes for the existing upstream dams at Challawa Gorge and Tiga, and have been reconsidering the construction of Kafin Zaki Dam. If these revised plans are fully implemented, then this suggests that some outcome between Scenarios 3 and 4 in Table 7.4 is likely for the Hadejia-Jama'are River Basin.

Finally, it should be noted that floodplain farmers downstream from the dam developments on the Hadejia and Jama'are Rivers have proven to be highly adaptive to changes in flood patterns that have occurred so far. For example, Thomas and Adams (1999) suggest that since the mid-1970s there have been considerable agrarian changes downstream in response to the construction of the Tiga Dam and subsequent drought years. The authors argue that "while in the short term the socioeconomic impacts of dams and drought were strongly negative, over a longer period the environmental changes caused by the dam and drought were strongly negative, over a longer period the environmental changes caused by the dam and drought gave added impetus to the diversification and expansion of agriculture" (Thomas and Adams 1999, p. 154). Table 7.5 summarizes some of the adaptive responses to changing flood patterns and environmental conditions that have occurred in the agricultural systems in the Hadejia-Jama'are floodplain.

The most important adaptive responses include expansion of rainfed farming on areas that no longer flood, and even the expansion of flood recession farming through the introduction of cowpeas; expansion of irrigated dry season farming and mechanized rice production; and increased off-farm employment (see Table 7.5). However, there are some important negative aspects to these trends. The sustainability of irrigated wheat and mechanized rice production has been questioned, especially due to the problems of soil erosion, declining fertility and overuse of water (Kimmage 1991; Kimmage and Adams 1992). Moreover, the expansion and shifting of agricultural production on to new lands has led to increased conflicts among farmers and between agriculturalists and the migrating *Fulani* pastoralists in the region, who for hundreds of years have had traditional communal dry season grazing rights to pasture within the floodplain area (Thomas and Adams 1999). While permanent emigration in search of new employment opportunities may in the short run reduce pressure on local land and water resources, in the long term it may affect the provision of rural health and educational services and the available pool of local agricultural labor.

Overall, the adaptive agrarian changes in response to the decline of flooding pattern downstream of the dams built in the Hadejia-Jama'are River Basin may mitigate somewhat the floodplain losses estimated for the different scenarios reported in Table 7.4. However, there are two notes of caution. First, as pointed out by Thomas and Adams (1999, p. 159) it is optimistic to consider all of the agrarian adaptations to be responses solely to the construction of Tiga Dam and the loss of downstream flood recession agricultural benefits: "most of the positive features of agricultural change in the Hadejia-Jama'are floodplain (new forms of recession farming, irrigation, improved marketing, etc.)

Table 7.5 Agrarian change downstream of the Tiga Dam, Nigeria

Adaptive response	Positive aspects	Negative aspects
Expansion of rainfed farming on areas that no longer flood	Increased rainfed area and yields at Zugobia. Relocated rainfed area at Dallah with higher yields.	Forest clearing, land use conflicts between Dallah and Gabaruwa, land use conflicts with Fulani pastoralists.
Expansion of flood recession farming	Introduction of drought-tolerant cow peas by migrants returning from Lake Chad to replace cassava.	Cassava would normally be preferred as it produces higher returns, uses less labor and is more pest resistant.
Expansion of dry season irrigated farming	Increased vegetable and wheat production through introduction of pumps, tubewells, credit and extension.	Forest clearing, increased erosion, crop and pest disease, agrochemical pollution. Conflicts with Fulani pastoralists.
Expansion of mechanized rice farming	In Tavurvur, increased yields and reduced labor costs.	Concentration of land ownership, reduced employment, agrochemical pollution. Dependence on government subsidies and special loans.
Increased off-farm employment	Increased income from salaried employment. Cash income safety net for drought years and crop failures.	Increased income inequality between wage earning and non-wage earning households. Increased rural–urban migration.

Source: Based on Thomas and Adams (1999).

would be likely to have happened anyway, without the dam, as they have elsewhere throughout northern Nigeria." Second, some of the farming innovations that have occurred in the floodplain, such as the expansion of dry season irrigated crop production, are themselves threatened by the impact of upstream water diversion on the downstream wetland areas and their ability to recharge the shallow aquifers that are used for tubewell irrigation (Acharya and Barbier 2000; DIYAM 1987; Thompson and Hollis 1995). It is the latter impacts on dry season irrigated agriculture that we now address.

Several hydrological studies of the Hadejia-Jama'are River Basin suggest that the "standing water" of the inundated areas of the downstream floodplains appears to percolate through the sub-soil to recharge many of the shallow aquifers in the area (DIYAM 1987; Thompson and Goes 1997; Thompson and Hollis 1995). As noted above, these shallow aquifers are increasingly being accessed through tubewell irrigation to expand dry season vegetable and wheat production. If upstream water diversion is causing less flooding and standing water downstream, then the resulting reduction in groundwater recharge could have important implications for dry season irrigated agricultural production downstream.

Acharya and Barbier (2000) have conducted an economic analysis of the impact of a decline in groundwater levels on dry season vegetable and wheat irrigated agricultural production in the floodplain region. They surveyed a sample of 37 farms in the Madachi area, out of a total 309 dry season farmers on 6,600 ha of cropland irrigated through tubewell abstraction from shallow aquifers. Wheat, tomato, onions, spring onions, sweet potatoes and pepper are the main cash crops grown by the farmers, although okra and eggplant are more minor crops grown principally for home consumption.[26] On average, irrigated dry season agriculture in the Madachi area is worth US$412.5 per ha, with a total estimated annual value of US$2.72 million over the entire 6,600 ha.

Employing a production function approach, Acharya and Barbier value the groundwater recharge function of the floodplain as an environmental input into the dry season agricultural production in the Madachi area.[27] They model crop-water production relationships for both vegetable and wheat production, and based on this analysis, the authors are able to calculate the welfare changes to farmers in Madachi of a one-meter fall in groundwater levels from six to seven meters in depth. The latter is the projected fall in mean water depth of the shallow aquifers in the area due to the declining flood extent and recharge function of the floodplain wetlands (Thompson and Goes 1997). The analysis was then extended to estimate the welfare impacts for all dry season irrigated farming on an estimated 19,000 ha throughout the floodplain.

Table 7.6 Welfare impacts on dry season farmers of a one-meter drop in groundwater levels, Hadejia-Jama'are river basin, Nigeria

	Average welfare loss per farmer (US$/year)	Total loss for all Madachi farmers (US$/year)[a]	Total loss for all dry season farmers (US$/year)[b]
Vegetable farmer	32.5	4,360	82,832
Wheat and vegetable farmers	330.8	57,890	1,099,905
All farmers		62,250 (2.3%)[c]	1,182,737 (15.1%)[d]

Notes:

[a] The Madachi farming area includes approximately 6,600 ha of irrigated dry season farming, comprising 134 vegetable farmers and 175 vegetable and wheat farmers.

[b] Based on an estimated total irrigated dry season farming area comprising 19,000 ha in the Hadejia-Jama'are floodplain area.

[c] Percentage of the annual net economic benefits of irrigated dry season agriculture in the Madachi area ($2.72 million).

[d] Percentage of the annual net economic benefits of irrigated dry season agriculture in the Hadejia-Jama'are floodplain area ($7.84 million).

Source: Acharya and Barbier (2000).

The results of the analysis are summarized in Table 7.6 suggest that a one-meter change in groundwater recharge would reduce the welfare by $32.5 annually on average for vegetable farmers (7.6% of annual income) in Madachi and by US$331 annually for farmers producing vegetables and wheat (77% of annual income). Total loss in annual income for all 134 vegetable farmers in Madachi is US$4,360, and for the 175 wheat and vegetable farmers US$57,890. The total loss for all 309 Madachi farmers of US$62,250 amounts to around 2.3% of the annual economic value of irrigated dry season farming in Madachi.

In the entire downstream region of the Hadejia-Jama'are River Basin, the annual losses to vegetable farmers amount to US$82,832. For wheat and vegetable farmers, the welfare loss is around US$1.1 million. The total welfare impact of around US$1.2 million annually is around 15.1% of the economic value of irrigated dry season agriculture in downstream areas.

Any impacts on the groundwater recharge of shallow aquifers due to a decline in the Hadejia-Jama'are flood inundation area will also have a major impact on village water wells that supply domestic water to households throughout the region. Villagers prefer to use well water for drinking, cooking and cleaning. Other activities such as watering of animals, washing clothes and utensils and house building may use water obtained directly from the wetlands in addition to well water. All households procure water from wells in one of three ways: i) they collect all their own well water, ii) they purchase all their water from vendors who collect well water, or iii) the households both collect and purchase their well water.

In order to estimate the value placed on groundwater either purchased or collected from village wells by households in the wetlands region, Acharya and Barbier (2002) have combined a hypothetical method of valuation, the contingent behavior method, with a household production model of observed behavior. Three villages in the Madachi region of the Hadejia-Jama'are floodplain and one village in the Sugum region were chosen for the economic valuation study, based on the hydrological evidence that the villages in these areas rely on groundwater recharged mainly by wetlands (Thompson and Goes 1997). The flooding in Madachi is caused by the floodwaters of the Hadejia River. The Sugum region is located in the eastern part of the wetlands and is influenced by the flooding of the Jama'are River.

The first step in the valuation approach was to derive and estimate the demand for water by the various types of households. To do this, a household production function model was constructed to determine the factors influencing a representative household's decision to choose its preferred method of water procurement – collect only, purchase only or both collect and purchase. The second step in the valuation procedure was to use the household water demand relationships to estimate the effect of a change in wetland flooding on the welfare of village households dependent on groundwater well supplies. As noted above, hydrological evidence suggests that reduced flooding in the wetlands will result in lower recharge rates and hence changes in groundwater levels in wells (Thompson and Hollis, 1995; Thompson and Goes, 1997). Changes in groundwater levels in turn affect collection time and the price of vended water, assuming all other household characteristics remain constant. The welfare impacts associated with

Table 7.7 Welfare impacts on households of a one-meter drop in groundwater levels, Hadejia-Jama'are river basin, Nigeria

Household type	Number of affected households in wetlands	Welfare loss per household (US$/ day)	Welfare loss for the wetlands (US$/day)
Purchase only	22,650	0.033	736
Collect only	57,013	0.137	7,833
Collect and purchase	28,302	0.226	6,410
All households	107,965	0.121	13,029

Source: Acharya and Barbier (2002).

these price changes were therefore estimated as changes in consumer surplus in the relevant household water demand equations.[28]

To value the change in the recharge function due to reduced flooding within the wetlands, it was hypothesized that a decrease of one meter in the level of water in village wells would result in an increased collecting time of 25% and an increase in the price of vended water of approximately one cent.[29] These assumptions are based on the evidence provided by the survey data on the relationship between collection time and well water levels and on the change in price indicated by vendors as likely to occur, in the event of a one meter decrease in water levels. Using the estimated demand equations, the welfare effects due to changes in both collection time and the price of vended water were calculated for the sample of households surveyed. These effects were then extrapolated to the entire population of the floodplain in order to calculate an aggregate welfare impact. The results are depicted in Table 7.7.[30]

The welfare estimates suggest the average welfare effect of a one-meter change in water levels is approximately US$0.12 per household per day. This impact is equivalent to a daily loss of approximately 0.23% of monthly income for purchase only households, 0.4% of monthly income for collect only households and 0.14% of monthly income for collect & purchase households. The total value across all floodplain households of maintaining the current groundwater recharge function (i.e. avoiding a one-meter drop in well water levels) amounts to US$13,029 per day. This translates into an annual value of US$4.76 million for the groundwater recharge of village wells by the floodplain wetlands. Such estimated welfare losses indicate that the failure of the Hadejia-Jama'are wetlands to provide the existing daily level of recharge would result in a substantial economic loss for wetland populations presently deriving benefit from groundwater use for domestic consumption.

Final remarks

There is no doubt that increased population growth and development needs will continue to place increasing stress on available freshwater supplies in developing economies. This is reflected in the "stylized facts" of water use highlighted in Chapter 1: Developing countries already account for 71% of global water withdrawal, and water demand in low and middle-income economies is expected to grow further by 27% over 1995 to 2025 (see Table 1.5). Moreover, the problem of water stress and scarcity is expected to worsen for key developing regions and countries, notably China, India, Pakistan, the Philippines, South Korea, Mexico, Egypt and virtually all other countries in West Asia/ North Africa, as well as for specific river basin regions within each of these countries (see Table 1.6).

However, the model of water use and economic growth presented in this chapter and estimated empirically for a broad cross-section of 163 countries suggests that it may be premature to consider that there is a widespread problem of "global water scarcity" in the sense that economic development worldwide is likely to be severely constrained by physical water limits. Increased water utilization may hamper growth in the near future, but if this does occur, it will most likely happen in the handful of countries that exhibit moderate or extreme water scarcity. Most of these countries are in the West Asia/North Africa region (Algeria, Djibouti, Libya, Bahrain, Israel, Jordan, Kuwait, Burundi, Oman, Qatar, Saudi Arabia, United Arab Emirates and Yemen). A few are from Sub-Saharan Africa (Cape Verde, Kenya, Rwanda and Uganda). Two are from Asia (Maldives and Singapore) and one is from Southern Europe (Malta). Some of the wealthier countries (e.g., Israel, Malta, Saudi Arabia and Singapore) have already invested heavily in improving economy-wide efficiency of water use, conserving available water supplies and finding new supplies (e.g. through developing de-salinization technology). But there is concern that the poorer countries may not be able to afford such investments. Also, if future trends in water stress and scarcity are accurate, then there is the possibility that other countries may also find themselves facing binding water conditions on their economic development. These latter countries include some of the more regionally important and populous economies of the developing world, notably China, India, Pakistan, the Philippines, South Korea, Mexico and Egypt.

As emphasized in this chapter, however, ensuring the water will be used efficiently in countries and not constrain growth and development will require further institutional reforms. For instance, it was noted that, given the rapid growth of water demands over recent decades, the public sector alone may be incapable of ensuring socially efficient levels of supply and water utilization in many countries. Instead, providing an adequate water supply to an economy and ensuring its efficient utilization will require increasingly both public and private sector participation, with some of the services more efficiently provided by the private sector. Thus, privatization, pricing reform and water markets all have the potential for establishing the incentives for more efficient use of water in the economy so as to maximize growth and development efforts, even in the poorest economies of the world.

However, perhaps the most important message of this chapter is that a developing country as a whole may appear to have sufficient freshwater supplies relative to demand, but specific regions and key sectors within the economy may not. Too often, such regional and sectoral water supply problems are exacerbated by poor policy decisions that lead to inefficient allocation of existing water supplies. The case study highlighted in this chapter of upstream water diversion on the Hadejia and Jama'are Rivers of Northern Nigeria illustrates this problem.

As the case study demonstrates, the substantial losses associated with upstream diversion suggest that the expansion of the existing irrigation schemes within the river basin is effectively uneconomic. The introduction of a regulated flooding regime would probably protect the groundwater recharge function of the downstream wetlands as well as reduce substantially the losses to floodplain recession agriculture, forestry and fishing, to around US$15.4–16.5 million (Table 7.4 Scenario 6). However, the latter losses could be reduced even further if the plans to construct Kafin Zaki Dam and to implement the Hadejia Valley Project fully are abandoned. The result would be an outcome between Scenarios 3 and 4 reported in Tables 7.3 and 7.4. The net downstream losses would therefore be in the region of US$2.2 to US$8.1 million.

This may be the best outcome, given that Tiga Dam, Challawa Gorge and many small dams on the tributaries of the Hadejia River have already been constructed.

There is an important lesson here from this case study for other developing countries: Upstream water investments and developments should not be based on the assumption that water is a "free" good. The correct economic approach to assessing dams and other water projects upstream that divert water is to consider the forgone net benefits of disruption to the natural environment and degradation downstream as part of the opportunity costs of the development investment. This is particularly important where substantial impacts on economic liveli-hoods will result from the hydrological and ecological impacts of upstream water diversion, as the case study of the Hadejia-Jama'are River Basin in Northern Nigeria illustrates.

Of course, an important question to ask with regard to the Hadejia-Jama'are Case Study is why were the dams constructed in the first place, given that the economic gains in terms of irrigation were so dispropor-tionately small compared to the economic losses imposed downstream due to widespread disturbances to the floodplain? Although the eco-nomic livelihoods of up to one million rural villagers downstream may have been affected by these losses, it is clear that they had little say in the water allocation decision to build the upstream dams. Instead, in the case of the decision to build dams on the Hadejia and Jama'are Rivers, this decision was taken mainly with the benefits of engineering and construc-tion companies and wealthier landowners, who could invest in large-scale irrigated agriculture, in mind. It appears that this case study is another example in the developing world where relatively poor rural populations that are most adversely affected by allocation of a critical natural resource for their livelihoods have little influence on the policy decisions determining this allocation.

As this problem is widespread, and has important implications for the role of natural resources in economic development in many poor regions of the world, it will be the main focus of the next chapter.

Notes

1. This model and subsequent empirical analysis is based on Barbier (2004c).
2. The increasing role of the private sector in the provision of water services in some economies is discussed further in the conclusion, particularly with

regard to improving the efficiency of water use. However, the use of institutions such as water markets and privatized water utilities does not necessarily detract from the overall view of water as a congestible non-excludable good, nor does it affect significantly the assumption that it is a public authority that is ultimately responsible for providing this good, even though the authority may decide that the most efficient way of providing some services is to allow regulated private entities be the ultimate end-use supplier. See Dosi and Easter (2000) and Johnstone and Wood (2001) for further discussion.

3. Interestingly, the authors suggest that "water systems" are a good example of this type of congestion model of economic growth Specifically, Barro and Sala-I-Martin (1992, p. 650) state: "The congestion model applies readily to highways and other transportation facilities, water and sewer systems, courts, etc." Futagami *et al.* (1993) extend the model by Barro (1990) to include both public and private capital, which allows the additional advantage of being able to analyze the transitional dynamics of an economy to its steady state. As public infrastructure is an important input in the supply of water provided to producers, depicting water supply as a non-excludable, congestible good produced through public capital accumulation would be an interesting theoretical extension of the current paper. For example, denoting g as public infrastructure per person and r as freshwater utilization per capita, one could depict $r = r(k_g), r' > 0, r'' < 0$, and equation (2) in the model of this paper, below, would be modified to $\dot{k}_g = z(\rho)$, with the function z having the same properties defined in (2).

4. As noted by Barro (1990), the government could be one of the producers in the economy with production function (1). Equally, the output, y_i, which results from production may itself be "delivered" water. Both factors may be particularly important with respect to domestic water use, where the producer supplying water directly to consumer households could be either a privately or publicly owned utility. However, regardless of who owns the water utility, this "producer" of "delivered" water to domestic households would have to compete with producers in the agricultural and industrial sectors for available water supplies in the entire economy. Such aggregate supplies of water therefore still have the characteristic of a public good subject to congestion, and thus equation (7.1) applies to all private and public production in the domestic, industrial and agricultural sectors of an economy that utilize water.

5. A specific functional form for $z(\rho)$ corresponding to (7.2) might be $\alpha \rho^\gamma$, $\beta = \alpha \gamma$.

6. If water scarcity is not binding, i.e. $\mu(t) = 0$, then condition (8) reduces to $f(z(\rho)) = (1 - z(\rho))f'(z(\rho))$. Efficient water use requires that the marginal benefit of an increase in the rate of water utilization, $f'(z(\rho))/f(z(\rho))$, must equal its marginal cost, $1/(1 - z(\rho))$. The benefit of increased water utilization in the economy is that it contributes to more aggregate per capita

output. The cost is that the government must appropriate a larger proportion of aggregate output to provide water supplies to the economy. The above equation is therefore the social efficiency condition determining the optimal rate of water utilization, if the economy does not face any binding water scarcity constraint.

7. If both α and w are constant then it follows from this constraint that y must also be constant; i.e. there is no growth in per capita income in the water-constrained economy. To rule out this outcome and to make this case interesting, we assume that, by appropriating output at its maximum rate, the government is able to increase freshwater availability, although not sufficiently to overcome the binding constraint, i.e. $\alpha y = w = r$. Essentially, there are two ways that a government might increase w in a water-constrained economy. First, it might invest in improved wastewater treatment to increase the rate of recovery and return of water withdrawals to the original freshwater sources. Second, it might invest in de-salinization plants to augment freshwater sources with converted sea and brackish water. Both approaches are common, albeit expensive, options currently being explored by water-constrained economies in the world (Gleick 2000).

8. It follows that, for the water-constrained economy, condition (7.8) is now
$$\lambda[(1 - \alpha)Akf'(\alpha)\beta - Akf(\alpha)\beta] = \mu[Akf(\alpha)\beta + \alpha Akf'(\alpha)\beta]$$
or $\mu = \lambda\left[\frac{f'(\alpha)}{f(\alpha)+\alpha f'(\alpha)} - 1\right] > 0$. The latter condition (7.17) determines the optimal use of water in the water-constrained economy. From the complementary slackness condition, $\mu > 0$, and as $\lambda > 0$, which means $\frac{f'(\alpha)}{f(\alpha)+\alpha f'(\alpha)} > 1$, i.e. in the water-constrained economy the marginal benefit of an extra unit of water in terms of its marginal productivity contribution always exceeds the social cost of providing water. A binding water scarcity constraint implies that it is socially optimal for the government to choose the maximum rate of appropriating economic output in order to supply freshwater, $\alpha y = r = w$, as the benefits of water use will always outweigh the costs of appropriation.

9. For the proof, see the previous note.

10. See Faurés *et al.* (2001) for the FAO AQUASTAT methodology. Surface water resources are usually computed by measuring total river flow occurring in a country on a yearly basis. Groundwater resources are expressed as a measure of aquifer recharge through infiltration. In arid areas, groundwater is estimated in terms of recharge from rainfall, whereas in humid areas aquifer recharge is associated with the base flow of connected river systems.

11. The original development of the water stress or scarcity index is attributed to the Swedish hydrologist Malin Falkenmark. The Falkenmark

index suggests that water stress for a country begins when there is less than 1,700 cubic meters of freshwater available per capita per year. When the index reaches 1,000 m³/year per capita, then water stress is severe. For further discussion, see Falkenmark (1989) and Falkenmark and Rockström (1998). Hydrologists also use the UN's "criticality ratio" of water withdrawals relative to the total freshwater renewable resources available to each country annually (Cosgrove and Rijsberman 2000; United Nations 1997). Vörösmarty *et al.* (2000) refer to the "cricitcality ratio" as "relative water demand" (RWD). An RWD value between 0.2 to 0.4 indicates medium to high stress, whereas a value greater than 0.4 reflect conditions of severe water limitation.

12. As discussed by Barbier (2004c) ideally one would want to test any relationship between growth and ρ through a pooled cross-sectional and time series (i.e. panel) analysis. However, the *World's Water* database reports only a single-year estimate of freshwater withdrawals and supplies for each country. In addition, because different sources are used to provide these estimates, the year in which *r* and *w* is estimated varies greatly from country to country. Given these limitations, it is therefore possible to estimate a cross-country relationship between per capita growth in GDP and ρ through a cross-sectional as opposed to a panel analysis.

13. The original "fixed" variables chosen by Sala-I-Martin (1999) included life expectancy in the initial year rather than the secondary-school enrolment rate. The author justifies the use of the latter two variables because "both are reasonable and widely used measures of the initial stock of human capital" (Sala-I-Martin 1999, p. 180). However, Temple (1999, p. 135) has argued that to include the primary-school enrolment rate without also including the secondary-school enrolment rate, or vice versa, "tends to exaggerate the variation in human capital across countries." Following this approach, we therefore include the secondary-school enrollment rate in the initial year as one of our three "fixed" variables. We exclude life expectancy because there were a significant number of missing observations in this data series for the countries in our sample.

14. The World Bank's governance data set covers 178 countries and therefore is the best match for the 163 countries of our sample of all the institutional data series currently available. The indicators in this data set are based on data referring to 1997–98 and are measured in units ranging from about −2.5 to 2.5, with higher values corresponding to better governance outcomes (e.g. greater political stability or control of corruption). The FAO classification of developing countries excludes the advanced economies of the Organization for Economic Cooperation and Development, the former Soviet republics and Eastern European countries in transition, South Africa and Israel.

15. See Barbier (2004c) for a discussion of the regression approach and the various statistical tests employed.
16. The countries are Bahrain, Kuwait, Libya, Malta, Qatar, Saudi Arabia and the United Arab Emirates. Note that Kuwait, Libya, Qatar and the United Arab Emirates do not appear in the regression sample as observations of five-year average annual growth rates could not be obtained for these countries over the specified time periods. Fifteen other countries also do not appear in the regression sample as observations of five-year average annual growth rates could not be obtained for these countries either. One additional country does not appear in the regression sample as an observation of its rate of water withdrawal could not be obtained. In sum, whereas the full sample contains 163 countries, due to missing observations the largest regression sample reported in Table 7.1 is 143 countries.
17. In fact the sample for the regression is even smaller as four of the countries, Jordan, Kuwait, Libya, Qatar and the United Arab Emirates, do not have observations for five-year annual growth rates.
18. The year 2000 level of population was preferred to population in 2025 because we are estimating the effects of potential water scarcity on five-year average annual growth rates during the 1980s and 1990s for most countries.
19. The four countries in the sample with moderate water scarcity are Burundi, Cape Verde, Kenya and Rwanda. The sixteen countries with extreme water scarcity are Algeria, Djibouti, Libya, Uganda, Bahrain, Israel, Jordan, Kuwait, Maldives, Oman, Qatar, Saudi Arabia, Singapore, United Arab Emirates, Yemen and Malta.
20. The same procedure for detecting and correcting for heteroskedasticity in the regressions for Table 7.1 was also followed for the regressions reported in Table 7.2 See Barbier (2004c) for further details.
21. Thus, as noted by Gleick (2000, p. 26), "the theoretical water availability rarely represents the actual water available to any particular person, which depends on economic factors, legal water rights, technical ability to capture, store, and move water from place to place, political agreements with neighboring countries, and so on ... On paper, the Sudan has a vast amount of water available on average, but it is compelled by a treaty signed with Egypt to pass on much of the water it receives in the Nile from upstream nations. In recent years, internal turmoil and civil war have prevented the Sudan from using even its legal share from the Nile treaty."
22. For example, Sullivan (2002, p. 1199) notes: "Almost all natural ecosystems can perform valuable hydrological functions, such as water purification, flood control, habitat provision and groundwater recharge, and many of these can help to reduce both water stress and poverty."
23. This case study is based on Acharya and Barbier (2000 and 2002); Barbier (2003b); Barbier and Thompson (1998) and Barbier et al. (1993).

24. Note that one reason for these high losses in floodplain benefits is that the total production area dependent on the wetlands is around 6.5 times greater than the actual area flooded. This critical feature of a semi-arid floodplain, its ability to "sustain" a production area much greater than the area flooded, is often underestimated and ignored. This in turn means that changes in flood extent have a greater multiplier impact in terms of losses in economic benefits in production areas within and adjacent to the floodplain, because of the high dependence of these areas on regular annual flooding. See Barbier and Thompson (1998) for more details.

25. Some of the upstream water developments are being used or have the potential to supply water to Kano City. Although these releases are included in the hydrological simulations, the economic analysis was unable to calculate the benefits to Kano City of these water supplies. However, the hydrological analysis shows that the proposed regulated water release from Tiga Dam to reduce downstream floodplain losses would not affect the ability of Tiga Dam to supply water to Kano. Although the potential exists for Challawa Gorge to supply additional water to Kano, it is unclear how much water could be used for this purpose. The resulting economic benefits are unlikely to be large enough to compensate for the substantial floodplain losses incurred by the Gorge and the additional upstream developments in the Hadejia Valley. Currently, there are no plans for Kafin Zaki Dam to be used to supply water to Kano. In addition, the economic analysis was unable to calculate other important floodplain benefits, such as the role of the wetlands in supporting pastoral grazing and in recharging groundwater both within the floodplain and in surrounding areas. Groundwater recharge by the floodplain may provide potable water supplies to populations within the middle and lower parts of the river basin, and supply tubewell irrigation for dry season farming downstream (Barbier *et al.* 1993).

26. Some farmers are also involved in mechanized rice production, but as this crop does not involve use of groundwater irrigation, it was excluded from the subsequent analysis.

27. See Chapter 9 for further discussion and examples of the application of the "production function" approach to valuing environmental functions in developing countries.

28. The estimated demand equations were Marshallian, or ordinary, demand functions. Consumer surplus measures based on ordinary demand functions will be a reasonable estimate of a multi-price change on welfare if the resulting income effects are small. It was assumed that this condition was likely for the price change in the Northern Nigeria case study.

29. The price of vended water in the surveyed villages ranged from 2.3 to 5.7 cents per 36 liters of water. The average amount of water collected either by vendors or households per trip is 36 liters, which is carried to houses in two 18-liter tins.

30. To calculate the consumer surplus effects of a change in collection time, a shadow value of time spent collecting water was estimated, using an approximate based on the local agricultural wage rate. See Acharya and Barbier (2002) for details.

8 | Rural poverty and resource degradation

> "People in poor countries are for the most part agrarian and pastoral folk ... Poor countries are for the most part *biomass-based subsistence economies*, in that their rural folk eke out a living from products obtained directly from plants and animals."
>
> (Dasgupta 1993, pp. 269 and 273)

P ART One of this book provided a broad overview of the role of natural resources in economic development. Part Two focused on the economic driving forces behind two key resource problems in many poor economies: widespread land conversion and the increasing demand for freshwater.

The following chapter, which begins Part Three, centers on a third important aspect of natural resources and economic development in poor countries, namely that much of the population in low and middle-income economies is concentrated in rural areas and remains dependent on agricultural and other renewable resources for their livelihoods, as emphasized by the above quote from Partha Dasgupta. This has two important implications for an economic approach to improved resource management for sustainable development in poor countries. First, we need to understand better the linkages between rural poverty and resource degradation in order to understand why the environment-poverty "trap" is so entrenched in many poor rural areas. Second, as we shall see in the final two chapters of this book, Chapters 9 and 10, understanding how this rural poverty-resource degradation arises in developing countries is critical to designing appropriate policies and reforms to improve overall resource-based development in developing economies.

The purpose of this chapter is to explore further a recurring theme touched on and illustrated in many chapters of this book: the problem of resource degradation and poverty in developing countries. As this is a potentially huge topic – over 1 billion people in the world live on less than US$1 day and most are dependent on some form of resource use – any meaningful analysis of the linkage between resource degradation and poverty must be organized around a consistent theme.

The four "stylized facts" highlighted in Chapter 1 suggests that there are currently two types of "dualism" in patterns of resource use within developing countries that are very much relevant to the problem of resource degradation and poverty.

The first "dualism" concerns aggregate resource use and dependency *within the global economy*. The main concern with this type of dualism is the tendency of resource-based development in many low and middle-income countries to be correlated with poor economic performance and development prospects. The second "dualism" concerns aggregate resource use and dependency *within a developing economy*. The main concern with this type of dualism is the tendency for a large number of the poorest members of the population of a developing country to be concentrated in marginal frontier areas and on ecologically "fragile" land, while any rents generated through exploitation of valuable natural resources accrue largely to wealthier households.

Most studies of resource degradation and poverty tend to focus on the problems posed by the second type of dualism, in particular the widespread land conversion and degradation caused by poor rural households. However, a major innovation of this chapter is to show that the observed "causation" between rural poverty and resource degradation in many developing countries often stems from important "cumulative causation" links between the two types of dualism described above. Because of these links, we refer to this process as the *"dualism within dualism" pattern of resource use*. As this chapter will show, it is this process that reinforces the entrenched relationships between rural poverty and resource degradation that are so endemic to many developing countries.

We begin by characterizing the main features of the "dualism within dualism" pattern of resource-based development. We will then focus in particular on how inequalities in wealth between rural households have an important impact on resource degradation processes, and how such problems are exacerbated by government policies that favor wealthier households in markets for key resources, such as land. Finally, we will discuss what policy measures are required to reverse this "cumulative causative" process that is reinforcing the environment-poverty "trap" that links rural poverty to resource degradation in developing economies.

The "dualism within dualism" pattern of resource use

As we discussed in Chapter 1, most low and middle-income economies are highly dependent on the exploitation of their natural resource endowments for commercial, export-oriented economic activities. However, an important outcome of this resource dependency is that the major investors in export-oriented resource-based economic activities, whether in commercial agriculture, mining, timber extraction or other activities, tend to be relatively wealthier households. These households generally have education and skilled labor advantages that allow them to attain higher income levels, accumulated wealth available for investment and the collateral for and access to formal credit markets for financial loans.

The process of resource exploitation in resource-dependent developing economies also tends to involve the following "cumulative causation" cycle. Development in low and middle-income economies is accompanied by substantial resource conversion. In particular, expansion of the agricultural land base in these economies is occurring rapidly through conversion of forests, wetlands and other natural habitat. In addition, many developing regions of the world are also placing greater stress on their freshwater resources as a result of increasing population and demand. Although it is commonly believed that poor rural households are mainly responsible for much of this resource conversion, what is often overlooked is that inequalities in wealth between rural households also have an important impact on resource degradation processes. Moreover, such problems are exacerbated by government policies that favor wealthier households in markets for key resources, such as land.

The consequence is that resource dependency of developing economies is usually accompanied by excessive resource conversion, and the benefits of this conversion are inequitably distributed. That is, the abundance of land and natural resources available in many developing countries does not necessarily mean that exploitation of this natural wealth will lead either to sustained economic growth, widespread benefits or substantial rural poverty alleviation. The increased concentration of the rural poor in marginal land and resource areas continues, and this in turn will generate the conditions for additional resource conversion through the process of frontier resource expansion.

The above processes of resource use and conversion suggest that there are currently two types of "dualism" in patterns of resource use within developing countries that are very much relevant to the problem of resource degradation and poverty. In addition, both types of dualism are also reflected in the four "stylized facts" highlighted in Chapter 1.

The first "dualism" is revealed by the first two stylized facts, and concerns aggregate resource use and dependency within the global economy. For example, the first stylized fact suggests that most low and middle-income economies are highly dependent on the exploitation of natural resources. For many of these economies, primary product exports account for the vast majority of their export earnings, and one or two primary commodities make up the bulk of exports. The second stylized fact suggests that, currently for developing countries, increasing economic dependence on natural resources is negatively correlated with economic performance. The implications for low income countries is that the "take-off" into sustained and structurally balanced economic growth and development is still some time away, and thus the dependence of their overall economies on natural resources will persist over the medium and long term.

Thus, one indicator of this first type of dualism might be the degree of resource dependency of an economy, as measured by the share of primary commodities in total exports. For instance, an economy with a primary product export share of 50% or more would be considered highly resource-dependent and more susceptible to this first type of dualism.

The second "dualism" is revealed by the last two stylized facts, and concerns aggregate resource use and dependency within a developing economy. The third stylized fact suggests that economic development in low-income countries is associated with high rates of land conversion and degradation as well as increased stress on available freshwater resources. However, the fourth stylized fact suggests that many poor people in rural areas may not necessarily be benefiting from this increased resource use. Instead, a substantial proportion of the population in low and middle-income countries is concentrated in marginal areas and on ecologically fragile land, such as converted forest frontier areas, poor quality uplands, converted wetlands and so forth. Households on these lands not only face problems of land degradation and low productivity but also tend to be some of the poorest in the world.

Two indicators of this second type of dualism might be the share of the total population concentrated on fragile lands, as defined by the World Bank (2003, p. 59) and discussed in Chapter 1, and the share of the rural population living under conditions of absolute poverty. Combining these two indicators gives us an approximate benchmark, or "20–20 rule," for the degree of rural poverty-resource use dualism within a developing economy: a country with 20% or more of its population concentrated on fragile land and 20% or more of its rural population living in rural poverty shows evidence of the second type of dualism.

Table 8.1 combines the above two sets of indicators to show the extent of "dualism within dualism" for seventy-two low and middle-income economies. The countries are grouped in terms of their degree of resource dependency, as measured by the share of primary products in total exports, and the extent to which their populations are concentrated on fragile land. The figure in the parentheses by each country also indicates the percentage of the rural population below the national poverty line.

According to the table, 56 out of the 72 economies have a primary product export share of 50% or more, and therefore display evidence of the first type of dualism, i.e. resource dependency within the global economy. All the economies have 20% or more of their population on fragile land and all but 7 also have 20% or more of the rural population living in absolute poverty. Thus by the "20–20 rule," virtually all the economies listed in Table 8.1 show signs of the second type of dualism, i.e. a high incidence of rural poverty-resource degradation linkage within the economy. What is more striking is that, with the exception of the Yemen Arab Republic and Indonesia, all 56 highly resource-dependent countries also satisfy the "20–20 rule."[1] That is, three-quarters of the countries listed in Table 8.1 show considerable evidence of "dualism-within-dualism" characteristics.

Of the 16 countries that do not show strong signs of the first type of dualism, i.e. they have a primary product export share of less than 50%, many of the countries nevertheless show a high degree of the second type of dualism. For example, Haiti, Lesotho, Nepal and

Table 8.1 Selective countries displaying "dualism within dualism" characteristics

	Share of population on fragile land ≥50%	Share of population on fragile land 30–50%	Share of population on fragile land 20–30%
Primary product export share ≥90%	Burkina Faso (61.2)	Algeria (30.3)	Ecuador (47.0)
	Chad (67.0)	Angola (NA)	Congo, Rep. (NA)
	Congo Dem. Rep. (NA)	Benin (33.0)	Liberia (NA)
	Laos (53.0)	Botswana (NA)	Zambia (88.0)
	Mali (72.8)	Cameroon (32.4)	
	Niger (66.0)	Comoros (NA)	
	Papua New Guinea (NA)	Eq. Guinea (NA)	
	Somalia (NA)	Ethiopia (31.3)	
	Sudan (NA)	Gambia (64.0)	
	Yemen A.R. (19.2)	Guyana (NA)	
		Iran (NA)	
		Mauritania (57.0)	
		Nigeria (36.4)	
		Rwanda (51.2)	
		Uganda (55.0)	
Primary product export share 50–90%	Egypt (23.3)	Central Af. Rep. (66.6)	Bolivia (79.1)
	Zimbabwe (31.0)	Chad (67.0)	Burundi (36.2)
		Guatemala (71.9)	Côte d'Ivoire (32.3)
		Guinea (40.0)	El Salvador (55.7)
		Kenya (46.4)	Ghana (34.3)
		Morocco (27.2)	Guinea-Bissau (48.7)
		Senegal (40.4)	Honduras (51.0)
		Sierra Leone (76.0)	Indonesia (15.7)

Table 8.1 (continued)

	Share of population on fragile land ≥50%	Share of population on fragile land 30–50%	Share of population on fragile land 20–30%
		Syria (NA)	Madagascar (77.0)
		Tanzania (51.1)	Mozambique (37.9)
			Myanmar (NA)
			Panama (64.9)
			Peru (64.7)
			Togo (32.3)
			Trinidad & Tobago (20.0)
			China (4.6)
			Dominican Rep. (29.8)
			India (36.7)
			Jamaica (33.9)
			Jordan (15.0)
			Malaysia (15.5)
			Mexico (10.1)
			Sri Lanka (20.0)
			Vietnam (57.2)
Primary product export share			
<50%		Costa Rica (25.5)	
		Haiti (66.0)	
		Lesotho (53.9)	
		Nepal (44.0)	
		Pakistan (36.9)	
		South Africa (11.5)	
		Tunisia (21.6)	

Notes:

Primary commodity export share is the average export share 1990/99 for low and middle-income countries (see Chapter 1).

Share of population on fragile land is from World Bank, *World Development Report 2003*, Table 4.3.

Figure in parenthesis is the percentage of the rural population below the national poverty line, from World Bank, 2002 World Development Indicators.

Pakistan have 30–50% of their populations on fragile land and display an incidence of rural poverty of 30–70%. The Dominican Republic, India, Jamaica and Vietnam have 20–30% of their populations living in fragile areas and around 30–60% of their rural populations in poverty. Only China and Mexico, and to a lesser extent Jordan and Malaysia, do not conform very strongly to the second type of dualism, according to the "20–20 rule" for population concentrated on fragile land and the degree of rural poverty.

In sum, the "dualism within dualism" characteristics of most developing countries suggest that the process of resource-based development undertaken by these economies is not yielding widespread benefits. As we have discussed throughout this book, agricultural land expansion, and natural resource exploitation by primary sector activities more generally, appears to be a fundamental feature of economic development in many of today's poorer economies. Yet, as we have seen, many developing economies have a large concentration of their populations on fragile land and high incidence of rural poverty. Also, developing countries that are highly dependent on exploiting their natural resource endowments tend to exhibit a relatively poor growth performance. This poses an intriguing paradox. Why is it that, despite the importance of natural capital for sustainable economic development, increasing economic dependence on natural resource exploitation appears to be a hindrance to growth and development in today's low and middle-income economies?

In Chapter 4 we provided one explanation of this paradox: most developing economies appear to be dependent on a process of frontier-based economic development that is yielding very little overall benefits. That is, this type of development is symptomatic of a pattern of economy-wide resource exploitation that: i) generates little additional economic rents, and ii) the rents that are generated are not being reinvested in more productive and dynamic sectors, such as manufacturing.

However, Chapter 4 also identified an important side effect of the process of resource exploitation associated with frontier-based development that has direct implications for the linkage between resource degradation and rural poverty in poor economies, and the consequent "dualism within dualism" characteristics of these economies.

First, frontier land expansion appears to be serving mainly as an outlet for the rural poor in many developing countries. This suggests that much of the output is for subsistence or local markets. Moreover, as we have seen, large segments of the rural poor end up being located on "marginal" or "fragile" land exhibiting low productivity as well as significant constraints for intensive agriculture. For example, the 1.2 billion people in developing countries occupying fragile lands include 518 million living in arid regions with no access to irrigation systems, 430 million on soils unsuitable for agriculture, 216 million on land with steep slopes and more than 130 million in fragile forest systems (World Bank 2003). This type of "marginal" agriculture typically generates very little rents or wealth for poor rural households, and provides very little opportunities for them to improve their economic livelihoods.

Second, an important outcome of the "resource dependency" of many low and middle-income countries is that the major investors in export-oriented resource-based economic activities, whether in commercial agriculture, mining, timber extraction or other activities, tend to be relatively wealthier households. The education, skills and wealth of these households allow them to maintain their advantage in key resource markets, as well as to generate the funds necessary for large-scale resource investments and the collateral for and access to formal credit markets for financial loans. In short, it is wealthier households that tend to invest in and benefit from many of the large-scale resource-extractive activities of resource-dependent developing economies, which are often responsible for initially opening up previously inaccessible frontier areas (Barbier 1997a). Investors in such activities are attracted to frontier areas because of the lack of government controls and property rights in these remote areas mean that resource rents are easily captured, and thus frontier resource-extractive activities are particularly prone to rent-seeking behavior (Ascher 1999).

Finally, this "dualism within dualism" economic structure in low and middle-income countries is often perpetuated by a policy climate that reinforces rent-seeking behavior by wealthier investors exploiting valuable natural resources while ignoring the resource degradation problems facing poorer rural households. As we have discussed in Chapter 3, it is well documented that resource sectors in many developing countries are prone to problems of rent-seeking and corruption, thus ensuring that natural resource assets, including land, are not being managed efficiently or sustainably (Ascher 1999; Tornell and Lane 1998; Torvik 2002). Many studies of resource-rich countries also emphasize how political economy factors more generally, and in particular the existence of policy and institutional failures that lead to myopic decision-making, fail to control rent-seeking behavior by wealthy investors in resource exploitation and weaken the political and legal institutions necessary to foster long-run growth as well to control rent seeking and corruption.[2] There is also an obvious link between rent-seeking activities in frontier areas and the lack of government enforcement of efficient regulation of these activities. For example, as Ascher (1999, p. 268) points out:

> The weak capacity of the government to enforce natural resource regulations and guard against illegal exploitation is an obvious factor in many of the cases reviewed. In every case of land and forest use, illegal extraction and failure to abide by conservation regulations reduce the costs to the resource exploiter and induce overexploitation, while failing to make the exploiter internalize the costs of resource depletion and pollution.

In Chapter 4, we emphasized how such processes lead to patterns of frontier land expansion and resource exploitation that are associated with poor economic performance in resource-dependent developing countries. In this chapter, we want to emphasize another important aspect of this "dualism within dualism" pattern of resource-based development, namely how the benefits of such development are often inequitably distributed between rich and poor households, and how such inequalities in wealth in turn have important impacts on resource degradation. In addition, such linkages between inequality, rural poverty and resource degradation are generally reinforced rather than mitigated by government policies that favor wealthier investors in markets for valuable natural resources, including arable land.

Rent-seeking and resource wealth

Several theoretical studies have shown that, in an economy with multiple powerful groups and "weak" political institutions, an increase in the availability of natural resources tends to foster rent-seeking behavior, which ultimately lowers overall "productive" economic activity and welfare. Lane and Tornell (1996) and Tornell and Lane (1998 and 1999) show that this is the case under "open access" production, which characterizes much resource exploitation especially in developing countries. An increase in the resource is tantamount to an increase in productivity, which through generating greater rents, induces each group to acquire a larger share of production by demanding more transfers. In turn, more transfers increase the tax rate and reduce the net return on capital, and if this redistribution effect outweighs the direct impact of increased productivity, the ultimate result is to lower the rate of return on investment and thus growth in the economy. Baland and Francois (2000) reach similar conclusions, but through a more specialized model where resource rents are generated by import quotas. The result is that, when the availability of natural resources increase, the value of an import quota rises more than that of productive production, causing economic resources to shift from that activity to rent seeking.

Torvik (2002) also shows that a greater amount of a natural resource causes wealthy individuals, or entrepreneurs, to shift from running productive firms in an economy to engage in rent seeking instead. Initially, the profits from rent seeking for these individuals increase unambiguously, but in the long run as more entrepreneurs switch to rent seeking, profits from both modern production and rent seeking fall and welfare in the economy is lower. As this model accords well with the pattern of large-scale extractive investments in frontier economies, where investors in such activities are attracted to frontier areas because of the lack of government controls and property rights in these remote areas mean that resource rents are easily captured, we will examine this model in a little more detail.

Torvik (2002) considers four sectors in an economy: a natural resource sector that contributes R units of good without any input requirements; a "backward" sector that produces with constant returns to scale with one unit of labor producing one unit of any good; a "modern" sector producing with increasing returns to scale, where production requires one entrepreneur and F units of labor but with each additional unit of labor producing $\alpha > 1$ units of output; and a "rent-seeking" sector whereby entrepreneurs can "bribe" or "lobby" the government in order to redistribute income in their favor.[3]

Torvik assumes that each firm in the modern sector has a fixed markup over marginal cost of $\tau = (\alpha - 1)/\alpha$, pays a share of production, t, as tax and generates total sales, y. Total profits in this sector are therefore $\pi = (\tau - t)y - F$.

In the rent-seeking sector, the total amount of rents that can be captured is the public sector income, which is income from taxes and the natural resources. If G is the total number of entrepreneurs engaged in rent seeking, then $1 - G$ entrepreneurs must be left in the modern sector. It follows that the total rents that can be captured from rent seeking are $\pi^T = t(1 - G)y + R$. But each entrepreneur engaged in rent seeking can only expect to receive a fraction $1/G$ of the total rents. Thus the expected income for an entrepreneur from competition for rents is $\pi^G = \pi^T/G$.

Finally, in this economy, total supply of all goods, $y + R$, must equal total demand for goods, which is simply equal to labor income plus profit income, $L + (1 - G)\pi + \pi^T$. Solving the latter equilibrium condition for the economy, Torvik finds that

$$y = y(G), \ y' < 0, \ y'' > 0, \ y(0) = \alpha(L - F), \ y(1) = L, \ y(0) > y(1)$$
$$(8.1)$$

In other words, not only does a higher G imply that fewer entrepreneurs engage in modern production and instead switch to rent seeking but also this reduces non-resource income, y. The reason is that, with fewer firms in the modern sector, workers are pushed from that sector into the backward sector. As this means that workers are transferred from increasing returns production to constant returns to scale production, overall non-resource income in the economy falls. At the extreme case, where all entrepreneurs engage in rent seeking ($G = 1$) and all workers are employed in the backward sector, total non-resource income is still lower than in the case when there is no rent seeking and all workers are employed in the modern sector ($G = 0$).

It follows that the equilibrium profits for an entrepreneur in the modern sector and an entrepreneur engaged in rent seeking are, respectively:

$$\pi = (\tau - t)y(G) - F = \pi(G), \ \pi'(G) < 0, \ \pi''(G) > 0 \qquad (8.2)$$

$$\pi_G = \frac{t(1 - G)y(G) + R}{G} = \pi_G(G), \ \pi'_G(G) < 0, \ \pi''_G(G) > 0. \quad (8.3)$$

It follows that in equilibrium, $\pi^G = \pi$, which implies that no entrepreneurs will want to shift between the modern sector and rent seeking. Figure 8.1 depicts the two profit curves and the case of a unique equilibrium, A.[4]

As Torvik (2002) demonstrates, an increase in the total amount of natural resources, R, means that it is now more profitable to be a rent seeker than an entrepreneur in the modern sector at all levels of rent

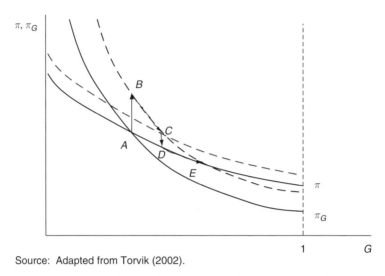

Source: Adapted from Torvik (2002).

Figure 8.1. Increased natural resource abundance and rent seeking

seeking. The profit curve for rent seeking thus shifts up to the dotted line curve in Figure 8.1. Initially, income for rent seekers increases by the amount of additional resource income, R, (point B), while profits from modern production are the same (point A). Entrepreneurs switch into rent seeking until the profit falls to what it used to be from modern production (point C). However, labor has also transferred to the backward sector, causing a fall in non-resource income, y. As the demand for goods produced in modern firms has now fallen, profits from modern production have decreased further (point D). Even more entrepreneurs flow into rent seeking, and profits from both rent seeking and modern production fall until a new stable equilibrium is reached (point E). At the new equilibrium, overall production, non-resource income and welfare are lower in the economy, and fewer workers are employed in the modern sector and more in the backwards sector.

Torvik (2002) also considers an open economy case, where the natural resource R is now entirely exported, and the increasing returns-to-scale modern sector produces a non-traded good.[5] Total supply of non-traded goods equals y, rather than $y + R$ in the previous model. There is now an export sector producing at constant returns to scale using one unit of labor at a given world market price set equal to one. The number of imported goods equals q, and consumers are assumed to have Cobb-Douglas utility preferences over $1 + q$ goods, where the number of non-traded goods consumed is normalized to one in the budget constraint. The demand for non-traded goods is now a share $1/(1 + q)$ of income, while a share $q/(1 + q)$ of income is used for imported goods. The reduced-form solution for the supply-demand equilibrium for non-traded goods, y, is therefore:

$$y = \frac{1}{1 + q}\left[L + (1 - G)\pi + \pi^T\right] = \frac{\alpha[L - (1 - G)F + R]}{1 + \alpha q + G(\alpha - 1)} \qquad (8.4)$$

The production of non-traded goods is affected not only by the amount of natural resources, R, indirectly through the amount of rent seekers, G, but also directly through R. For a given G, more natural resources raise income and thus demand for non-traded goods, which is the classic "Dutch disease" effect in an open economy (see Chapter 3). Also, demand for non-traded goods is affected by the openness of the economy. A more open economy, with greater imports q, means less demand and production of non-traded goods.

Condition (8.4) implies that a rise in natural resource abundance will increase not only profits from rent seeking but also profits from modern production, as the demand for non-traded goods in the economy increases with income. As shown in Figure 8.1, both the π and π^G curves shift up, but the vertical shift in the profit curve for rent seeking is always larger. The new equilibrium will be point C, at a higher number of rent seekers, G, for the same level of profit as before.

Although profits from rent seeking have increased, total income, and thus welfare, in the economy is unchanged. The reason is straightforward. Suppose R increases by one unit. Despite this marginal increase, income and all prices are not affected as they are independent of R. It follows that consumption of all goods, imported and non-traded, is also the same as before. Thus the impact of an increase in R is on the supply side, shifting one unit of labor from the export sector to enter the non-traded sector and leaving the total supply of export goods unaltered. Therefore, as in "Dutch disease" models, more natural resources lead to a transfer of labor from the export to the non-traded sector. However, unlike "Dutch disease" models, the increased amount of labor in the non-traded sector does not lead to increased production. The reason is that, for any given number of rent seekers G, profits in rent seeking will have increased with a rise in R so that more entrepreneurs will switch from the modern sector to rent seeking. Entrepreneurs switch into rent seeking until the profit falls to what it used to be from modern production (point C). However, although production in the modern sector has not increased, there are now fewer firms but more labor employed. Average productivity in the modern non-traded sector has fallen.

It follows that, in an open economy, a rise in natural resource wealth leads to increased rent-seeking and a fall in the number of entrepreneurs engaged in modern production. Although the equilibrium profits from rent seeking have increased, the profits from modern production are unchanged (point C). In turn, the fall in the average productivity in the modern sector equals the sum of the profit for the entrepreneurs that have shifted from this sector into rent seeking. But this sum is only just equal to the increase in the natural resource. Consequently, more natural resources in the economy decrease productivity in the non-traded sector sufficiently to keep aggregate income the same as before.

To summarize, in an open economy in the early stages of developing a domestic manufacturing capacity, the availability of additional natural resources is likely to stimulate rent-seeking behavior and to deter industrial development.[6] Entrepreneurs who switch from productive investment to rent seeking clearly benefit, but the economy as a whole does not. Of course, Torvik (2002) is assuming that weak political and legal institutions prevent the government from deterring the rent-seeking stimulus of additional natural resources. However, as we have seen, many studies of resource-rich countries emphasize that the inability of their governments to control rent-seeking behavior by wealthy investors is often the norm in these countries (Ascher 1999; Barbier 2004a; Auty 1994 and 1997; Broad 1995; Gylfason 2001b; Karl 1997; López 2003; Ross 1999 and 2001; Stevens 2003; Torvik 2002).

What does this analysis of rent-seeking behavior and resource wealth imply for patterns of natural resource exploitation, poverty and development in poor resource-rich countries? It is easy to see that, if resource wealth triggers rent-seeking behavior, then this process will only serve to perpetuate the "dualism within dualism" structure of many poor economies.

The relationship with the first pattern of "dualism" is fairly straightforward to establish. The prospect of increased rents from natural resource exploitation will clearly attract wealthy investors to this activity and away from investments in manufacturing and other dynamic sectors of the economy. The latter sectors do not develop, and may even decline, thus reinforcing the continued and overwhelming dependence of the economy on natural resource exploitation for the majority of its exports and for overall development.

The relationship with the second type of "dualism" found in most poor countries is more indirect but also extremely important. Simply put, if weak political and legal institutions in these countries encourage rent-seeking behavior by wealthy investors in the natural resource sectors of the economy, then the same poor institutions are essentially allowing the most valuable natural resources of the economy to be "transferred" to wealthy individuals. There are many ways that this may occur, but the outcome is usually always the same: poor rural households are unable to compete in existing markets or to influence policy decisions that determine the allocation of more valuable natural resources, and thus the rural poor continue to be confined to marginal land and resource areas to exploit for their economic livelihoods. Moreover, since these areas and resources generate little aggregate rents or overall "wealth" for the economy, very little public or private investments to improve the productivity or livelihoods of these poor households occur. Thus the "second" dualism of the continuing concentration of the rural poor in marginal land and resource areas is perpetuated.

The remainder of the chapter will focus on this second pattern of inequality, poverty and resource degradation.

Inequality, poverty and resource degradation

Inequality in access to valuable natural resources is therefore an important component of the "cumulative causative" environment-poverty trap found in many rural areas of poor countries (Dasgupta 1993).[7] For one, and as we shall discuss further below, inequalities in wealth between rural households seem to have an important impact on land degradation and deforestation processes, which in turn appear to have a greater impact on the livelihoods of the rural poor (Barbier 1999; Dasgupta 1993). As we have just discussed in the context of rent seeking and resource wealth, there is also increasing evidence in developing countries that more powerful groups use their social and economic power to secure greater access to valuable environmental resources, including land, minerals, energy, gems, water and even fuelwood, (Alston *et al.* 1999; Barbier 1999; Barbier and Homer-Dixon 1999; Binswanger and Deininger 1997; Fairhead 2001; Homer-Dixon 1999; Lonegran 1999; Swain 2001). Such problems are exacerbated by government policies that favor wealthier households in markets for these key natural resources, and especially land. For example, "rural elites" in developing countries are often "able to steer policies and programs meant to increase rural productivity into capital-intensive investment programs for large farms, thus perpetuating inequality and inefficiency" (Binswanger and Deininger 1997, p. 1996).

The role that inequality plays in the allocation of land resources is a good example of the problem.

First, poorer households are often unable to compete with wealthier households in land markets for existing agricultural land. The result is a segmented land "market": Formal markets exist only for better quality arable land, and the wealthier rural households tend to dominate these markets. Excluded from the latter markets, the poorer and landless households either trade in less productive land or migrate to marginal lands.

Second, although poorer households may be the initial occupiers of converted forestland they are rarely able to sustain their ownership. As the frontier develops economically and property rights are established, the increase in economic opportunities and potential rents makes ownership of the land more attractive to wealthier households. Because of their better access to capital and credit markets, they can easily bid current owners off the land, who in turn may migrate to other frontier forest regions or marginal lands.

Third, because of their economic and political importance, wealthier households are able to lobby and influence government officials to ensure that resource management policies favorable to them continue. This means that policy reform is very difficult to implement or sustain.

For example, in Colombia distortions in the land market prevent small farmers from attaining access to existing fertile land (Heath and Binswanger 1996). That is, as the market value of farmland is only partly based on its agricultural production potential, the market price of arable land in Colombia generally exceeds the capitalized value of farm profits. As a result, poorer smallholders and of course landless workers cannot afford to purchase land out of farm profits, nor do they have the non-farm collateral to finance such purchases in the credit market. In contrast, large land holdings serve as a hedge against inflation for wealthier households, and land is a preferred form of collateral in credit markets. Hence the speculative and non-farming benefits of large land holdings further bid up the price of land, thus ensuring that only wealthier households can afford to purchase land, even though much of the land may be unproductively farmed or even idled.

Similar to Colombia, land titling, tax and credit policies in Brazil generally reinforce the dominance of wealthier households in credit markets and the speculative investment in land as tax shelters (Alston *et al.* 1999; Caviglia-Harris 2004; Mahar and Schneider 1994). Because poorer households on the frontier do not benefit from such policies, their ability to compete in formal land markets is further diminished. This reinforces the "sell-out" effect of transferring frontier land ownership from poorer initial settlers to wealthier and typically urban-based arrivals, forcing the poorer households to drift further into the frontier, or enter into land use conflicts with wealthier land-owners (Alston *et al.* 1999; Schneider 1994).[8]

Throughout the developing world, the ability of poor farmers to obtain credit for land improvements is limited either by restrictions on the availability of rural credit for this purpose, or because insecure property rights mean that poor farmers are not eligible for credit programs. In particular, legal land titles prove to be significant in helping alleviate liquidity constraints affecting the purchase of working inputs, as well as land improvements generally, yet many smallholders do not have legally recognized titles to their land (Feder and Onchon 1987; López and Valdés 1998). In any case, often the only asset available to poor rural households for collateral is their land, and this may not always be allowed as the basis for acquiring loans (Zeller *et al.* 1997). In addition, for many poor rural households, "imperfect insurance markets, spatial dispersion, and covariant incomes add to the difficulties of obtaining access to credit" (Binswanger and Deininger 1997, p. 1971; see also Hoff and Stiglitz 1990; Stiglitz 1987).

Thus even if formal credit is available in rural areas, poor smallholders usually are not eligible or unable to take advantage of it to finance the inputs needed for improved land management and productivity (Binswanger and Deininger 1997; Dasgupta 1993; Feder 1985). Estimates suggest that only 5% of farmers in Africa and around 15% in Latin America and Asia have access to formal credit. Moreover, around 5% of all borrowers receive 80% of all credit (Hoff *et al.* 1993). A study across five countries in Latin America indicates that access to either extension assistance or credit for input purchases by smallholders ranges between 13% and 33% (López and Valdés 1998). Of the rural producers surveyed across Mexico who received rural credit, only 9.6% had holdings of 0–2 ha (Deininger and Minten 1999). In Malawi, although approximately 45% of rural smallholders have holdings of less than 1 ha and over 21% are "core poor" households with less than 0.5 ha, only 17% of medium-term credit is allocated to households with less than 2 ha of land (Barbier and Burgess 1992). Many poor smallholders in developing countries are therefore forced to meet both consumption and input needs by borrowing from informal credit sources, often at much higher effective rates of interest (Binswanger and Sillers 1983; Chaves and Sánchez 1998; Zeller *et al.* 1997).

As summarized by Dasgupta (1993, p. 475) "in rural communities of poor countries a great many markets of significance (e.g. credit, capital, and insurance) are missing, and a number of commodities of vital importance for household production (potable water, sources of fuel and fodder, and so forth) are available only at considerable time and labour cost." Given these constraints, Dasgupta argues that the landless and near landless in rural communities depend critically on exploitation of common property resources for their income and nutritional needs. This will be particularly the case if agricultural labor markets are incapable of absorbing all the poor and landless households looking for work. Through a series of models, Dasgupta (1993, p. 476) demonstrates that the initial distribution of assets, and particularly agricultural land, is critical to this outcome:

Consider then an economy that is neither rich in assets nor vastly poor. The theory to be developed will show that, were such an economy to rely on the market mechanism, the initial distribution of assets would play a crucial role in determining whether or not all citizens have their basic needs met. For example, we will confirm that, if a large fraction of the population were to be assetless, markets on their own would be incapable of enabling all to obtain an adequate diet ... On the other hand, were the distribution of assets sufficiently equal, the labour market would be capable of absorbing all, and no one would suffer from malnutrition ...

The following approach summarizes in a modified (and highly simplified) form the main theoretical framework and results developed by Dasgupta (1993, ch. 16).

Assume that a country has a fixed rural population that can be normalized to one. A large proportion of this population, $\bar{n}$, is landless, and the remaining $1 - \bar{n}$ proportion owns all the available arable land, T. Both individuals with land and the landless have an opportunity to work as agricultural laborers in the rural economy, and they will choose such employment if it satisfies the efficient piece-rate wage, ω^*, which is minimum wage per unit of agricultural work that an individual will accept. This wage rate is defined as

$$\omega^* = \frac{w^*}{\phi(x)} = \frac{w^*}{\phi(w^* + \rho N)}, \tag{8.5}$$

where w^* is the efficiency wage, i.e. the minimum wage necessary to induce an individual to accept agricultural employment, and $\phi(x)$ is the maximum labor power that an individual can offer in agricultural production. The latter expression is an increasing function of x, the nutritional intake of an individual, which in this simplified model is assumed be the individual's income. For a landed individual, his or her income will consist of wages from employment, w^*, and total rental income, with N representing the land holding of each individual and ρ the rental rate.[9]

Defining $\hat{x}$ as the level of nutritional intake, or income, that provides an individual with his or her most efficient level of productivity in agricultural work, $\phi(\hat{x})$, Dasgupta identifies the efficient piece-rate wage for three different groups of rural workers. For landless workers, all their income is from wage employment, which will allow them to attain their nutritional requirement necessary for efficient agricultural productivity, i.e. $w^* = \hat{x}$. It follows from (8.5) that the efficient piece-rate wage of the landless is $\omega^* = \hat{x}/\phi(\hat{x})$.[10] In contrast, large landowners will have significant rental income, and so if they engage in agricultural work, they will require a piece-rate wage well in excess of that of the landless. Thus for large landowners, $w^* > \hat{x}$, and $\omega^* > \hat{x}/\phi(\hat{x})$. Finally, there is a third group of "near landless" who have very small landholdings. Because they must spend some labor on working their smallholdings, the near landless do not command an efficiency wage that meets their nutritional requirement, i.e. $w^* < \hat{x}$. Although they earn some rental income, the piece-rate wage of smallholders will therefore be even less than that of the landless, i.e. $\omega^* < \hat{x}/\phi(\hat{x})$.[11]

The distribution of land and the efficiency piece-rate wage is graphed in Figure 8.2. The bottom half of the diagram shows the distribution of land, $t(n)$, as a continuous, non-decreasing function of

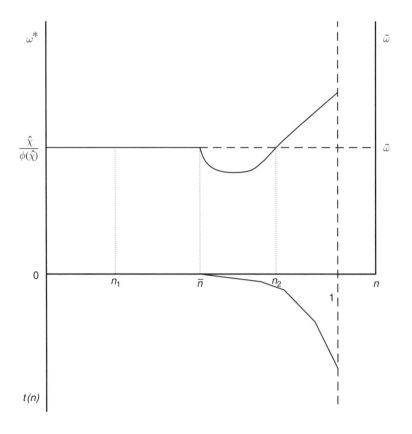

Source: Dasgupta (1993).

Figure 8.2. Land distribution and rural labor market equilibrium

different types of landholding people, n. Persons labeled 0 to $\bar{n}$ are landless, and $t(n)$ is an increasing function for the landed, $1 - \bar{n}$. Thus the diagram "orders" the rural population by the size of their land-holdings. The solid curve in the upper diagram of Figure 8.2 therefore shows how the piece-rate wage varies for three types of rural people: the landless, smallholders and large landowners. The proportion of the rural population that is without any land, $\bar{n}$, is willing to work at the same efficient piece-rate wage, $\omega^* = \hat{x}/\phi(\hat{x})$. However, the wage of the near landless, $n_2 - \bar{n}$, is lower than that of the landless. In contrast, large landowners, $1 - n_2$, are willing to work if they receive a relatively large piece-rate wage, and this wage rises sharply the larger the landholding.

We now assume that agricultural output in the rural economy is produced under constant returns to scale technology and is dependent on two factors, aggregate arable land (T) and aggregate labor power (E). Then under competitive market conditions and assuming that the price of agricultural output is normalized to one, the market equilibrium piece-rate wage, $\tilde{\omega}$, is determined by the marginal productivity of aggregate labor, i.e. $\tilde{\omega} = \partial F(E, T)/\partial E$. Figure 8.2 depicts the situation for a "labor surplus" economy, in which the prevailing equilibrium wage (the dotted line in the top diagram) is just sufficient to meet the nutritional requirement of the landless who find employment, i.e. $\tilde{\omega} = \omega^* = \hat{x}/\phi(\hat{x})$.[12] The economy can be characterized as labor surplus, because although there is a sufficiently large amount of arable land, T, used in agricultural production to generate demand for employing the landless at their efficiency piece-rate wage, the "pool" of landless seeking employment at this wage rate far exceeds aggregate demand for labor power in the rural economy.[13] As shown in Figure 8.2, the result is that only a fraction of the landless, $1 - n_1/\bar{n}$, find employment as agricultural workers at the equilibrium wage, $\tilde{\omega} = \omega^* = \hat{x}/\phi(\hat{x})$, whereas the rest, $n_1/\bar{n}$, are involuntarily unemployed. Note as well that only persons between n_1 and n_2 are employed as agricultural workers; land-owning individuals to the right of n_2 are also unemployed. But the latter individuals are voluntarily unemployed, unlike the landless, as these landowners clearly have a "reservation" wage, ω^*, that is higher than the prevailing equilibrium wage for agricultural work in the rural economy, $\bar{\omega}$.

Dasgupta (1993, ch. 16) demonstrates formally that such an outcome in the rural economy has several implications for economic livelihoods, especially for the landless:

- It is clear that such a labor surplus economy "equilibrates by rationing landless people in the labour market."
- Because of the combination of the lack of assets and work, the fraction of the landless, $n_1/\bar{n}$, that is involuntarily unemployed are forced to "live on common property resources."
- In addition, because these individuals are destitutes, they are unable to meet their nutritional requirements from living just

off common property resources (or "begging"), i.e. "they are undernourished."[14]

- Because they are chronically undernourished, the unemployed landless are unable to compete in the labor market, particularly compared to an individual with assets (land); "in a poor economy she enjoys an advantage over her assetless counterpart, in that she can undercut the assetless in the labour market."

Thus what Dasgupta (1993, p. 475) calls "economic disfranchisement," or "the inability to participate in the labour market," is the direct consequence of an inequitable distribution of assets in the economy. Increased disfranchisement in turn leads more and more of the "assetless" poor in the economy to become dependent on exploitation of common property environmental resources.

The scale of this dependence may be very extensive in some developing regions. For example, in Southern Malawi it was found that surveyed households derived 30% of their income on average from exploiting "common" forests (Fisher 2004). However, households that are poor in land, education, and goat holdings are more reliant on "low-return" forest activities (LRFA).[15] As noted by the author, this dependence of poorer households on exploiting forests appear to be part of their "coping" strategies: "reliance on LRFA was associated with lower measured income over the course of the survey year. Participation in LRFA therefore did not reduce poverty during the survey year, though it may have helped the poor survive their poverty, providing supplementary income and a means to cope with adverse shocks" (Fisher 2004, p. 150). Such findings appear to be consistent with studies of income diversification across Africa, which show that the "assetless" poor diversify into low-return activities based on exploiting common property environmental resources, but with little hope of escaping the "poverty trap" (Barrett *et al.*, 2001; Dercon, 1998). This link between asset poverty and resource extraction as insurance may also be very significant in many tropical forest regions, where the livelihoods of the poor often depend on the extraction of biological resources in fragile environments (Takasaki *et al.* 2004; Wunder, 2001).

In addition to exploiting common property environmental resources, the "assetless" poor are also likely to convert any sources of land available to them. The result is often over-use of environmental resources, frontier land expansion and widespread problems of land degradation on "marginal" agricultural land.

The "assetless" poor, rural labor employment and resource degradation

As the rural poor have few assets other than their own labor power, it is not surprising that the availability of "outside" or "off-farm" labor opportunities will be a key determinant in whether or not the "assetless" are driven to over-exploiting available natural resources, including engaging in agricultural land expansion. The analysis by Dasgupta (1993) summarized above suggests that the inability of rural labor markets to absorb the "disfranchised" rural poor forces them to become more dependent on "common property" environmental resources.[16]

Early models addressing the basic conservation/deforestation problem of a farmer in a frontier region implicitly recognized this link between outside employment and allocation of labor either to improve existing cropland or to clear more forest for new arable land, even if they did not explicitly include this link (Larson 1991; Southgate 1990). For example, in the Southgate-Larson model of "spontaneously" expanding agricultural frontiers, it is assumed that a farmer with H hectares (ha) of initial cropland and unlimited access to uncleared forest land will decide to improve N_c ha of his cropland (i.e. invest in soil erosion control) and leave $H - N_c$ ha unimproved (no erosion control). In addition, the farmer could decide to clear N_d ha of forest land to add to the stock of unimproved land. As labor is the only input available to the frontier farmer for these activities, how much the farmer decides to "invest" in improving existing land as opposed to clearing new forest land depends on the present value of the returns to labor from all three activities over the farmer's planning horizon. However, as Southgate (1990, p. 95) comments: "The opportunity costs of labor allocated to erosion control and deforestation do not depend only on N_c, N_d, and the intensity of farming in the frontier region. They are also a function of off-farm employment opportunities in the frontier region and the performance of other regions' labor markets."

More recent models have attempted to explore formally this link between exploitation of forests, land and other frontier natural resources and off-farm labor employment opportunities (Barbier and Cox 2004b; Bluffstone 1995; Caviglia-Harris 2004; Cooke 1998; Coxhead and Jayisuriya 2003; Dasgupta 1993; Shively 2001). For example, using a slightly different model in a two-period framework,

Dasgupta (1993, p. 508) demonstrates that, because the prevailing casual wage for agricultural work will be a function of the "productivity of the commons" as well as the size of the population that it must sustain, then "in any cross-section of villages those possessing a richer stock of common property resources per person during the slack season are the ones that would be expected to sustain casual wages during the busy season." This result also implies the opposite relationship; i.e., as common property resources are degraded or depleted, we would expect households dependent on their exploitation to seek more hours in casual wage employment and thus command lower wages.

Some evidence in support of these propositions comes from a study of the effects of mangrove loss on the labor allocation decisions of households living along the coastal areas of Thailand (Barbier and Cox 2004b). As noted in Chapter 6, the economic livelihoods of coastal communities in Southern Thailand have been affected by the widespread mangrove deforestation that has occurred since the mid-1970s. These livelihoods have consisted traditionally of two types of "mangrove-dependent" activities. First, households depend on direct use of mangrove forests for various wood products, including construction timber, fuelwood and charcoal production, and for harvesting of fish and shellfish in mangrove swamps. The net annual income from these activities is estimated to be around US$88 per hectare (ha) of mangrove forest in Surat Thani Province (Sathirathai and Barbier 2001). Second, households may also harvest fish from a coastal fishery, which is indirectly dependent on the mangroves as a breeding nursery habitat. Barbier *et al.* (2002) estimate that the marginal value of this indirect use from a one-hectare change in mangrove area across Southern Thailand ranges from US$33 to US$135 per ha, if the elasticity of demand for fish is -0.1 to -1.0.

Barbier and Cox (2004b) model the labor allocation of these coastal households in Thailand under the assumption that they have three possible uses of their labor: i) for one or both of the above "mangrove-dependent" activities; ii) for another production activity, such as agriculture, which is not directly or indirectly dependent on the mangrove forest; and iii) for paid work "outside" of the household, for which it receives a market wage. The authors are able to show that the total effect of mangrove deforestation on a household's supply of labor for "outside" employment occurs both directly and indirectly through impacts on the household's wage-offer equation and its income function for mangrove-based activity. Household labor supply and employment are in turn disaggregated into effects on male and female household members. Four key results emerge from this analysis:

• A one-hectare reduction in mangrove area is estimated to increase the average outside employment hours for males by 1% and for females by 2%.

• As the degree of mangrove-dependent income of the household increases, so does the male wage rate.

• A reduction in mangrove area leads to a fall in overall household income.

• As the time devoted by both males and females to mangrove-dependent activities falls, so does overall household income.[17]

These results suggest that, for coastal households in Thailand, mangrove-dependent activities are important to their economic livelihoods and overall income, and that mangrove deforestation would force these households to seek outside employment opportunities. However, it is possible that the result may be loss of income and declining household welfare from a switch from mangrove-dependent activities to outside employment.

For many poor rural households in marginal and frontier lands, declining outside employment opportunities may also mean that the only alternative is to convert even more land. As argued by Rodríguez-Meza *et al.* (2004), this is because for poor households in these areas demand for land is dominated by a *precautionary* motive rather than the usual *investment* motive. For relatively wealthy households with access to credit and land markets, expansion in farmed area is driven by the normal rent-seeking investment motive to exploit untapped profits from highly productive arable land. In contrast, the precautionary motive for agricultural land use is important for a large number of rural families, which depend on subsistence farming to cushion consumption in the face of adverse shocks in earnings. As noted by Rodríguez-Meza *et al.* (2004, p. 229), declining outside employment is the major "shock" driving increased precautionary demand for land and forest conversion in the "marginal" agricultural areas of rural El Salvador:

Because of limited education, high transaction costs resulting from inadequate physical and institutional infrastructure, and policy-induced inefficiencies in markets for labor, land, and financial services, households below the poverty line have found it difficult to compete for non-agricultural work in rural areas. With little chance of encountering alternative employment, many of the rural poor have responded to the loss of agricultural wages by dedicating more labor and land to subsistence production of corn, beans, and other basic grains. This response is observed even though newly cleared fields are typically in places where risks of erosion and other forms of land degradation are acute.

The links between rural livelihoods, outside employment opportunities and resource degradation may have important implications for patterns of deforestation, agricultural intensification and migration at the regional level. Recent studies from Southeast Asia confirm some of these potential effects (Coxhead and Jayisuriya 2003; Shively 2001; Shively and Pagiola 2004). Such models highlight the "lowland–upland" dualism of the rural regional economy, which is summarized by Shively (2001, p. 270) as follows: "Lowland households are viewed as agricultural in their orientation. Upland households, because of their limited agricultural capacity, are recognized as engaging in a range of income-generating activities. These include low-input and shifting agriculture in the uplands, forest clearing, exploitation of upland forest resources, and sales of labor in the lowlands when opportunities arise." As a result, "the net migration rate is a response to the relative returns to labour in upland and lowland regions, and within uplands, between more and less intensive forms of agricultural land use." Simultaneously, the models "identify economy-wide driving forces behind the two main sources of environmental problems in uplands: agricultural land expansion, which is associated with deforestation; and intensification, which is associated with soil depletion and erosion" (Coxhead and Jayisuriya 2003, p. 95).

For example, for the Philippines, Shively (2001) finds that irrigation development in lowland agriculture increases the probability of employment for upland residents, more than doubled the number of days of employment for those working on lowland irrigated farms, and increased the wage income of farms in the upland by a factor of three. In addition, these changes also cause upland households to reduce the time allocated to forest clearing and hillside farming, especially of annual cash crops. In an additional study of the impacts of lowland irrigation on the employment, incomes and activities of households at the forest margin, Shively and Pagiola (2004) estimate that annual labor use rose approximately 50% following irrigation development in the lowlands, primarily because of increases in cropping intensity. The increased employment for upland households meant that the latter were drawn away from forest-degrading activities. Upland households also had higher incomes from outside employment, which facilitated purchases of inputs, especially fertilizer, for use on their upland farms. The increase in intensification and agricultural productivity of already-cleared farmland reduced even further the demand for additional forest clearing in the uplands.

Coxhead and Jayisuriya (2003) relate the typical upland-lowland "dualistic" rural economy through applied general equilibrium analysis to the overall economic structure and policy orientation of Southeast Asian economies in different eras. They characterize four types of economies:

- The "jeepney" economy, which is a net food importer and bases industrial development on import-competing, mainly capital-intensive industries (the Philippines before economic and trade liberalization in the 1990s).
- The "tuk-tuk" economy, which is a net food exporter and bases industrial development on export-oriented, labor-intensive manufacturing (Thailand after the 1970s).
- The "becak" economy, which exports plantation crops (including timber) and bases industrial development on import-competing, mainly capital-intensive industries (Indonesia after the 1970s; Sri Lanka prior to trade policy reforms; Malaysia at an earlier stage of its development).
- The "proton" economy, which exports plantation crops (including timber) and bases industrial development on export-oriented, labor-intensive manufacturing (present-day Malaysia).

Coxhead and Jayisuriya (2003) show that the deforestation and land degradation impacts in the uplands from economy-wide policies and shocks will vary with the type of representative economy. In the "jeepney" economy, any price, endowment or policy changes that increase factor productivity in the lowlands will induce "down-slope migration" from the uplands, thus reducing pressures for deforestation and land degradation. In the "becak" economy, shocks that increase lowland productivity will also facilitate down-slope migration, but if the plantation crops in the uplands are mainly labor-intensive, then food production will increase as a proportion of agricultural land in the uplands and be accompanied by greater deforestation. In the "tuk-tuk" economy, traded food production dominates both upland and lowland farming, and so the pressures on upland forests are solely determined by inter-regional labor migration. Any increase in labor demand in the lowlands will result in reduced deforestation as the total area of upland agriculture declines. In contrast, in the "proton" economy, relatively capital-intensive plantation crops dominate upland agriculture. Although increased down-slope migration will again reduce deforestation pressures, there is the additional possibility of increased investment, including foreign investment, in the plantation sector. This could lead to expansion of upland agriculture at the expense of forests.

Barbier and Burgess (1996) also find that in Mexico inter-regional labor migration may be key to understanding the potential impacts on rural poverty and deforestation of the maize sector reforms as part of the North American Free Trade Agreement (NAFTA). Trade liberalization in the maize sector of Mexico as a result of NAFTA reforms has led to a substantial reduction in the producer price of maize. Barbier and Burgess show that the reduction in output and planted area ought to have a direct effect of reducing deforestation pressures in rural areas, and that consumers in Mexico benefit from lower food prices. However, the value of rainfed land is predicted to fall to nearly one quarter that of irrigated land, thereby making subsistence farmers, rainfed farmers who are net sellers of maize, and landless rural workers dependent on agricultural employment worse off. These latter impacts could have a "second-order" impact on deforestation that could be substantial. The overall lack of employment and income opportunities in existing rainfed cropland areas could induce rural workers and subsistence farmers to migrate towards frontier forest areas, or to convert remaining forestland that is available to them locally. Deforestation in Mexico might even increase in the long run, if these "second-order" employment and income effects outweigh the initial impacts of a reduction in maize producer prices on planted agricultural area.

To summarize, there is substantial evidence that the "assetless" poor in developing countries are dependent, on the one hand, on outside employment opportunities particularly as agricultural workers, and on the other, on exploiting common property environmental resources as well as converting any additional forest, wetland and other marginal land available to them for subsistence needs. This implies that increased natural resource degradation and a scarcity of new land to convert will mean that the rural poor will become more reliant on finding employment opportunities. If these opportunities are not available in their immediate rural regions, then the "assetless" poor are likely to be driven to over-exploiting available natural resources, including engaging in agricultural land expansion, migrating to other areas where they can find employment, including urban areas, or moving to "frontier" regions where new land to convert is likely to be available.

Final remarks: implications for resource-based development

It is clear that the "dualism within dualism" found in so many low and middle-income countries is symptomatic of a pattern of resource-based development that is leading to an inequitable distribution of benefits between rich and poor households, and such inequalities in wealth in turn have important impacts on resource degradation. First, the main beneficiaries of the dependency of many developing economies are mainly wealthier households who can afford to invest in rent-extracting resource-based activities. If weak political and legal institutions in these countries encourage rent-seeking behavior by wealthy investors, then the most valuable natural resources of the economy are likely to be "transferred" to the rich. A second implication is that poor rural households are unable to compete in existing markets or to influence policy decisions that determine the allocation of more valuable natural resources, and thus the rural poor continue to be confined to marginal land and resource areas to exploit for their economic livelihoods. Finally, as we have just discussed, if rural labor markets are unavailable to absorb the "assetless" poor, then their only recourse is to become more dependent on exploiting available natural resources, including engaging in agricultural land expansion.

A new insight offered by this chapter is to characterize and analyze the "dualism within dualism" nature of resource use. As Table 8.1 indicates, this pattern of "dualism within dualism" is widely prevalent in the developing world. That is, three-quarters of the countries listed in the table show considerable evidence of "dualism within dualism" characteristics, and virtually all the economies display signs of the second type of dualism, i.e. a high incidence of rural poverty-resource degradation linkage within the economy.

Perhaps the most important implication highlighted by this chapter is that these two types of dualisms found in developing economies appear to be linked. As stressed throughout this book, the "resource dependency" of low and middle-income countries is not a novel observation, and indeed is often thought to be an important "stage" for these economies in their process of "taking off" into sustained growth and development. In recent decades, more attention has also been devoted to observing and understanding why the rural poor are often "trapped" in a vicious poverty-environmental degradation cycle. But, as this chapter has attempted to demonstrate, it is no coincidence that these two types of dualism are occurring simultaneously in many poor economies; rather, they appear to be inexorably linked.

This pattern of "dualism within dualism" also explains why, despite the abundance of land and natural resources available in many developing countries, exploitation of this natural wealth is not leading either to sustained economic growth, widespread benefits or substantial rural poverty alleviation. This is despite the considerable resource conversion, frontier land expansion and extractive activities that occur in these countries. Throughout this book we have referred to this process as frontier-based economic development, which is symptomatic of economy-wide resource exploitation that: i) generates little additional economic rents, and ii) the rents that are generated are not being reinvested in more productive and dynamic sectors, such as manufacturing. "Dualism within dualism" appears to be a systematic feature of poor economies dependent on such frontier-based development.

How can developing countries break out of this pattern of development and ensure that natural resource exploitation does confer sustained growth and poverty alleviation? There are several broad objectives that need to be attained. First, the resource rents generated in the economy must be reinvested in more productive and dynamic sectors, which in turn are linked to the resource-exploiting sectors of the domestic economy. Second, political and legal institutions in these countries must be developed to discourage rent-seeking behavior by wealthy investors in the natural resource sectors of the economy. Third, there needs to be widespread reform of government policies that favor wealthier investors in markets for valuable natural resources, including arable land. Finally, additional policies and investments need to be targeted to improve the economic opportunities and livelihoods of the rural poor, rather than relying on frontier land expansion and urban migration as the principal outlet for alleviating rural poverty.

These four objectives do pose a daunting challenge. However, they are not an insurmountable challenge, once it is recognized that the policies and reforms necessary to achieve these objectives are complementary and mutually reinforcing. To understand why requires explaining in more detail the importance of these objectives and the necessary steps to achieve them. To do that is beyond the scope of this chapter. Instead, we shall take up this task in the final two chapters of this book.

Notes

1. In fact, with over 50% of its population in fragile areas and with a rural poverty incidence of 19.2%, Yemen shows distinct signs of the second type of dualism. Indonesia is also not far off from satisfying the "20–20 rule," given that the country has over 20% of its population on fragile land and 15.7% of its rural population in absolute poverty.
2. See, for example, Ascher (1999), Barbier (2004a), Auty (1994) and (1997), Broad (1995), Gylfason (2001b), Karl (1997), López (2003), Ross (1999) and (2001), Stevens (2003) and Torvik (2002).
3. Torvik (2002) assumes that there are a given number of goods normalized to one, and an equal number of entrepreneurs, and that the economy is populated by L workers. Also, in the modern sector there must be one increasing returns firm producing each good, with the price of each good normalized to one since this is the price charged by potential competitors in the constant returns to scale backwards sector. Production units in the latter sector pay the lowest possible wage to attract workers, which is also equal to one, since this constant returns to scale sector is the workers fallback employment option. This implies in turn that the wage rate in the economy is one.
4. As indicated by Torvik (2002) the equilibrium depicted in Figure 8.1 occurs if $R < (\tau-t)L-F$ so that $\pi(1) > \pi_G(1)$.
5. Although this is clearly a highly specialized case of a very resource-dependent economy, Torvik (2002) refers to the work of Davies *et al.* (1994) who note that heavy import restrictions have made the manufacturing sector in sub-Saharan African countries a sector with non-traded characteristics, whereas the agricultural sector is the main traded sectors. See also Chapter 1 and its appendix, which suggests that many low and middle-income countries have a high percentage of primary product exports to total exports. Presumably, this also implies that any nascent manufacturing in these highly resource-dependent economies is generally non-traded.

6. As noted by Torvik (2002, p. 469), any attempt to isolate the economy from these effects through import substitution policy will backfire: "Import substitution policies that were meant to create domestic industrialization deliver deindustrialization with natural resource abundance."

7. Dasgupta (1993) develops a compelling theory of this cumulative causative environment-poverty trap by linking inequality in access to assets, including land and other valuable natural resources, to problems of malnutrition and general "destitution" of poor rural households, and finally to the chronic "economic disfranchisement" of theses households. He outlines this theory through the following thought experiment: "A theory of economic disfranchisement and undernourishment, which links their incidence and extent to the distribution of assets, can be fashioned out of these ingredients. The theory makes precise the intuitive idea we carry with us when we use the term *economic disfranchisement*; it also identifies the assetless as those who are particularly vulnerable. The economic outcasts are for the most part from this segment of the population ... Economic disfranchisement will be interpreted here as the inability to participate in the labour market. We will think of the outcasts as living on common property resources (or alternatively, as beggars). They gradually waste away; their life expectancy is low even by standards prevailing in poor countries. Such people exist in large numbers; they are the outsiders ... Suppose the landless are all identical to begin with. Assume too that living on common property resources involves an ever-so-slight deterioration in nutritional status, and therefore in their efficient productivity. In the first period a fraction of the landless are employed ... We can't tell in advance which particular fraction, because a lottery is in use. But in the next period the previously employed face an ever-so-slight advantage (because of their better nutritional history). Subsequently, most of the same people will find employment, and all who languished in the first period through bad luck will continue to languish – no longer through bad luck, but through *cumulative causation*." (Dasgupta 1993, pp. 473–474 and 502).

8. Access to credit and bank accounts can also influence the pattern of agricultural land use on the frontier. Caviglia-Harris (2004) finds that in Rondônia, Brazil large landowners with access to credit and bank accounts are likely to invest in cattle ranching, for beef and milk production, rather than in crop production, resulting in greater deforestation.

9. To simplify the analysis, I have skipped over the important analytical distinction wage made initially by Dasgupta (1993, pp. 479–484) between the efficiency and reservation wage. However, as Dasgupta proves, the outcome of this formal analysis is that in fact the reservation and efficiency wages of an individual will be the same. Note as well that, as

Dasgupta (1993, p. 484) demonstrates, the efficiency (reservation) wage should be written as a function of n and ρ, i.e. $w^* = w^*(n, \rho)$: "it is a function of n, not because people differ physiologically (in our model they don't), but because different people possess different landholdings. This explains why a person's efficiency wage depends in general on the rental rate on land. (A person's efficiency wage depends on his 'unearned' income)." It follows from (8.5) that the efficiency piece-rate wage must also be a function of n and ρ. Finally, the landholding of each individual, n, is defined as $N = t(n)T$, where T is the total quantity of arable land and $t(n)$ is the proportion of land owned by person n.

10. As noted by Dasgupta (1993, p. 485), $\omega^* = \hat{x}/\phi(\hat{x})$ means that the piece-rate wage for a landless individual is equal to the inverse of "a person's efficient productivity." That is, the right-hand side of this expression can be defined as "the nutrition intake per unit of agricultural work an individual is capable of performing when his intake equals his requirement."

11. See Dasgupta (1993, pp. 479–484) for proof of this outcome for the near landless. However, an intuitive explanation can be derived with the aid of (8.5). Assume that a smallholder will combine rental and wage income in order to attain the nutritional requirement, i.e. $w^* + \rho N = \hat{x}$. It therefore follows that the denominator of (8.5) is $\phi(\hat{x})$. However, this implies that wages alone are insufficient to meet this requirement, i.e. $w^* < \hat{x}$. Thus, for the near landless, (8.5) becomes $\omega^* < \hat{x}/\phi(\hat{x})$.

12. This equilibrium corresponds to "Regime 2" in Dasgupta (1993, ch. 16).

13. As maintained by Dasgupta (1993, p. 479) such labor surplus conditions are prevalent in the rural economies of the developing world, mainly because large-scale landlessness is a widespread problem: "A value of $\bar{n}$ in the region of 0.5–0.7 does not appear to be uncommon."

14. As argued by Dasgupta (1993, p. 482): "The key assumption I now make is that the reservation wage of a landless person is less than $\hat{x}$. The thought here is that income from common property resources is less than $\hat{x}$, and that is quite inadequate even when allowance is made of the fact that gathering and tapping involve less work than agriculture."

15. These include sales of "forest-based" crafts (bamboo baskets and mats, grass brooms, and wood-fired pots), roof thatching and brick-burning, sales of prepared foods and drink, sales of firewood and bamboo, and traditional medicines. See Fisher (2004) for further details.

16. As noted by López (1998a, p. 445), many rural households often depend on both common property resources and agricultural production from their smallholdings: "Households produce agricultural commodities in their own private lots and at the same time engage in extractive activities to obtain what we henceforth call 'resource goods' from common

lands." López goes on to model the affects of various agricultural policies on these households under two situations: i) the case where competition between agricultural and common property activities is restricted to the use of labor; and ii) the case where such activities compete for the allocation of both household labor and land. However, there may also be complementarities between use of common property and private resources, to the extent that rural households with more private assets also exploit more of the commons. Adhikari *et al.* (2004) find this to be the case for the exploitation of community forests (CF) in rural areas of Nepal. For example, Adhikari *et al.* (2004, pp. 253–254) note: "There is a distinguishable pattern in the household ownership of private resources and corresponding dependency on CF whereby households with more land and cattle spend more time gathering tree and grass fodder and bedding materials from the forest than did households with few or no cattle. Forest biomass especially fodder, grasses and leaf litter were important forest products for subsistence use for large agricultural households. However, due to the lack of complementary resources (land, cattle, etc.) the poorest of the poor use less quantities of these products."

17. The analysis was based on a survey of 201 households in four representative coastal villages in Southern Thailand, Ban Khlong Khut and Ban Gong Khong in Nakhon Si Thammarat Province and Ban Sam Chong Tai and Ban Bang Pat in Phangnga Province.

9 | Can frontier-based development be successful?

C
AN frontier-based development be successful? The short answer to this question is "why not?" As we have discussed, since 1500 "frontier expansion" has been a major part of global economic development. Such frontier-based economic development is characterized by a pattern of capital investment, technological innovation and social and economic institutions dependent on "opening up" new frontiers of natural resources once existing ones have been "closed" and exhausted. Most of this development has been incredibly successful, particularly during the Golden Age of Resource-Based Development (1870–1913). So why shouldn't present-day developing economies dependent on frontier-based development also be able to attain such success?

One reason is that the current process of frontier-based development in low and middle-income economies is fundamentally different from the exploitation of the "Great Frontier" in previous eras, including the Golden Age. Frontier expansion in today's developing countries is not facilitating take off into sustained and balanced growth; rather, it is symptomatic of a "dualism within dualism" economic structure that is perpetuating underdevelopment. This "dualism within dualism" structure reinforces the dependence of the overall economy on mainly primary product exports, the concentration of a large proportion of the population on fragile land, and a high incidence of rural poverty.

There is clearly a "vicious cycle" at work here: in many of today's developing economies, any resource rents that are generated and appropriated from frontier "reserves" are simply leading to further frontier land expansion and resource exploitation. The result is very little economy-wide efficiency gains and benefits. In addition, this process tends to be inequitable. What resource rents are available from the frontier and existing natural capital for exploitation accrue mainly to a wealthy elite, who have increased incentives for "rent-seeking" behavior, which in turn leads to increased policy distortions to reinforce the existing pattern of allocating and distributing natural resources. The poor are therefore left with marginal resources and frontier land areas to exploit, further reducing their ability to improve their livelihoods significantly, and of course, to generate and appropriate significant rents.

Breaking free of this vicious cycle and instilling instead a "virtuous cycle" of successful resource-based development in developing economies is likely to depend on attaining four broad objectives:

- First, the resource rents generated in the economy must be reinvested in more productive and dynamic sectors, which in turn are linked to the resource-exploiting sectors of the domestic economy.
- Second, political and legal institutions in these countries must be developed to discourage rent-seeking behavior by wealthy investors in the natural resource sectors of the economy.
- Third, there needs to be widespread reform of government policies that favor wealthier investors in markets for valuable natural resources, including arable land.
- Finally, additional policies and investments need to be targeted to improve the economic opportunities and livelihoods of the rural poor, rather than relying on frontier land expansion and urban migration as the principal outlet for alleviating rural poverty.

How can developing countries achieve these four objectives for encouraging a more "virtuous" cycle of successful frontier expansion and resource-based development? The final two chapters of this book are an attempt to provide an answer to this important question. In this chapter we will examine more closely the first objective, which is concerned with the conditions that could make frontier-based development compatible with successful resource-led growth. Building on this analysis, Chapter 10 will in turn explore more fully the other three policy objectives.

Historical evidence suggests that there are three conditions for "successful" resource-based development in a small open economy: exogenous technological change in resource use, complete integration between a frontier, resource-extracting sector and a mainstay sector, and knowledge spillovers. The following chapter extends the model of frontier resource exploitation first developed in Chapter 4 to demonstrate how these three conditions can lead to sustained growth, even if the economy is fundamentally dependent on frontier-based development.

To understand more fully how frontier-based development might lead to sustainable growth, we need first to summarize the frontier expansion hypothesis and the conditions for successful resource-based development that were discussed in Chapter 4.

Frontier expansion and successful resource-based development revisited

Recall that Chapter 4 proposed the *frontier expansion hypothesis* as a possible explanation of why many resource-dependent low and middle-income economies may not be benefiting from frontier-based development today.

It is important to keep in mind that this hypothesis suggests that frontier land expansion and resource exploitation may be *associated* with poor economic performance in resource-dependent developing countries but not necessarily a *cause* of it. This distinction is vital, because it implies that the pattern of frontier expansion observed in developing countries today is symptomatic of an overall structure of resource-based development that is unlikely to lead to sustained economic growth in many low and middle-income economies. Thus, frontier-based development today in many developing economies is fundamentally different from the "successful" cases of resource-based development that occurred in the past, such as during the Golden Age (1870–1914), or among a handful of (mainly mineral-based) countries in recent decades.

To recap, Chapter 4 identified four key aspects of the process of frontier expansion and economy-wide resource exploitation in present-day low and middle-income countries that prevent this process from generating widespread economic benefits and growth (see also Barbier 2003a and 2004a). These key factors are:

- Frontier land expansion in these economies often generates little additional economic rents as it serves mainly as an outlet for the rural poor on low-productive "marginal" or "fragile" land (World Bank 2003). Consequently, there is little investment, either by the households working this land or government agricultural research and extension activities, in developing *country-specific knowledge* for improving the productivity and sustainable exploitation of frontier land and natural resources used by the rural poor.

- If rents are generated through resource exploitation and frontier expansion, they will accrue mainly to larger scale resource-extractive activities. Although these activities may generate substantial exports and rents, they are more likely to result in either imported consumption or imported capital goods for the frontier resource-extractive industries rather than in economy-wide investments (e.g. in manufacturing, productive services or human capital).

- The result is that there are *weak linkages* between more dynamic sectors (i.e. manufacturing) in the economy and the frontier resource sector. This in turn limits any *economy-wide knowledge spillovers* arising from the exploitation and conversion of frontier resources, including land. Thus frontier-based economic activities, which are already located far away from urban and industrial centers, are unlikely to be integrated with the rest of the economy.
- This process is further exacerbated by policy and market failures, such as rent-seeking behavior, corruption and ill-defined property rights, which are prevalent in the resource sectors of many developing economies (Ascher 1999). Investors in large-scale resource-extractive activities are often attracted to frontier areas because the lack of government controls and property rights in these remote areas mean that resource rents are easily captured, and thus frontier resource-extractive activities are particularly prone to rent-seeking behavior.

In essence, the frontier sector operates as a separate "enclave" in the developing economy. This lack of integration of frontier-based economic activities with the rest of the economy also decreases the likelihood that any rents generated by these activities will be reinvested in more productive and dynamic sectors, such as manufacturing.

In Chapter 4, we developed a model of a small resource-dependent economy to illustrate the implications for long-run growth of these key structure features of this pattern of frontier-based development. The model demonstrates that, although such frontier-based economic development can lead to an initial economic boom, it is invariably short-lived and the economic benefits are quickly dissipated. If the additional frontier "reserves" are used mainly to expand domestic consumption and exports (in exchange for imported consumption), then there will be little additional capital accumulation outside of the frontier resource-extractive sector. This implies that any economic boom will continue only as long as the frontier resource reserves last. Once resource rents are dissipated and the frontier is effectively closed, there will be no long-term take off into sustained growth for the economy as a whole.

If during the frontier expansion phase some rents are invested in capital accumulation in other sectors of the economy as well, then the initial boom period will coincide with increased growth. However, this growth path cannot be sustained. The additional capital accumulation is unlikely to overcome the poor linkages between other economic sectors (i.e. manufacturing) and frontier-based economic activities, and is therefore unlikely to yield substantial economy-wide knowledge spillovers. As a result, any additional growth generated by this capital accumulation will last only as long as frontier expansion continues. Once the frontier is "closed" and any reserves of land and natural resources available to an economy have been fully exploited or converted, some economic retrenchment is inevitable, and an economic bust will occur.

However, the results of the frontier expansion hypothesis and model explored in Chapter 4 raises an important issue, which is the key question to be addressed by the remainder of this chapter. *Can frontier resource exploitation ever be compatible with successful resource-based development in a small open economy, or will growth in such an economy always be limited to a short-run economic "boom" that occurs only as long as new frontier resources are available to exploit?*

In the next section, we adapt the model of Chapter 4 to show that it is possible for frontier expansion in a small open economy to lead to sustained long-run growth. The key to this outcome appears to be the three conditions for "successful" resource-based development identified in Chapter 4: i) *exogenous technological change in resource use*, ii) *complete integration between the frontier and mainstay sectors*, and iii) *economy-wide knowledge spillovers* (David and Wright 1997; Wright and Czelusta 2002). In addition, of course, the model assumes that frontier resources or "reserves" are extracted efficiently, i.e. there are no market and policy failures encouraging rent seeking, corruption or open access behavior.

Several key results stem from this model. First, the availability of a "frontier" resource still remains a pervasive influence on the economy. As long as some frontier resource is available, it is always optimal for the economy to extract and use the resource. The first condition for successful resource-based development, exogenous technological change in resource use, does help to extend the life of the available frontier resource stock. However, this condition on its own is not sufficient to prevent economic growth from ending once the frontier is fully exploited, or closed. But if the resource output from the frontier serves as an input into the mainstay production sector, then this ensures that frontier resource exploitation will contribute to some capital investment by entrepreneurs in the latter sector. More importantly, the presence of knowledge spillovers means that capital accumulation in that sector contributes to overall innovation in the economy. It therefore follows that, once the frontier is "closed" and all resource extraction stops, it is still possible to generate sustained growth in the small open economy, as knowledge spillovers prevent any diminishing returns to capital. In essence, the economy has transitioned from a frontier resource-dependent economy to a fully "modernized" capital-labor economy with knowledge spillovers leading to endogenous growth (Arrow 1962; Romer 1986).

If frontier resources are exploited at the maximum rate or when the frontier is closed, we find that a subsidy is necessary because the presence of an economy-wide knowledge spillover means that the private return to capital investment is lower than the social return. If the government subsidizes the contribution of capital to firms' production, the difference between social and private returns to capital in the economy could be eliminated, and the growth rate generated by the decentralized economy would also be socially optimal.

These outcomes define important policy issues, which we touch on in the final remarks of this chapter and discuss in more detail in Chapter 10. First, however, we present a model of "successful" frontier-based development in a resource-dependent economy.

The small open economy model revisited

Recall from Chapter 4 that we assume that a small open economy comprises two sectors, an "established" or "mainstay" sector and a "frontier" sector. The latter includes all economic activities, such as agriculture, forestry, ranching, mining or any other basic extractive industries that are dependent on the exploitation or conversion of "newly acquired" resources available on an open, but ultimately limited, frontier. Although clearly heterogeneous, these available "frontier resources" will be viewed in the following model as an aggregate, homogeneous stock, which we can also refer to broadly as "land." Equally, the extractive activities and economic uses of these resources will be aggregated into a single sectoral output.

Chapter 4 also suggested that there is a "mainstay" sector of the economy, and it was assumed that this sector contained all the other economic activities, industrial and agricultural, which are not directly dependent on the exploitation of frontier resources. However, now we want to make the opposite assumption. Although we can still consider the mainstay economic activities to be separate from the frontier sector, *the two sectors are fully integrated through backward and forward linkages.* That is, the output produced through exploiting frontier "reserves" is an intermediate input into all mainstay production activities. The latter activities can be considered the manufacturing and industrial processing industries of the economy that utilize the "raw material" frontier resources as inputs, e.g. agro-industrial and mineral processing industries.

As in Chapter 4, at some initial time $t = 0$, the frontier sector of the economy is assumed to be endowed with a given stock of natural resources, F_0, which acts as a "reserve" that can be potentially tapped through the rate of extraction, N. Hence, the process of "frontier expansion" is essentially marked by the continual use and depletion of the fixed stock of frontier resources, F_0. To sharpen the analysis, once again we will not include explicitly a cost of frontier resource conversion but postulate that the existence of institutional, geographical and economic constraints limits the maximum amount of frontier resource exploitation at any time t to $\overline{N}$.[1] Over a finite planning horizon, T, it follows that

$$F_0 \geq \int_0^T N\,dt, \quad 0 \leq N \leq \overline{N}, \quad F_0 = F(0) \qquad (9.1)$$

Again, it will be convenient to express the rate of resource extraction in per capita terms. We consider aggregate labor supply, L, and population in the economy to be the same, and we assume that both are growing at the exogenous rate θ. We make the standard assumption that the initial stock of labor, L_0, is normalized to one. Utilizing the relationship $N = ne^{\theta t}$, condition (9.1) can be rewritten as

$$F_0 \geq \int_0^T ne^{\theta t}\,dt, \quad 0 \leq n \leq \overline{n}, \quad F_0 = F(0) \qquad (9.2)$$

where $\overline{n}$ is the maximum per capita amount of frontier resource conversion that can occur at any time t. Since from labor supply grows exogenously, the maximum conversion rate, $\overline{n}$, must decline over time.

So far, our model is consistent with the one developed in Chapter 4. Now, however, we want to deviate from the previous version of the model and introduce a mainstay sector that is *fully* linked with resource exploitation in the frontier sector. To sharpen the analysis, we link the sectors in the following simplified way: let's assume that each firm i in the mainstay sector combines natural resources from the frontier and other inputs to produce output, M_i

$$M_i = M(K_i, N_i, B_i L_i) \tag{9.3}$$

where K_i is the capital stock and L_i is the labor employed by the firm, and B_i is the index of knowledge available to the firm.

We now introduce the classic *knowledge spillover* assumptions concerning productivity growth in the mainstay sector (Arrow 1962; Romer 1986). First, learning-by-doing innovation works through each firm's investment. An increase in a firm's capital stock leads to a parallel increase in its stock of knowledge, B_i. Second, each firm's knowledge is a public good that any other firm can access at zero cost. In other words, once discovered, any new technology spills over instantly across the whole mainstay sector. This assumption implies that the change in each firm's technology term, dB_i/dt, corresponds to the overall learning in the mainstay sector and is therefore proportional to the change in the aggregate capital stock, dK/dt.[2] These assumptions allow B_i to be replaced by K in (9.3), so that $M_i = M(K_i, N_i, KL_i)$.

The second technological change occurs in resource production. That is, we assume that *exogenous technological change contributes to an effective increase in the amount of resources extracted and available to each mainstay firm*. In essence, this source of technological innovation represents increased knowledge in the frontier sector that essentially extends the life of the available frontier resource stock, F. Thus, if N is the aggregate amount of "raw" resource stock extracted at any time t from the frontier resource, the effective amount of resource available for use by any mainstay firm is $a(t)N_i$ with $a(t) = a_0 e^{\alpha t}$.

The above assumptions allow the production function for each firm i in the mainstay sector to be written in intensive form as

$$m_i = m(k_i, n_i, K; a(t)) = a(t)n_i + f(k_i, K),$$
$$m_i = \frac{M_i}{L_i}, \quad k_i = \frac{K_i}{L_i}, \quad n_i = \frac{N_i}{L_i}. \tag{9.4}$$

To facilitate our analysis, we separate the spillover investment effects from the exogenous resource technological change effects on mainstay production. If k and l_i are constant, then each firm faces diminishing returns to k_i as in a standard neoclassical production function. However, if each producer expands k_i, then K rises accordingly across the entire mainstay sector and provides a spillover benefit that raises the productivity of all firms. Moreover, $f(\bullet)$, which represents the function for the contribution of capital to mainstay production, is homogeneous of degree one in k_i and K for given l_i. This implies that there are constant returns to capital at the social level, when k_i and K expand together for a fixed l. Technological change in resource use implies that, for each firm, the marginal productivity of n_i is not diminishing but grows at the exogenous rate α.

A firm's profit function can be written as

$$\pi_i = L_i\big[a(t)n_i + f(k_i, K) - w^N n_i - w - (r + \omega)k_i\big] \qquad (9.5)$$

where w^N is the rental price of the frontier resource, w is the wage rate, $r + \omega$ is the rental price of capital (i.e. the interest rate, r, plus capital depreciation, ω), and output price is normalized to one. Each perfectly competitive firm takes these prices as given. In addition, each firm is small enough to neglect its own contribution to the aggregate capital stock and therefore treats K as given.

Profit maximization and the zero profit condition imply

$$\frac{\partial \pi_i}{\partial k_i} = \frac{\partial m_i}{\partial k_i} = f_1(k_i, K) = r + \omega$$

$$\frac{\partial \pi_i}{\partial n_i} = \frac{\partial m_i}{\partial n_i} = a(t) = w^N \qquad (9.6)$$

$$\frac{\partial \pi_i}{\partial L_i} = \frac{\partial M_i}{\partial L_i} = f(k_i, K) - k_i f_1(k_i, K) = w$$

In equilibrium, all firms make the same choices so that $k_i = k$, $n_i = n$, $m_i = m$ and $K = kL$. Since $f(\bullet)$ is homogeneous of degree one in k_i and K, we can write the average product of capital as

$$\frac{m}{k} = \frac{a(t)n + f(k, K)}{k} = \frac{a(t)n}{k} + \tilde{f}\left(\frac{K}{k}\right) = \frac{a(t)n}{k} + \tilde{f}(L) \qquad (9.7)$$

where $\tilde{f}(L)$ is the function for the average contribution of capital to mainstay production.[3] This function is invariant with respect to k and increases with L but at a diminishing rate, $\tilde{f}''(L) < 0$. It follows from (9.7)

$$m = a(t)n + \tilde{f}(L)k \quad \text{and} \quad \frac{\partial m}{\partial k} = \tilde{f}(L) - L\tilde{f}'(L). \qquad (9.8)$$

Thus the private marginal product of capital is invariant with k and n, increasing in L and is less than the average product.

Per capita output from the mainstay sector may be used for domestic consumption, c, or exported, x. To focus the analysis, we will treat domestic consumption and exports as homogeneous commodities. Let $q = c + x$ be defined as aggregate consumption, both domestic and foreign, of the economy's total output. If households own all the assets in the economy, and s is the net assets per person measured in real terms (i.e. in terms of units of consumables), then real wealth per capita in the economy will increase according to

$$\dot{s} = rs + w + w^N n - \theta s - q. \qquad (9.9)$$

If all the capital stock in the economy is owned by households, then $s = k$. Substituting this condition and (9.6) into the budget constraint (9.9) yields

$$
\begin{aligned}
\dot{k} &= [f_1(k, K) - \omega]k + f(k, K) - f_1(k, K)k + a(t)n - \theta k - q \\
&= \tilde{f}(L)k + a(t)n - (\omega + \theta)k - q
\end{aligned} \qquad (9.10)
$$

In exchange for its exports, the economy imports a consumption good, z. As the country is a small open economy, the terms of trade are fixed and defined as $p = p^x/p^z$. Thus the balance of trade condition for the economy is

$$px = z \qquad (9.11)$$

Finally, all consumers in the economy share identical preferences over the finite time horizon $[0, T]$ given by

$$W = \int_0^T [\beta \log(c) + \log(z)]e^{-\rho t}dt + \psi_T k(T)e^{-\rho T}, \quad \rho = \delta - \theta, \ \beta > 0,$$

$$(9.12)$$

where δ is the discount rate and ψ_T is the scrap value of the terminal capital stock, $k(T)$.

The social planner's problem

Any social planner in the small open economy will recognize that each firm's increase in its capital stock adds to the aggregate capital stock, thus contributing to the productivity of all other firms in the economy. This implies that the social planner will take into account, or internalizes, the knowledge spillovers across all firms. The planner's objective is therefore to maximize the welfare function (9.12) over finite time T with respect to aggregate per capita consumption, q, exports, x, and frontier resource exploitation, n, subject to capital accumulation in the entire economy (9.10), the resource constraint (9.2), and the balance of trade condition (9.11).

The corresponding Hamiltonian for maximizing W is

$$H = [\beta \log(q - x) + \log(px)]e^{-\rho t} + \lambda \left[\tilde{f}(L)k + a(t)n - (\omega + \theta)k - q \right]$$
$$- \mu n e^{\theta t} \tag{9.13}$$

The resulting first-order conditions are

$$e^{-\rho t} \frac{\beta}{c} = \lambda \tag{9.14}$$

$$\frac{\beta}{c} = \frac{p}{z} \quad \text{or} \quad \frac{c}{\beta} = \frac{z}{p} = x \tag{9.15}$$

$$\lambda a(t) - \mu e^{\theta t} \begin{array}{c} < \\ = \\ > \end{array} 0 \Rightarrow \begin{array}{c} n = 0 \\ 0 < n < \bar{n} \\ n = \bar{n} \end{array} \tag{9.16}$$

$$\dot{\lambda} = \lambda \left[(\omega + \theta) - \tilde{f}(L) \right], \quad \lambda(T) = \psi_T e^{-\rho t} \tag{9.17}$$

$$\dot{\mu} = 0, \ \mu \geq 0, \ F_0 - \int_0^T n e^{\theta t} dt \geq 0, \ \mu \left[F_0 - \int_0^T n e^{\theta t} dt \right] = 0 \tag{9.18}$$

plus the equation of motion (9.10).

Equation (9.14) is the usual condition requiring that the discounted marginal utility of consumption equals the shadow price of capital. Equation (9.15) is the open economy equilibrium condition, which indicates that the relative marginal value of domestic to imported consumption must equal the terms of trade, p. This condition can be rewritten using (9.11) to indicate the marginal tradeoff between additional exports and domestic consumption in the economy.

Condition (9.16) governs the optimal rate of frontier resource extraction, n. The first term represents the benefit of extraction, $\lambda a(t)$. This is the marginal product of additional resource exploitation (see (9.6)) expressed in terms of the value of capital. In other words, any additional extraction and use of frontier resources has a potential for increasing valuable capital stock in the economy. However, the second term in (9.16), $\mu e^{\theta t}$, represents the user cost of exploitation; i.e. depletion today means less of the frontier resource available in the future for extraction and use. The latter cost consists of the scarcity value of the resource, μ, weighted by population growth, as larger future populations in the economy imply that greater resource extraction will be required in later periods. Condition (9.16) states that, if the value marginal product of frontier resource exploitation exceeds its marginal cost, then per capita resource extraction will be at the maximum rate, $\bar{n}$. If extraction costs are greater than the benefits, then no frontier resource exploitation will occur. When benefits equal costs, then extraction is at the rate n where $0 < n < \bar{n}$.

Equation (9.17) determines the change over time in the value of the capital stock of the economy. This value will grow if $\tilde{f}(L)$ is less than any capital depreciation and population growth, $\omega + \theta$. In addition, the terminal value of the capital stock, $\lambda(T)$, combined with (9.14) – (9.16) will determine the final levels of per capita domestic consumption plus exports, $c(T) + x(T)$, in the economy.

Finally, condition (9.18) states that the marginal value, μ, of the fixed stock of frontier resources, F_0, is essentially unchanging over the planning horizon. Instead, whether the scarcity value of frontier resources is positive or zero depends on whether the available stock of frontier resources, F_0, is completely exhausted through extraction, n, by terminal time, T. Combined with the other first-order conditions, (9.18) proves to be important in characterizing the optimal "frontier resource exploitation" path of the economy.

For example, suppose that by the end of the planning horizon at time T the stock of frontier resources is not completely exhausted through frontier exploitation, i.e. $F_0 > \int_0^T n e^{\theta t} dt$ over $[0,T]$ such that $F(T) > 0$. From (9.18) it follows that $\mu = 0$. The unlimited availability of frontier resources to the economy over the entire planning period means that these reserves have no scarcity value. However, from (9.14), the marginal value of accumulated capital in the economy is always positive, $\lambda > 0$. As a consequence, leftover resource stocks imply that in (9.16) the value marginal product of frontier resource exploitation, $\lambda a(t)$, will exceed the costs, and thus the economy will exploit frontier resources at the maximum per capita rate, $\bar{n}$, throughout $[0, T]$.

Alternatively, suppose that $F_0 = \int_0^T n e^{\theta t} dt$ so that frontier resources are exhausted at least by the end of the time horizon, T, if not at some time $t^F < T$. These resources now have positive scarcity value, $\mu > 0$, throughout the planning period. This in turn implies that optimal paths of frontier exploitation may have either an interior solution, $0 < n < \bar{n}$, or corner solutions, $n = \bar{n}$ and $n = 0$. Since these paths have interesting and differing economic implications, we will focus mainly on them. Thus the rest of the chapter will consider only the case where frontier resource exploitation comes to an end some time during the planning horizon of the open economy.

We begin with the conditions for an interior solution to the choice of frontier resource extraction, $0 < n < \bar{n}$:

According to (9.12), an interior solution for n requires that the benefits of frontier exploitation equal the cost. This condition can be rewritten as

$$\lambda = \frac{\mu e^{(\theta - \alpha)t}}{a_0} \quad \text{and} \quad \dot{\lambda} = (\theta - \alpha)\lambda \qquad (9.19)$$

given that μ is constant. Substituting (9.19) into (9.17) yields

$$(\theta - \alpha)\lambda = \lambda[(\rho + \omega + \theta) - \tilde{f}(L)] \quad \text{or} \quad \tilde{f}(L) = \rho + \omega + \alpha \qquad (9.20)$$

The latter expression implies that $\tilde{f}'(L) = 0$, and from (9.8), that the marginal productivity of capital is constant, i.e. $\frac{\partial m}{\partial k} = \tilde{f}(L) = \rho + \omega + \alpha$.

Combining (9.11), (9.14), (9.15) and (9.17) yields

$$\dot{c} = c\left[\tilde{f}(L) - (\rho + \omega + \theta)\right]$$
$$\dot{q} = \dot{c} + \dot{x} = \left(1 + \frac{1}{\beta}\right)c\left[\tilde{f}(L) - (\rho + \omega + \theta)\right] \qquad (9.21)$$

Since $\tilde{f}(L) = \rho + \omega + \alpha$, it follows that q and c will increase over time if $\alpha > \theta$, i.e. if exogenous resource technological change exceeds population growth in the economy. Thus, the interior solution for frontier resource extraction in this frontier open economy with spill-overs can be consistent with an optimal path leading to growth in per capita consumption and exports, provided that $\alpha > \theta$. If this is the case, which we will also assume throughout the rest of the chapter, then frontier resource extraction under the interior solution will lead to the following growth conditions

$$g = \frac{\dot{q}}{q} = \frac{\dot{c}}{c} = \alpha - \theta \qquad (9.22)$$

$$\dot{k} = a(t)n + (\rho + \alpha - \theta)k - q, \ q(t) = q_0 e^{(\alpha-\theta)t}, \ q(0) = q_0, \ 0 < n < \bar{n} \qquad (9.23)$$

Growth in per capita consumption, exports and thus aggregate consumption, q, is therefore constant and equal to $\alpha - \theta$.[4] Because of the knowledge spillovers across firms, the marginal productivity of capital in the economy is constant but invariant with respect to capital per worker, k. In other words, there are no diminishing returns to capital in the economy, and thus as long as frontier resources can be exploited at the rate $0 < n < \bar{n}$, economic growth will occur at the constant rate $\alpha - \theta$.

However, because of exogenous population growth, the key condition for the interior solution, $\tilde{f}(L) = \rho + \omega + \alpha$, is likely to hold for only an instant of time. Thus, along the optimal path for the economy, there may be only one instant in which the interior solution is feasible.

The remaining two choices for the economy are the corner solutions $n = 0$ and $n = \bar{n}$. Both corner solutions yield the same dynamic equations (9.21) for q and c as the interior solution. It follows from (9.21) that, for both corner solutions to yield economic growth, requires $\tilde{f}(L) > \rho + \omega + \theta$. Note as well that, since the labor force, L, is increasing over time, the average contribution of capital, $\tilde{f}(L)$, will also rise over time. Thus the growth rate of the economy will increase due to this scale effect of population growth on the average contribution of capital to production. Consequently, the two corner solutions for frontier resource extraction will lead to the following growth conditions, respectively

$$g = \frac{\dot{q}}{q} = \frac{\dot{c}}{c} = \tilde{f}(L) - (\rho + \omega + \theta) \qquad (9.24)$$

$$\dot{k} = \tilde{f}(L)k + a(t)\bar{n} - (\omega + \theta)k - q, q(t) = q_0 e^{\int_0^t [\tilde{f}(L)-(\rho+\omega+\theta)]dt},$$

$$q_0 = q(0), n = \bar{n} \tag{9.25}$$

$$\dot{k} = \tilde{f}(L)k - (\omega + \theta)k - q, q(t) = q_0 e^{\int_0^t [\tilde{f}(L)-(\rho+\omega+\theta)]dt},$$

$$q_0 = q(0), n = 0 \tag{9.26}$$

Note that, just as both corner solutions differ in the rate of capital accumulation (compare (9.25) and (9.26)), they also differ in terms of the productivity of capital. For example, if frontier extraction is at the maximum rate, $n = \bar{n}$, the average and marginal productivity of capital are determined by (9.7) and (9.8). However, when frontier exploitation stops, $n = 0$, the average productivity of capital falls to equal the average contribution of capital, i.e. $m/k = \tilde{f}(L)$. Nevertheless, both the marginal and average productivity of capital remain invariant with respect to capital. Thus, once frontier resource extraction halts, the economy is no longer dependent on natural resource exploitation, but the "spillover" effects eliminate the tendency for diminishing returns as capital per worker accumulates, and growth can be sustained if condition (9.24) holds. A final result of the model is that, if the economy is generating economic growth, it is never optimal to halt resource extraction as long as there is some frontier stock remaining. To see this, note that in the case of zero resource extraction, $n = 0$, positive growth also implies that the value of the capital stock, λ, is positive but declining over time (see equations (9.24) and (9.17)).[5] From (9.16), halting frontier resource extraction will be an optimal choice only if $\lambda < \frac{\mu e^{(\theta-\alpha)t}}{a_0}$. However, from (9.18), $n = 0$ also requires $\mu F_0 = 0$ and $\mu \geq 0$, whereas (9.14) indicates that $\lambda(t) > 0$ always. Together, these conditions imply that the zero extraction policy is only optimal once the frontier resource stock is completely exhausted, i.e. when $F_0 = 0$.

To summarize, as long as some of the frontier resource is available and its exploitation generates economic growth, it is always optimal to exploit it. Frontier resource extraction will only be halted once the resource is completely exhausted. During the period of time in which frontier reserves are available, the economy is likely to be exploiting it at the maximum rate, then in the instant before the reserves are exhausted, the reserves will be exploited at optimal rate less than the maximum (i.e. the interior solution for n).

As maximum frontier resource exploitation occurs, the economy can sustain growth provided that the average contribution of capital exceeds the sum of population growth, capital depreciation and the discount rate. Once the frontier resource is completely exhausted, growth can still be sustained. Although the economy is no longer dependent on the resource for production, knowledge spillovers eliminate the tendency for diminishing returns from accumulation of capital per worker and can therefore allow growth to continue indefinitely.

Equilibrium in the decentralized economy

A key issue is whether a social planner is necessary to achieve the optimal growth rates in the economy for aggregate consumption depicted in the previous section. In other words, in the absence of a social planner, will the equilibrium growth rates for q chosen through the decentralized decisions of individual consumers and producers also yield the optimal growth rates?

The decentralized outcome can be found by assuming that the representative infinite-lived household seeks to maximize overall utility over the time period $[0, T]$, given by

$$U = \int_0^T [\beta \log(c) + \log(z)] e^{-\rho t} dt + \psi_T s(T) e^{-\rho T}, \quad \rho = \delta - \theta, \ \beta > 0,$$

$$(9.27)$$

subject to the household budget constraint (9.9), the resource constraint (9.2), and the balance of trade condition (9.11). From this maximization problem, the key conditions governing economic growth in the economy are

$$\lambda w^N = \lambda a(t) \begin{array}{c} < \\ = \\ > \end{array} \mu e^{\theta t} \Rightarrow \begin{array}{c} n = 0 \\ 0 < n < \bar{n} \\ n = \bar{n} \end{array} \qquad (9.28)$$

$$\tilde{g} = \frac{\dot{q}}{q} = \frac{\dot{c}}{c} = [r - \theta - \rho] = \left[\tilde{f}(L) - L\tilde{f}'(L) - (\rho + \omega + \theta)\right], \quad (9.29)$$

where we make use of the conditions for the marginal products of resource use and capital (see (9.6) and (9.8)). We denote the decentralized growth rate as $\tilde{g}$ in order to distinguish it from socially optimal growth, g. It is clear from (9.29) that what determines the growth rate of aggregate consumption in the decentralized solution is the magnitude of the marginal product of capital, $\tilde{f}(L) - L\tilde{f}'(L)$.

However, it is easy to see that for the interior solution, $0 < n < \bar{n}$, growth condition (9.29) reduces to $\tilde{g} = -\dot{\lambda}/\lambda = \alpha - \theta$. Comparing the latter expression to (9.22), it appears that the decentralized and socially optimal growth rates are the same, i.e. $\tilde{g} = g$. That is, as long as the economy is pursuing a path in which some frontier expansion occurs but at a rate less than the maximum, the decentralized decisions of individual consumers and producers will yield socially optimal growth in aggregate consumption. In both the decentralized and optimal solutions, growth in aggregate consumption is constant and is determined by the difference between resource technological change and population growth. However, as noted above, the interior solution will occur only at an instant along the optimal path of the economy. Thus, the decentralized decisions of consumers and producers will coincide with the socially optimal outcome only at this instant.

In the case of the two corner solutions, $n = 0$ and $n = \bar{n}$, the decentralized growth rate is determined by (9.29). Comparing the latter to (9.24), it is clear that $\tilde{g} < g$. When the economy is either extracting resources at the maximum rate, $n = \bar{n}$, or when the frontier is closed, $n = 0$, the decentralized growth rate is lower than the planner's growth rate. This occurs because the presence of economy-wide knowledge spillover means that the private return to capital investment is lower than the social return. Unlike any social planner, individual producers do not internalize the knowledge spillovers, and so the decentralized growth rate (9.29) is set in accordance with the private marginal product of capital, $\tilde{f}(L) = L\tilde{f}'(L)$, which is less than the average contribution of capital in production, $\tilde{f}(L)$. In contrast, a social planner will take into account the spillovers, and the average contribution of capital is the determinant of the socially optimal growth rate in (9.24).[6]

Policy implications

However, the social optimum could be attained in a decentralized economy if the government chooses to subsidize the contribution of capital to firm's production. Such a subsidy would raise the private return to capital, thus eliminating the difference between social and private returns. To illustrate this, let's assume that the function for the contribution of capital to mainstay production takes the following Cobb-Douglas form, $f(k_i, K) = \gamma k_i^{\eta} K^{1-\eta}$, $0 < \eta < 1$. It follows that a subsidy to each producer of $(1 - \eta)/\eta$ on the average contribution of capital would result in the following outcome in the decentralized economy

$$
m_i = a(t)n_i + \left(1 + \frac{1}{\eta}\right)f(k_i, K) = a(t)n_i + \frac{1}{\eta}\gamma k_i^{\eta}K^{1-\eta}
$$

$$
\frac{\partial m_i}{\partial k_i} = \frac{1}{\eta}f_1(k_i, K) = \gamma\left(\frac{K}{k_i}\right)^{1-\eta} = \gamma L^{1-\eta} = \tilde{f}(L)
$$

$$(9.30)$$

Thus the effect of the subsidy is to ensure that the private marginal product of capital in the economy equals the average contribution of capital. From (9.29), it is easy to see that the growth rate in aggregate consumption produced by the decentralized decisions of individual producers and consumers now equals the socially optimal rate of growth

$$
\tilde{g} = \left[\tilde{f}(L) - (\rho + \omega + \theta)\right] = g \tag{9.31}
$$

In sum, only when the economy is exploiting frontier resources at less than the maximum rate, $0 < n < \bar{n}$, will the decentralized decisions of individual consumers and producers also yield the optimal growth rate. Any economic growth will be constant and equal to the difference between resource technological change and population growth. This result occurs because, despite the presence of knowledge spillovers in the economy, there is no difference between the social and private returns to capital investment. Unfortunately, however, this result will occur only at an instant along the optimal path of the economy; for the remainder of this path the optimal and decentralized growth rates will diverge. For instance, if frontier resources are exploited at the maximum rate, $n = \bar{n}$, or when the frontier is closed, $n = 0$, then the decentralized growth rate is lower than the planner's growth rate. In the latter cases, the presence of economy-wide knowledge spillover does ensure that the private return to capital investment is lower than the social return. However, the difference between social and private returns to capital in the economy could be eliminated if the government chooses to subsidize the contribution of capital to firms' production. Such a policy would then enable the growth rate generated by the decentralized economy to be socially optimal.

There is evidence from past examples of successful resource-based development that government subsidies, or at least complementary public investment, have played a pivotal role in generating the economy-wide increasing returns from such development (David and Wright 1997; Romer 1996; Wright and Czelusta 2002). For example, in explaining the world-wide ascendancy of the US copper industry during the 1880–1920 era, David and Wright (1997, p. 239) maintain that: "Capital requirements and long term horizons made copper an industry for corporate giants ... These large enterprises internalized many of the complementarities and spillovers in copper technology, but they also drew extensively on national infrastructural investments in geological knowledge and in the training of mining engineers and metallurgists."

What is needed, perhaps, is a similar set of policies for agricultural and other resource-based activities in the frontier sectors of developing countries, provided of course that the incentives for encouraging corruption and rent-seeking and the problems of ill-defined property rights can be corrected in frontier areas.

Final remarks

This chapter has demonstrated that it is theoretically possible at least that frontier-based development can lead to successful resource-based development in a small open developing economy. This could, in turn, reverse the current "vicious" cycle of resource exploitation and frontier land expansion in the economy and instead create a "virtuous" cycle leading to sustainable, long-run growth.

Following recent studies of successful mineral-based development, we have argued that under certain conditions frontier expansion in a small open economy can be associated with sustained growth. These conditions include: i) resource-enhancing technological change; ii) strong linkages between the resource and manufacturing sectors; and iii) substantial knowledge spillovers across producers in the economy. These conditions are incorporated into a modified version of the small open economy model first developed in Chapter 4 by assuming that output produced through exploiting frontier "reserves" is an intermediate input into all manufacturing and industrial processing activities, capital accumulation by each firm engaged in the latter activities leads to knowledge spillovers across the entire sector, and exogenous technological change increases the effective stock of resources extracted available as intermediate inputs.

The modified model leads to several important results in terms of optimal frontier resource exploitation and economic growth.

First, as long as some frontier resource is available, it is always optimal for the economy to extract and use the resource. Optimal extraction will occur at the maximum rate possible, except in the instant before the frontier reserves are exhausted, and economic growth can be sustained provided that the average contribution of capital exceeds the sum of population growth, capital depreciation and the discount rate. Because any social planner will take into account the presence of knowledge spillovers, the average contribution of capital represents the social return to capital in the economy and thus determines the socially optimal growth rate.

Second, once the frontier is "closed" and all resource extraction stops, it is still possible to generate sustained growth in the small open economy. Although the economy is no longer dependent on the resource for production, knowledge spillovers eliminate the tendency for diminishing returns from accumulation of capital per worker and can therefore allow growth to continue indefinitely. The average contribution of capital once again represents the social return to capital, and thus determines the socially optimal growth rate. Moreover, since the labor force, L, is increasing over time, the average contribution of capital, $\tilde{f}(L)$, will also rise over time. Thus the growth rate of the economy will increase due to this scale effect of population growth on the average contribution of capital to production. In essence, the economy has transitioned from a frontier resource-dependent economy to a fully "modernized" capital-labor economy with knowledge spillovers leading to endogenous growth (Arrow 1962; Romer 1986).

Third, we also examined whether it is necessary for producers to receive a subsidy in order for the decentralized economy to attain the socially optimal growth rate. As we have shown, except for possibly one instant in time when frontier resources are exploited at less than the maximum rate, there will be a divergence between the social and private returns to capital investment. For instance, if frontier resources are exploited at the maximum rate or when the frontier is closed, a subsidy is necessary because the presence of an economy-wide knowledge spillover means that the private return to capital investment is lower than the social return. In the latter two cases, if the government subsidizes the contribution of capital to firms' production, the difference between social and private returns to capital in the economy could be eliminated, and the growth rate generated by the decentralized economy would also be socially optimal. As discussed above, evidence from past examples of successful resource-based development indicates that government subsidies, or at least complementary public investments, played an important role in generating the economy-wide benefits from such development (David and Wright 1997; Romer 1996; Wright and Czelusta 2002).

However, as we discussed in Chapter 4, there are three important caveats attached to the above conditions for successful resource-based development, which served as the basis of the model of this chapter.

First, there is unfortunately plenty of evidence that government investment and subsidies in resource sectors of developing countries are not aimed at promoting economy-wide knowledge spillovers but encouraging problems of rent seeking and corruption (Ascher 1999; Barbier 2003a and 2004a). Such policies not only dissipate resource rents and militate against efficient management of natural resources, but also ensure that whatever rents are being generated are not being channeled into productive investments elsewhere in the economy. As we saw in Chapter 8, perverse government policies in many resource-dependent economies are not aimed at promoting knowledge spillovers but encouraging problems of rent seeking and corruption, especially in frontier resource-extractive activities. As the model of this chapter also suggests, a second consequence of such misallocation of government investments and subsidies is that the private returns to investment in the resource-based economy will fall short of the social returns. The result is that private firms will under-invest in resource-based production, thus leading to lower economic growth.

A second caveat, which was also highlighted in Chapter 4, is that all of the past and present examples of development with the above three conditions for success – *resource-augmenting technological change*, *frontier-mainstay integration* and *knowledge spillovers* – are associated with minerals-based development (David and Wright 1997; Wright and Czelusta 2002). It remains to be seen whether a small open economy dependent on frontier agricultural land expansion is likely to foster the above conditions for successful resource-based development. In fact, there is some evidence that agricultural-based development based on land expansion may be negatively correlated with economic growth and development (Barbier 2003a and 2004a; Stijns 2001). On the other hand, as we demonstrate in the next chapter, Thailand and Malaysia may be important counter-examples of countries that have attained long-run successful resource-based development and economic diversification that is linked to frontier resource extraction and land expansion.

Finally, as discussed in Chapter 8, in many developing economies, inequalities in wealth between rural households also have an important impact on land degradation and deforestation processes, which may explain why so many poorer households find themselves confined to marginal lands. This structural feature of present-day developing countries translates into a particular pattern of resource-based development that is characterized by a large proportion of the population concentrated on fragile land, and a high degree of rural poverty, and a frontier land expansion process that generates little rents and is largely divorced from the rest of the economy.

It is important to address these three caveats, in order to understand how the conditions for successful resource-based development illustrated by the model of this chapter might translate into specific policies that will overcome the key features of the "dualism within dualism" economic structure that is perpetuating underdevelopment in many poor economies. This will be the focus of the next, and final, chapter of this book, which examines both recent country case studies of successful resource-led development and the key policies and reforms underlying this success.

Notes

1. The reason for this assumption is the same as in Chapter 4: many frontier resources are located far from population centers, and thus the rate at which these resources may be profitably converted or exploited may be constrained by distance to market and accessibility. In this regard, we follow in spirit the approach to institutions as defined by North (1990). See also studies that have explored the impact on frontier resource extraction and land conversion of institutional factors, such as land use conflict, security of ownership or property rights, political stability, and the "rule

of law" (e.g. Alston *et al.* 2000; Barbier 2002; Deacon 1999; Godoy *et al.* 1998). Bohn and Deacon (2002) illustrate that reduction of ownership risk is also fundamental to reducing over-exploitation of a variety of natural resources.

2. The specification that all discoveries are unintended by-products of investment and that these discoveries immediately become common knowledge allows the framework of perfect competition to be retained for the mainstay sector, although as we see below the decisions of consumers and producers even under perfect competition do not always turn out to be socially optimal.

3. It is clear from (9.7) that the average contribution of capital to production, $\tilde{f}(L)$, is not the same as the average product of capital in mainstay production. That is, $\tilde{f}(L) = m/k$ only if there is no resource extraction, i.e. $n = 0$.

4. In the remainder of the chapter we will use the term "economic growth" as shorthand for growth in aggregate consumption, $q = x + c$.

5. In fact, for all three solutions to generate economic growth results in a positive but declining value of the capital stock, λ.

6. Note that, in the case of the interior solution, we proved that the private marginal product of capital is constant and equal to the average contribution of capital in the economy. Thus, there is no difference between the social and private returns to capital investment, and the decentralized and socially optimal growth rates are the same.

10 | Policies for sustainable resource-based development in poor economies

As discussed in Part One, the very minimum criterion for attaining sustainable development in an economy dependent on exploiting natural resources is that this exploitation satisfies "weak sustainability" conditions. That is, the development path must ensure that, first, natural resources must be managed efficiently so that any rents earned are maximized, and second, the rents resulting from the depletion of natural capital must be invested into other productive assets in the economy.

Historically successful examples of resource-based development have largely adhered to these principles. This includes the past 500 years or so of frontier-based economic development, which is characterized by a pattern of capital investment, technological innovation and social and economic institutions dependent on "opening up" new frontiers of natural resources once existing ones have been "closed" and exhausted. Such development has been mainly successful, particularly during the Golden Age of Resource-Based Development (1870–1913).

However, as maintained throughout this book, frontier-based development in many present-day low and middle-income economies has been much less successful. A key reason is that this development often falls far short of the minimum conditions for attaining sustainable development. What little rents have been generated from this development process have not led to sufficient investments in other productive assets and in more dynamic sectors of the economy. Instead, many poor economies exhibit a "dualism within dualism" economic structure characterized by continuing dependence of the overall economy on mainly primary product exports, a large proportion of the population concentrated on fragile land, and a high degree of rural poverty. These conditions are symptomatic of a "vicious cycle" of underdevelopment: any resource rents that are earned from frontier "reserves" are often reinvested in further land expansion and resource exploitation. The frontier remains an isolated enclave, and there are very little economy-wide efficiency gains and benefits. In addition, this process tends to be inequitable. The resource rents accrue mainly to wealthy individuals, who have increased incentives for "rent-seeking" behavior that is in turn supported by policy distortions that reinforce the existing pattern of allocating and distributing natural resources. The poor are therefore left with marginal resources and frontier land areas to exploit, further reducing their ability to improve their livelihoods, and of course, to generate and appropriate significant rents.

The model of frontier-based development and long-run growth presented in Chapter 9 demonstrates that it is at least *theoretically* possible to break this vicious cycle. Under the right conditions, a process of frontier resource exploitation and land expansion can be compatible with successful resource-based development in a small open economy. The conditions include: i) resource-enhancing technological change; ii) strong linkages between the resource and manufacturing sectors; and iii) substantial knowledge spillovers across producers in the economy. In addition, of course, the model assumes that frontier resources or "reserves" are extracted efficiently, i.e. there are no market and policy failures encouraging rent-seeking, corruption or open access behavior. Under both sets of conditions, frontier-based development appears to lead to sufficient reinvestment of resource investments to allow the economy to "take off" into sustained growth and development.

But as indicated in the outset of Chapter 9, the model developed in that chapter addresses really only one of the four objectives highlighted in the conclusion to Chapter 8 as being necessary for overcoming the "dualism within dualism" pattern of development that is a persistent structural feature of many poor economies. The four goals are:

- Reinvesting resource rents in more productive and dynamic sectors of the economy, which in turn are linked to the resource-exploiting sectors of the domestic economy.
- Developing political and legal institutions to discourage rent-seeking behavior by wealthy investors in the natural resource sectors of the economy.
- Instigating widespread reform of government policies that favor wealthier investors in markets for valuable natural resources, including arable land.
- Targeting additional policies and investments to improve the economic opportunities and livelihoods of the rural poor, rather

than relying on frontier land expansion and urban migration as the principal outlet for alleviating rural poverty.

As noted at the end of Chapter 9, for a small open economy dependent on frontier agricultural land expansion to achieve the first goal requires fostering resource-augmenting technological change, frontier-mainstay integration and economy-wide knowledge spillovers. On available evidence, this seems to be a tall order for many present-day low and middle-income economies. As we shall discuss later in this chapter, however, Botswana, Malaysia and Thailand may provide instructive examples as to how this might be accomplished.

As for the other three objectives, achieving them will mean over-coming pervasive policy, market and institutional distortions that, on the one hand, encourage problems of rent-seeking and corruption, especially in frontier resource-extractive activities, and on the other, perpetuate inequalities in wealth and rural poverty. The latter in turn have an important impact on land degradation and deforestation processes, which may explain why so many poorer households are confined to marginal lands and are dependent on open-access resource exploitation. Thus, for a very large number of developing economies, their "dualism within dualism" structure reflects a particular pattern of resource-based development and frontier land expansion that is characterized by a large proportion of the population concentrated on fragile land, and a high degree of rural poverty, and a frontier land expansion process that generates little rents and is largely divorced from the rest of the economy.

It is of course tempting to end this book with these rather pessimistic observations. However, that would be neither fruitful nor helpful for anyone interested in encouraging successful resource-based development in today's low and middle-income economies.

Instead, this concluding chapter will end the book by asking one last, very pertinent question. Is there some way in which policies and institutions in developing countries could be modified to change the pattern of frontier-based development from a "vicious" to a "virtuous" cycle. The short answer is "yes," but not without difficulty.

The purpose of this chapter is to provide some discussion and illustrative cases indicating what type of policy and institutional reforms might be necessary to instigate a more successful pattern of resource-based development in developing countries. The next section provides a broad overview of the type of institutional and policy reforms that are necessary for such a transformation. We then discuss the lessons learned from three present-day examples of successful resource-based development: Botswana, Malaysia and Thailand. We end this book with some final remarks concerning natural resources and economic development in today's low and middle-income economies.

Policies and institutions for successful resource-based development: an overview

If the "vicious cycle" of present-day frontier-based development is to be shifted to a "virtuous cycle," there are essentially two roles for institutional and policy reform within developing economies. First, specific policies must be aimed at overcoming the structural features in resource use patterns implied by this vicious cycle. Second, policies must also be introduced that improve the overall success of resource-based development that is accompanied by frontier land expansion. As we shall see, these two sets of reform are inherently inter-related.

One straightforward, but often politically difficult, approach to the problem is economy-wide land reform. As noted by Binswanger and Deininger (1997, p. 1972), "where rural capital markets are highly imperfect and the distribution of wealth is unequal, a one-time redistribution of wealth, such as a land reform, may largely eliminate the need for distortionary redistributive policies later." As the authors point out, the experience of Japan, South Korea and Taiwan indicate that land reform is also likely to alter the growth path of the economy and lead to permanently higher levels of growth as well as improvement in the livelihoods of the rural poor. As demonstrated by Dasgupta (1993, p. 496), this may be due to three effects of land redistribution to the landless and near-landless:

First, because their rental income increases, the unemployed become more attractive to employers. Second, those among the poor who are employed become more productive to the extent that they too receive land. And third, by taking land away from the gentry their reservation wages are lowered, and when this effect is strong enough it induces them to forsake leisure and enter the agricultural labour market.

Finally, the "greater wealth" arising through land reform "also increases the ability of the poor to directly participate in the political process" (Binswanger and Deininger 1997, p. 1999).[1]

Improving the security of property rights over land is another important reform that can contribute to both increased growth and improvement in rural livelihoods. In particular, empirical evidence across many developing regions suggest that legal land titles prove to be significant in helping alleviate liquidity constraints affecting the purchase of working inputs, as well as land improvements generally (Alston *et al.* 1996; Besley 1995; Feder and Feeny 1991; Feder and Noronha 1987; Feder and Onchon 1987; López and Valdés 1998). Greater land tenure security for initial agricultural smallholder settlers in frontier areas also appears to slow down the incentive for these migrants to engage in subsequent deforestation for land conversion (Alston *et al.* 1999; Barbier 1998a; Barbier and Burgess 2001b; Cattaneo 2001; Godoy *et al.* 1998; Nelson *et al.* 2001). Finally, providing legal and institutional support for existing common property regimes may lead to better protection of encroachment and degradation of key natural resources. For example, legal enforcement of the *ejido* rural community ownership rules in Mexico has been significant in slowing down cropland expansion and deforestation (Barbier 2002; Deininger and Minten 1999; see also Chapter 6). In contrast, historically ill-defined common property rights in Thailand have accelerated the rapid conversion of forests to agriculture in upland areas and mangroves to shrimp farms in coastal regions (Barbier and Sathirathai 2004; Feder *et al.* 1988; Feeny 2002).

A related, but equally difficult, task is reform of tax, credit and other economic policies that generally reinforce the dominance of wealthier households in natural resource and land markets and promote the speculative investment in these resources as tax shelters. According to López (2003, p. 271) such policies in Latin America over the past 50 years are symptomatic of the general economic policy failure in the region that has "focused on the generation of an expensive and often incoherent system of short-run incentives to promote investment in physical capital … by undertaxing capital income and wasted in massive subsidies to the corporate sector in a futile effort to promote investment and economic growth." This has had two overall consequences on the land degradation and deforestation process in the region. First, as described above, the resulting market and tax distortions promote this process directly, in a deliberate strategy of "wasting natural resources as a way of enticing investors" (López 2003, p. 260). Second, Latin American governments are dissipating scarce revenues and financial resources "instead of concentrating their efforts in raising enough public revenues to finance the necessary investment in human and natural capital and the necessary institutional capacities to effectively enforce environmental regulations" (López 2003, p. 271).

Finally, the third structural problem associated with frontier-based development today is the under-investment in human capital in rural areas, particularly by those poor households concentrated on fragile land. As noted above, these households generate insufficient savings, suffer chronic indebtedness and rely on informal credit markets with high short-term interest rates. As a result, private investment in human capital improvement is a luxury for most poor rural households, and similarly the lack of education and marketable skills limits not only the earning potential of the rural poor but also their political bargaining power relative to wealthier rural and urban households. As argued by Binswanger and Deininger (1997, pp. 1988–1989): "Primary education and health services, especially for the poor, rural inhabitants, and women, are important not only because they foster growth and help reduce poverty through several well known channels, but also because they reduce income inequality, and thereby enhance the collective action potential of the poor."

Clearly, if resource-dependent development in poor economies is associated with frontier land expansion and resource exploitation, then the critical issue for these economies is how to improve the sustainability of such development. Based on our previous discussion in this chapter, the key to sustainable economic development will be improving the economic integration between frontier and other sectors of the economy, targeting policies to improved resource management in frontier areas and overcoming problems of corruption and rent seeking in resource sectors.

Particularly for those economies that do not have substantial mineral wealth, better integration between frontier-based activities and more dynamic economic sectors means a greater commitment to promoting "agro-industrialization" generally. As argued by Reardon and Barrett (2000), such a strategy comprises three related sets of changes: i) growth of commercial, off-farm agro-processing, distribution and input provision activities; ii) institutional and organizational change in relations between farms and firms both upstream and downstream, such as marked increased in vertical integration and contract-based procurement; and iii) related changes in product composition, technologies, and sectoral and market structure. Such an integrated approach to agro-industrialization is essential for developing *country-specific knowledge* in improving the productivity and sustainable exploitation of land resources, *strong forward and backward linkages* between more dynamic economic sectors (i.e. manufacturing) and agricultural activities, and finally, the opportunities for *substantial knowledge spillovers* from the farm to firm level.

However, frontier-based agricultural activities will be largely left out of the development of such agro-industrial capacity in low and middle-income economies unless specific policy reforms are aimed at improving resource management and productivity of frontier lands, and targeted especially at poor rural households farming these lands. Nevertheless, recent economic analyses are beginning to indicate what kind of policy reforms may be necessary to improve the incentives for better land management in the frontier areas and marginal farmlands of developing countries. The good news is that overall agricultural sector policy reforms that reduce price distortions, promote efficient operation of rural financial markets, and make property rights enforceable should support these incentives (Barbier 1997b). In some countries, there may be a win-win situation between general macroeconomic and sectoral reforms and improved land management. For example, in the Philippines and other Southeast Asian countries it was found that reducing import tariffs and export taxes may also reduce the rate of upland degradation (Coxhead and Jayasuriya 1995 and 2003). Similarly, in Indonesia reducing fertilizer, pesticide and other subsidies for irrigated rice could be compatible with improved investment and credit strategies for the uplands of Java (Pearce *et al.* 1990).

One of the important consequences of better integration of farming systems in "frontier" areas with commercial and national agro-industry is that this may actually increase the range of policy options for influencing land and farming decisions on the frontier. For example, Coxhead *et al.* 2001, pp. 264–265) argue, in the case of Filipino upland farmers: "If market-driven incentives dominate in farmers' decisions, there is a case for broadening the range of policy instruments brought to bear on the upland environmental problem; moreover, project design may be improved by a different balance of local action and national-level information dissemination and policy advocacy." The authors go on to note (p. 265) that, "in spite of remoteness, the farmers in our study area produce for markets that are integrated in the national system." As a consequence, Coxhead *et al.* demonstrate that upland deforestation, soil erosion and watershed degradation could be substantially reduced through a combination of a "national-level" policy of trade liberalization of maize and vegetables, which will reduce the farm-gate prices for the two most environmentally damaging crops in upland areas, and "local-action" consisting of projects to support soil-conserving technologies and adoption of improved farming systems.

The latter example illustrates an important point: Neither economy-wide reforms aimed at increasing production through price incentives nor local projects aimed at influencing smallholders' land conversion and land use decisions is sufficient *on their own* to overcome the "vicious cycle" of present-day frontier-based development in many developing economies. As we have seen, economy-wide and sectoral reforms, especially those aimed at increasing aggregate production, may have unknown – and possibly negative – aggregate impacts on land and resource use strategies of rural households. Equally, the "sustainability" of local "land improvement" projects is often undermined by policy and price changes that reinforce the incentives driving rural households to convert land and over-exploit other environmental resources.

A good example of the latter problem is the case of smallholder pricing and policy reforms instigated in Malawi throughout the 1980s (Barbier 1998c). The main aim of the policies was to increase smallholder production of key food and cash crops. At the same time, substantial project investments were taking place in Malawi to encourage farmers to adopt improved soil conservation and cropping methods. However, an economic analysis of the policy reforms showed that the resulting fluctuations in relative crop prices and returns were exerting a significant impact on the incentives for smallholders to invest in cropping systems and land management by increasing the degree of price risk. As summarized by Barbier (1998c), the dynamics of price risk were producing the following effects on smallholder incentives:

- Given the very small margins for risk among most smallholders and the widespread prevalence of household food insecurity, the uncertainty arising from fluctuating prices and returns was not conducive to improving farming systems, incorporating new crops into farming systems, and investing in substantial improvements in existing cropping patterns, cultivation practices and conservation efforts.
- The impacts of the policies on the relative returns of the less erosive crops (groundnuts and pulses) to the erosive crops (maize, cassava,

cotton and tobacco) was not considered in the pricing decisions, and therefore the resulting decline in the relative returns per labor unit for the less erosive crops caused smallholders to reject new farming systems that promoted intercropping with groundnuts and pulses, which had long-run implications for both soil conservation and household income.

• The asymmetrical impacts of pricing for most households – i.e. food-deficit households in Malawi tend to be influenced by higher food prices as consumers rather than responding as producers to increase output – may have reinforced both the disincentive effect of price fluctuations on investment in improved farming systems and land management and the income constraints faced by poorer households.

To reverse such counter-productive policies and investments requires a dual strategy that combines both "national-level" policies with local-action. In particular, to improve the effectiveness of economy-wide and sectoral reforms will require complementing these reforms with specific, targeted policies to generate direct incentives for improved rural resource management in "fragile" areas where many of the rural poor are located. The main purpose of such policies should be to increase the economic returns of existing as opposed to frontier lands; improve the access of poorer rural households to credit and land markets; and alleviate any remaining policy biases in these markets that favor relatively wealthy farmers and individuals (Barbier 1997b). In some cases, specific non-price transfers in the form of targeted subsidies could reduce significantly the incentives for land degradation and forest conversion in developing countries. This is particularly true for expenditures that aimed to improve access by the rural poor to credit, research and extension, investments to disseminate conservation, information and technologies to smallholders, and investments in small-scale irrigation and other productivity improve-ments on existing smallholder land. For example, in Mexico there is some evidence that a land improvement investment program for exist-ing rainfed farmers, particularly in States and regions prone to high deforestation rates, could provide direct and indirect incentives for controlling deforestation by increasing the comparative returns to farming existing smallholdings as well as the demand for rural labor (Barbier 2002; Barbier and Burgess 1996).

Targeting public investments and expenditures to the agricultural sector to provide effective credit markets and services to reach poor rural households, while continuing to eliminate subsidies and credit rationing that benefit mainly wealthier households, may also be important in achieving a more efficient pattern of land use – and a less extensive one – in many developing countries. An important inducement for many poor smallholders to invest in improved land management is to establish proper land titling and ownership claims on the land they currently occupy. To improve land tenure services in frontier areas it may be necessary to develop more formal policies for smallholder settlement, such as a policy to allocate preferentially public land with fully demarcated ownership and tenure rights to smallholders.

In addition, policies that have increased processes of land degradation and deforestation as an unintended side effect should be mitigated. For example, expansion of the road network in frontier areas has been identified as a major factor in opening up forestlands and thus making these lands artificially cheap and abundantly available (Barbier 1998a; Cattaneo 2001; Chomitz and Gray 1996; Cropper *et al.* 2001). This suggests the building of new roads and large-scale infrastructure investments in tropical forest areas need to be evaluated routinely for their potential impacts on subsequent frontier migration and deforestation. Tax policies that encourage the holding of agricultural land as a speculative asset not only artificially inflate the price of existing arable land but promote much idling of potentially productive land (Heath and Binswanger 1996; Cattaneo 2001; Vincent *et al.* 1997).

Finally, in many developing countries policy reform will have to be complemented by investments in key infrastructural services. Several have been mentioned already – availability of rural credit, conservation and general extension services, land tenure and titling services, and irrigation and other land improvement investments for existing smallholder land. However, other services may also be important. For example, in most rural areas there needs to be a general development of adequate post-harvest and marketing facilities targeted to smallholder production, in order to ensure that such production participates in an overall agro-industrial development strategy. In frontier areas, there is a need not only to increase credit and extension services to initial settlers but also more basic services such as improved community, education and health care services.

Perhaps one of the greatest challenges for policy reform in developing countries will be to reduce the propensity for corruption and rent-seeking in resource-based sectors. The institutional "failures" that promote such practices appear to be deep-seated and endemic, and will be difficult to change. Nevertheless, as argued by Ascher (1999, p. 299) there is some hope for reform even in this difficult area:

The fact that some government officials may intend to sacrifice resource-exploitation soundness for other objectives does not mean that they will necessarily have their way, even if they are chiefs of state. Prior arrangements, public outcry, and adverse reactions by international institutions can raise the political or economic costs too high. Other officials may be in a position to block their actions, especially if the structures of natural resource policymaking reveal policy failures for what they are.

Reinvesting resource rents: Malaysia and Thailand

Gylfason (2001b) indicates that, out of sixty-five resource-rich countries, only four managed to achieve i) long-term investment exceeding 25% of GDP on average over 1965–98, equal to that of industrialized countries lacking raw materials, and ii) average annual per capita economic growth rates exceeding 4% during the same period. The four countries are Botswana, Indonesia, Malaysia and Thailand. As noted by Gylfason (2001b, p. 566), "the three Asian countries achieved this success by diversifying their economies and by industrialising; Botswana without doing so." As noted by Coxhead and Jayasuriya (2003, p. 61), the extent of diversification in Malaysia and Thailand is particularly noteworthy for the profound structural changes occurring in those economies: "In Thailand and Malaysia, the fastest-growing resource-rich economies of tropical Asia, labour productivity growth in manufacturing caused rural wages to rise sharply and the agricultural labor force to decline not merely in relative terms but absolutely."

Table 10.1 provides some key economic indicators for Botswana, Indonesia, Malaysia and Thailand as a comparison to averages for the ninety-five low and middle-income economies of Table 1.1, high-income economies and the world. However, despite its favorable economic indicators, Indonesia may not necessarily be considered a long-term "success" story compared to the other three resource-rich economies, as according to Gylfason (2001b, p. 566), "a broader measure of economic success – including the absence of corruption, for instance – would put Indonesia in less favourable light. Moreover, Indonesia has weathered the crash of 1997–98 much less well than either Malaysia or Thailand." For example, Table 10.2 shows that Indonesia performs relatively

Table 10.1 Successful resource-rich countries: key economic indicators

(a) Dualism within dualism (%)

Country	Primary product export share[a]	Share of population in rural areas[b]	Share of population on fragile land[c]	Share of rural population in poverty[a]
Botswana	100	51	30–50	..
Indonesia	54	59	20–30	15.7
Malaysia	33	43	20–30	15.5
Thailand	30	80	..	18.0
95 Low & middle income[d]	71	53	..	42.8
High income[e]	17	23	..	..
World	22	53	..	..

(b) Long-run growth and investment (%, 1965–2001)[c]

Country	Annual growth in GDP per capita	Investment share of GDP	Primary-school enrolment rate[f]	Secondary-school enrolment rate[f]
Botswana	6.9	28	103	51
Indonesia	4.0	25	108	42
Malaysia	4.0	28	98	57
Thailand	4.7	28	92	42
95 Low & middle income	1.4	20	86	39
High income	2.5	23	102	98
World	1.7	23	100	55

(c) Long-run land use trends (% of total land area)[c]

Country	Arable cropland 1970	Arable cropland 2000	Permanent cropland 1970	Permanent cropland 2000
Botswana	0.7	0.7	0.002	0.005
Indonesia	9.9	11.3	4.4	7.2
Malaysia	2.8	5.5	10.7	17.6

Table 10.1 (continued)

Country	Arable cropland 1970	Arable cropland 2000	Permanent cropland 1970	Permanent cropland 2000
Thailand	24.1	28.8	2.9	6.5
95 Low & middle income	11.1	12.9	2.7	4.1
High income	12.0	11.6	0.5	0.5
World	9.9	10.5	0.8	1.0

Notes:
[a] World Bank, World Development Indicators 2001.
[b] World Bank, World Development Indicators 2003.
[c] World Bank, World Development Report 2003.
[d] The 95 economies listed in Table 1.1.
[e] High-income economies are those in which 2001 GNI per capita was US$9,206 or more.
[f] Gross rates, which may exceed 100%.

poorly with regard to a number of key governance indicators, including control of corruption.

Finally, it has been pointed out that Malaysia, Thailand and Indonesia can be considered "rapidly growing countries with open land frontiers," in the sense that their economic success corresponded with continued agricultural land expansion (Coxhead and Jayasuriya 2003, p. 61). In this regard, these three countries, or at least Malaysia and Thailand, can be considered examples of "successful" frontier-based development as defined throughout this book.

In the remainder of this section, we will focus on the policies and development strategies in Malaysia and Thailand as examples of successful "diversification" through reinvesting resource rents from frontier-based development. In the next section we will discuss the case of Botswana as an example of a resource-rich country that has developed favorable institutions and policies for managing its natural wealth for extensive economy-wide benefits.

Malaysia

As we discussed in Chapter 8, present-day Malaysia is the classic case of the "proton" economy, which exports plantation crops (including timber)

Table 10.2 Successful resource-rich countries: key governance indicators[a]

Country	Voice and accountability	Political stability/ lack of violence	Government effectiveness	Regulatory framework	Rule of law	Control of corruption
Botswana	0.779	0.743	0.221	0.572	0.502	0.535
Indonesia	−1.165	−1.289	−0.528	0.121	−0.918	−0.799
Malaysia	−0.144	0.552	0.714	0.477	0.834	0.633
Thailand	0.215	0.246	0.010	0.192	0.413	−0.165
95 Low & middle income[b]	−0.321	−0.406	−0.350	−0.174	−0.393	−0.377
High income[c]	0.910	0.908	1.026	0.714	1.180	1.143
World	0.000	−0.020	−0.014	0.002	0.004	−0.001

Notes:
[a] Indicators range from −2.5 (lowest) to 2.5 (highest).
[b] The 95 economies listed in Table 1.1.
[c] High-income economies are those in which 2001 GNI per capita was US$9,206 or more.
Source: Kaufmann *et al.* (1999a).

and bases industrial development on export-oriented, labor-intensive manufacturing (Coxhead and Jayasuriya 2003). As indicated in Table 8.1 of that chapter, Malaysia is one of the few developing countries that appears to have emerged from the classic "dualism within dualism" pattern of underdevelopment. Although 20–30% of Malaysia's population is still concentrated on fragile land, over 1990–99 the share of primary product to total exports was 33%, and the share of the rural population living in poverty had fallen to 15.5% (see Table 10.1(a)). The decline in Malaysia's resource dependency is particularly remarkable given that primary product export share was 94% in 1965 and still 80% as recently as 1980–81 (see Table 1.1).

Malaysia's long-run economic growth performance has been strong, reflecting the reinvestment of resource rents over the decades in physical and human capital (see Table 10.1(b)). Over 1965–2001, annual growth in Malaysia has averaged 4.0%. During this period, investment in gross fixed capital formation as a share of gross domestic product (GDP) has averaged 28%, which is greater than the world average or that of higher income economies. Vincent *et al.* (1997) calculate that in the 1970s and 1980s that net investment in Malaysia, adjusted for depletion of minerals and timber, was positive in all years but one, and net domestic product rose by 2.9% per year. Gross primary and secondary school enrolment rates in Malaysia have been considerably higher than in other low and middle-income countries, and in the case of primary-school enrolment, the rates match that of higher income economies. As noted above, this reinvestment of resource rents has been the key to the diversification of the Malaysian economy, including the rapid decline in its resource dependency, rising rural wages and the absolute as well as relative fall in the agricultural labor force. Other economy-wide benefits also occurred. During the 1970s and 1980s Malaysia increased rapidly the number of urban and rural households with access to piped, treated water (Vincent *et al.* 1997).

As in the case of other low and middle-income economies, Malaysia's development has been accompanied by significant agricultural land expansion, especially at the expense of tropical forests. However, an important difference for Malaysia is that much frontier land expansion has occurred through the use of new land for perennial plantation crops such as oil palm and rubber (see Table 10.1(c)). Malaysia is also a major world exporter of tropical timber products, and is the leading world exporter of wood-based panels (Barbier

1998b). Thus considerable investments have occurred in Malaysia in agro-industrial and forest-based industries, with extensive forward and backward linkages to domestic plantation crops and tropical forestry.

With regard to governance, Table 10.2 indicates that Malaysia ranks comparably with high-income economies in terms of political stability, government effectiveness, regulatory framework, rule of law and control of corruption. Although at the time the governance indicators in the table were formulated (1997/8), political "voice" and accountability in Malaysia were considered relatively low. However, recent elections and transfer of power over 2002–3 would suggest that even this political economy indicator has improved. The long-term political stability of Malaysia is particularly remarkable, given that the population is ethnically diverse, containing a Malay majority with a sizable Chinese and Indian minority. Overall, Malaysia appears to have the "good governance" necessary for long-run management of its natural resource wealth and the reinvestment of resource rents to achieve a more diversified and prosperous economy.

Vincent *et al.* (1997) identify several policies that were critical to the successful strategy of reinvesting resource rents in Malaysia. First, rents from minerals and timber amount to about one third of gross domestic investment during the 1970s and 1980s, and the most effective policies were aimed at capturing and reinvesting these key resource rents. These policies included petroleum-sharing contracts, which both attracted investment from international oil companies to provide essential capital and technology while at the same time ensuring that substantial oil rents were retained within Malaysia. The establishment of the Permanent Forest Estate in Peninsular Malaysia also enhanced the development of long-term timber management for forest-based industries as well as maintaining a sustained flow of timber rents. Although substantial tropical deforestation did occur, forest and land use policies were implemented to ensure that deforestation led to the expansion of tree-crop plantations for export. As argued by Vincent *et al.* (1997, p. 353), this is "evidently a sustainable land use, thanks in large part to the country's investment in agricultural research. This contrasts with the situation in many other tropical countries, where the end result of deforestation has been unproductive, degraded land." Finally, the substantial reinvestment of resource rents from minerals, timber and plantation crop exports was vital to the industrial development of export-oriented, labor-intensive manufacturing, which has in turn led to the diversification of the present-day Malaysian economy (Coxhead and Jayasuriya 2003). Thus, these polices ensured that "Malaysia as a nation succeeded in using investible funds from resource rents and other sources to build up stocks of physical capital that more than offset the depletion of mineral and timber resources" (Vincent *et al.* 1997, pp. 351–352).

Diversification of the Malaysian economy has created its own "virtuous circle" with regard to reducing land degradation and deforestation, halting depletion of fisheries and other renewable resources and combating rural poverty:

For example, reductions in deforestation and traditional fishing effort in Peninsular Malaysia owed much to the region's rapid economic growth and diversification. Superior employment opportunities raised production costs in traditional activities as labor flowed out of rural areas, resulting in less land clearing and less demand for fishing licenses. Although state governments could in principle still excise areas from the Permanent Forest Estate for development, reduced returns to agricultural expansion diminished this threat (Vincent *et al.* 1997, pp. 353–354)

Increased rural-urban migration and the absolute decline in the agricultural labor force were accompanied by rising rural wages and better employment prospects for the rural poor (Coxhead and Jayasuriya 2003). As a consequence, the share of the population living in rural poverty in Malaysia has fallen to 15.5%, one of the lowest rates among low and middle-income economies (see Table 10.1(a)). Finally, the declining pressure on rural resources and land has also enabled Malaysia to implement better resource management policies in agriculture and fisheries. For example, the government has implemented land rehabilitation programs for smallholder rice and rubber, which has overcome problems of land fragmentation and improved the economic viability of these smallholdings. In marine fisheries, several policies have been instigated to reduce overfishing in commercial and traditional coastal fisheries through controlling fishing effort and increasing rents (Vincent *et al.* 1997).

However, not all resource management strategies have been successful in Malaysia (Vincent *et al.* 1997). In agriculture, some government programs wasted substantial subsidies on attempting to rehabilitate smallholder land that was not economically viable, while at the same time policy-induced rigidities in land markets actually increased the amount of productive land that was idled. Although policies to control overfishing in coastal areas were implemented, deep-sea fishing remained largely open access. In addition, too often resource management strategies in Malaysia have been driven by an emphasis on maximizing physical production rather than on maximizing net economic benefits. This has been exacerbated by direct involvement of public enterprises in key sectors, such as forestry, petroleum and fishing. Finally, "over-mining"of Malaysia's remaining tropical timber reserves in Sabah and Sarawak to feed the forest-based industries in Peninsular Malaysia is a worrisome problem, which has been fueled by long-term policies of log export restrictions and protection of wood panels and furniture industries that has led to over-capacity and inefficiencies in timber processing (Barbier 1998b).

Thailand

In many ways, Thailand's success resembles that of Malaysia. As noted in Chapter 8, since the 1970s Thailand has been the prototype "tuk-tuk" economy, which is a net food exporter that bases industrial development on export-oriented, labor-intensive manufacturing (Coxhead and Jayasuriya 2003). As a consequence, resource dependency in the Thai economy has declined steadily; primary product export share was 95% in 1965, 68% in 1980–81 and 30% in 1990–99 (see Table 1.1). Although 80% of the population still lives in rural areas, the share of the rural population living in poverty is only 18% (see Table 10.1(a)). As in the case of Malaysia, diversification of the Thai economy and the decline in its resource dependency has been accompanied by rising rural wages and the absolute as well as relative fall in the agricultural labor force.

The successful diversification of the Thai economy is reflected in its long-run growth and investment patterns (see Table 10.1(b)). Annual growth in GDP per capita has averaged 4.7% over 1965–2000, and the share of gross fixed capital formation in GDP has averaged 28% over the same period. Both of these trends exceed world averages or those of high-income economies. In addition, primary and secondary school enrolment rates are above those of low and middle-income economies and comparable with world rates.

Like Malaysia, Thailand's development has been accompanied by significant agricultural land expansion at the expense of tropical forests, mainly through new land for perennial plantation crops (see Table 10.1(c)). However, unlike Malaysia, Thailand has never had substantial mineral and timber reserves. Thus, Thailand's remarkable success with resource-based development has occurred without the benefit of large resource rents to tap. Instead, this development has been accomplished through considerable investments in agro-industrial industries, with extensive forward and backward linkages to domestic plantation crops, food crops and fisheries. Again, "good governance" appears to be crucial to the success of this long-term development strategy in Thailand (see Table 10.2).

In Thailand's economy, traded food production and plantation crops dominate both upland and lowland farming, and so the pressures on upland forests are solely determined by inter-regional labor migration. Any increase in labor demand in the lowlands will result in reduced deforestation as the total area of upland agriculture declines (Coxhead and Jayasuriya 2003). Thus the emphasis on agro-industrialization, with forward and backward linkages, and on reinvestment of rents in labor-intensive manufacturing has generated a "virtuous cycle" of reducing land degradation and deforestation, better management of fisheries and other renewable resources and improving rural livelihoods. However, the key to this process was a profound structural change in the Thai economy, reflected in rising prices for non-trade, mainly non-agricultural goods, growth of non-agricultural investment and rising labor productivity outside of the farm sector. The result has been increased employment opportunities outside of agriculture, rising rural wages, declining relative agricultural prices and thus a reduction in farm profits and investment (Coxhead and Jayasuriya 2003; Pingali 2001). The overall outcome was a relative decline in the agricultural sector relative to the rest of the Thai economy, accompanied by a fall in total planted area, which in turn reduced pressures for land conversion and deforestation. Meanwhile, the agricultural sector has been forced to become more efficient, commercially oriented and internationally competitive (Pingali 2001). As a result, substantial inter-regional migration has occurred from highland to lowland areas to take advantage of rising rural wages accompanying the commercialization of agriculture on favorable and productive lands, even as total rural employment opportunities and planted area across Thailand have declined. In addition, the economy-wide trade reforms implemented in Thailand provided further stimulus to labor-intensive manufacturing industries, greater employment opportunities outside of rural areas, and significantly reduced pressures on frontier agricultural soils, forests and watersheds (Coxhead and Jayasuriya 2003).

In other sectors, such as fisheries, Thailand has also promoted export-oriented industries, particularly shrimp. Since 1979, Thailand has been the world's major shrimp producer, and one third of all shrimp marketed internationally is from Thailand. Although shrimp are also caught in coastal fisheries, the vast majority of Thailand's shrimp production now comes from aquaculture. In the late 1990s, the total value of export earnings for shrimp was around US$1–2 billion annually, and the government has been keen to expand these exports (Jitsanguan *et al.* 1999; Tokrisna 1998). Thailand has also sought to manage its coastal fisheries through zoning (Kaosa-ard and Pednekar 1998). Since 1972, the 3 km off-shore coastal zone in Southern Thailand has been reserved for small-scale, traditional marine fisheries. The Gulf of Thailand is divided into four such major zones, and the Andaman Sea (Indian Ocean) comprises a separate fifth zone.

However, there have been problems with some resource management strategies pursued in Thailand. First, ill-defined property rights for forest areas have contributed to excessive upland deforestation and the rapid conversion of mangroves to shrimp farms in Thailand. Historically, this has been a common problem for all forested areas in Thailand (Feder *et al.* 1988; Feeny 2002). Although the state through the Royal Forestry Department ostensibly owns and controls forest areas, in practice they are *de facto* open access areas onto which anyone can encroach. Estimates of the amount of mangrove conversion due to shrimp farming vary, but studies suggest that up to 50–65% of Thailand's mangroves have been lost to shrimp farm conversion since 1975 (Barbier and Sathirathai 2004; Dierberg and Kiattisimkul 1996; Tokrisna 1998). In provinces close to Bangkok, such as Chanthaburi, mangrove areas have been devastated by shrimp farm developments (Raine 1994). This has led to substantial losses to local communities dependent on mangrove-based activities and the habitat support provided by the mangroves for coastal fisheries (Barbier and Sathirathai 2004; see also Chapter 6). Second, the build-up of manufacturing and agro-industries coupled with the increasing commercialization of agriculture may lead to better land and water management but is worsening other environmental problems, such as pollution and congestion in cities (particularly Bangkok), industrial and toxic waste, over-use of pesticides and non-point pollution in agriculture. Finally, the increasing commercialization of agriculture is likely to continue the trends towards consolidation of land holdings, adoption of labor-saving innovations and reductions in cropping intensities, which is likely to further labor substitution and declining employment opportunities in agriculture (Pingali 2001). Although this may have removed less productive, marginal upland areas from food production, rural employment opportunities in lowland areas are likely to slow down and provide less work for the rural poor from upland areas. In Thailand, there does not appear to be a set of policies targeted at the upland areas to i) manage the transition from movement of rice and subsistence-crop production to a variety of commercial-oriented agricultural enterprises, such as maize, horticulture, tree crops, dairy and livestock-raising, ii) promote these enterprises in those upland areas with the most suitable agro-ecological conditions, i.e. areas that are less susceptible to erosion and have favorable micro-climates, iii) provide research and development support to develop adequate post-harvest and marketing facilities, targeted to smallholder production, and to facilitate the integration of these upland enter-prises with the economy's agro-industrial development strategy and iv) encourage the commercialization of upland agriculture as an alter-native source of employment for the rural poor in these areas.

Sound policies and good institutions: Botswana

In Chapter 3 it was noted that many studies of the "resource curse" hypothesis suggest that this hypothesis cannot be explained adequately without also examining political economy factors, in particular the exist-ence of policy and institutional failures that lead to myopic decision-making, failure to control rent-seeking behavior by resource users and weaken the political and legal institutions necessary to foster long-run growth. However, this perspective leads logically to the conclusion that if "bad" policies and institutions lie at the heart of translating resource abundance and windfall gains into negative economy-wide effects, then "good" policies and institutions may explain why some developing economies with resource wealth may have avoided the "resource curse." In other words, "the natural resource curse is not necessarily the fate of resource abundant countries ... sound economic policies and good management of windfall gains can lead to sustained eco-nomic growth" (Sarraf and Jiwanji 2001, p. 3).

Botswana is a particularly Interesting case because its economy has remained heavily dependent on mineral export earnings, principally diamonds (see Table 10.1(a) and Table 1.1). Thus, unlike Malaysia and Thailand, Botswana's economy remains fundamentally resource-dependent in all senses of the term. Not only are all of its exports from primary products but also minerals, especially diamonds, account for one-third of GDP and half of government revenue (Lange and Wright 2004). Because of its high resource dependency, since the 1970s Botswana has experienced periodic and substantial commodity export booms and windfalls (Hill 1991; Sarraf and Jiwanji 2001). Yet the economy appears to show no classic signs of the "resource curse": since 1965 the country had one of the highest rates of long-term growth in the world, and in the 1990s the highest ratios of government expenditures on education to GDP (Gylfason 2001b and Table 10.1(b)). As indicated in Table 10.1(b), Botswana's long-run share of investment in GDP is equivalent to that of Malaysia and Thailand, and Botswana also has comparably high rates of primary and secondary-school enrolment. Thus, usually for most resource-dependent economies, Botswana has achieved substantial economic success through reinvesting its resource wealth in physical and human capital.

As noted in Chapter 3, Botswana's success in managing cycles of resource booms and busts is attributed largely to its adoption of appropriate and stable economic policies, including managing the exchange rate to avoid excessive appreciation during boom periods, using windfalls to build up international reserves and government balances that provide a cushion when booms end, avoiding large-scale increases in government expenditure and instead targeting investments to public education and infrastructure, and finally, pursuing an economic diversification strategy that has led to modest increases in labor-intensive manufactures and services (Hill 1991; Sarraf and Jiwanji 2001). However, such long-term policies for stable management of the economy are only possible if legal and political institutions function well. Botswana has had considerable political stability and lack of civil conflict that are on par with high-income economies (see Table 10.2). In addition, the government has an international reputation for honest public administration, and overall Botswana is generally rated the least corrupt country in Africa (Gylfason 2001b).

The cornerstone of the Government of Botswana's long-run development policy has been the recovery and reinvestment of resource rents. Over 1980–97, the government has collected on average 75% of mining rents through taxes and royalties (Lange and Wright 2004). Over this period, these mineral revenues have been reinvested in public capital, and public sector investment has accounted for 30–50% of total gross fixed capital formation in the economy. Although much of this public expenditure has been on infrastructure, such as roads, expansion of water connections, electricity and communications, there has been an increasing emphasis on investment in education and health, which in recent years has averaged 24% of the capital development budget.

Since the mid-1990s, the main planning tool for guiding this public investment in Botswana has been the Sustainable Budget Index (SBI). This index is simply the ratio of non-investment spending to recurrent revenues. As summarized by Lange and Wright (2004, pp. 15–16):

An SBI value of 1.0 or less has been interpreted to mean that public consumption is sustainable because it is financed entirely out of revenues other than from minerals, and that all the revenue from minerals is used for public investment. An SBI value greater than 1.0 means that consumption relies in part on the mineral revenues, which is unsustainable in the long term.

However, as summarized by Lange and Wright (2004), there are some problems with using the SBI as an economic planning tool. First, the SBI is simply an expenditure allocation rule and cannot by itself be used to interpret the usefulness of the allocation in terms of long-run welfare for the economy. Second, there is an implicit assumption underlying the SBI that all development spending is productive investment. Third, the SBI encourages the over-reliance of the economy on public sector investments, even though they are often insulated from market competition and have not always been justified on project appraisal criteria such as expected economic returns. Over the long term, continued growth in public sector investment might lead to problems of diminishing returns to an expanding stock of public infrastructure, which could precipitate a decline in total factor productivity in the economy. Lange and Wright (2004) calculate that the SBI for Botswana remained well under 1.00 until the 1999s, but has been well over 1.00 since 1994–95. The SBI is even higher over recent years if it is adjusted to omit capital expenditures for defense or for other non-productive investments, such as agricultural subsidies and assistance programs, and some pure transfer payments. One reason for the rise of the SBI in recent years has been the efforts of the government to combat the HIV/AIDS epidemic in Botswana, including its recent commitment to provide affordable medicine to all of its people.

One of the key investment strategies of the government has been to increase foreign exchange reserves and financial assets (Sarraf and Jiwanji 2001). The main rationale has been to save windfall gains from mineral revenues for use when export earnings decline, both during short-term busts and in the long run once mineral reserves are depleted. Overall, this strategy has been successful. By 1995 the government had accumulated foreign exchange reserves equal to 25 months of import cover. In recent years, income from foreign financial assets has become the next largest source of government revenue after mineral taxes and royalties (Lange and Wright 2004).

The government has also been able to foster modest diversification of the economy, particularly in labor-intensive manufactures and services (Sarraf and Jiwanji 2001). This was achieved both directly through public investment in the manufacturing sector and indirectly through adopting stabilization policies that prevented appreciation of the domestic currency, even during periods of commodity booms. Although the share of manufacturing value added in GDP remains only 5%, the sector is expanding. Employment in manufacturing and services has also grown, and accounts for 25% and 32% of formal employment respectively.

Less successful have been the government programs to promote agricultural growth. Although on average 7% of the government's development budget has gone to agriculture, and over the period 1973–96 public sector expenditure in support of agriculture averaged more than 40% of agricultural GDP, over the past twenty-five years the sector's contribution to overall GDP has declined to less than 4% (Lange and Wright 2004). Between 1990 and 1996, agricultural GDP in Botswana contracted by 1.2% (Sarraf and Jiwanji 2001). The main reason for the decline has been prolonged periods of drought combined with continuing over-pressure on rural resources, including depletion of village water reserves, water pollution problems, over-grazing, range-land degradation and depletion of wood supplies.

In sum, there is no question that "good governance" in Botswana including political stability and control of corruption has been the key factor enabling the government to pursue long-term development strategies, combined with short-run stabilization policies in times of commodity booms and busts, which have allowed the economy to benefit from its resource riches. Overall, these policies have worked; as noted by Lange and Wright (2004, p. 28): "Botswana's long-lasting economic success and political stability attest to the strength of its processes." Or, as Davis (1998, p. 226) points out, Botswana is a clear and exemplary case of "the more passive neoclassical recommendations of correcting the market externalities and imperfections within mineral economies, while saving enough of the resource rents to ensure at least a sustainable level of consumption."

However, to sustain and build on its economic success, there are clearly some additional structural imbalances that Botswana needs to tackle in the near future. First, the economy is overly reliant on public sector investment. Since 1980, private sector capital has grown about 7% annually, but over the same period domestic public sector investment plus net foreign financial assets held by the government grew at 15.5% per year. As a result, the relative share of private sector capital in the economy declined significantly, from 29 to 22% (Lange and Wright 2004). Second, the growth in manufacturing and services shows signs that the economy is diversifying, but these sectors produce mainly non-tradable goods. Overall, the economy is still dominated by mining, especially for export earnings, and the declining relative share of private capital in the economy suggests that full economic diversification is likely to be unrealized for some time. Finally, the government programs for investing in agriculture have been largely a failure. Yet agricultural development is still critical for the economy. Agriculture accounts for over 70% of the labor force, and will remain a significant source of income for the rural poor (Sarraf and Jiwanji 2001). As indicated in Table 10.1(a) over half of the population still lives in rural areas, and 30–50% of the population is on fragile land. Moreover, in the mid-1990s around 38% of all households (equivalent to 47% of the population) still live in poverty (Lange and Wright 2004). Thus, by the criteria established in Chapter 8, even though it is hailed as a "successful" resource-rich developing economy, Botswana shares with many low and middle-income countries the classic characteristics of "dualism within dualism."

Final remarks

The examples of Botswana, Malaysia and Thailand remind us that the "resource curse" is not an inevitable outcome. Simply because a developing economy is well endowed with natural resource wealth, it is not always doomed to poor economic performance. Malaysia and Thailand appear to have harnessed their respective natural resource endowments to diversify their economies successfully. Botswana has exploited its mineral wealth for high rates of sustained economic growth through a sustained policy of capturing and reinvesting resource rents. Perhaps there are important lessons that can be learned by other resource-dependent low and middle-income economies from these three success stories.

Interestingly, all three "resource-rich" countries have achieved their success through exploiting very different natural endowments. In Malaysia, the main source of resource rents has come from petroleum and timber, and more recently plantation crops. For Thailand, it has been exports of food, plantation crops and fisheries, and for Botswana diamonds and other minerals. Thus these three country case studies are encouraging in another important way, as they suggest that not only is abundant resource wealth not necessarily an obstacle to good economic performance but also the *type* of resource wealth may not be an obstacle either. This should not be a surprising conclusion. As Davis (1998, p. 225) has argued, "we have no consistent statistical evidence that mineral dependence leads to either faster or slower economic growth." Hence, why should we find it amazing that Botswana has managed to exploit its mineral-based wealth beneficially? The examples of Thailand and Malaysia suggest that agricultural wealth or timber wealth or even fisheries wealth should not be an inherent obstacle to successful resource-based development either.

The examples of Malaysia and Thailand also provide some hope that a process of frontier resource exploitation and land expansion can be compatible with sustainable development in a small open economy. As pointed out by Coxhead and Jayasuriya (2003, p. 61), these two countries are "rapidly growing countries with open land frontiers." Perhaps, then, Malaysia and Thailand can be considered the first economies to display some of the key characteristics of "successful" frontier-based development that were discussed and modeled in Chapter 9. Although hardly any land expansion has occurred in Botswana (see Table 10.1(c)), its vast mineral reserves can be considered a vertical frontier, as suggested by Findlay and Lundahl (1999). Hence, we could conceivably consider Botswana also to be an example of an economy that is successfully exploiting its frontier reserves, in the manner indicated in Chapter 9, albeit without yet reaching the comparable stage of development of Malaysia and Thailand where successful economic diversification has occurred through the reinvesting of rents from frontier-based development.

However, as noted at the beginning of this chapter, reinvesting the rents from frontier resource exploitation is only one of four objectives necessary to overcoming the dualism within dualism pattern of development that is a structural feature of many poor economies. Botswana, Malaysia and Thailand may have achieved this first objective, but they may also have been less successful in attaining the other three goals. For these economies, perhaps the next stage of development should focus on these goals, especially targeting additional policies and investments to improve further the economic opportunities and livelihoods of the rural poor.

For Botswana, Malaysia and Thailand, reaching this next stage of development appears to be a realistic goal. As stressed in this chapter, if the "vicious cycle" of dualism within dualism economic structure is to be reversed in a developing country, then important institutional and policy reforms are required. Already, Botswana, Malaysia and Thailand appear to be on this path, because all three countries already appear to have in place good institutions and sound economic management policies. At the heart of these institutions and policies is the realization that "good governance" is the key to discouraging rent-seeking behavior, managing resources more efficiently to capture rents, and then reinvesting these rents in more productive and dynamic sectors of the economy. Further developing policies and institutions to ensure that the benefits of resource-based development are more fairly distributed and in particular reach the rural poor is clearly an attainable objective for these three resource-rich countries in the near future.

Can other resource-dependent low and middle-income economies emulate Botswana, Malaysia and Thailand and also launch themselves on a "virtuous cycle" growth path of reinvesting resource rents, developing sound policies and institutions and lessening dualism within dualism? Both the previous chapter and this one suggest that the answer is "yes." Unfortunately, however, breaking out of the dualism-within-dualism pattern of development appears to be a difficult task for most present-day economies. If this were not so, then clearly we would have more success stories than the three countries we have discussed in this chapter.

This book has attempted to explain why it is that so many low and middle-income economics appear to be trapped in a pattern of frontier land expansion and resource exploitation that is not conducive to sustained growth and poverty alleviation but instead perpetuates a dualism-within-dualism structure of underdevelopment.

First, it is clear that, throughout history, simply because a developing economy or region is endowed with abundant natural resources, the country may not necessarily end up exploiting this natural wealth efficiently and generating productive investments. Or, as Wright (1990, p. 666) suggests: "there is no iron law associating natural resource abundance with national industrial strength."

On the other hand, even in the present age when so many resource-dependent developing economies appear to perform relatively poorly, one should not draw the conclusion that, simply because a developing economy is well endowed with natural resource wealth, it is always doomed to slow growth and widespread poverty. Present-day Botswana, Malaysia and Thailand are the counter-examples that there is also no "iron law" associating natural resource abundance, or even a particular type of natural resource endowment, with poor economic performance.

Instead, the key to successful resource-based development appears to be sound policies and favorable institutions, especially those aimed at attaining the "virtuous cycle" growth path of reinvesting resource rents, developing sound policies and institutions and lessening dualism within dualism. Unfortunately, most developing countries appear to be trapped in the opposite, "vicious cycle" of unsuccessful frontier land expansion and resource exploitation that is perpetuating, rather than alleviating, dualism within dualism.

One reason that this "vicious cycle" may be so difficult for poor economies to break is because environmental conditions, including resource endowments, have had a long-term impact on the institutional development of these economies. For instance, Acemoglu *et al.* (2001), Engerman and Sokoloff (1997), and Sokoloff and Engerman (2000) have all suggested that the key to successful resource-based development over the long run may have to do mainly with the interplay of critical exogenous factors, such as geography, climate and institutional legacy. This hypothesis that environmental conditions and factor endowments may be important in determining whether or not countries develop "good" institutions conducive to long-run development has received sup-port from the econometric analysis by Easterly and Levine (2003). That is, the inhospitable tropical climate and diseases prevalent in many African,

Asian and Latin American countries may explain why these countries failed to attract mass European settlement, and thus to develop into "neo-Europes" with favorable institutions for economic development. The fact that many of the low and middle-income economies may still be dependent on resource exploitation and frontier land expansion for their economic development may in turn be perpetuating their "extractive state" institutions. These "extractive state" institutions then further reinforce the pattern of frontier-based development that is so inimical to development in many poor economies today: rent-seeking resource extraction by a wealthy elite and frontier land expansion as an outlet for the rural poor.

Yet, as this chapter maintains, breaking out of this pattern is possible. To do this, a long-run development strategy in a resource-dependent low and middle-income economy must set four long-term goals. As a fitting end to this book, we repeat these goals once more:

- Reinvesting resource rents in more productive and dynamic sectors of the economy, which in turn are linked to the resource-exploiting sectors of the domestic economy.
- Developing political and legal institutions to discourage rent-seeking behavior by wealthy investors in the natural resource sectors of the economy.
- Instigating widespread reform of government policies that favor wealthier investors in markets for valuable natural resources, including arable land.
- Targeting additional policies and investments to improve the economic opportunities and livelihoods of the rural poor, rather than relying on frontier land expansion and urban migration as the principal outlet for alleviating rural poverty.

Note

1. As in the case of any economic reform, if implemented poorly land reform can be ineffective, highly costly and even counter-productive. A good example is the disastrous efforts of the Mugabe Government in Zimbabwe to allow party loyalists to incite poor black landless and near landless farmers to take over by force large-scale commercial farms owned mainly by white Zimbabweans.

References

Acemoglu, Daron, Simon Johnson and James A. Robinson. 2001. "The Colonial Origins of Comparative Development: An Empirical Investigation." *American Economic Review* **91**(5): 1369–1401.

Acharya, Gayatri and Barbier, Edward B. 2000. "Valuing Groundwater Recharge Through Agricultural Production in the Hadejia-Hguru Wetlands in Northern Nigeria." *Agricultural Economics* **22**: 247–259.

2002. "Using Domestic Water Analysis to Value an Environmental Function: Groundwater Recharge in the Hadejia-Jama'are Floodplain, Northern Nigeria." *American Journal of Agricultural Economics* **84**(2): 415–426.

Adams, William M. 1992. *Wasting the Rains: Rivers, People and Planning in Africa*. Earthscan, London.

Adhikari, Bhim, Salvatore Di Falco and Jon C. Lovett. 2004. "Household Characteristics and Forest Dependency: Evidence from Common Property Forest Management in Nepal." *Ecological Economics* **48**: 245–257.

Agénor, Pierre-Richard. 2000. *The Economics of Adjustment and Growth*. Academic Press, San Diego.

Alston, Lee J., Gary D. Libecap and Bernardo Mueller. 1999. *Titles, Conflict, and Land Use: The Development of Property Rights and Land Reform on the Brazilian Amazon Frontier*. The University of Michigan Press, Ann Arbor.

2000. "Land Reform Policies, the Sources of Violent Conflict, and Implications for Deforestation in the Brazilian Amazon." *Journal of Environmental Economics and Management* **39**(2): 162–188.

Alston, Lee J., Gary D. Libecap and Robert Schneider. 1996. "The Determinants and Impact of Property Rights: Land Titles on the Brazilian Frontier." *The Journal of Law, Economics and Organization* **12**(1): 25–61.

Amin, Samir. 1974. *Accumulation on a World Scale: A Critique of the Theory of Underdevelopment*. Monthly Review Press, New York.

Anderson, L. E., C. W. J. Granger, J. R. Eustaquio, D. Weihold and S. Wunder, 2003. *The Dynamics of Deforestation and Economic Growth in the Brazilian Amazon*. Edward Elgar, London.

Anderson, Terry L. and Peter J. Hill. 1975. "The Evolution of Property Rights: A Study of the American West." *The Journal of Law and Economics* 18: 163–179.

———. 1990. "The Race for Property Rights." *The Journal of Law and Economics* 33: 177–197.

Andreoni, J. R. and A. Levinson 2001. "The Simple Analytics of the Environmental Kuznets Curve." *Journal of Public Economics* 80: 269–286.

Angelsen, A. 1999. "Agricultural Expansion and Deforestation: Modelling the Impact of Population, Market Forces and Property Rights." *Journal of Development Economics* 58: 185–218.

Ansuategi, Alberto, Edward B. Barbier and Charles A. Perrings. 1998. "The Environmental Kuznets Curve." In J. C. J. M. van den Bergh and M. W. Hofkes (eds.) *Theory and Implementation of Economic Models for Sustainable Development*, Kluwer Academic Publishers, Dordrecht, pp. 139–164.

Antle, John M. and George Heidebrink. 1995. "Environment and Development: Theory and International Evidence." *Economic Development and Cultural Change* 43(3): 603–625.

Antweiler, Werner, Brian R. Copeland and M. Scott Taylor. 2001. "Is Free Trade Good for the Environment?" *American Economic Review* 91: 877–908.

Appendini, K. 1998. "Changing Agrarian Institutions – Interpreting the Contradictions." In W. A. Cornelius and D. Myhre (eds.) *The Transformation of Rural Mexico: Reforming the Ejido Sector*. Center for US-Mexican Studies, University of California, San Diego, pp. 25–38.

Arrow, Kenneth J. 1962. "The Economic Implications of Learning By Doing." *Review of Economic Studies* 29: 155–173.

Arrow, Kenneth, Bert Bolin, Robert Costanza, Partha Dasgupta, Carl Folke, C. S. Holling, Bengt-Owen Jansson, Simon Levin, Kal-Göran Mäler, Charles A. Perrings and David Pimentel. 1995. "Economic Growth, Carrying Capacity, and the Environment." *Science* 268: 520–521.

Ascher, William 1999. *Why Governments Waste Natural Resources: Policy Failures in Developing Countries*. Johns Hopkins University Press, Baltimore.

Asheim, Geir B. 1986. "Hartwick's Rule in Open Economies." *Canadian Journal of Economics* 19: 395–402.

———. 1996. "Capital Gains and Net National Product in Open Economies." *Journal of Public Economics* 59: 419–434.

Auty, Richard M. 1993. *Sustaining Development in Mineral Economies: The Resource Curse Thesis*. Routledge, London.

1994. "Industrial Policy Reform in Six Large Newly Industrializing Countries: The Resource Curse Thesis." *World Development* **22**(1), January: 11–26.

1997. "Natural Resource Endowment, the State and Development Strategy." *Journal of International Development* **9**(4), June: 651–663.

2001a. "The Political Economy of Resource-Driven Growth." *European Economic Review* **45**(4–6): 839–846.

2001b. "Introduction and Overview." In Richard M. Auty (ed.) *Resource Abundance and Economic Development*. Oxford University Press, Oxford, pp. 3–18.

Baland, Jean-Marie and Patrick Francois. 2000. "Rent-Seeking and Resource Booms." *Journal of Development Economics* **61**: 527–542.

Baland, Jean-Marie and Jean-Philippe Plateau. 1996. *Halting Degradation: Is there a Role for Rural Communities?* Clarendon Press, Oxford.

Baltagi, B. 1995. *Econometric Analysis of Panel Data*. John Wiley, Chichester and Johns Hopkins University Press, Baltimore.

Baran, Paul A. 1957. *The Political Economy of Growth*. Monthly Review Press, New York.

Barbier, Edward B. 1989. *Economics, Natural Resource Scarcity and Development: Conventional and Alternative Views*. Earthscan Publications, London.

1997a. "Introduction to the Environmental Kuznets Curve Special Issue." *Environment and Development Economics* **2**(4): 369–382.

1997b. "The Economic Determinants of Land Degradation in Developing Countries." *Philosophical Transactions of the Royal Society of London, Series B* **352**: 891–899.

1998a. "Rural Poverty and Natural Resource Degradation." In Ramón López and Alberto Valdés (eds.) *Rural Poverty in Latin Amercia*. The World Bank, Washington DC, pp. 152–184.

1998b. "The Economics of the Tropical Timber Trade and Sustainable Forest Management." In F. B. Goldsmith (ed.) *Tropical Rain Forest: A Wider Perspective*. Chapman and Hall, London, pp. 199–254.

1998c. "The Role of Smallholder Producer Prices in Land Degradation: The Case of Malawi." In Edward B. Barbier (ed.) *The Economics of Environment and Development: Selected Essays*. Edward Elgar, Cheltenham, pp. 254–280.

1999. "Poverty, Environment and Development." In J. C. J. M. van den Bergh (ed.) *The Handbook of Environmental and Resource Economics*. Edward Elgar, London, pp. 731–744.

2000. "Biodiversity, Trade and International Agreements." *Journal of Economic Studies* **27**(1/2): 55–74.

2001. "The Economics of Tropical Deforestation and Land Use: An Introduction to the Special Issue." *Land Economics* 77: 155–171.

2002. "Institutional Constraints and Deforestation: An Application to Mexico." *Economic Inquiry* 40(3): 508–519.

2003a. "The Role of Natural Resources in Economic Development." *Australian Economic Papers* 42(2): 253–272.

2003b. "Upstream Dams and Downstream Water Allocation – The Case of the Hadejia-'Jama'are Floodplain, Northern Nigeria." *Water Resources Research* 39(11): 1311–1319.

2004a. "Agricultural Expansion, Resource Booms and Growth in Latin America: Implications for Long-Run Economic Development." *World Development* 32(1): 137–157.

2004b. "Explaining Agricultural Land Expansion and Deforestation in Developing Countries." *American Journal of Agricultural Economics*, forthcoming.

2004c. "Water and Economic Growth." *Economic Record* 80: 1–16.

2005. "Frontier Expansion and Economic Development." *Contemporary Economic Policy*, forthcoming.

Barbier, Edward B. and Joanne C. Burgess. 1992. "Malawi – Land Degradation in Agriculture." Environment Department, Divisional Working Paper No. 1992–37, The World Bank, Washington DC.

1996. "Economic Analysis of Deforestation in Mexico." *Environment and Development Economics* 1(2): 203–240.

1997. "The Economics of Tropical Forest Land Use Options." *Land Economics* 73(2): 174–195.

2001a. "The Economics of Tropical Deforestation." *Journal of Economic Surveys* 15(3): 413–432.

2001b. "Tropical Deforestation, Tenure Insecurity, and Unsustainability." *Forest Science* 47(4): 497–509.

Barbier, Edward B. and Mark Cox. 2004a. "An Economic Analysis of Shrimp Farm Expansion and Mangrove Conversion in Thailand." *Land Economics* 80(3): 389–407.

2004b. "The Effects of Mangrove Loss on the Labor Allocation of Households." Ch. 8 in Edward B. Barbier and Suthawan Sathirathai (eds.) *Shrimp Farming and Mangrove Loss in Thailand*. Edward Elgar, Northampton, Mass., pp. 131–153.

Barbier, Edward B. and Thomas Homer-Dixon. 1999. "Resource Scarcity, Institutional Adaptation, and Technical Innovation." *Ambio* 28(2): 144–147.

Barbier, Edward B. and Suthawan Sathirathai (eds.) 2004. *Shrimp Farming and Mangrove Loss in Thailand*. Edward Elgar, London.

Barbier, Edward B. and Julian R. Thompson. 1998. "The Value of Water: Floodplain versus Large-Scale Irrigation Benefits in Northern Nigeria." *Ambio* 27(6): 434–440.

Barbier, Edward B., William M. Adams and Kevin Kimmage. 1993. "An Economic Valuation of Wetland Benefits." In G. E. Hollis, W. M. Adams and M. Aminu-Kano (eds.) *The Hadejia-Nguru Wetlands: Environment, Economy and Sustainable Development of a Sahelian Floodplain Wetland.* IUCN, Geneva.

Barbier, Edward B., Joanne C. Burgess, Joshua T. Bishop and Bruce A. Aylward 1994. *The Economics of the Tropical Timber Trade.* Earthscan Publications, London.

Barbier, Edward B., Joanne C. Burgess and Carl Folke. 1994. *Paradise Lost? The Ecological Economics of Biodiversity Loss.* Earthscan Publications, London.

Barbier, Edward B., Ivar Strand and Suthawan Sathirathai. 2002. "Do Open Access Conditions Affect the Valuation of an Externality? Estimating the Welfare Effects of Mangrove-Fishery Linkages in Thailand." *Environmental and Resource Economics* 21(4): 343–367.

Barrett, Christopher B., Thomas Reardon and P. Webb. 2001. "Nonfarm Income Diversification and Household Livelihood Strategies in Rural Africa: Concepts, Dynamics and Policy Implications." *Food Policy* 26: 315–331.

Barro, Robert J. 1990. "Government Spending in a Simple Model of Endogenous Growth." *Journal of Political Economy* 98(5): S103–S124.

Barro, Robert J. and Xavier Sala-I-Martin. 1992. "Public Finance in Models of Economic Growth." *Review of Economic Studies* 59: 645–661.

Beckerman, Wilfred A. 1992. "Economic Growth and the Environment: Whose Growth? Whose Environment?" *World Development* 20: 481–496.

Benhin, James K. A. and Edward B. Barbier. 2001. "The Effects of the Structural Adjustment Program on Deforestation in Ghana." *Agricultural and Resource Economics Review* 30(1): 66–80.

Besley, Timothy. 1995. "Property Rights and Investment Incentives: Theory and Evidence from Ghana." *Journal of Political Economy* 103(5): 903–937.

Bhattarai, Madhusudan and Michael Hammig. 2004. "Governance, Economic Policy, and the Environmental Kuznets Curve for Deforestation." *Environment and Development Economics* 30(3): 367–382.

Binswanger, Hans P. and Klaus Deininger. 1997. "Explaining Agricultural and Agrarian Policies in Developing Countries." *Journal of Economic Literature* 35: 1958–2005.

Binswanger, Hans P. and D. A. Sillers. 1983. "Risk Aversion and Credit Constraints in Farmers' Decisionmaking: A Reinterpretation." *Journal of Development Studies* 22: 504–539.

Bishop, Richard C. 1993. "Economic Efficiency, Sustainability and Biodiversity." *Ambio* 22(2–3): 69–73.

Bleany, M. F. and David Greenaway. 1993. "Long-Run Trends in the Relative Price of Primary Commodities and in the Terms of Trade of Developing Countries." *Oxford Economic Papers* 45: 349–363.

Bloom, David E. and Jeffrey D. Sachs. 1998. "Geography, Demography, and Economic Growth in Africa." *Brookings Papers on Economic Activity* 1998, (2): 207–273.

Bluffstone, Randall A. 1995. "The Effect of Labor Market Performance on Deforestation in Developing Countries Under Open Access: An Example from Rural Nepal." *Journal of Environmental Economics and Management* 29: 42–63.

Bohn, Henning and Robert T. Deacon. 2000. "Ownership Risk, Investment, and the Use of Natural Resources." *American Economic Review* 90(3): 526–549.

Bolte, Katharine, Mampite Matete and Micheal Clemens. September 2002. *Manual for Calculating Adjusted Savings*. Environment Department, The World Bank, Washington DC.

Brander, James A. and M. Scott Taylor. 1997. "International Trade and Open-Access Renewable Resources: The Small Open Economy." *Canadian Journal of Economics* 30(3): 526–552.

1998a. "Open Access Renewable Resources: Trade and Trade Policy in a Two-Country Model." *Journal of International Economics* 44: 181–209.

1998b. "The Simple Economics of Easter Island: A Ricardo-Malthus Model of Renewable Resource Use." *American Economic Review* 88: 119–138.

Briscoe, John. 1996. "Managing Water as an Economic Good: Rules for Reformers." *Water Supply* 15(4): 153–172.

Broad, Robin. 1995. "The Political Economy of Natural Resources: Case Studies of the Indonesian and Philippine Forest Sectors." *The Journal of Developing Areas* 29: 317–340.

Bromley, Daniel W. 1989. "Property Relations and Economic Development: The Other Land Reform." *World Development* 17: 867–877.

1991. *Environment and Economy: Property Rights and Public Policy.* Basil Blackwell, Oxford.

Brown, K. and D. W. Pearce (eds.) 1994. *The Causes of Tropical Deforestation: The Economic and Statistical Analysis of Factors Giving Rise to the Loss of the Tropical Forests.* University College London Press, London.

Brown, P. 1997. "Institutions, Inequalities, and the Impact of Agrarian Reform on Rural Mexican Communities." *Human Organization* 56(1): 102–110.

Burger, J., E. Ostrom, R. B. Norgaard, D. Policansky and B. D. Goldstein (eds.) 2001. *Protecting the Commons: A Framework for Resource Management in the Americas.* Island Press, Washington DC.

Burgstaller, André and Nicolás Saavedra-Rivano. 1984. "Capital Mobility and Growth in a North–South Model." *Journal of Development Economics* 15: 213–237.

Carson, Richard T., Yongil Jeon and Donald R. McCubbin. 1997. "The Relationship Between Air Pollution Emissions and Income: US Data." *Special Issue on Environmental Kuznets Curves, Environment and Development Economics* 2(4): 433–450.

Cattaneo, Andrea. 2001. "Deforestation in the Brazilian Amazon: Comparing the Impacts of Macroeconomic Shocks, Land Tenure, and Technological Change." *Land Economics* 77(2): 219–240.

Caviglia-Harris, Jill L. 2004. "Household Production and Forest Clearing: The Role of Farming in the Development of the Amazon." *Environment and Development Economics* 9: 181–202.

Chambers, E. J. and D. F. Gordon. 1966. "Primary Products and Economic Growth: An Empirical Measurement." *Journal of Political Economy* 74(4): 315–332.

Chaves, R. A. and S. M. Sánchez 1998. "Poverty, Entrepreneurs and Financial Markets in the Rural Areas of Mexico." In R. López and A. Valdés (eds.) *Rural Poverty in Latin America.* The World Bank, Washington DC.

Chew, Sing C. 2001. *World Ecological Degradation: Accumulation, Urbanization, and Deforestation 3000 BC–AD 2000.* Altamira Press, New York.

Chichilnisky, Graciela. 1994. "North–South Trade and the Global Environment." *American Economic Review* 84: 851–874.

Chomitz, Kenneth M. and David A. Gray. 1996. "Roads, Land Markets and Deforestation: A Spatial Model of Land Use in Belize." *The World Bank Economic Review* 10(3): 487–512.

Cipolla, Carlo M. 1976. *Before the Industrial Revolution: European Society and Economy, 1000–1700.* Methuen, London.

1962. *The Economic History of World Population.* Penguin Books, Harmondsworth.

Cole, Matthew A. 2003. "Development, Trade, and the Environment: How Robust is the Environmental Kuznets Curve?" *Environment and Development Economics* 8(4): 557–581.

Cole, Matthew A., A. J. Rayner and J. M. Bates. 1997. "The Environmental Kuznets Curve: An Empirical Analysis. *Special Issue on Environmental*

Kuznets Curves, Environment and Development Economics 2(4): 401–416.

Cooke, Priscilla A. 1998. "The Effect of Environmental Good Scarcity on Own-Farm Labor Allocation: The Case of Agricultural Households in Rural Nepal." *Environment and Development Economics* 3(4): 443–470.

Corden, W. Max. 1984. "Booming Sector and Dutch Disease Economics: Survey and Consolidation." *Oxford Economic Papers* 36: 359–380.

Cornelius, W. A. and D. Myhre. (eds.) 1998. *The Transformation of Rural Mexico: Reforming the Ejido Sector.* Center for US-Mexican Studies, University of California, San Diego.

Cosgrove, William J. and Frank R. Rijsberman. 2000. *World Water Vision: Making Water Everybody's Business.* World Water Council and Earthscan Publications, London.

Coxhead, Ian and Sisira Jayasuriya. 1995. "Trade and Tax Policy Reform and the Environment: The Economics of Soil Erosion in Developing Countries." *American Journal of Agricultural Economics* 77: 631–644.

2003. *The Open Economy and the Environment: Development, Trade and Resources in Asia.* Edward Elgar, Northampton, Mass.

Coxhead, Ian, Agnes Rola and Kwansoo Kim. 2001. "How Do National Markets and Price Policies Affect Land Use at the Forest Margin? Evidence from the Philipines." *Land Economics* 77(2): 250–267.

Cropper, M., C. Griffiths, and M. Mani. 1999. "Roads, Population Pressures, and Deforestation in Thailand, 1976–1989." *Land Economics* 75(1): 58–73.

Cropper, Maureen and Charles Griffiths. 1994. "The Interaction of Population Growth and Environmental Quality." *American Economic Review*, AEA Papers and Proceedings, 84(2): 250–254.

Cropper, Maureen, Jyotsna Puri and Charles Griffiths. 2001. "Predicting the Location of Deforestation: The Role of Roads and Protected Areas in Northern Thailand." *Land Economics* 77(2): 172–186.

Crosby, Alfred. 1986. *Ecological Imperialism: The Biological Expansion of Europe 900–1900.* Cambridge University Press, New York.

Dasgupta, Partha. 1993. *An Inquiry into Well-Being and Destitution.* Oxford University Press, New York.

Dasgupta, Partha S. and Geoffrey Heal. 1974. "The Optimal Depletion of Exhaustible Resources." *Review of Economic Studies* 41(Symposium Issue): 3–28.

1979. *The Economics of Exhaustible Resources.* Cambridge University Press, Cambridge.

Dasgupta, Partha S. and Karl-Göran Mäler. 1991. "The Environment and Emerging Development Issues." In *Proceedings of the Annual World Bank Conference on Development Economics 1990*, pp. 101–132.
  2000. "Net National Product, Wealth and Social Well-Being." *Environment and Development Economics* 5(1–2): 69–94.
Dasgupta, S., B. Laplante, H. Wang and D. Wheeler. 2002. "Confronting the Environmental Kuznets Curve." *Journal of Economic Perspectives*, 16: 147–168.
David, Paul A. and Gavin Wright. 1997. "Increasing Returns and the Genesis of American Resource Abundance." *Industrial and Corporate Change* 6: 203–245.
Davies, R., J. Rattsø and R. Torvik. 1994. "The Macroeconomics of Zimbabwe in the 1980s: A CGE-Model Analysis." *Journal of African Economies* 3: 153–198.
Davis, Graham A. 1995. "Learning to Love the Dutch Disease: Evidence from the Mineral Economies." *World Development* 23(1): 1765–1779.
  1998. "The Minerals Sector, Sectoral Analysis, and Economic Development." *Resources Policy* 24(4): 217–228.
de Bruyn, Sander. 1997. "Explaining the Environmental Kuznets Curve: Structural Change and International Agreements in Reducing Sulphur Emissions." *Special Issue on Environmental Kuznets Curves, Environment and Development Economics* 2(4): 484–504.
De Groot, Herni L., Cees A. Withagen and Zhou Minliang. 2004. "Dynamics of China's Regional Development and Pollution: An Investigation into the Environmental Kuznets Curve." *Environment and Development Economics* 9(4): 507–538.
Deacon, Robert T. 1994. "Deforestation and the Rule of Law in a Cross-Section of Countries." *Land Economics* 70(4): 414–430.
  1999. "Deforestation and Ownership: Evidence from Historical Accounts and Contemporary Data." *Land Economics* 75(3): 341–359.
Deininger, K. W. and B. Minten. 1999. "Poverty, Policies and Deforestation: The Case of Mexico." *Economic Development and Cultural Change* 47(2): 313–344.
Dercon, S. 1998. "Wealth, risk and activity choice: cattle in Western Tanzania." *Journal of Development Economics* 55: 1–42.
di Tella, G. 1982. "The Economics of the Frontier." In C. P. Kindleberger and G. di Tella (eds.) *Economics in the Long View*. Macmillan, London, pp. 210–227.
Diamond, Jared. 1999. *Guns, Germs, and Steel: The Fates of Human Societies*. WW. Norton & Co., New York.

Dierberg, F. E. and W. Kiattisimkul. 1996. "Issues, Impacts and Implications of Shrimp Aquaculture in Thailand." *Environmental Management* 20(5): 649–666.

Dixit, Avinash P., Peter Hammond and Michael Hoel. 1980. "On Hartwick's Rule for Regular Maxmin Paths of Capital Accumulation and Resource Depletion." *Review of Economic Studies* 47: 551–556.

Dixon, R. and A. P. Thirwall. 1975. "A Model of Regional Growth Rate Differences on Kaldorian Lines." *Oxford Economic Papers* 27: 201–214.

DIYAM. 1987. *Shallow Aquifer Study*, 3 vols., Kano State Agricultural and Rural Development Authority, Kano, Nigeria.

Dosi, Cesare and William K. Easter. 2000. "Water Scarcity: Institutional Change, Water Markets and Privatisation." *Nota di Lavoro 102.2000*. Fondazione Eni Enrico Mattei Working Paper Series, Milan, Italy.

Easterly, William. 2001. *The Elusive Quest for Growth: Economists' Adventures and Misadventures in the Tropics*. The MIT Press, Cambridge, Mass.

Easterly, William and Ross Levine. 2003. "Tropics, Germs and Crops: How Endowments Influence Economic Development." *Journal of Monetary Economics* 50: 3–39.

Ehui, Simeon K. and Thomas W. Hertel. 1989. "Deforestation and Agricultural Productivity in the Côte d'Ivoire." *American Journal of Agricultural Economics* 71(August): 703–711.

Emmanuel, Arrighi. 1972. *Unequal Exchange: A Study in the Imperialism of Trade*. Monthly Review Press, New York.

Engerman, Stanley L. 2003. "Comment on: Tropics, Germs and Crops: How Endowments Influence Economic Development." *Journal of Monetary Economics* 50: 41–47.

Engerman, Stanley L. and Kenneth L. Sokoloff. 1997. "Factor Endowments, Institutions, and Differential Paths of Growth Among New World Economies." In Stephen Haber (ed.) *How Latin America Fell Behind: Essays on the Economic Histories of Brazil and Mexico*. Stanford University Press, Stanford, pp. 260–304.

Erftemeijer, P. L. A. and R. R. Lewis, III. 2000. "Planting Mangroves on Intertidal Mudflats: Habitat Restoration or Habitat Conversion?" In V. Sumantakul *et al.* (eds.) *Enhancing Coastal Ecosystem Restoration for the 21st Century*. *Proceedings of the Regional Seminar for East and Southeast Asian Countries: ECOTONE VIII*. Ranong and Phuket, Thailand, May 23–28 1999. Royal Forestry Department, Bangkok, Thailand, pp. 156–165.

Fairhead, James. 2001. "The Conflict over Natural and Environmental Resources." In E. W. Nafziger, F. Stewart and R. Väyrynen (eds.) *War,*

Hunger, and Displacement: The Origins of Humanitarian Emergencies. Volume 1: Analysis. Oxford University Press, Oxford, pp. 147–178.

Falkenmark, Malin. 1989. "The Massive Water Scarcity Now Threatening Africa – Why Isn't It Being Addressed?" *Ambio* 18(2): 112–118.

Falkenmark, Malin and Johan Rockström. 1998. "Water in Emergencies." In S. Fleming (ed.) *Forum: War and Water.* International Committee of the Red Cross, Geneva, pp. 22–29.

Falkenmark, Malin, Wolf Klohn, Jan Lundqvist, Sandra Postel, Johan Rockström, David Seckler, Jillel Shuval and James Wallace. 1998. "Water Scarcity as a Key Factor Behind Global Food Insecurity: Round Table Discussion." *Ambio* 27(2): 148–154.

Faurés, Jean-Marc, Domitille Vallée, Åse Eliasson, Jipe Hoogeveen. 2001. "Statistics on Water Resources by Country in FAO's AQUASTAT Programme." Paper presented at the Joint ECE/EUROSTAT Work Session on Methodological Issues of Environmental Statistics. Ottawa, Canada, October 1–4, 2001.

Feder, G. 1985. "The Relation between Farm Size and Farm Productivity: The Role of Family Labor, Supervision and Credit Constraints." *Journal of Development Economics* 18: 297–313.

Feder, Gershon and David Feeny. 1991. "Land Tenure and Property Rights: Theory and Implications for Development Policy." *World Bank Economic Review* 5(1): 135–153.

Feder, Gershon and Raymond Noronha. 1987. "Land Rights Systems and Agricultural Development in Sub-Saharan Africa." *World Bank Research Observer* 2: 143–169.

Feder, Gershon and Tongroj Onchan. 1987. "Land Ownership Security and Farm Investment in Thailand." *American Journal of Agricultural Economics* 69(2): 311–320.

Feder, Gershon, Tongroj Onchan, Yongyuth Chalamwong and Chira Hongladarom. 1988. "Land Policies and Farm Performance in Thailand's Forest Reserve Areas." *Economic Development and Cultural Change* 36(3): 483–501.

Feeny, David. 1988. "Agricultural Expansion and Forest Depletion in Thailand, 1900–1975." In John F. Richards and Richard Tucker (eds.) *World Deforestation in the Twentieth Century.* Duke University Press, Durham, pp. 112–143.

——— 2002. "The Co-evolution of Property Rights Regimes for Man, Land, and Forests in Thailand, 1790–1990." In John F. Richards (ed.) *Land Property and the Environment.* Institute for Contemporary Studies Press, San Francisco, pp. 179–221.

Findlay, Ronald. 1980. "The Terms of Trade and Equilibrium Growth in the World Economy." *American Economic Review* 70: 291–299.

1992. "The Roots of Divergence: Western Economic History in Comparative Perspective." *American Economic Review* **82**(2): 158–161.

1993. "The 'Triangular Trade' and the Atlantic Economy of the Eighteenth Century: A Simple General-Equilibrium Model." In R. Findlay (ed.) *Trade, Development and Political Economy: Essays of Ronald Findlay.* Edward Elgar, London, pp. 321–351.

1995. *Factor Proportions, Trade, and Growth.* MIT Press, Cambridge, Mass.

1998. "The Emergence of the World Economy." In Daniel Cohen (ed.) *Contemporary Economic Issues: Proceedings of the Eleventh World Congress of the International Economics Association, Tunis. Volume 3. Trade Payments and Debt.* St Martin's Press, New York, pp. 82–122.

Findlay, Ronald and Mats Lundahl. 1994. "Natural Resources, 'Vent-for-Surplus,' and the Staples Theory." In G. Meier (ed.) *From Classical Economics to Development Economics: Essays in Honor of Hla Myint.* St. Martin's Press, New York, pp. 68–93.

1999. "Resource-Led Growth – a Long-Term Perspective: The Relevance of the 1970–1994 Experience for Today's Developing Economies." UNU/WIDER Working Papers No. 162. World Institute for Development Economics Research, Helsinki.

Findlay, Ronald and Stanislaw Wellisz (eds.) 1993. *The Political Economy of Poverty, Equity and Growth: Five Small Open Economies, a World Bank Comparative Study.* Oxford University Press, New York.

Fischer, Günther and Gerhard K. Heilig. 1997. "Population Momentum and the Demand on Land and Water Resources." *Philosophical Transactions of the Royal Society Series B* **352**(1356): 869–889.

Fisher, Monica. 2004. "Household Welfare and Forest Dependence in Southern Malawi." *Environment and Development Economics* **9**: 135–154.

Flaherty, M. and C. Karnjanakesorn. 1995. "Marine Shrimp Aquaculture and Natural Resource Degradation in Thailand." *Environmental Management* **19**(1): 27–37.

Food and Agricultural Organization (FAO). 1993. *Forest Resources Assessment 1990: Tropical Countries.* FAO Forestry Paper 112. FAO, Rome.

1995. *World Agriculture: Towards 2010 – An FAO Study.* FAO and John Wiley & Sons, Rome and New York.

1997. *State of the World's Forests 1997.* FAO, Rome.

2001. *Forest Resources Assessment 2000: Main Report.* FAO Forestry Paper 140. FAO, Rome.

2003. *State of the World's Forests 2003*. FAO, Rome.

Frank, André Gunder. 1967. *Capitalism and Underdevelopment in Latin America: Historical Studies of Chile and Brazil*. Monthly Review Press, New York.

1978. *Dependent Accumulation and Development*. Macmillan, London.

Freeman, A. M. III. 2003. *The Measurement of Environmental and Resource Values: Theory and Methods*. 2nd ed. Washington DC: Resources for the Future, Washington DC.

Furtado, Celso. 1970. *Economic Development of Latin America: A Survey from Colonial Times to the Cuban Revolution*. Cambridge University Press, Cambridge.

Futagami, Koichi, Yuichi Morita and Akihisa Shibata. 1993. "Dynamic Analysis of an Endogenous Growth Model with Public Capital." In T. Andersen and Karl Moene (eds.) *Endogenous Growth*. Basil Blackwell, Oxford, pp. 217–235.

Galor, Oded and David N. Weil 1998. "From Malthusian Stagnation to Modern Growth." *American Economic Review* 89(2): 150–154.

Gelb, Alan. 1986a. "Adjustment to Windfall Gains: A Comparative Analysis of Oil-Exporting Countries." In J. Peter Neary and Sweder van Wijnbergen (eds.) *Natural Resources and the Macroeconomy*. MIT Press, Cambridge, Mass., pp. 54–93.

1986b. "The Oil Syndrome: Adjustment to Windfall Gains in Oil-Exporting Countries." In Deepak Lal and Martin Wolf (eds.) *Stagflation, Savings, and the State: Perspectives on the Global Economy*. World Bank Research Publication Series, Oxford University Press for the World Bank, New York, Oxford, Toronto, and Melbourne, pp. 115–130.

Gelb, Alan and Associates. 1988. *Oil Windfalls: Blessing or Curse?* Oxford University Press for the World Bank, New York.

Gibson, C. C. 2001. "Forest Resources: Institutions for Local Governance in Guatemala." In J. Burger, E. Ostrom, R. B. Norgaard, D. Policansky and B. D. Goldstein (eds.) *Protecting the Commons: A Framework for Resource Management in the Americas*. Island Press, Washington DC, pp. 71–90.

Gleick, Peter H. 1998. *The World's Water 1998–1999: The Biennial Report on Freshwater Resources*. Island Press, Washington DC.

2000. *The World's Water 2000–2001: The Biennial Report on Freshwater Resources*. Island Press, Washington DC.

Godoy, Ricardo, Marc Jacobson, Joel De Castro, Vianca Aliaga, Julio Romero and Allison Davis. 1998. "The Role of Tenure Security and Private Preference in Neotropical Deforestation." *Land Economics* 74(2): 162–170.

Goss, J., D. Burch, and R. E. Rickson. 2000. "Agri-Food Restructuring and Third World Transnationals: Thailand, the CP Group and the Global Shrimp Industry." *World Development* 28(3): 513–530.

Goss, J., M. Skladany, and G. Middendorf. 2001. "Dialogue: Shrimp Aquaculture in Thailand: A Response to Vandergeest, Flaherty and Miller." *Rural Sociology* 66(3): 451–460.

Green, Alan and M. C. Urquhart. 1976. "Factor and Commodity Flows in the International Economy of 1870–1914: A Multi-Country View." *Journal of Economic History* 36: 217–252.

Grossman, Gene M. and Alan B. Kreuger. 1995. "Economic Growth and the Environment." *Quarterly Journal of Economics* 110(2): 353–377.

Gylfason, Thorvaldur. 2001a. "Natural Resources, Education, and Economic Development." *European Economic Review* 45: 847–859.

2001b. "Nature, Power, and Growth." *Scottish Journal of Political Economy* 48(5): 558–588.

Gylfason, Thorvadulr, T. T. Herbertsson and G. Zoega. 1999. "A Mixed Blessing: Natural Resources and Economic Growth." *Macroeconomic Dynamics* 3: 204–225.

Hall, Robert E. and Charles I. Jones. 1999. "Why Do Some Countries Produce So Much More Output Per Worker Than Others?" *Quarterly Journal of Economics* 114(1): 83–116.

Hamilton, Kirk. 2003. "Sustaining Economic Welfare: Estimating Changes in Total and Per Capita Wealth." *Environment, Development and Sustainability* 5: 419–436.

Hamilton, Kirk and Michael Clemens. 1999. "Genuine Savings Rates in Developing Countries." *The World Bank Economic Review* 13(2): 333–356.

Hannesson, R. 2000. "Renewable Resources and the Gain from Trade." *Canadian Journal of Economics* 33: 122–132.

Hansen, B. 1979. "Colonial Economic Development with Unlimited Supply of Land: A Ricardian Case." *Economic Development and Cultural Change* 27: 611–627.

Hartwick, John M. 1977. "Intergenerational Equity and the Investing of Rents from Exhaustible Resources." *American Economic Review* 66: 972–974.

1978. "Investing Returns from Depleting Renewable Resource Stocks and Intergenerational Equity." *Economic Letters* 1: 85–88.

1995. "Constant Consumption Paths in Open Economies with Exhaustible Resources." *Review of International Economics* 3(3): 275–285.

Hausmann, Ricardo and Roberto Rigobon. 2002. "An Alternative Interpretation of the 'Resource Curse': Theory and Policy Implications." NBER Working Paper No. 9424. Cambridge, Mass.

Hayami, Yujiro. 2001. *Development Economics: From the Poverty to the Wealth of Nations*. 2nd ed. Oxford University Press, New York.

Heal, G. 1982. "The Use of Common Property Resources." In V. K. Smith and J. V. Krutilla (eds.) *Explorations in Natural Resource Economics*. Johns Hopkins University Press, Baltimore, pp. 72–106.

Heath, John and Hans Binswanger. 1996. "Natural Resource Degradation Effects of Poverty and Population Growth Are Largely Policy-Induced: The Case of Colombia." *Environment and Development Economics* 1(1): 65–84.

Hill, Catherine B. 1991. "Managing Commodity Booms in Botswana." *World Development* 19(9): 1185–1196.

Hoff, Karla and Joseph E. Stiglitz. 1990. "Introduction: Imperfect Information and Rural Credit Markets – Puzzles and Policy Perspectives." *World Bank Economic Review* 4(3): 235–250.

Hoff, Karla, Avishay Braverman and Joseph E. Stiglitz (eds.) 1993. *The Economics of Rural Organization: Theory, Practice and Policy*. Oxford University Press, New York.

Hollis, G. Edward, William M. Adams and M. Aminu-Kano (eds.) 1993. *The Hadejia-Nguru Wetlands: Environment, Economy and Sustainable Development of a Sahelian Floodplain Wetland*. IUCN, Geneva.

Holtz-Eakin, D. and Thomas M. Selden. 1995. "Stoking the Fires? CO_2 Emissions and Economic Growth." *Journal of Public Economics* 57: 85–101.

Homer-Dixon, Thomas F. 1999. *Environment, Scarcity, and Violence*. Princeton University Press, Princeton.

Horan, Richard D., Jason F. Shogren and Erwin Bulte. 2003. *Scottish Journal of Political Economy* 50(2): 19–36.

Hotte, Louis, Ngo Van Long and Huilan Tian. 2000. "International Trade with Endogenous Enforcement of Property Rights." *Journal of Development Economics* 62: 25–54.

Howarth, Richard B. and Richard B. Norgaard. 1995. "Intergenerational Choices under Global Environmental Change." In D. Bromley (ed.) *The Handbook of Environmental Economics*. Basil Blackwell, Oxford, pp. 111–138.

Howe, Charles W. 1976. "The Effects of Water Resource Development on Economic Growth: The Conditions for Success." *Natural Resources Journal* 16(4): 939–955.

Innis, Harold A. 1930. *The Fur Trade in Canada: An Introduction to Canadian Economic History*. Yale University Press, New Haven.

1940. *The Cod Fisheries: The History of an International Economy*. Yale University Press, New Haven.

Jitsanguan, T., B. Sootsukon and S. Tookwinas. 1999. "Estimation of Environmental Costs from Shrimp Farming." A report submitted to Office of Environmental Policy and Planning, Ministry of Science, Technology and Environment by the Department of Agricultural and Resource Economic, Faculty of Economics, Kasetsart University.

Johnstone, Nick and Libby Wood (eds.) 2001. *Private Firms and Public Water: Realizing Social and Environmental Objectives in Developing Countries*. Edward Elgar, London.

Jones, Eric L. 1987. *The European Miracle: Environments, Economics and Geopolitics in the History of Europe and Asia*. 2nd ed. Cambridge University Press, Cambridge.

Jones, G. A. and P. M. Ward. 1998. "Privatizing the Commons: Ejido and Urban Development in Mexico." *International Journal of Urban and Regional Research* 22(1): 76–95.

Kaimowitz, D. and A. Angelsen. 1998. *Economic Models of Tropical Deforestation: A Review*. Center for International Forestry Research, Bogor, Indonesia.

Kamarck, A. M. 1976. *The Tropics and Economic Development*. Johns Hopkins University Press, Baltimore.

Kaosa-ard, M. and S. S. Pednekar. 1998. "Background Report for the Thai Marine Rehabilitation Plan 1997–2001." Report submitted to the Joint Research Centre of the Commission of the European Communities and the Department of Fisheries, Ministry of Agriculture and Cooperatives, Thailand Development Research Institute, Bangkok.

Karl, Terry L. 1997. *The Paradox of Plenty: Oil Booms and Petro-States*. University of California Press, Berkeley.

Kaufmann, Daniel, Aart Kraay and Pablo Zoido-Lobaton. 1999a. "Aggregating Governance Indicators." World Bank Policy Research Department Working Paper No. 2195.

1999b. "Governance Matters." World Bank Policy Research Department Working Paper No. 2196.

Keefer, Philip and Stephen Knack. 1997. "Why Don't Poor Countries Catch Up? A Cross-National Test of an Institutional Explanation." *Economic Inquiry* 35: 590–602.

Kennedy, Paul. 1988. *The Rise and Fall of the Great Powers: Economic Change and Military Conflict from 1500 to 2000*. Fontana Press, London.

Kimmage, Kevin. 1991. "Small-scale Irrigation Initiatives in Nigeria: The Problem of Equity and Sustainability." *Aplied Geography* 11: 5–20.

Kimmage, Kevin and William M. Adams. 1992. "Wetland Agricultural Production and River Basin Development in the Hadejia-Jama'are Valley, Nigeria." *The Geographical Journal* 158(1): 1–12.

Komen, Marinus H. C., Shelby Gerking and Henk Folmer. 1997. "Income and Environmental R&D: Empirical Evidence from OECD Countries." *Special Issue on Environmental Kuznets Curves, Environment and Development Economics* 2(4): 505–515.

Kongkeo, H. 1997. "Comparison of Intensive Shrimp Farming Systems in Indonesia, Philippines, Taiwan and Thailand." *Aquaculture Research* 28: 89–796.

Koop, Gary and Lise Toole. 1999. "Is There an Environmental Kuznets Curve for Deforestation?" *Journal of Development Economics* 58(July): 231–244.

Kooten, van G. C., R. A. Sedjo and E. H. Bulte. 1999. "Tropical Deforestation: Issues and Policies," ch.5 in H. Folmer and T. Tietenberg (eds.) *The International Yearbook of Environmental and Resource Economics 1999/2000*. Edward Elgar, London, pp. 199–248.

Kremer, Michael. 1993. "Population Growth and Technological Change: One Million BC to 1990." *Quarterly Journal of Economics* 108(3): 681–716.

Krugman, Paul R. 1981. "Trade, Accumulation, and Uneven Development." *Journal of Development Economics* 8: 149–161.

1987. "The Narrow Moving Band, the Dutch Disease, and the Competitive Consequences of Mrs Thatcher: Notes on Trade in the Presence of Dynamic Scale Economies." *Journal of Development Economics* 27: 41–55.

Kuznets, Simon. 1955. "Economic Growth and Income Inequality." *American Economic Review* 49: 1–28.

La Porta, Rafael, Florencio Lopez-de-Silanes, Andrei Shleifer and Robert W. Vishny. 1998. "Law and Finance." *Journal of Political Economy* 106(6): 1113–1155.

1999. "The Quality of Government." *Journal of Law, Economics and Organization* 15(1): 222–279.

Landes, David S. 1998. *The Wealth and Poverty of Nations: Why Some Are So Rich and Some So Poor*. W. W. Norton and Co., New York.

Lane, Philip R. and Aaron Tornell. 1996. "Power, Growth and the Voracity Effect." *Journal of Economic Growth* 1: 213–241.

Lange, Glenn-Marie and Matthew Wright. 2004. "Sustainable Development in Mineral Economies: The Example of Botswana." *Environment and Development Economics*, forthcoming.

Larson, Bruce A. 1991. "The Causes of Land Degradation along 'Spontaneously' Expanding Agricultural Frontiers in the Third World: A Comment." *Land Economics* 67(2): 260–266.

Larson, Bruce A. and Bromley, Daniel W. 1990. "Property Rights, Externalities, and Resource Degradation: Locating the Tragedy." *Journal of Development Economics* 33: 235–262.

Leite, Carlos and Jens Weidmann. 1999. "Does Mother Nature Corrupt? Natural Resources, Corruption and Economic Growth." IMF Working Papers WP/99/85. International Monetary Fund, Washington DC.

Lewis, R. R. III, P. L. A. Erftemeijer, A. Sayaka, and P. Kethkaew. 2000. "Mangrove Rehabilitation after Shrimp Aquaculture: A Case Study in Progress at the Don Sak National Forest Reserves, Surat Thani, Southern Thailand." *Mimeo*, Mangrove Forest Management Unit, Surat Thani Regional Forest Office, Royal Forest Department, Surat Thani, Thailand.

Lieb, Christoph M. 2002. "The Environmental Kuznets Curve and Satiation: A Simple Static Model." *Environment and Development Economics* 7(3): 429–448.

Livi-Bacci, Massimo. 1997. *A Concise History of World Population*. 2nd ed. Blackwell Publishers, Oxford.

Lonegran, Steven C. 1999. *Environmental Change, Adaptation, and Security. NATO ASI Series*. Kluwer, Dordrecht.

López, Ramón. 1989. "Exchange Rate Determination in Natural Resource-Rich Economies." *Revista de Análisis Económico* 4(1): 91–105.

———. 1994. "The Environment as a Factor of Production: The Effects of Economic Growth and Trade Liberalization." *Journal of Environmental Economics and Management* 27(2): 163–184.

———. 1997. "Environmental Externalities in Traditional Agriculture and the Impact of Trade Liberalization: The Case of Ghana." *Journal of Development Economics* 53(July): 17–39.

———. 1998a. "Agricultural Intensification, Common Property Resources and the Farm-Household." *Environmental and Resource Economics* 11(3–4): 443–458.

———. 1998b. "Where Development Can or Cannot Go: The Role of Poverty-Environment Linkages." In B. Pleskovic and J. E. Stiglitz (eds.) *Annual Bank Conference on Development Economics 1997*. The World Bank, Washington DC, pp. 285–306.

———. 2003. "The Policy Roots of Socioeconomic Stagnation and Environmental Implosion: Latin America 1950–2000." *World Development* 31(2): 259–280.

López, Ramón and Siddhartha Mitra. 2000. "Corruption, Pollution and the Kuznets Environment Curve." *Journal of Environmental Economics and Management* 40(2): 137–150.

López, Ramón and Alberto Valdés (eds.) 1998. *Rural Poverty in Latin America*. The World Bank, Washington DC.

Lundahl, Mats. 1998. "Staples Trade and Economic Development." In M. Lundahl (ed.) *Themes of International Economics*. Ashgate Publishing, Boston, pp. 45–68.

McConnell, Kenneth E. 1997. "Income and the Demand for Environmental Quality." *Special Issue on Environmental Kuznets Curves, Environment and Development Economics* 2(4): 383–399.

McNeil, John R. and William H. McNeil. 2003. *The Human Web: A Bird's Eye View of Human History*. W. W. Norton & Co., New York.

McNeil, William H. 1999. *A World History*. 4th ed. Oxford University Press, New York.

Maddison, Angus. 2003. *The World Economy: Historical Statistics*. Organization for Economic Cooperation and Development, Paris.

Mahar, Dennis and Robert R. Schneider. 1994. "Incentives for Tropical Deforestation: Some Examples from Latin America." In Katrina Brown and David W. Pearce (eds.) *The Causes of Tropical Deforestation*. University College London Press, London, pp. 159–170.

Mahon, J. E. 1992. "Was Latin America Too Rich to Prosper? Structural and Political Obstacles to Export-Led Industrial Growth." *Journal of Development Studies* 28: 241–263.

Mäler, Karl-Göran. 1991. "National Accounts and Environmental Resources." *Environmental and Resource Economics* 1(1): 1–15.

1995. "Economic Growth and the Environment." In C. A. Perrings, K-G. Mäler, C. Folke, C. S. Holling, and B-O. Jansson (eds.) *Biodiversity Loss: Economic and Ecological Issues*. Cambridge University Press, Cambridge, UK, pp. 213–224.

Manning, Patrick. 2003. *Negotiating World History: Historians Create a Global Past*. Palgrave Macmillan, New York.

Manzano, Osmel and Roberto Rigobon. 2001. "Resource Curse or Debt Overhang?" NBER Working Paper No. 8390. Cambridge, Mass.

Marks, Robert B. 2002. *The Origins of the Modern World*. Rowman & Littlefield, Lanham, Maryland.

Matsuyama, Kimoru. 1992. "Agricultural Productivity, Comparative Advantage, and Economic Growth." *Journal of Economic Theory* 58: 317–334.

Matthews, E., Payne, R., Rohweder, M. and Murray, S. 2000. *Pilot Analysis of Global Ecosystems: Forest Ecosystems*. World Resources Institute, Washington DC.

Mauro, Paulo. 1995. "Corruption and Growth." *Quarterly Journal of Economics* 110(3): 681–712.

Murphy, Kevin, A. Shleifer and R. Vishny. 1993. "Why is Rent-Seeking So Costly to Growth?" *American Economic Review Papers and Proceedings* 83: 409–414.

Myint, Hla. 1958. "The Classical Theory of International Trade and the Underdeveloped Countries." *Economic Journal* 68: 315–337.

Myrdal, Gunnar. 1957. *Economic Theory and Under-Developed Regions.* Duckworth, London.

Neary, Peter J. and S. van Wijnbergen (eds.) 1986. *Natural Resources and the Macro-Economy.* MIT Press, Cambridge, Mass.

Nelson, G. C. and D. Hellerstein. 1997. "Do Roads Cause Deforestation? Using Satellite Images in Econometric Analysis of Land Use." *American Journal of Agricultural Economics* 79(2): 80–88.

Nelson, Gerald C., V. Harris and S. W. Stone. 2001. "Deforestation, Land Use, and Property Rights: Empirical Evidence from Darién, Panama." *Land Economics* 77(2): 187–205.

North, Douglass C. 1990. *Institutions, Institutional Change and Economic Performance.* Cambridge University Press, Cambridge.

North, Douglass C. and Robert P. Thomas. 1973. *The Rise of the Western World: A New Economic History.* Cambridge University Press, Cambridge, UK.

Ostrom, E. 2001. "Reformulating the Commons." In J. Burger, E. Ostrom, R. B. Norgaard, D. Policansky and B. D. Goldstein (eds.) *Protecting the Commons: A Framework for Resource Management in the Americas.* Island Press, Washington DC, pp. 17–44.

Ostrom, Elinor. 1990. *Governing the Commons: The Evolution of Institutions for Collective Action.* Cambridge University Press, Cambridge.

Pack, H. 1994. "Endogenous Growth Theory: Intellectual Apeal and Empirical Shortcomings." *Journal of Economic Perspectives* 8(1): 55–72.

Panayotou, Theodore. 1995. "Environmental Degradation at Different Stages of Economic Development." In I. Ahmed and J. A. Doeleman (eds.) *Beyond Rio: The Environmental Crisis and Sustainable Livelihoods in the Third World.* Macmillan Press, London.

1997. "Demystifying the Environmental Kuznets Curve: Turning a Black Box into a Policy Tool." *Special Issue on Environmental Kuznets Curves, Environment and Development Economics* 2(4): 465–484.

Panayotou, Theodore and Somthawin Sungsuwan. 1994. "An Econometric Analysis of the Causes of Tropical Deforestation: The Case of Northeast Thailand." In K. Brown and D. W. Pearce (eds.) *The Causes of Tropical Deforestation: The Economic and Statistical Analysis of Factors Giving Rise to the Loss of the Tropical Forests.* University College London Press, London, pp. 192–210.

Parker, Douglas D. and Yacov Tsur (eds.) 1997. *Decentralization and Coordination of Water Resource Management.* Kluwer Academic Publishers, Dordrecht.

Pearce, David W. and Giles Atkinson. 1993. "Capital Theory and the Measurement of Sustainable Development: An Indicator of Weak Sustainability." *Ecological Economics* 8: 103–108.

Pearce, David W. and Edward B. Barbier. 2000. *Blueprint for a Sustainable Economy*. Earthscan Publications, London.

Pearce, David W., Edward B. Barbier and Anil Markandya. 1990 *Sustainable Development: Economics and Environment in the Third World*. Edward Elgar, London.

Pearce, David W., Anil Markandya and Edward B. Barbier. 1989. *Blueprint for a Green Economy*. Earthscan Publications, London.

Pezzey, John C. V. 1989. "*Economic Analysis of Sustainable Growth and Sustainable Development*." Environment Department Working Paper No. 15. The World Bank, Washington DC.

Pingali, Prabhu L. 2001. "Environmental Consequences of Agricultural Commercialization in Asia." *Environment and Development Economics* 6(4): 483–502.

Pomeranz, Kenneth. 2000. *The Great Divergence: Europe, China, and the Making of the Modern World Economy*. Princeton University Press, Princeton.

Pomeranz, Kenneth and Steven Topik. 1999. *The World that Trade Created: Society, Culture and the World Economy, 1400 – the Present*. M. E. Sharpe, New York.

Population Division of the United Nations Secretariat. 2001. *World Urbanization Prospects: The 2001 Revision*. United Nations, New York.

Prebisch, Raúl. 1950. "The Economic Development of Latin America and its Principal Problems." *Economic Bulletin for Latin America* 7(1): 1–22. 1959. "Commercial Policy in the Underdeveloped Countries." *American Economic Review* 59(2): 251.

Raffer, Kunibert and Hans W. Singer. 2001. *The Economic North–South Divide: Six Decades of Unequal Development*. Edward Elgar, London.

Raine, R. M. 1994. "Current Land Use and Changes in Land Use Over Time in the Coastal Zone of Chathaburi Province, Thailand." *Biological Conservation* 67: 201–204.

Reardon, Thomas and Christopher B. Barrett. 2000. "Agroindustrialization, Globalization, and International Development: An Overview of Issues, Patterns, and Determinants." *Agricultural Economics* 23(3): 195–205.

Rebelo, Santiago. 1991. "Long Run Policy Analysis and Long Run Growth." *Journal of Political Economy* 99: 500–521.

Revenga, Carmen, Jake Brunner, Norbert Henninger, Ken Kassem and Richard Payne. 2000. *Pilot Analysis of Global Ecosystems: Freshwater Systems*. World Resources Institute, Washington DC.

Richards, M. 1997. "Common Property Resource Institutions and Forest Management in Latin America." *Development and Change* 28: 95–117.

Rodríguez, Francisco and Jeffrey D. Sachs. 1999. "Why Do Resource-Abundant Economies Grow More Slowly?" *Journal of Economic Growth* 4: 277–303.

Rodríguez-Meza, Jorge, Douglas Southgate and Claudio González-Vega. 2004. "Rural Poverty, Household Responses to Shocks, and Agricultural Land Use: Panel Results for El Salvador." *Environment and Development Economics* 9: 225–240.

Romer, Paul M. 1986. "Increasing Returns and Long-Run Growth." *Journal of Political Economy* 94(5): 1002–1037.

1996, "Why, Indeed, in America? Theory, History, and the Origins of Modern Economic Growth." *American Economic Review* 86(2): 202–212.

Rosegrant, Mark W. and Ximing Cai. 2001. "Water for Food Production." In Ruth S. Meinzen-Dick and Mark W. Rosegrant (eds.) *2020 Vision Focus 9: Overcoming Water Scarcity and Quality Constraints.* International Food Policy Research Institute, Washington DC.

Rosegrant, Mark W., Ximing Cai and Sarah A. Cline. 2002. *World Water and Food to 2025: Dealing with Scarcity.* International Food Policy Research Institute, Washington DC.

Ross, Michael L. 1999. "The Political Economy of the Resource Curse." *World Politics* 51: 297–322.

2001. *Timber Booms and Institutional Breakdowns in Southeast Asia.* Cambridge University Press, Cambridge, UK.

Sachs, Jeffrey D. and Andrew M. Warner. 1995a. "Economic Reform and the Process of Global Integration." *Brookings Papers on Economic Activity* Spring (1): 1–118.

1995b. "Natural Resource Abundance and Economic Growth." National Bureau of Economic Research Working Paper No. 5398, December.

1997. "Fundamental Sources of Long-Run Growth." *American Economic Review* 87(2): 184–188.

1999a. "The Big Push, Natural Resource Booms and Growth." *Journal of Development Economics* 59: 43–76.

1999b. "Natural Resource Intensity and Economic Growth." In. J. Mayer, B. Chambers and A. Farooq (eds.) *Development Policies in Natural Resource Economies.* Edward Elgar, Cheltenham, pp. 13–38.

2001. "The Curse of Natural Resources." *European Economic Review* 45: 827–838.

Sahlins, Marshall. 1974. *Stone Age Economics*. Tavistock Publications, London.

Sala-I-Martin, Xavier. 1999. "I Just Ran Two Million Regressions." *American Economic Review* 87(2): 178–183.

Sala-I-Martin, Xavier and Arvind Subramanian. 2003. "Addressing the Natural Resource Curse: An Illustration from Nigeria." NBER Working Paper No. 9804. Cambridge, Mass.

SARH. 1988. *Estadisticas Basics 1960–1980 para la Planeqcion del Dsarollo Rural Integral*. Tomo 1. Sector Agropeuario Forestal, Mexico City.

Sarraf, Maria and Moortaza Jiwanji. 2001. "Beating the Resource Curse: The Case of Botswana." *Environmental Economics Series*. The World Bank Environment Department, The World Bank, Washington DC.

Sarukhán, J. and Jorge Larson. 2001. "When the Commons Become Less Tragic: Land Tenure, Social Organization, and Fair Trade in Mexico." In J. Burger, E. Ostrom, R. B. Norgaard, D. Policansky and B. D. Goldstein (eds.) *Protecting the Commons: A Framework for Resource Management in the Americas* Island Press, Washington DC, pp. 45–70.

Sathirathai, S. 1998. "Economic Valuation of Mangroves and the Roles of Local Communities in the Conservation of the Resources: Case Study of Surat Thani, South of Thailand." Final report submitted to the Economy and Environment Program for Southest Asia (EEPSEA), Singapore.

Sathirathai, Suthawan and Edward B. Barbier. 2001. "Valuing Mangrove Conservation in Southern Thailand." *Contemporary Economic Policy* 19(2): 109–122.

Schedvin, C. B. 1990. "Staples and Regions of Pax Britannica." *Economic History Review* 43: 533–559.

Schneider, Robert R. 1994. *Government and the Economy on the Amazon Frontier*. Latin America and the Caribbean Technical Department, Regional Studies Program, Report No. 34. The World Bank, Washington DC.

Schumpeter, Joseph A. 1961. *A Theory of Economic Development: An Inquiry into Profits, Capital, Credit, Interest, and the Business Cycle*. Oxford University Press, New York.

Seckler, David, Randolph Barker and Upali Amarasinghe. 1999. "Water Scarcity in the Twenty-first Century." *International Journal of Water Resources Development* 15(1/2): 29–42.

Seers, Dudley. 1962. "A Model of Comparative Rates of Growth in the World Economy." *Economic Journal* 72: 285.

Selden, Thomas M. and D. Song. 1994. "Environmental Quality and Development: Is There a Kuznets Curve for Air Pollution Emissions?" *Journal of Environmental Economics and Management* 27: 147–162.

Shafik, Nemat. 1994. "Economic Development and Environmental Quality: An Econometric Analysis." *Oxford Economic Papers* 46(October): 757–773.

Shively, Gerald E. 2001. "Agricultural Change, Rural Labor Markets, and Forest Clearing." *Land Economics* 77(2): 268–284.

Shively, Gerald E. and Stefano Pagiola. 2004. "Agricultural Intensification, Local Labor Markets and Deforestation in the Philipines." *Environment and Development Economics* 9: 241–266.

Singer, Hans W. 1950. "The Distribution of Gains between Investing and Borrowing Countries." *American Economic Review* 40: 478.

Singh, I., Squire, L. and Strauss, J. (eds.) 1986. *Agricultural Household Models: Extensions, Aplications and Policy.* Johns Hopkins University Press, Baltimore.

Smith, S. 1976. "An Extension of the Vent-for-Surplus Model in Relation to Long-Run Structural Change in Nigeria." *Oxford Economic Papers* 28(3): 426–446.

Smith, Vernon L. 1975. "The Primitive Hunter Culture, Pleistocene Extinction, and the Rise of Agriculture." *Journal of Political Economy* 83(4): 727–756.

Sokoloff, Kenneth L. and Stanley L. Engerman. 2000. "Institutions, Factor Endowments, and Paths of Development in the New World." *Journal of Economic Perspectives* 14(3): 217–232.

Solow, Robert M. 1974. "Intergenerational Equity and Exhaustible Resources." *Review of Economic Studies* 41(Symposium Issue): 29–45.

Southey, C. 1978. "The Staples Thesis, Common Property and Homesteading." *Canadian Journal of Economics* 11(3): 547–559.

Southgate, Douglas. 1990. "The Causes of Land Degradation along 'Spontaneously' Expanding Agricultural Frontiers in the Third World." *Land Economics* 66(1): 93–101.

  1994. "Tropical Deforestation and Agricultural Development in Latin America." In K. Brown and D. W. Pearce (eds.) *The Causes of Tropical Deforestation: The Economic and Statistical Analysis of Factors Giving Rise to the Loss of the Tropical Forests.* University College London Press, London, pp. 134–145.

Stern, David, Michael S. Common and Edward B. Barbier. 1996. "Economic Growth and Environmental Degradation: The Environmental Kuznets Curve and Sustainable Development." *World Development* 24(7): 1151–1160.

Stevens, Paul. 2003. "Resource Impact: Curse or Blessing? A Literature Survey." *The Journal of Energy Literature* 9: 3–42.

Stevenson, N. J., R. R. Lewis, III and P. R. Burbridge. 1999. "Disused Shrimp Ponds and Mangrove Rehabilitation." In W. Streever (ed.) *An*

International Perspective on Wetland Rehabilitation. Kluwer Academic Publishers, Dordrecht, pp. 277–297.

Stiglitz, Joseph E. 1987. "Some Theoretical Aspects of Agricultural Policies." *World Bank Research Observer* 2(1): 43–53.

2003. *Globalization and its Discontents*. W. W. Norton, New York.

Stijns, Jean-Phillipe C. 2001. "Natural Resource Abundance and Economic Growth Revisited." *Mimeo*. University of California at Berkeley.

Stokey, Nancy L. 1998. "Are There Limits to Growth?" *International Economic Review* 39: 1–31.

Sullivan, Caroline. 2002. "Calculating a Water Poverty Index." *World Development* 30(7): 1195–1210.

Swain, Ashok. 2001. "Water Scarcity as a Source of Crisis." In E. W. Nafziger, F. Stewart and R. Väyrynen (eds.) *War, Hunger, and Displacement: The Origins of Humanitarian Emergencies. Volume 1: Analysis*. Oxford University Press, Oxford, pp. 179–206.

Takasaki, Yoshito, Bradford L. Barham and Oliver T. Coomes. 2004. "Risk Coping Strategies in Tropical Forests: Floods, Illness, and Resource Extraction." *Environment and Development Economics* 9: 203–224.

Taylor, Alan M. and Jeffrey G. Williamson. 1994. "Capital Flows to the New World as an Intergenerational Transfer." *Journal of Political Economy* 102(2): 348–371.

Temple, Jonathon. 1999. "The New Growth Evidence." *Journal of Economic Literature* 37(March): 112–156.

Thomas, David H. L. and William M. Adams. 1999. "Adapting to Dams: Agrarian Change Downstream of the Tiga Dam, Northern Nigeria." *World Development* 6: 919–935.

Thomas, Vinod, Mansoor Dailami, Ashok Dhareshwar, Daniel Kaufmann, Nalin Kishor, Ramón López and Yan Wang. 2000. *The Quality of Growth*. Oxford University Press, New York.

Thompson, Julian R. and B. Goes. 1997. "Inundation and Groundwater Recharge in the Hadejia-Nguru Wetlands, Northeast Nigeria: Hydrological Analysis." Report for the Hadejia-Nguru Wetlands Conservation Project, Kano, Nigeria and the Wetland Research Unit, University College London.

Thompson, Julian R. and G. Edward Hollis. 1995. "Hydrological Modelling and the Sustainable Development of the Hadejia-Nguru Wetlands, Nigeria." *Hydrological Science Journal* 40: 97–116.

Thompson, Julian R. and Gert Polet. 2000. "Hydrology and Land Use in a Sahelian Floodplain Wetland." *Wetlands* 20(4): 639–659.

Thomson, James T., David H. Feeny and Ronald J. Oakerson. 1992. "Institutional Dynamics: The Evolution and Dissolution of Common

Property Resource Management." In Daniel W. Bromley (ed.) *Making the Commons Work: Theory, Practice, and Policy*. San Francisco, Institute for Contemporary Studies Press, San Francisco, pp. 129–160.

Thongrak, S., T. Prato, S. Chiayvareesajja and W. Kurtz. 1997. "Economic and Water Quality Evaluation of Intensive Shrimp Production Systems in Thailand." *Agricultural Systems* 53: 121–141.

Tokrisna, R. 1998. "The Use of Economic Analysis in Suport of Development and Investment Decision in Thai Aquaculture: With Particular Reference to Marine Shrimp Culture." A paper submitted to the Food and Agriculture Organisation of the United Nations.

Toman, Michael A., John C. V. Pezzey and Jeffrey Krautkramer. 1995. "Neoclassical Economic Growth Theory and 'Sustainability'". In D. Bromley (ed.) *The Handbook of Environmental Economics*. Basil Blackwell, Oxford, pp. 139–165.

Tornell, Aaron and Philip R. Lane. 1998. "Are Windfalls a Curse? A Non-Representative Agent Model of the Current Account." *Journal of International Economics* 44: 83–112.

1999. "The Voracity Effect." *American Economic Review* 89: 22–46.

Torvik, Ragnar. 2001. "Learning by Doing and the Dutch Disease." *European Economic Review* 45(2), February: 285–306.

2002. "Natural Resources, Rent Seeking and Welfare." *Journal of Development Economics* 67: 455–470.

Toynbee, Arnold. 1978. *Mankind and Mother Earth*. Granada Publishing, London.

Turner, Frederick J. 1986. "The Significance of the Frontier in American History." In F. J. Turner, *The Frontier in American History*. University of Arizona Press, Tucson, pp. 1–38.

Turner, R. Kerry. 1993. "Sustainability Principles and Practice." In R. K. Turner (ed.) *Sustainable Environmental Management: Principles and Practice*. 2nd ed. Belhaven Press, London, pp. 3–36.

United Nations. 1997. *Comprehensive Assessment of the Freshwater Resources of the World*. World Meteorological Organization, Geneva.

Van Wijnbergen, S. 1984. "The 'Dutch Disease': A Disease After All?" *Economic Journal* 94: 41–55.

Vandergeest, P., M. Flaherty and P. Miller. 1999. "A Political Ecology of Shrimp Aquaculture in Thailand." *Rural Sociology* 64(4): 573–596.

Vincent, Jeffrey R. 1997. "Testing for Environmental Kuznets Curves within a Developing Country." *Special Issue on Environmental Kuznets Curves, Environment and Development Economics* 2(4): 417–432.

Vincent, Jeffrey R., Razali M. Ali and Associates. 1997. *Environment and Development in a Resource-Rich Economy: Malaysia under the New*

Economic Policy. Harvard Institute for International Development, Harvard University Press, San Diego CA.

Vincent, Jeffrey R., Theodore Panayotou and John M. Hartwick. 1997. "Resource Depletion and Sustainability in Small Open Economies." *Journal of Environmental Economics and Management* 33: 274–286.

Vörösmarty, Charles J., Pamela Green, Joseph Salisbury and Richard B. Lammers. 2000. "Global Water Resources: Vulnerability from Climate Change and Population Growth." *Science* 289(14 July): 284–288.

Wahba, Jackline. 1998. "The Transmission of Dutch Disease and Labour Migration." *Journal of International Trade and Economic Development* 7(3), September: 355–365.

Wallerstein, Immanuel. 1974. *The Modern World-System*. Academic Press, New York.

Watkins, M. H. 1963. "A Staple Theory of Economic Growth." *The Canadian Journal of Economics and Political Science* 29(2): 141–158.

Webb, W. P. 1964. *The Great Frontier*. University of Nebraska Press, Lincoln.

Weitzman, Martin L. 1976. "On the Welfare Significance of National Product in a Dynamic Economy." *Quarterly Journal of Economics* 90(1): 156–162.

1997. "Sustainability and Technological Progress." *Scandinavian Journal of Economics* 99: 1–13.

1998. "On the Welfare Significance of National Product under Interest Rate Uncertainty." *European Economic Review* 42(8): 1581–1594.

Wood, Adrian and Kersti Berge. 1997. "Exporting Manufactures: Human Resources, Natural Resources, and Trade Policy." *The Journal of Development Studies* 34(1): 35–59.

Wood, Adrian and Jörg Mayer. 2001. "Africa's Export Structure in a Comparative Perspective." *Cambridge Journal of Economics* 25: 369–394.

Wood, Adrian and Cristóbal Ridao-Cano. 1999. "Skill, Trade and International Inequality." *Oxford Economic Papers* 51: 89–119.

World Bank. 1989. *Mexico – Agricultural Sector Report*. The World Bank, Washington DC.

1992. *World Development Report 1992*. World Bank, Washington DC.

1994. *Mexico – Resource Conservation and Forest Sector Review*. World Bank, Washington DC.

1997. *Expanding the Measure of Wealth: Indicators of Environmentally Sustainable Development*. World Bank, Washington DC.

2001. *World Development Indicators 2001 CD-ROM*. The World Bank, Washington DC.

2003. *World Development Report 2003*. World Bank, Washington DC.

World Commission on Environment and Development (WCED). 1987. *Our Common Future.* Oxford University Press, Oxford and New York.

Wright, Gavin. 1990. "The Origins of American Industrial Success, 1879–1940." *American Economic Review* 80(4): 651–668.

Wright, Gavin and Jesse Czelusta. 2002. "Exorcizing the Resource Curse: Minerals as a Knowledge Industry, Past and Present." *Mimeo.* Department of Economics, Stanford University.

Wunder, Sven. 2001. "Poverty alleviation and tropical forests – what scope for synergies?" *World Development* 29: 1817–1833.

2003. *Oil Wealth and the Fate of the Forest: A Comparative Study of Eight Tropical Countries.* Routledge, London.

Zeller, M., G. Schreider, J. von Braun and F. Heidhues 1997. *Rural Finance for Food Security for the Poor.* Food Policy Review No. 4, International Food Policy Research Institute, Washington DC.

Ziesemer, Thomas. 1995. "Economic Development and Endogenous Terms-of-Trade Determination: Review and Reinterpretation of the Prebisch-Singer Thesis." *UNCTAD Review* 6: 17–33.

Index